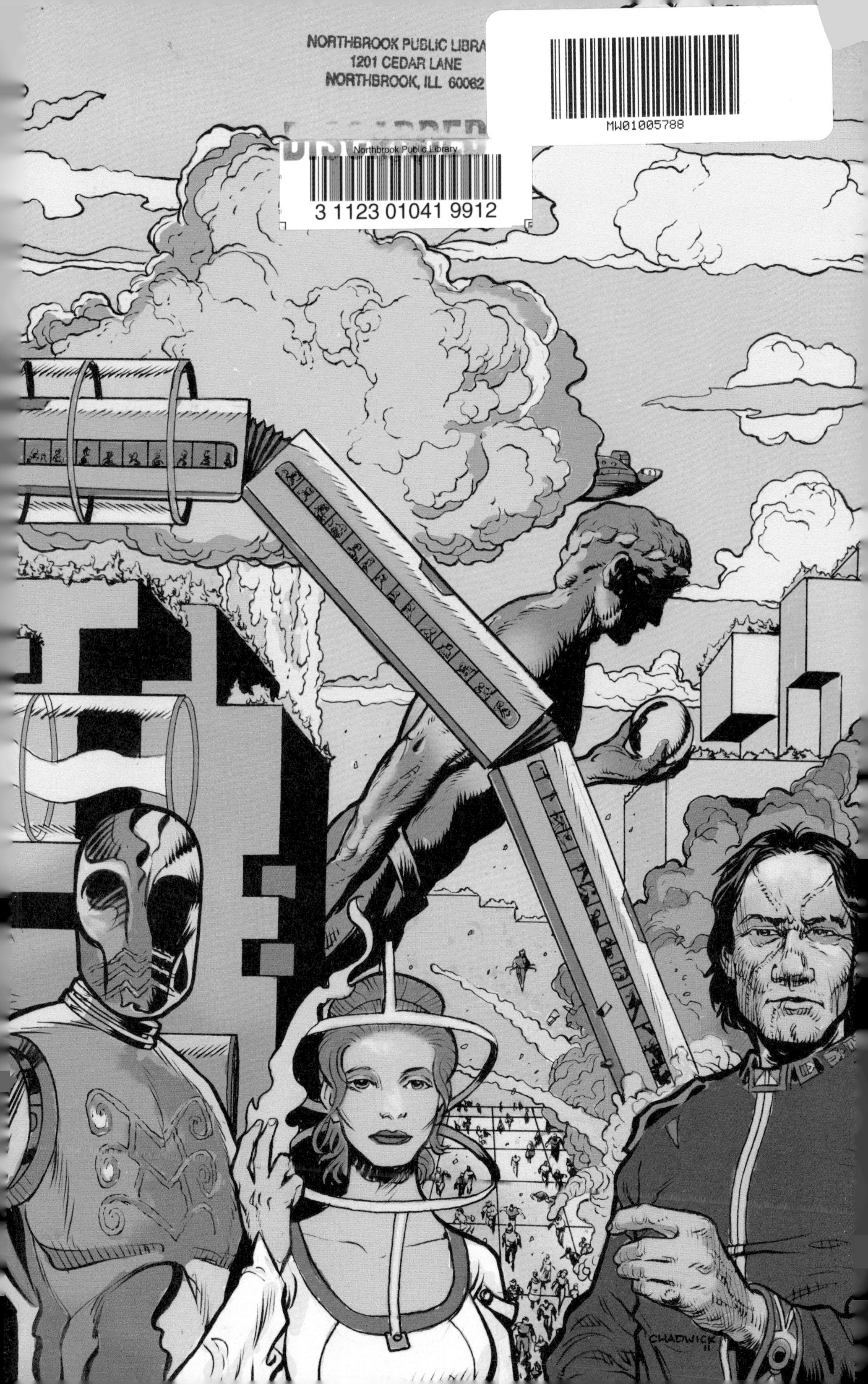
CHADWICK

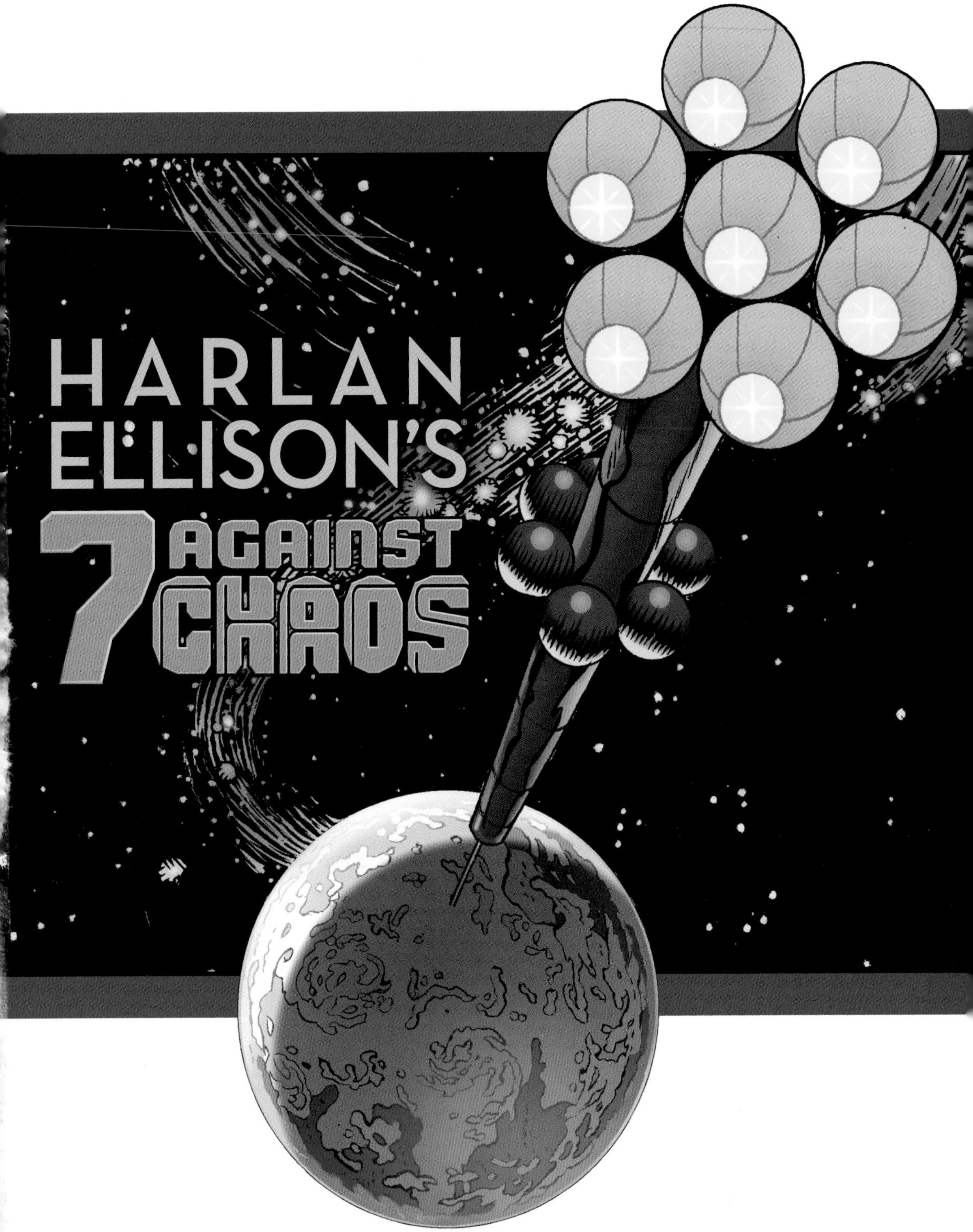
HARLAN
ELLISON'S
7 AGAINST
CHAOS

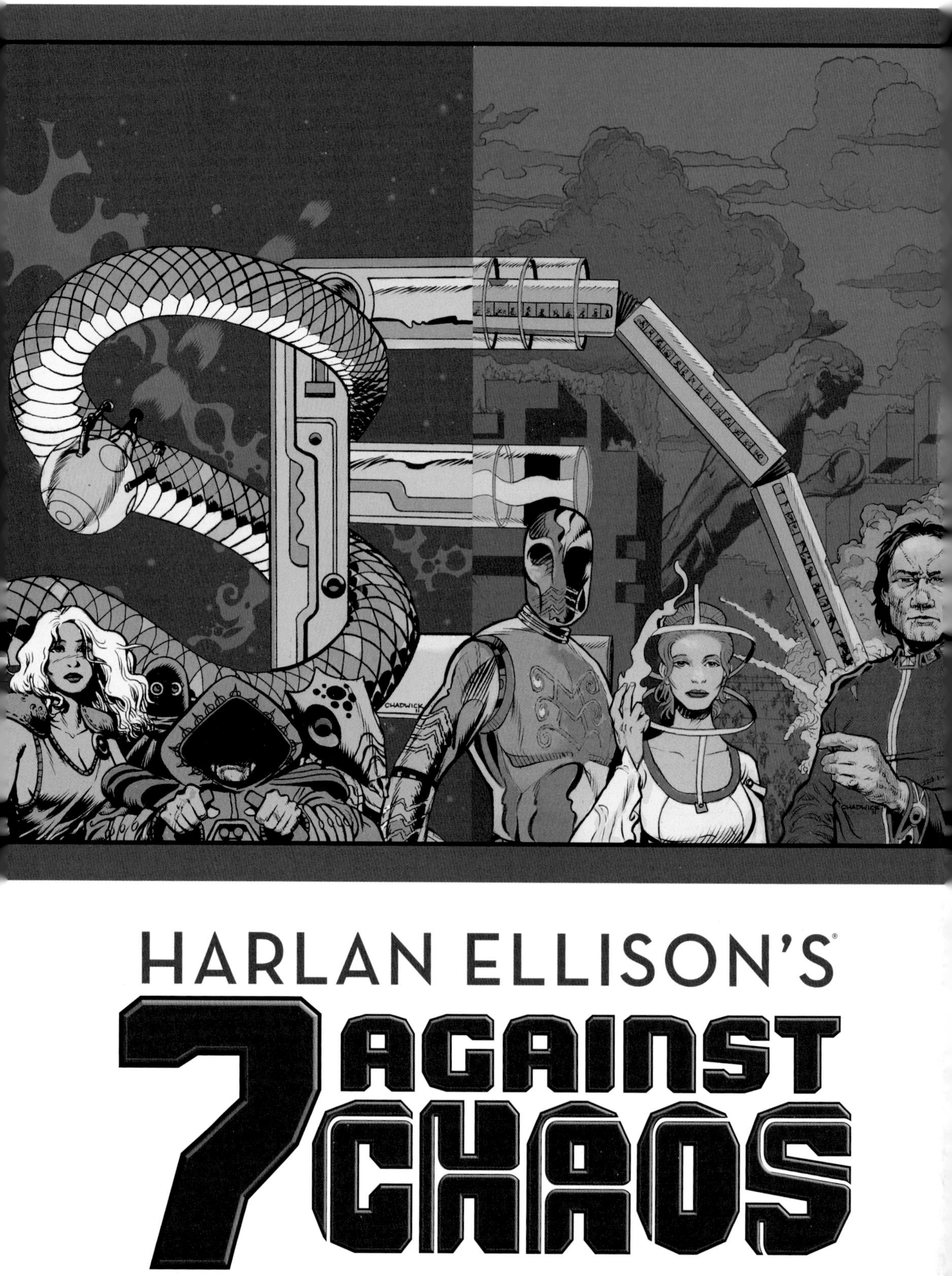
CHADWICK
CHADWICK

HARLAN ELLISON'S®

7 AGAINST CHAOS

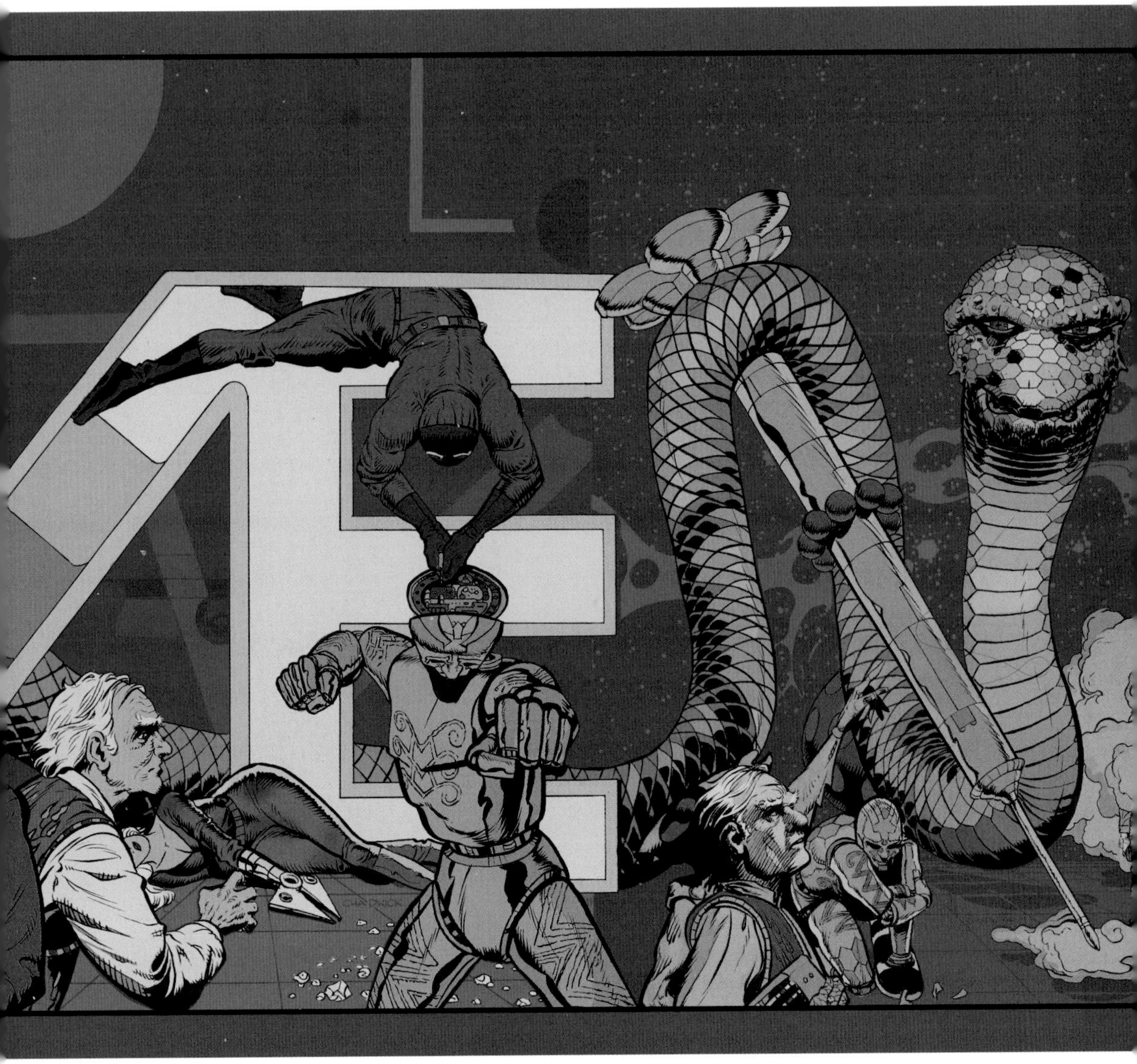

STORY AND ART BY

HARLAN ELLISON & PAUL CHADWICK

KEN STEACY
Colorist

TODD KLEIN
Letterer

PAUL CHADWICK
Cover art

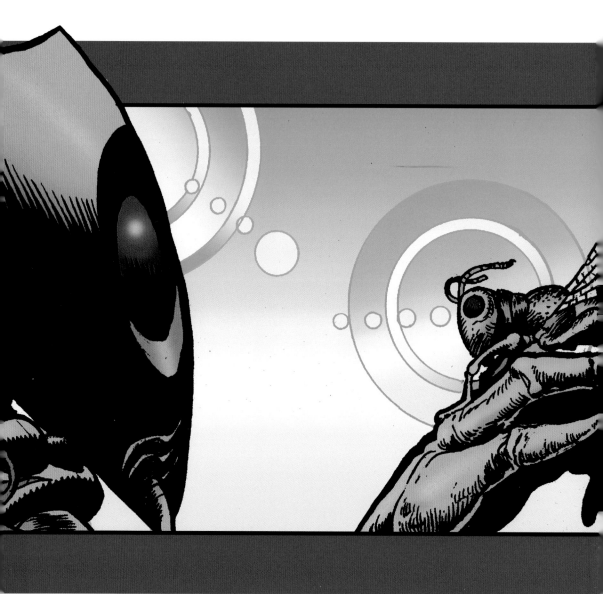

Bobbie Chase Peter Hamboussi Editors
Robbin Brosterman Design Director - Books
Curtis King Jr. Publication Design

Bob Harras Senior VP - Editor-in-Chief, DC Comics

Diane Nelson President
Dan DiDio and **Jim Lee** Co-Publishers
Geoff Johns Chief Creative Officer
John Rood Executive VP - Sales, Marketing and Business Development
Amy Genkins Senior VP - Business and Legal Affairs
Nairi Gardiner Senior VP - Finance
Jeff Boison VP - Publishing Planning
Mark Chiarello VP - Art Direction and Design
John Cunningham VP - Marketing
Terri Cunningham VP - Editorial Administration
Alison Gill Senior VP - Manufacturing and Operations
Hank Kanalz Senior VP - Vertigo and Integrated Publishing
Jay Kogan VP - Business and Legal Affairs, Publishing
Jack Mahan VP - Business Affairs, Talent
Nick Napolitano VP - Manufacturing Administration
Sue Pohja VP - Book Sales
Courtney Simmons Senior VP - Publicity
Bob Wayne Senior VP - Sales

HARLAN ELLISON'S® 7 AGAINST CHAOS

DC Comics, 1700 Broadway, New York, NY 10019.
A Warner Bros. Entertainment Company
Printed in the USA. 6/7/13. First Printing.
HC ISBN: 978-1-4012-3910-7

SUSTAINABLE
FORESTRY
INITIATIVE

Certified Chain of Custody
At Least 20% Certified Forest Content
www.sfiprogram.org
SFI-01042
APPLIES TO TEXT STOCK ONLY

Library of Congress Cataloging-in-Publication Data

Ellison, Harlan.
  Harlan Ellison's 7 against chaos / Harlan Ellison, Paul Chadwick.
    pages cm
  ISBN 978-1-4012-3910-7
  1. Graphic novels. I. Chadwick, Paul (Paul H.) illustrator. II. Title. III. Title: 7
against chaos. IV. Title: Seven against chaos.
  PN6728.E45A63 2013
  741.5'973—dc23
                                      2013009147

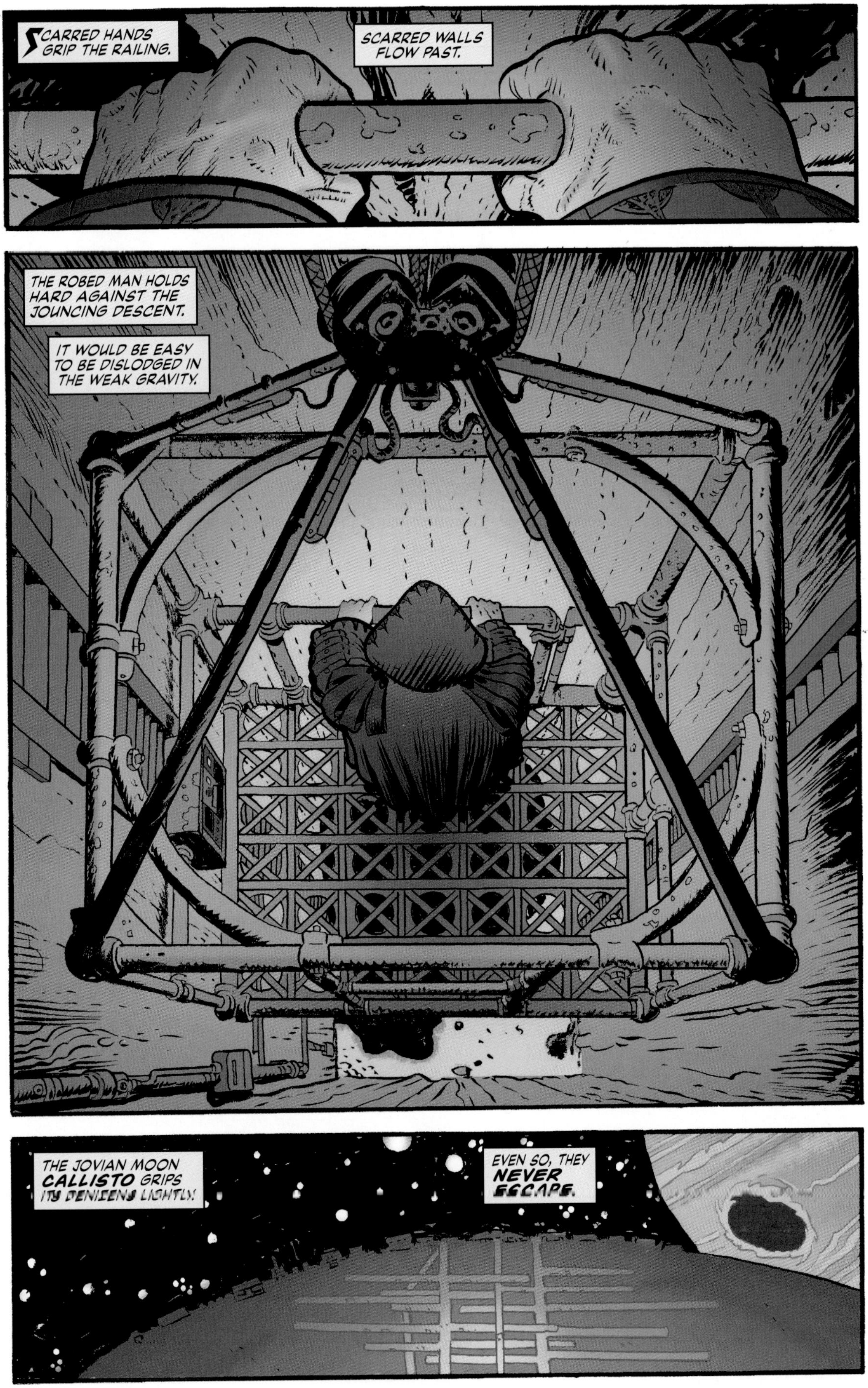
SCARRED HANDS GRIP THE RAILING.
SCARRED WALLS FLOW PAST.
THE ROBED MAN HOLDS HARD AGAINST THE JOUNCING DESCENT.
IT WOULD BE EASY TO BE DISLODGED IN THE WEAK GRAVITY.
THE JOVIAN MOON CALLISTO GRIPS ITS DENIZENS LIGHTLY.
EVEN SO, THEY NEVER ESCAPE.

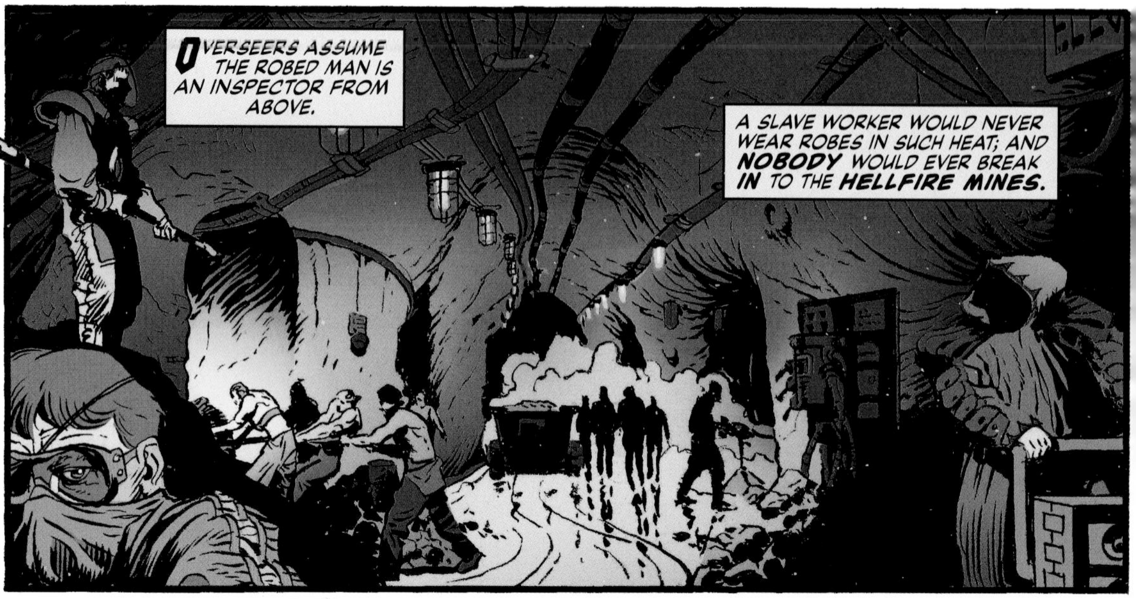
OVERSEERS ASSUME THE ROBED MAN IS AN INSPECTOR FROM ABOVE.
A SLAVE WORKER WOULD NEVER WEAR ROBES IN SUCH HEAT; AND **NOBODY** WOULD EVER BREAK **IN** TO THE **HELLFIRE MINES.**

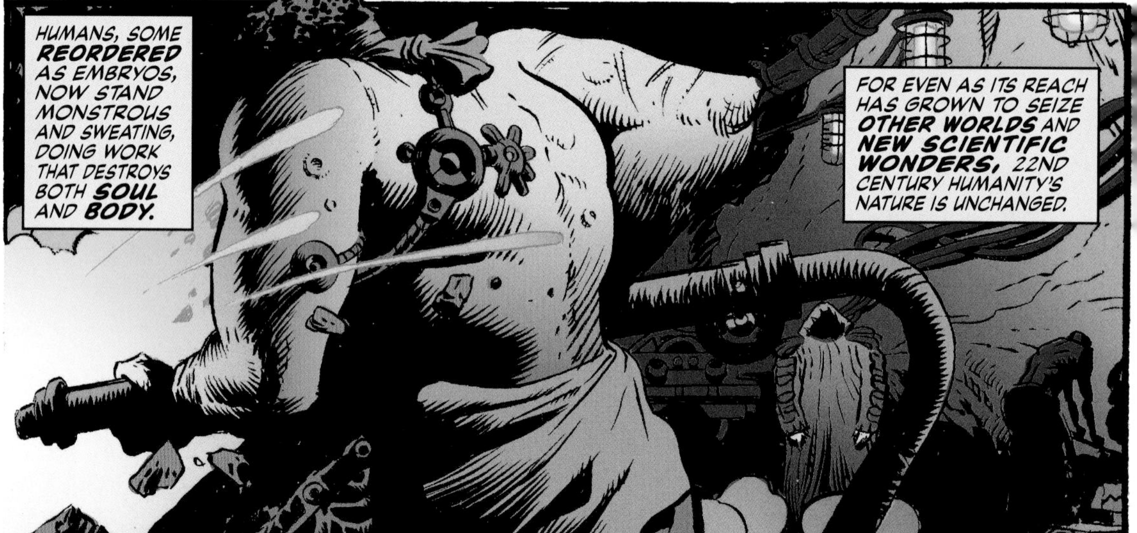
HUMANS, SOME **REORDERED** AS EMBRYOS, NOW STAND MONSTROUS AND SWEATING, DOING WORK THAT DESTROYS BOTH **SOUL** AND **BODY.**
FOR EVEN AS ITS REACH HAS GROWN TO SEIZE **OTHER WORLDS** AND **NEW SCIENTIFIC WONDERS,** 22ND CENTURY HUMANITY'S NATURE IS UNCHANGED.

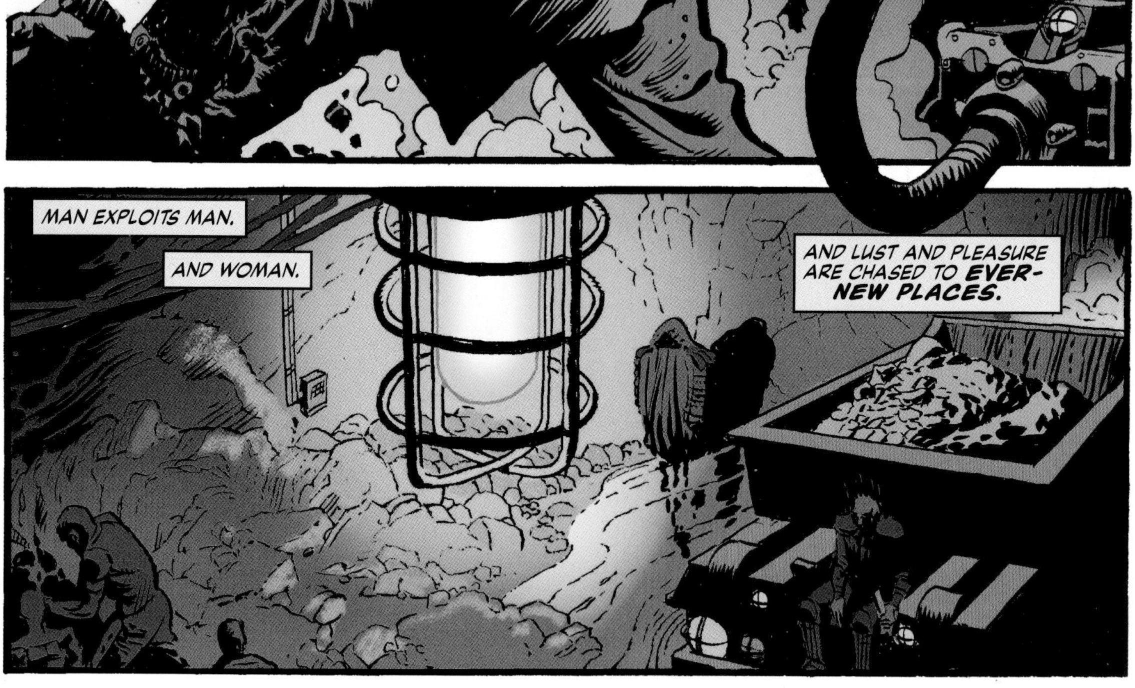
MAN EXPLOITS MAN.
AND WOMAN.
AND LUST AND PLEASURE ARE CHASED TO **EVER-NEW PLACES.**

THEY MINE A COLLOIDAL SUBSTANCE FOUND NO-WHERE ELSE.

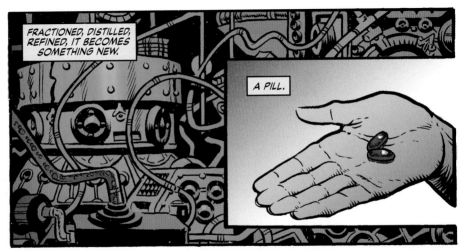

FRACTIONED, DISTILLED, REFINED, IT BECOMES SOMETHING NEW.

A PILL.

CALLISTAN FREEBOOTERS, USING SLAVES STOLEN FROM EVERY PLANET IN THE SYSTEM, PRODUCE AND SELL IT **THROUGHOUT THE CIVILIZED WORLDS.**

AAAH.

USERS THINK LITTLE OF ITS PROVENANCE.

THEY'RE TOO THRILLED BY THE **MOST POWERFUL APHRODISIAC NARCOTIC** EVER KNOWN TO CARE.

HE'S DONE. CYCLE HIM, MOURNA.

UHHHH.

BUT HE ISN'T DEAD!

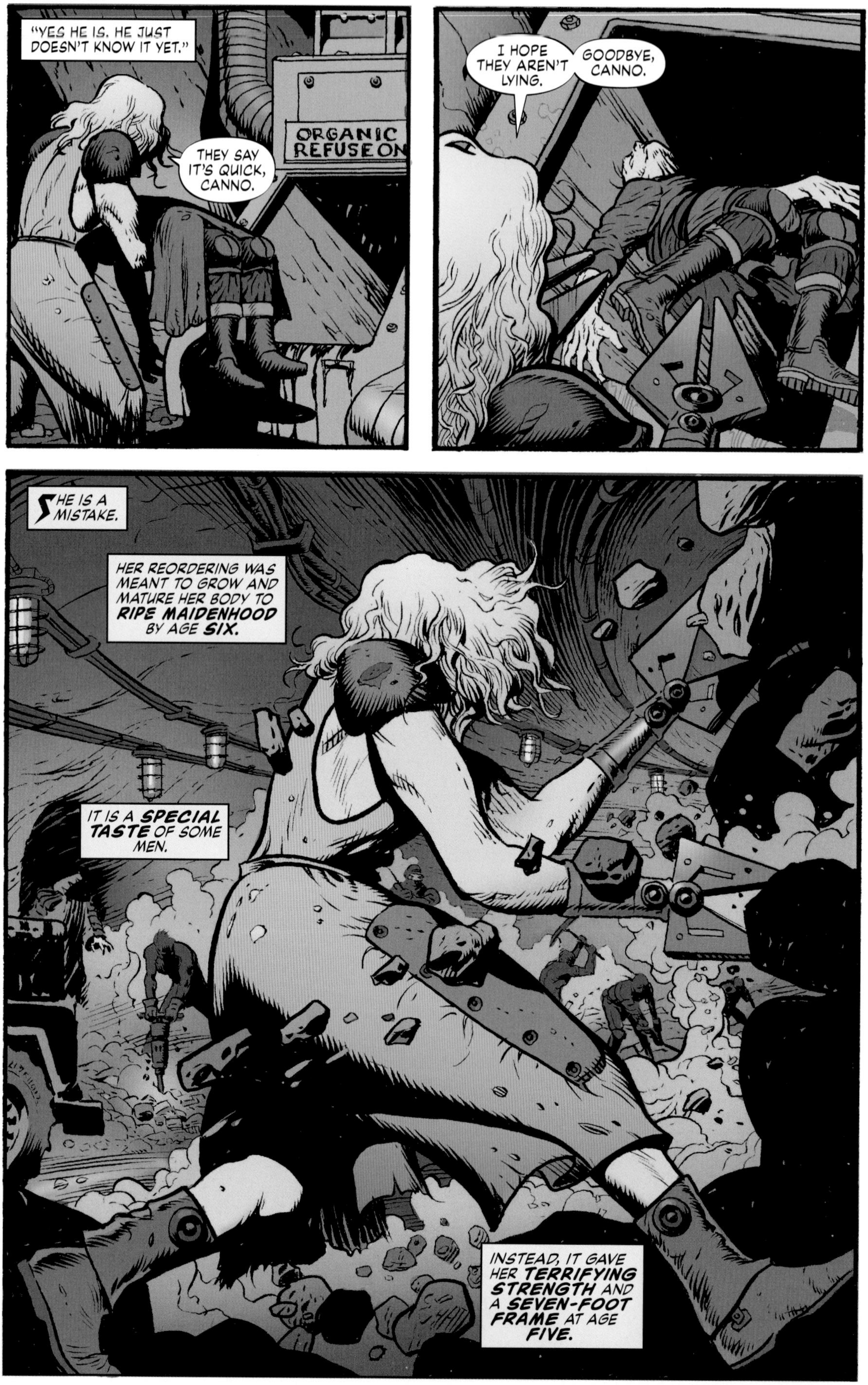
"YES HE IS. HE JUST DOESN'T KNOW IT YET."
ORGANIC REFUSE ON
THEY SAY IT'S QUICK, CANNO.
I HOPE THEY AREN'T LYING.
GOODBYE, CANNO.
SHE IS A MISTAKE.
HER REORDERING WAS MEANT TO GROW AND MATURE HER BODY TO RIPE MAIDENHOOD BY AGE SIX.
IT IS A SPECIAL TASTE OF SOME MEN.
INSTEAD, IT GAVE HER TERRIFYING STRENGTH AND A SEVEN-FOOT FRAME AT AGE FIVE.

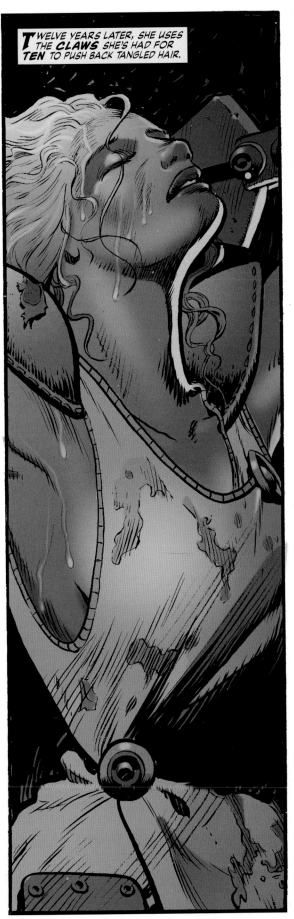

TWELVE YEARS LATER, SHE USES THE **CLAWS** SHE'S HAD FOR **TEN** TO PUSH BACK TANGLED HAIR.

THE ACT IS APPRECIATED BY A FELLOW SLAVE...

...A MOMENT OF BEAUTY IN A HIDEOUS WORLD.

IT CONFIRMS TO THE ROBED MAN THAT HERE IS **MOURNA**, THE WOMAN HE SEEKS.

WHAT REMAINS IS HOW TO GET HER OUT.

HE REVIEWS SEVERAL PLANS.

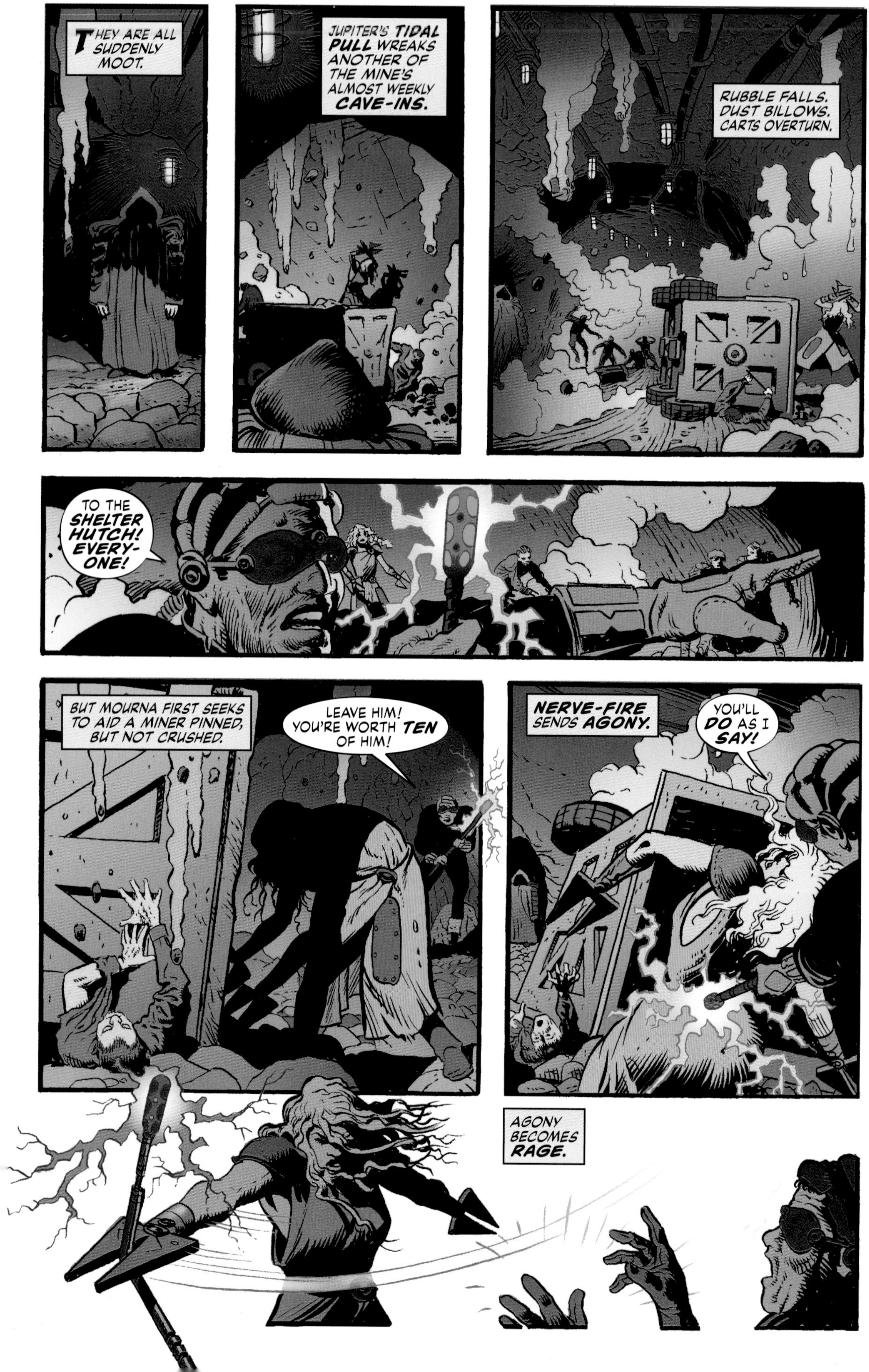
THEY ARE ALL SUDDENLY MOOT.
JUPITER'S TIDAL PULL WREAKS ANOTHER OF THE MINE'S ALMOST WEEKLY CAVE-INS.
RUBBLE FALLS. DUST BILLOWS. CARTS OVERTURN.
TO THE SHELTER HUTCH! EVERY-ONE!
BUT MOURNA FIRST SEEKS TO AID A MINER PINNED, BUT NOT CRUSHED.
LEAVE HIM! YOU'RE WORTH TEN OF HIM!
NERVE-FIRE SENDS AGONY.
YOU'LL DO AS I SAY!
AGONY BECOMES RAGE.

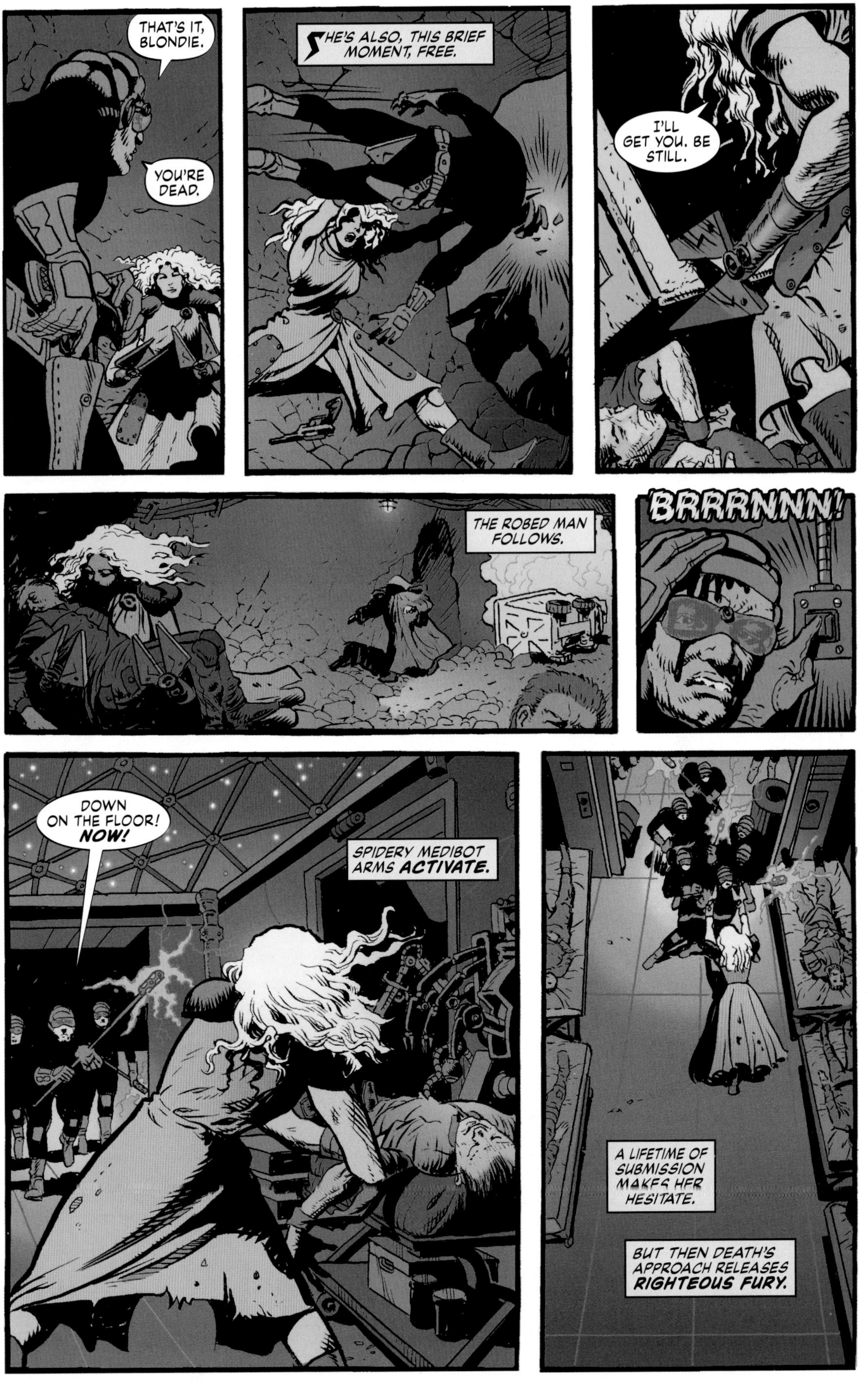
THAT'S IT, BLONDIE.
YOU'RE DEAD.
SHE'S ALSO, THIS BRIEF MOMENT, FREE.
I'LL GET YOU. BE STILL.
THE ROBED MAN FOLLOWS.
BRRRNNN!
DOWN ON THE FLOOR! NOW!
SPIDERY MEDIBOT ARMS ACTIVATE.
A LIFETIME OF SUBMISSION MAKES HER HESITATE.
BUT THEN DEATH'S APPROACH RELEASES RIGHTEOUS FURY.

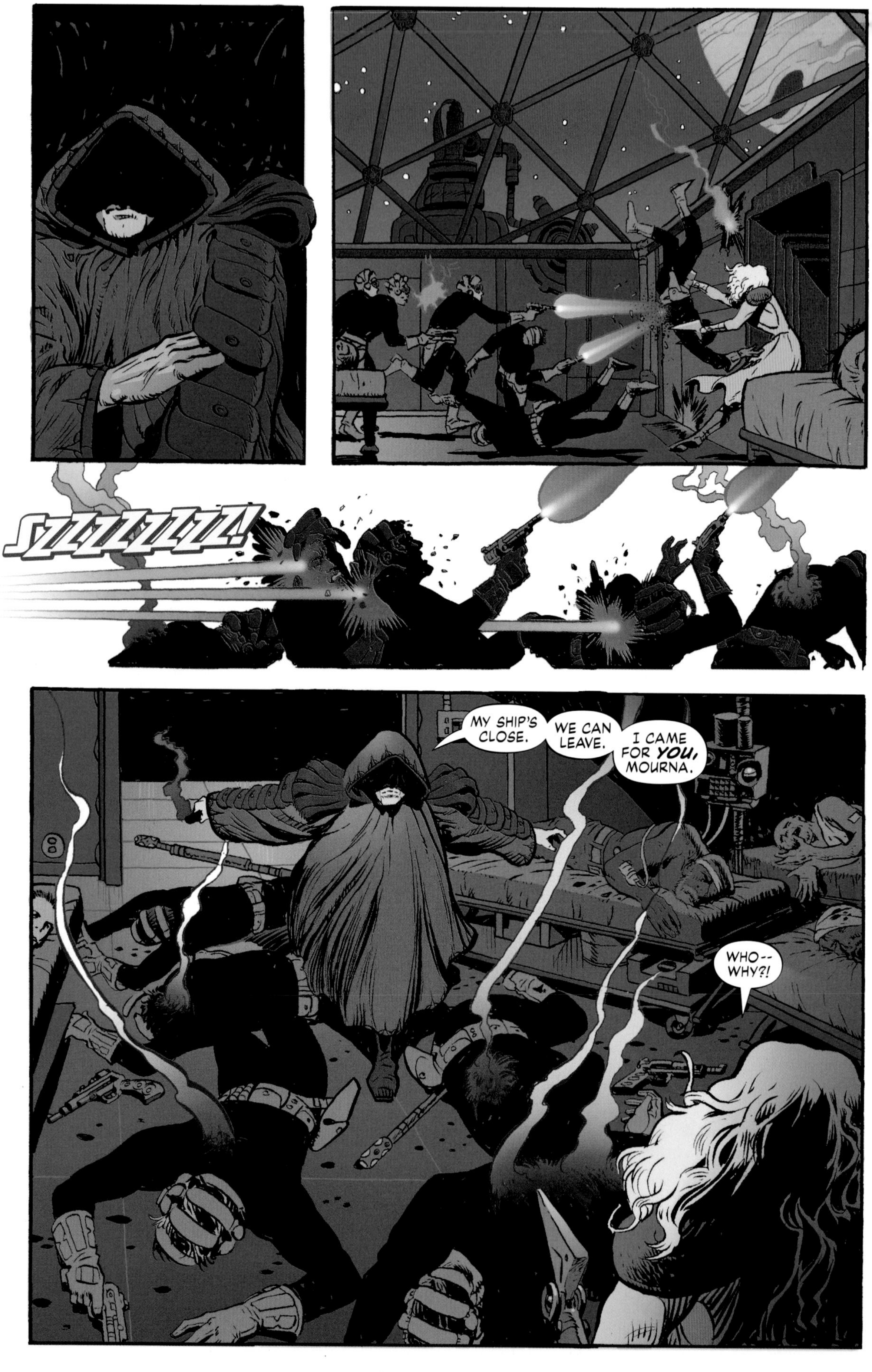
SZZZZZZZZZ!
MY SHIP'S CLOSE.
WE CAN LEAVE.
I CAME FOR YOU, MOURNA.
WHO-- WHY?!

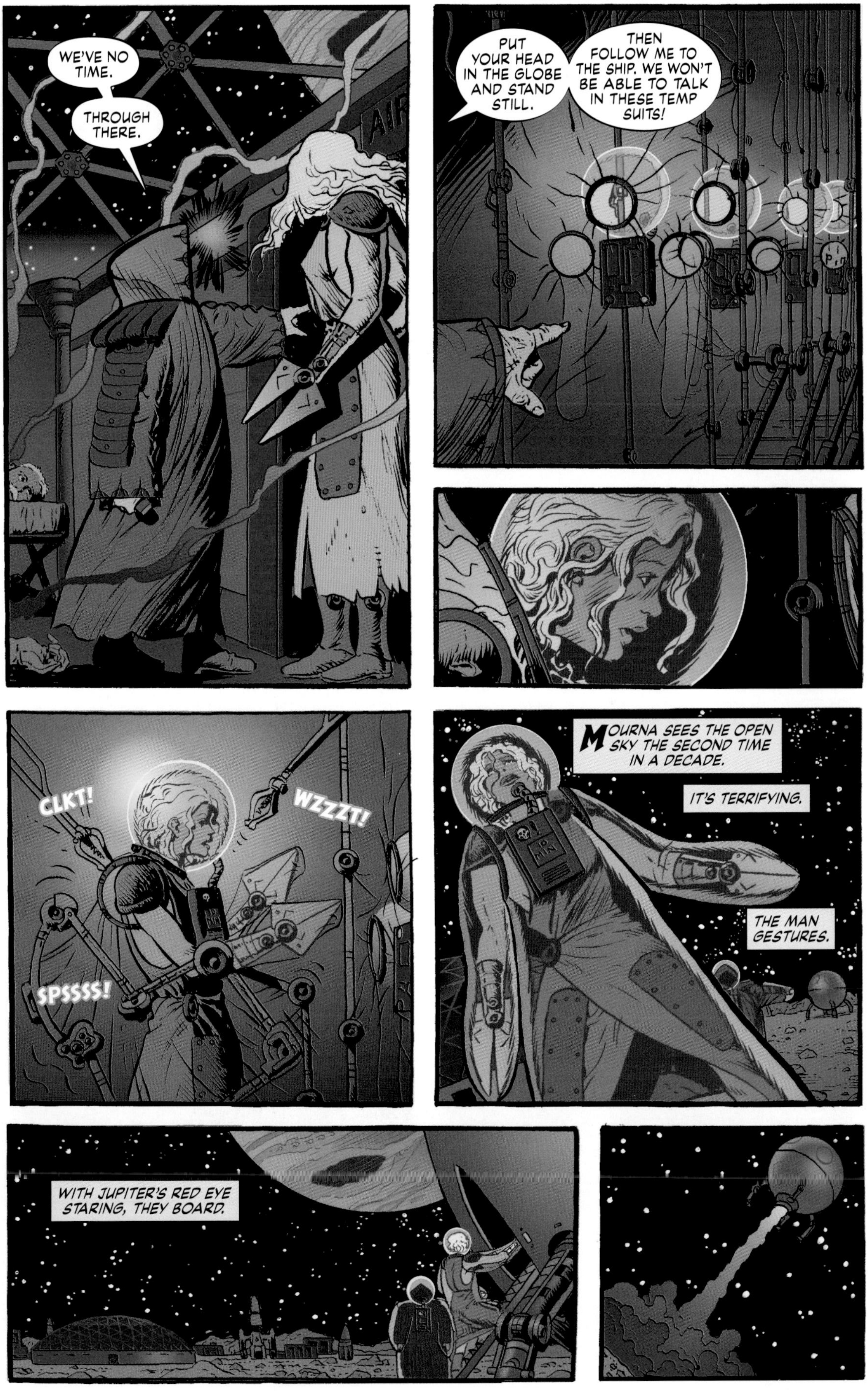
WE'VE NO TIME.
THROUGH THERE.
PUT YOUR HEAD IN THE GLOBE AND STAND STILL.
THEN FOLLOW ME TO THE SHIP. WE WON'T BE ABLE TO TALK IN THESE TEMP SUITS!
CLKT!
WZZZT!
SPSSSS!
MOURNA SEES THE OPEN SKY THE SECOND TIME IN A DECADE.
IT'S TERRIFYING.
THE MAN GESTURES.
WITH JUPITER'S RED EYE STARING, THEY BOARD.

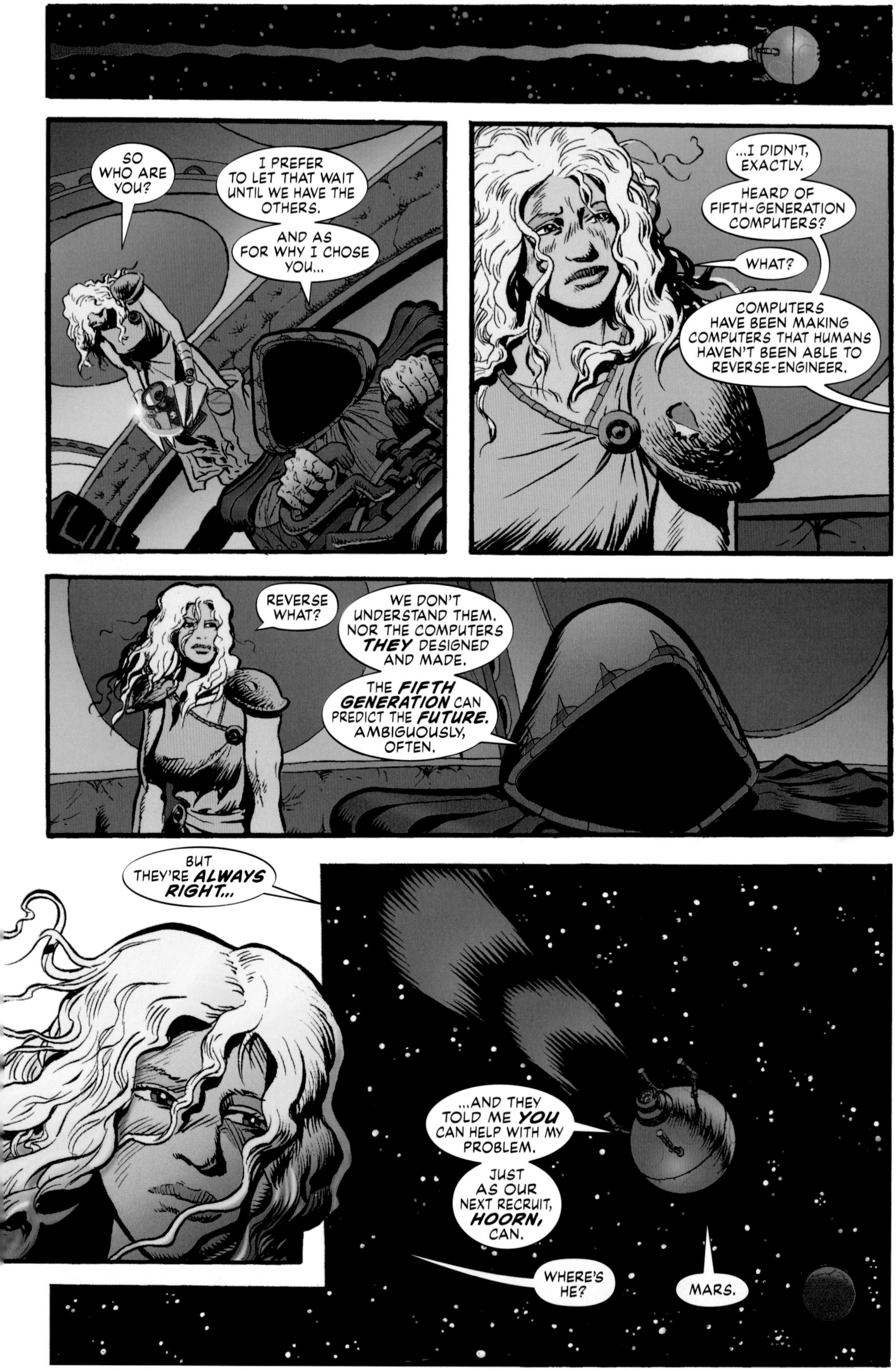
SO WHO ARE YOU?
I PREFER TO LET THAT WAIT UNTIL WE HAVE THE OTHERS.
AND AS FOR WHY I CHOSE YOU...
...I DIDN'T, EXACTLY.
HEARD OF FIFTH-GENERATION COMPUTERS?
WHAT?
COMPUTERS HAVE BEEN MAKING COMPUTERS THAT HUMANS HAVEN'T BEEN ABLE TO REVERSE-ENGINEER.
REVERSE WHAT?
WE DON'T UNDERSTAND THEM. NOR THE COMPUTERS THEY DESIGNED AND MADE.
THE FIFTH GENERATION CAN PREDICT THE FUTURE. AMBIGUOUSLY, OFTEN.
BUT THEY'RE ALWAYS RIGHT...
...AND THEY TOLD ME YOU CAN HELP WITH MY PROBLEM.
JUST AS OUR NEXT RECRUIT, HOORN, CAN.
WHERE'S HE?
MARS.

GALIOPOLIS, CAPITAL CITY OF MARS.

ROCOCO TOWERS HOUSE THE **SUPER-RICH.**

THEY ARE NEARLY IMPREGNABLE.

NEARLY.

THE **FACELESS MAN HOORN** SURVEYS THE PENTHOUSE.

RICHES ARE HERE.

BUT WHERE? A SCANNING INTUITAB WEIGHS PROBABILITIES.

AH, THE BED. TO WORK.

A WHIRRING-- SPY-EYES!

LASER-EQUIPPED!

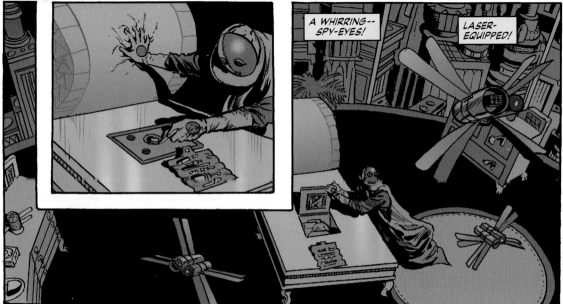

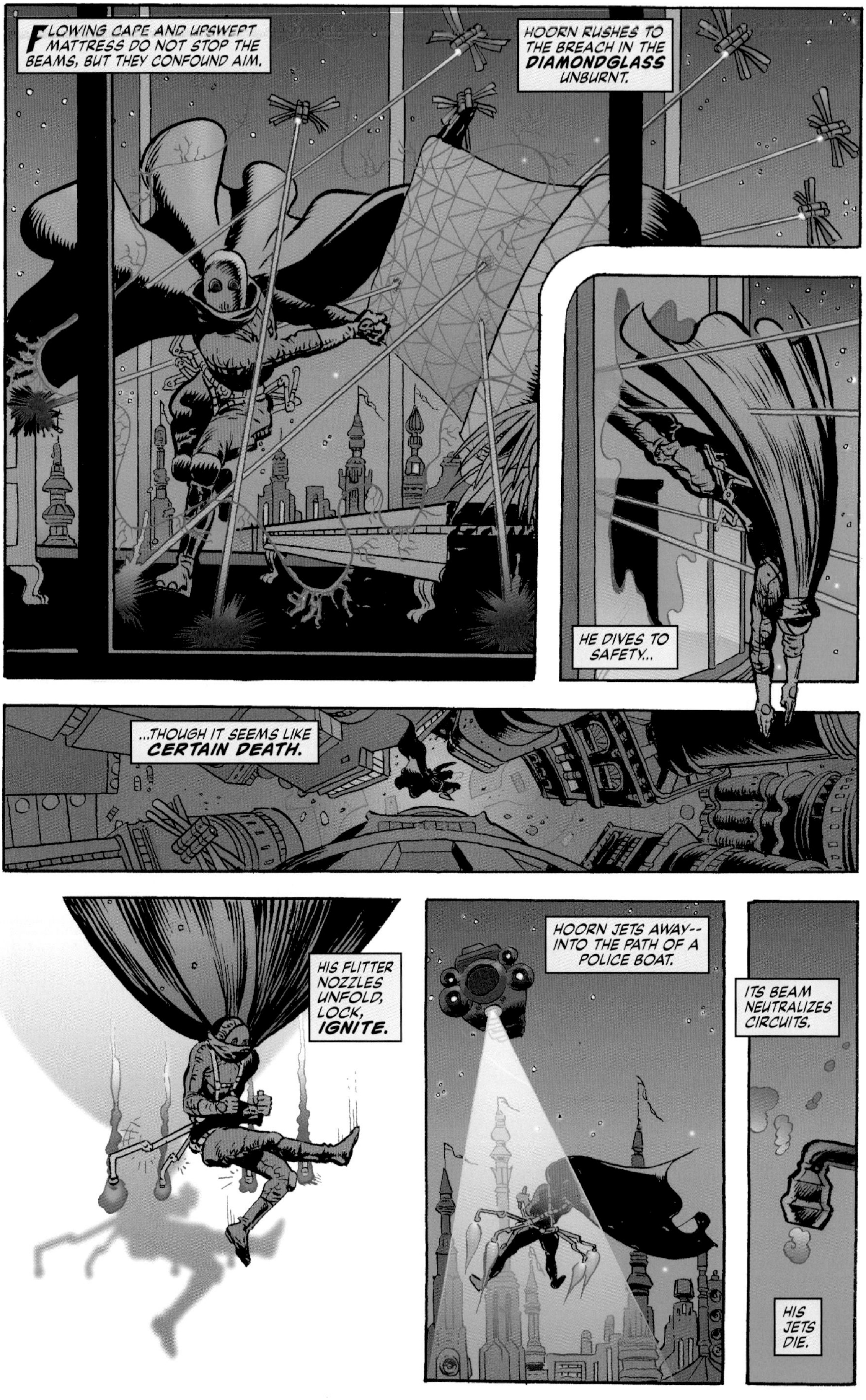
FLOWING CAPE AND UPSWEPT MATTRESS DO NOT STOP THE BEAMS, BUT THEY CONFOUND AIM.
HOORN RUSHES TO THE BREACH IN THE DIAMONDGLASS UNBURNT.
HE DIVES TO SAFETY...
...THOUGH IT SEEMS LIKE CERTAIN DEATH.
HIS FLITTER NOZZLES UNFOLD, LOCK, IGNITE.
HOORN JETS AWAY-- INTO THE PATH OF A POLICE BOAT.
ITS BEAM NEUTRALIZES CIRCUITS.
HIS JETS DIE.

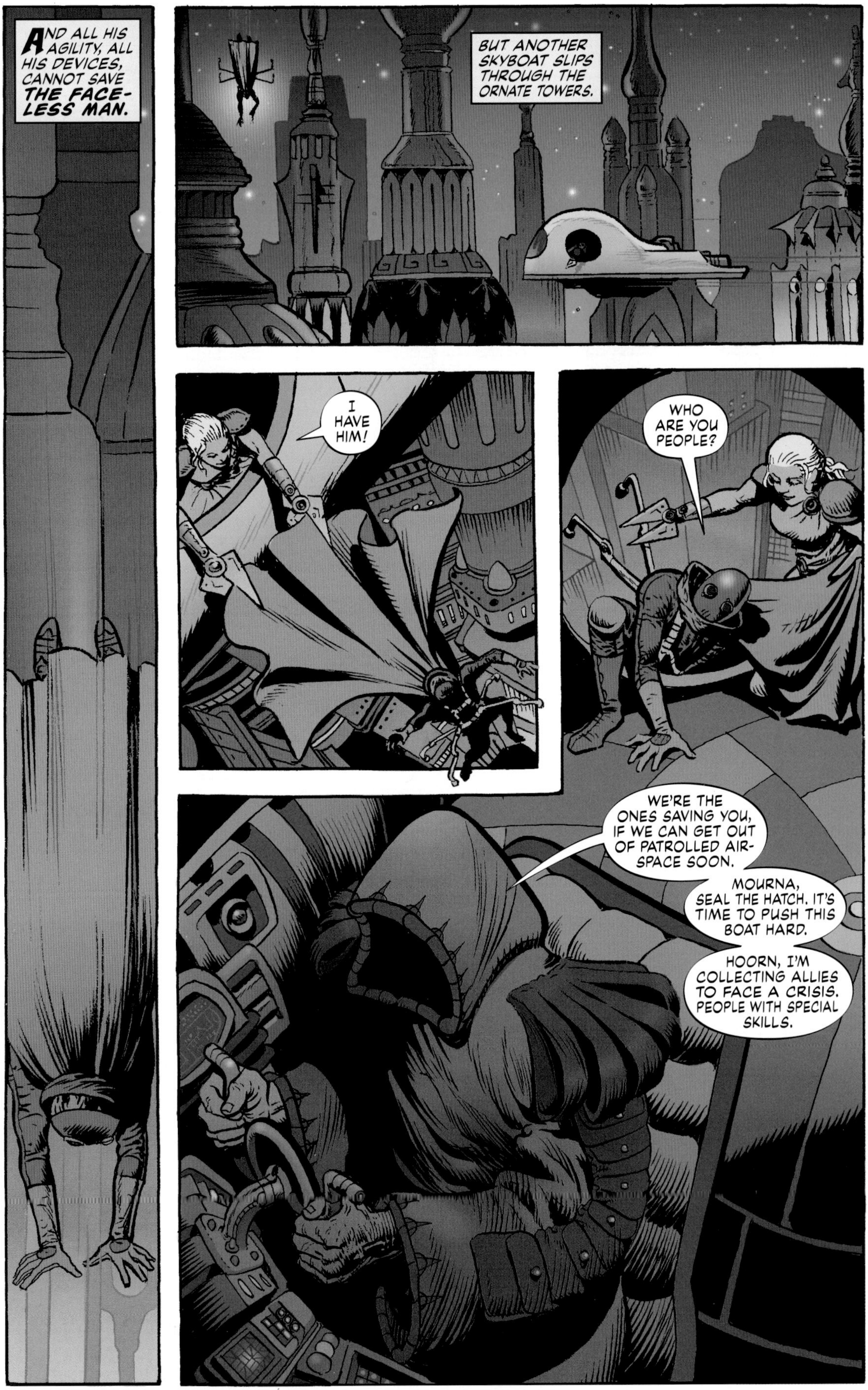
AND ALL HIS AGILITY, ALL HIS DEVICES, CANNOT SAVE THE FACE-LESS MAN.
BUT ANOTHER SKYBOAT SLIPS THROUGH THE ORNATE TOWERS.
I HAVE HIM!
WHO ARE YOU PEOPLE?
WE'RE THE ONES SAVING YOU, IF WE CAN GET OUT OF PATROLLED AIR-SPACE SOON.
MOURNA, SEAL THE HATCH. IT'S TIME TO PUSH THIS BOAT HARD.
HOORN, I'M COLLECTING ALLIES TO FACE A CRISIS. PEOPLE WITH SPECIAL SKILLS.

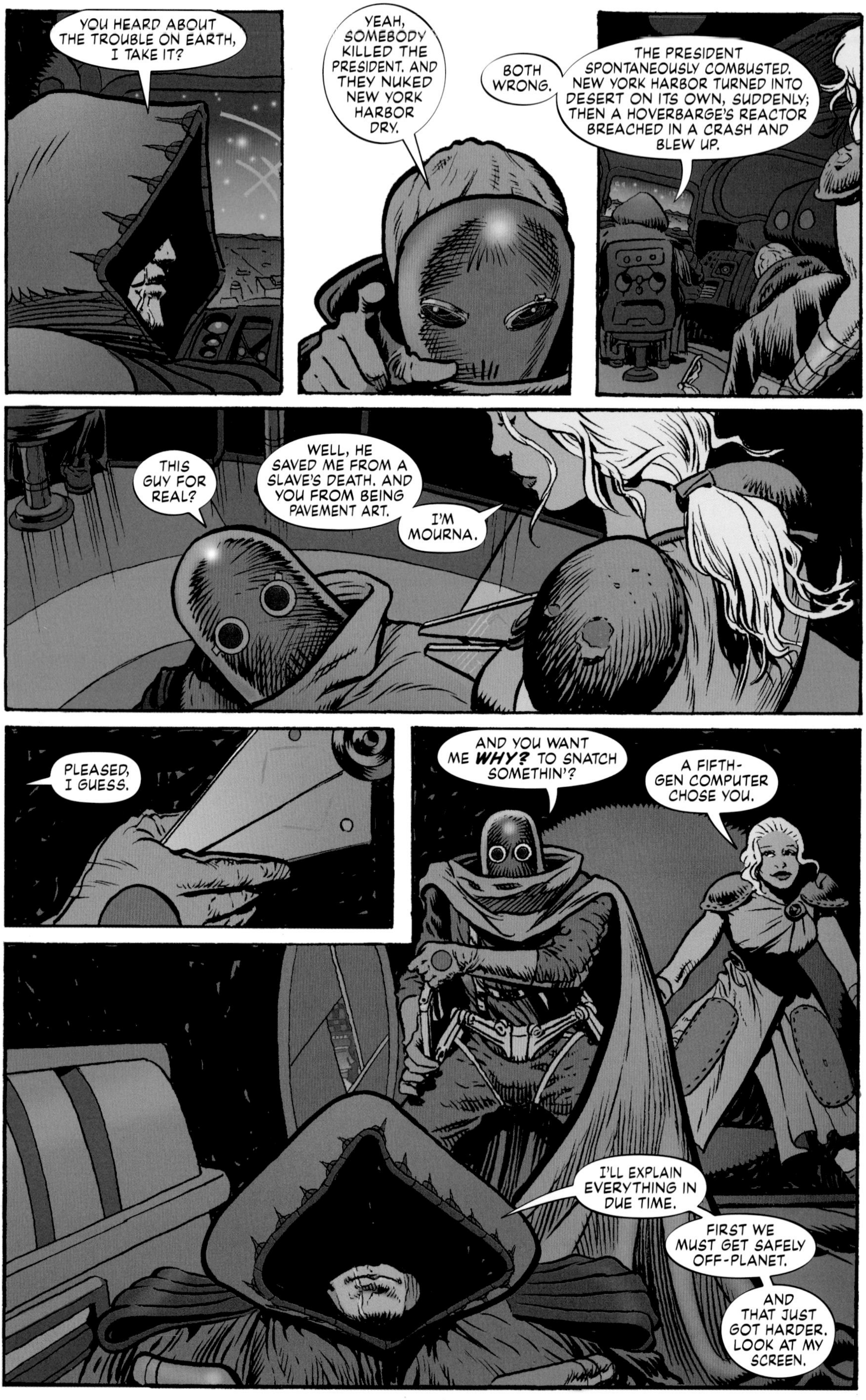
YOU HEARD ABOUT THE TROUBLE ON EARTH, I TAKE IT?
YEAH, SOMEBODY KILLED THE PRESIDENT. AND THEY NUKED NEW YORK HARBOR DRY.
BOTH WRONG.
THE PRESIDENT SPONTANEOUSLY COMBUSTED. NEW YORK HARBOR TURNED INTO DESERT ON ITS OWN, SUDDENLY; THEN A HOVERBARGE'S REACTOR BREACHED IN A CRASH AND BLEW UP.
THIS GUY FOR REAL?
WELL, HE SAVED ME FROM A SLAVE'S DEATH. AND YOU FROM BEING PAVEMENT ART.
I'M MOURNA.
PLEASED, I GUESS.
AND YOU WANT ME WHY? TO SNATCH SOMETHIN'?
A FIFTH-GEN COMPUTER CHOSE YOU.
I'LL EXPLAIN EVERYTHING IN DUE TIME.
FIRST WE MUST GET SAFELY OFF-PLANET.
AND THAT JUST GOT HARDER. LOOK AT MY SCREEN.

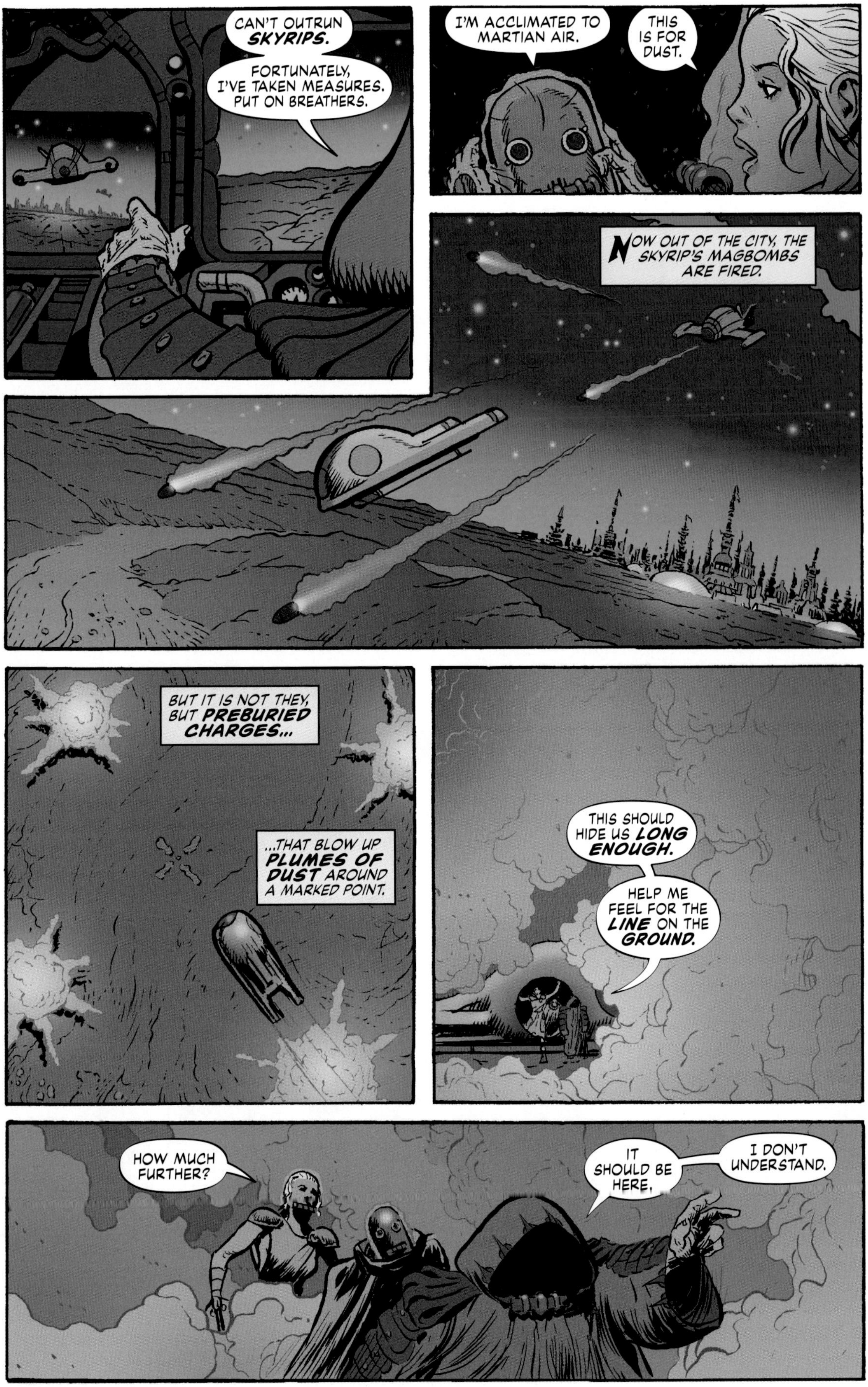
CAN'T OUTRUN SKYRIPS.
FORTUNATELY, I'VE TAKEN MEASURES. PUT ON BREATHERS.
I'M ACCLIMATED TO MARTIAN AIR.
THIS IS FOR DUST.
NOW OUT OF THE CITY, THE SKYRIP'S MAGBOMBS ARE FIRED.
BUT IT IS NOT THEY, BUT PREBURIED CHARGES...
...THAT BLOW UP PLUMES OF DUST AROUND A MARKED POINT.
THIS SHOULD HIDE US LONG ENOUGH.
HELP ME FEEL FOR THE LINE ON THE GROUND.
HOW MUCH FURTHER?
IT SHOULD BE HERE.
I DON'T UNDERSTAND.

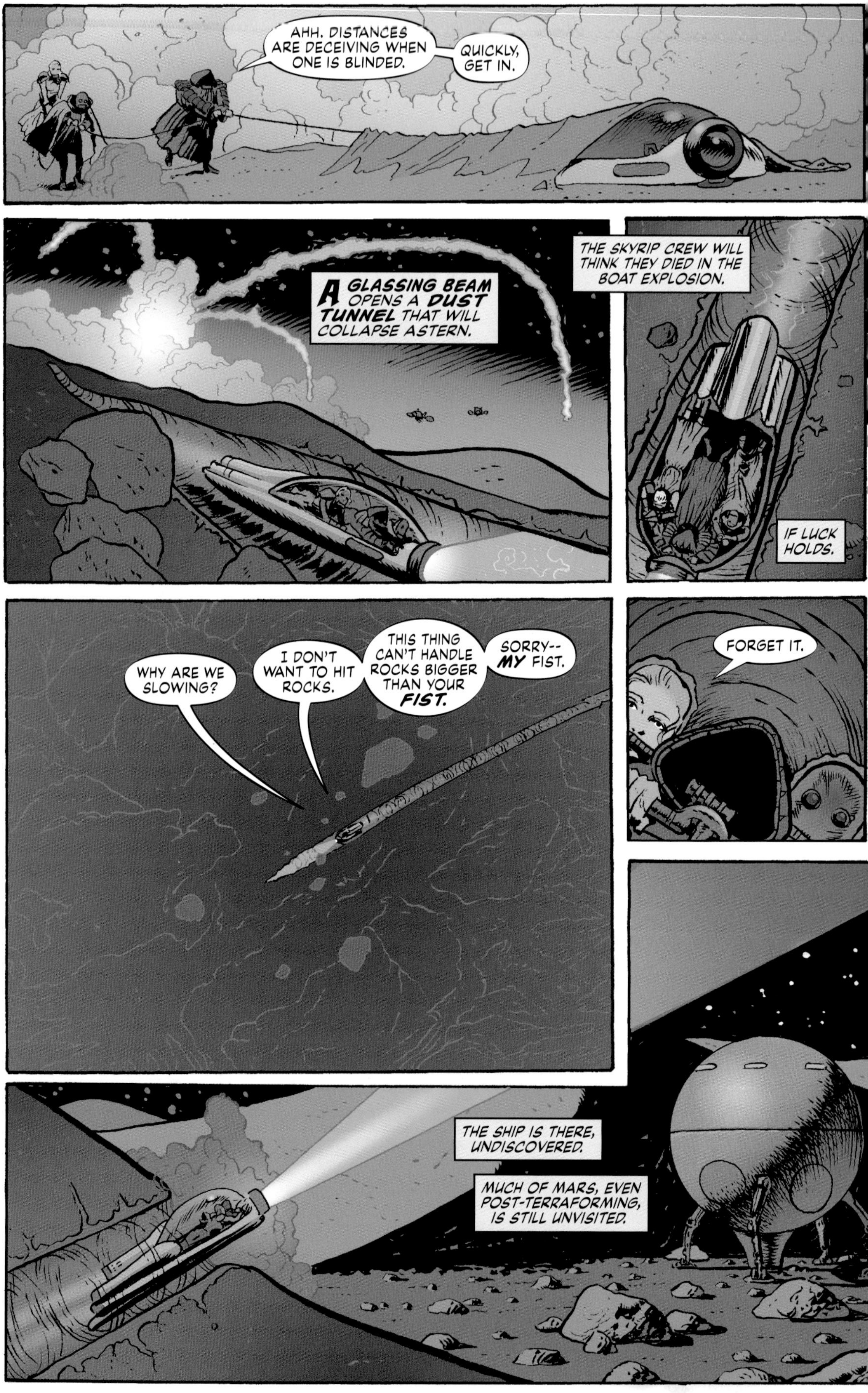
AHH. DISTANCES ARE DECEIVING WHEN ONE IS BLINDED.
QUICKLY, GET IN.
A GLASSING BEAM OPENS A DUST TUNNEL THAT WILL COLLAPSE ASTERN.
THE SKYRIP CREW WILL THINK THEY DIED IN THE BOAT EXPLOSION.
IF LUCK HOLDS.
WHY ARE WE SLOWING?
I DON'T WANT TO HIT ROCKS.
THIS THING CAN'T HANDLE ROCKS BIGGER THAN YOUR FIST.
SORRY-- MY FIST.
FORGET IT.
THE SHIP IS THERE, UNDISCOVERED.
MUCH OF MARS, EVEN POST-TERRAFORMING, IS STILL UNVISITED.

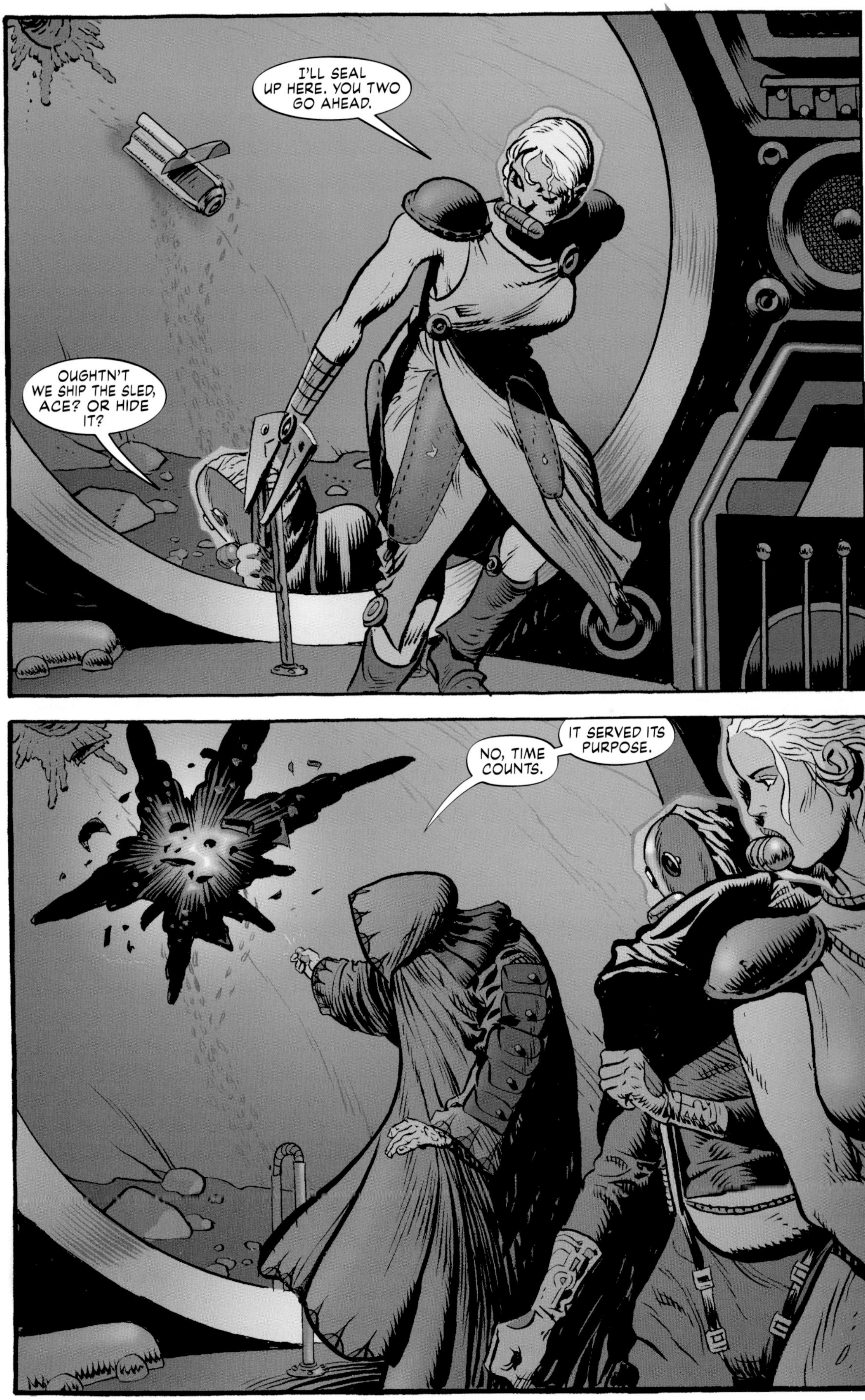
I'LL SEAL UP HERE. YOU TWO GO AHEAD.
OUGHTN'T WE SHIP THE SLED, ACE? OR HIDE IT?
NO, TIME COUNTS.
IT SERVED ITS PURPOSE.

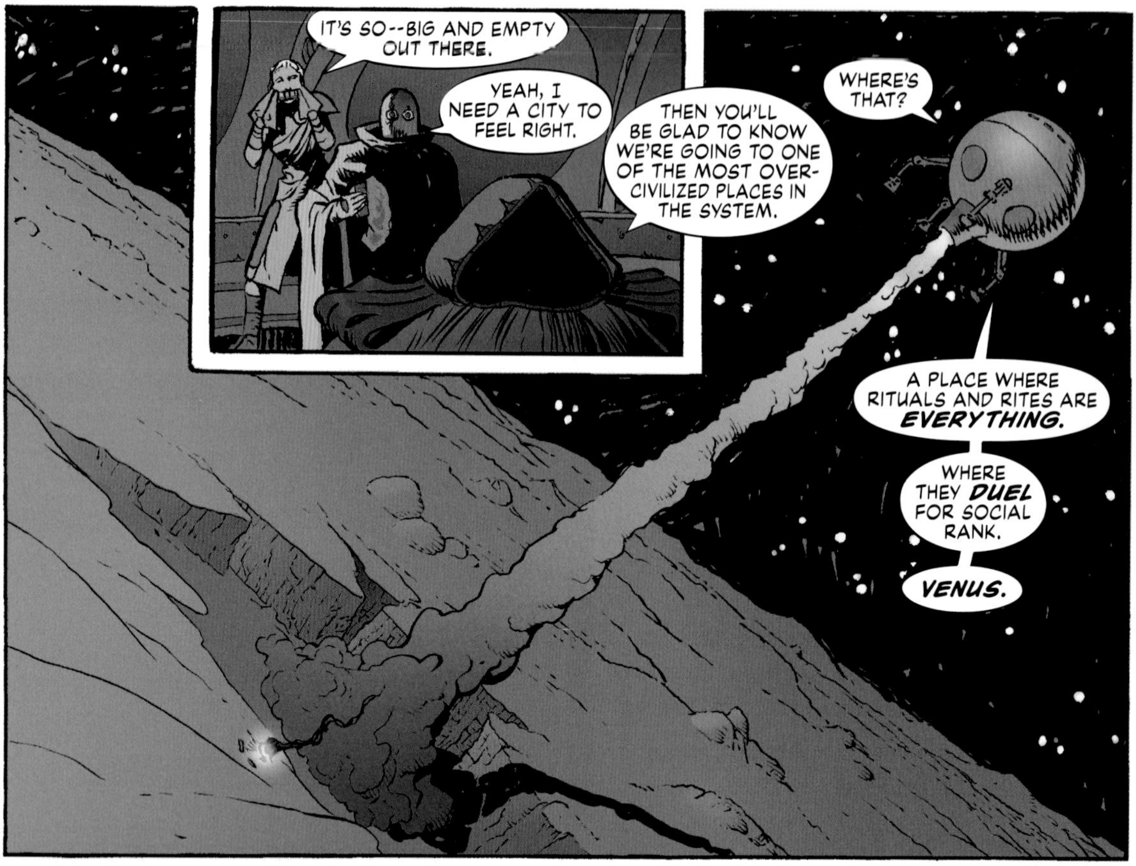
IT'S SO--BIG AND EMPTY OUT THERE.
YEAH, I NEED A CITY TO FEEL RIGHT.
THEN YOU'LL BE GLAD TO KNOW WE'RE GOING TO ONE OF THE MOST OVER-CIVILIZED PLACES IN THE SYSTEM.
WHERE'S THAT?
A PLACE WHERE RITUALS AND RITES ARE EVERYTHING.
WHERE THEY DUEL FOR SOCIAL RANK.
VENUS.

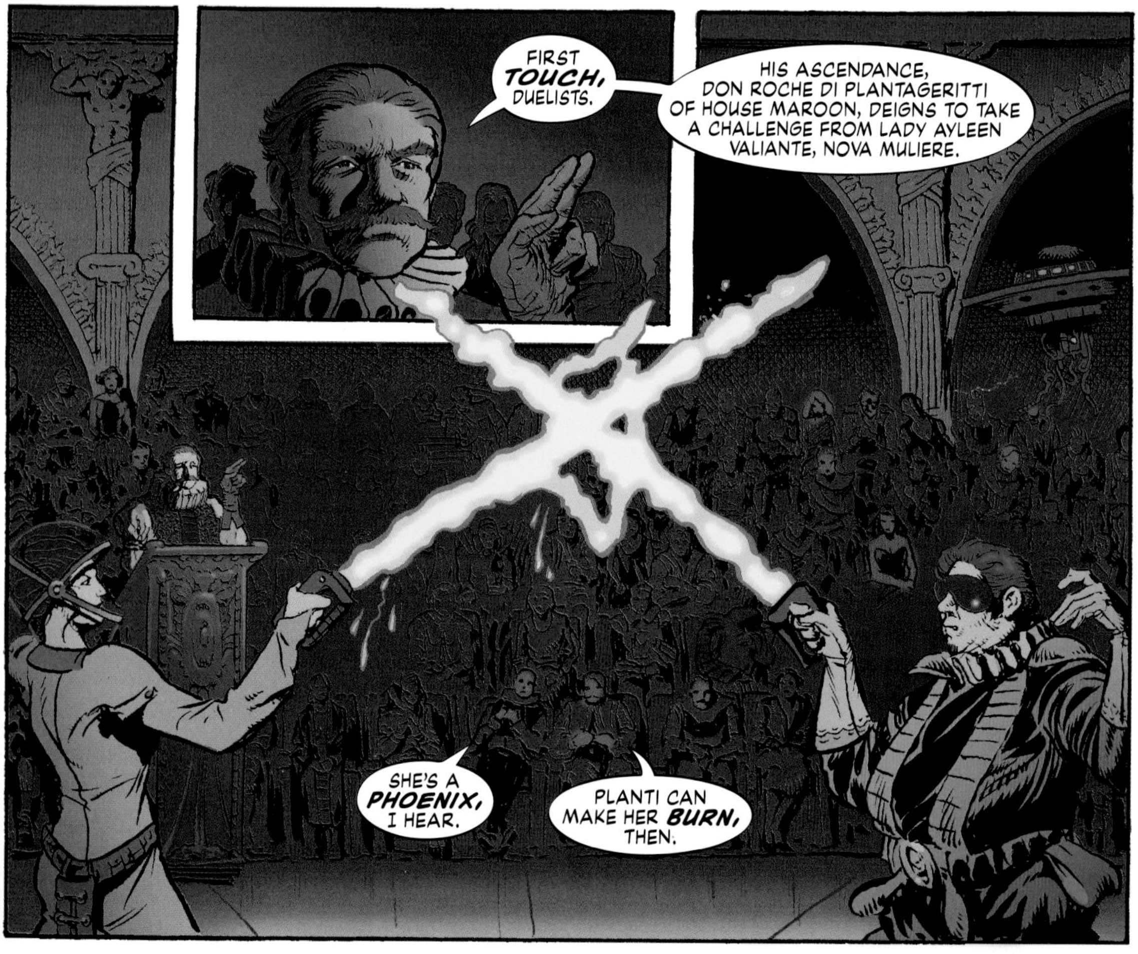
FIRST TOUCH, DUELISTS.
HIS ASCENDANCE, DON ROCHE DI PLANTAGERITTI OF HOUSE MAROON, DEIGNS TO TAKE A CHALLENGE FROM LADY AYLEEN VALIANTE, NOVA MULIERE.
SHE'S A PHOENIX, I HEAR.
PLANTI CAN MAKE HER BURN, THEN.

IT IS LADY AYLEEN'S ENTRY INTO ELITE SOCIETY, IF SHE CAN **DISARM** THE DON.

NO EASY TASK.

VETERAN OF THIRTY MATCHES--THOUGH SURGERIES AND **NANOMENDS** HAVE ERASED THEIR MARKS-- HE KNOWS ALL THE GAMBITS.

AND HE **RESENTS** THIS UPSTART. THEY **ALL** DO.

ENGAGE!

GZZZZT!!

SHE'S **FAST.**

PHOENIXES HAVE TO BE.

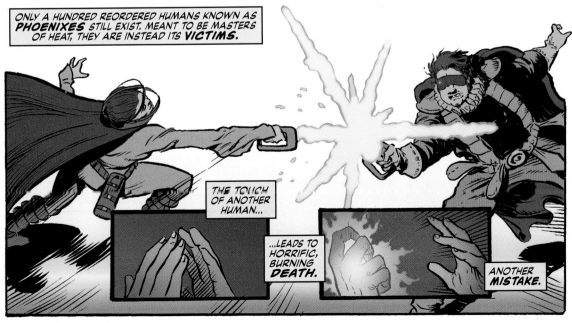

ONLY A HUNDRED REORDERED HUMANS KNOWN AS **PHOENIXES** STILL EXIST. MEANT TO BE MASTERS OF HEAT, THEY ARE INSTEAD ITS **VICTIMS.**

THE TOUCH OF ANOTHER HUMAN...

...LEADS TO HORRIFIC, BURNING **DEATH.**

ANOTHER **MISTAKE.**

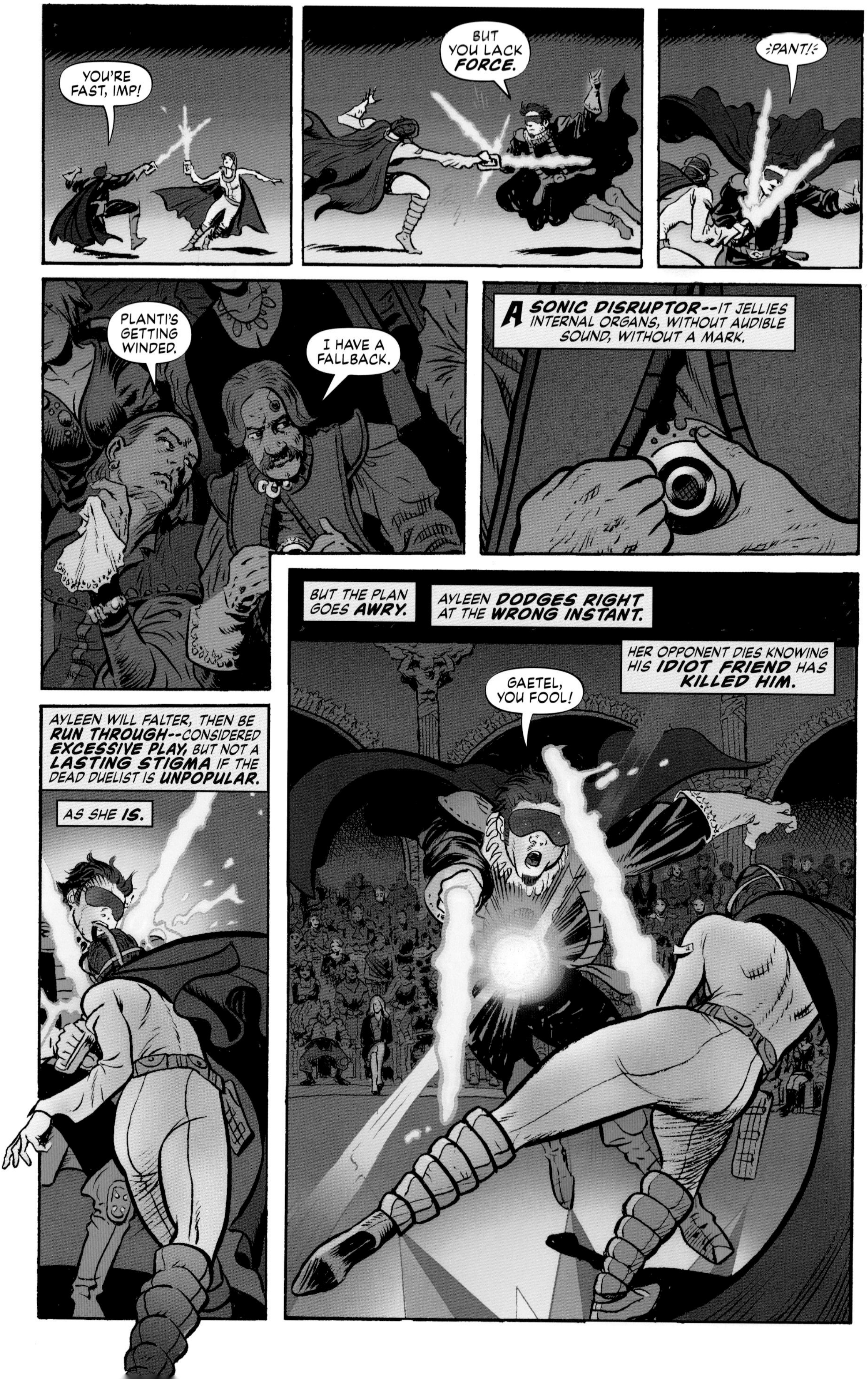
YOU'RE FAST, IMP!
BUT YOU LACK FORCE.
:PANT!:
PLANTI'S GETTING WINDED.
I HAVE A FALLBACK.
A SONIC DISRUPTOR--IT JELLIES INTERNAL ORGANS, WITHOUT AUDIBLE SOUND, WITHOUT A MARK.
AYLEEN WILL FALTER, THEN BE RUN THROUGH--CONSIDERED EXCESSIVE PLAY, BUT NOT A LASTING STIGMA IF THE DEAD DUELIST IS UNPOPULAR.
AS SHE IS.
BUT THE PLAN GOES AWRY.
AYLEEN DODGES RIGHT AT THE WRONG INSTANT.
HER OPPONENT DIES KNOWING HIS IDIOT FRIEND HAS KILLED HIM.
GAETEL, YOU FOOL!

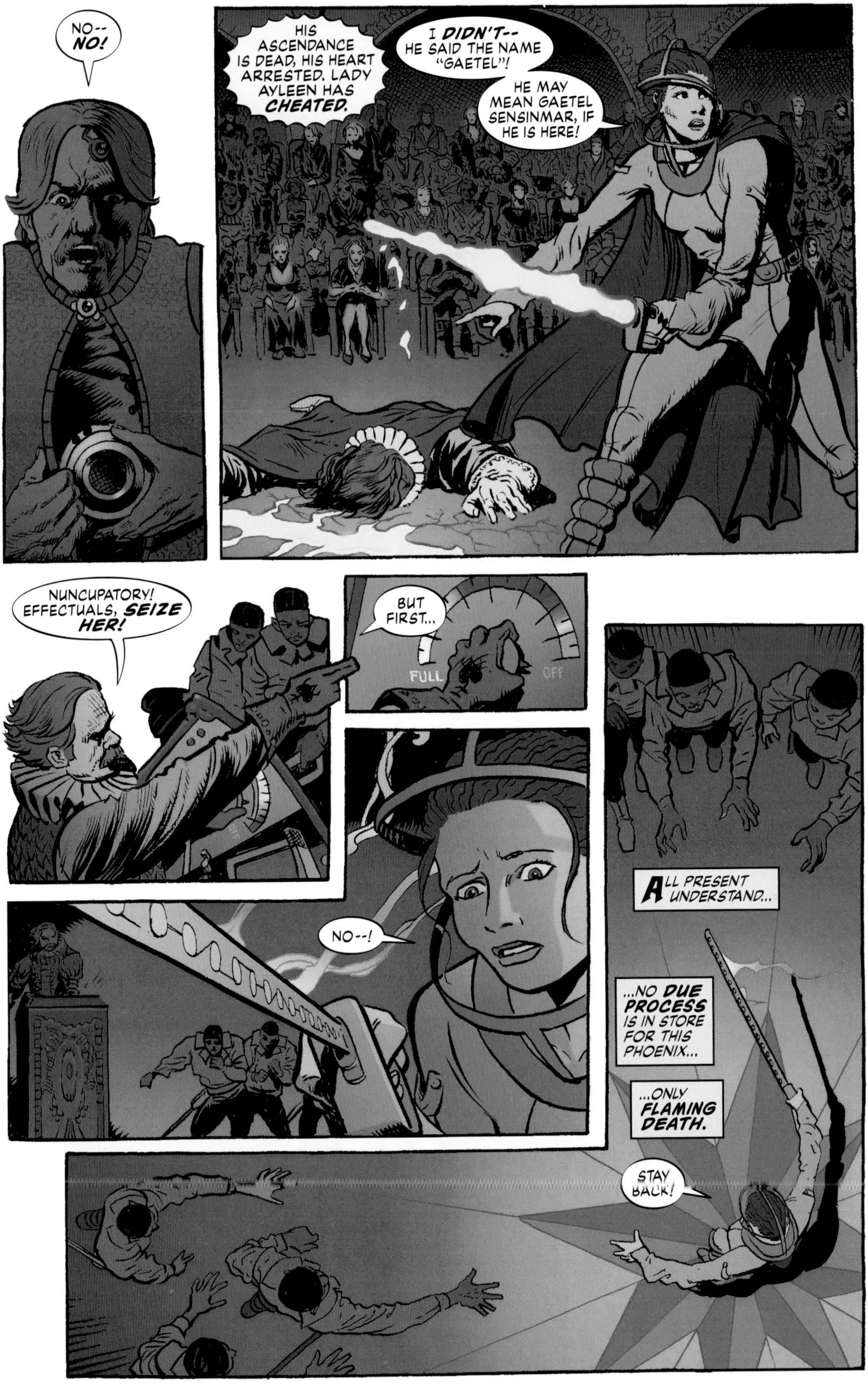
NO-- NO!
HIS ASCENDANCE IS DEAD, HIS HEART ARRESTED. LADY AYLEEN HAS CHEATED.
I DIDN'T-- HE SAID THE NAME "GAETEL"!
HE MAY MEAN GAETEL SENSINMAR, IF HE IS HERE!
NUNCUPATORY! EFFECTUALS, SEIZE HER!
BUT FIRST...
FULL
OFF
NO--!
ALL PRESENT UNDERSTAND...
...NO DUE PROCESS IS IN STORE FOR THIS PHOENIX...
...ONLY FLAMING DEATH.
STAY BACK!

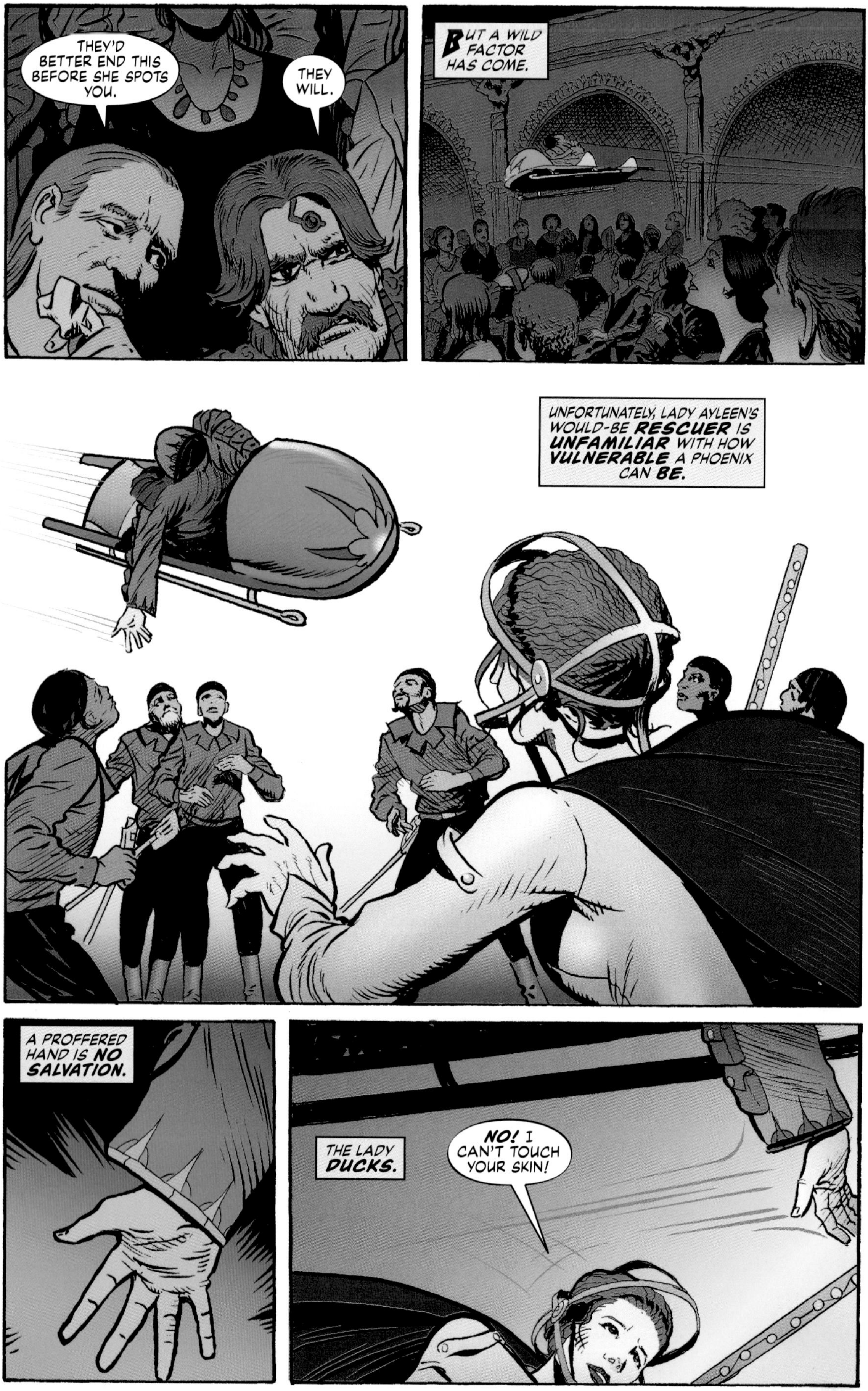
THEY'D BETTER END THIS BEFORE SHE SPOTS YOU.
THEY WILL.
BUT A WILD FACTOR HAS COME.
UNFORTUNATELY, LADY AYLEEN'S WOULD-BE RESCUER IS UNFAMILIAR WITH HOW VULNERABLE A PHOENIX CAN BE.
A PROFFERED HAND IS NO SALVATION.
THE LADY DUCKS.
NO! I CAN'T TOUCH YOUR SKIN!

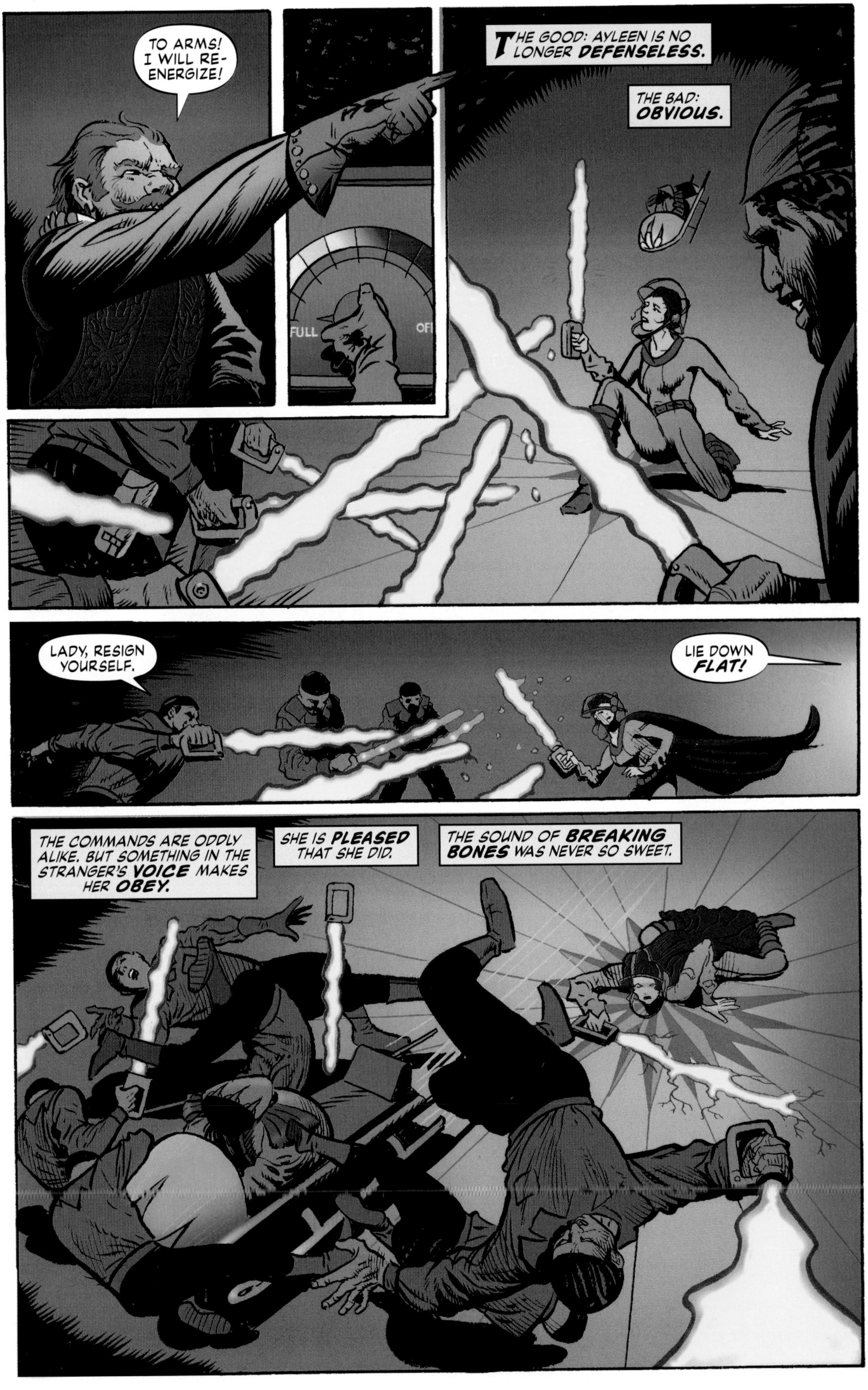
TO ARMS! I WILL RE-ENERGIZE!
FULL
OFF
THE GOOD: AYLEEN IS NO LONGER DEFENSELESS.
THE BAD: OBVIOUS.
LADY, RESIGN YOURSELF.
LIE DOWN FLAT!
THE COMMANDS ARE ODDLY ALIKE. BUT SOMETHING IN THE STRANGER'S VOICE MAKES HER OBEY.
SHE IS PLEASED THAT SHE DID.
THE SOUND OF BREAKING BONES WAS NEVER SO SWEET.

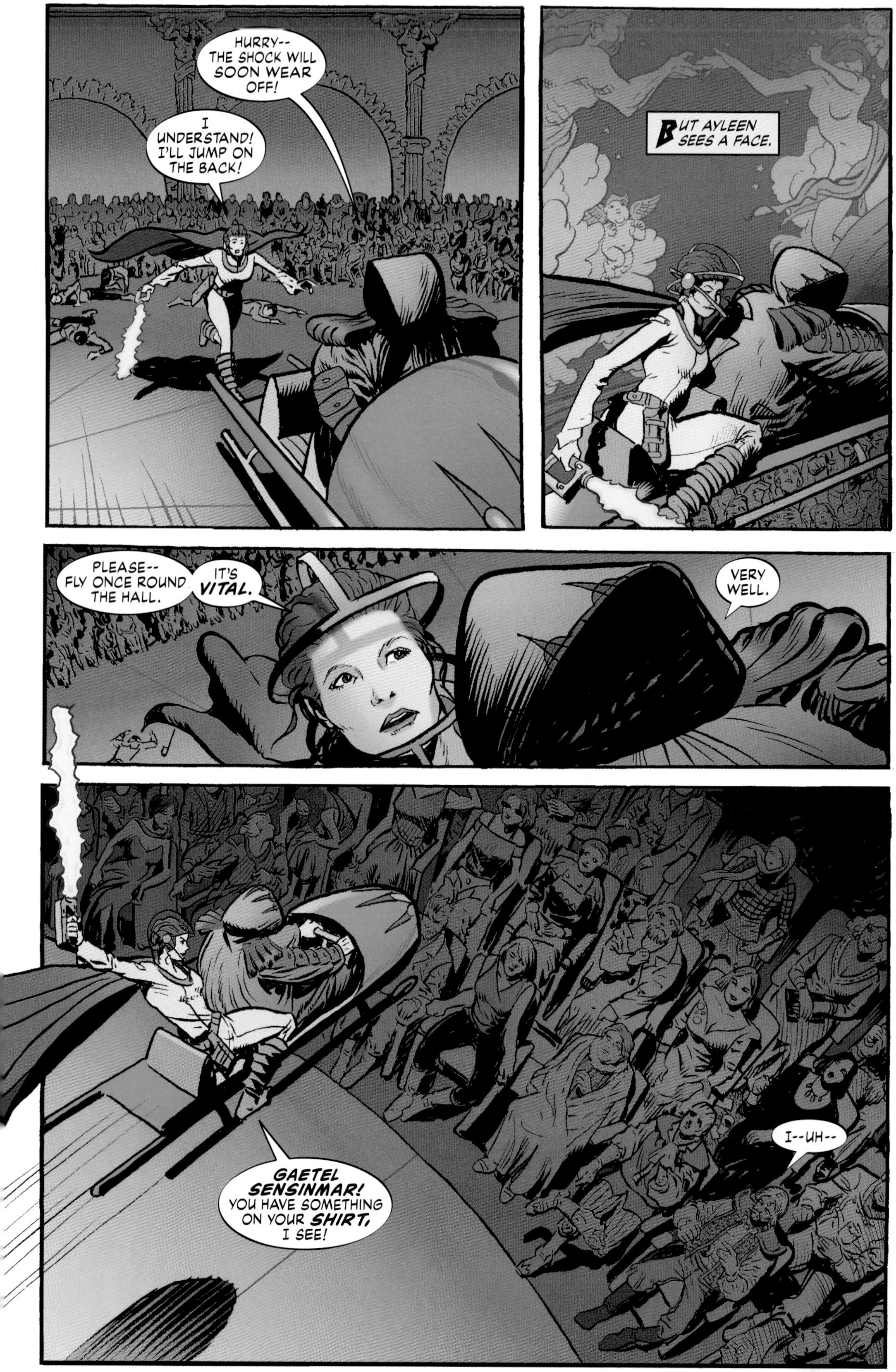
HURRY-- THE SHOCK WILL SOON WEAR OFF!
I UNDERSTAND! I'LL JUMP ON THE BACK!
BUT AYLEEN SEES A FACE.
PLEASE-- FLY ONCE ROUND THE HALL.
IT'S VITAL.
VERY WELL.
GAETEL SENSINMAR! YOU HAVE SOMETHING ON YOUR SHIRT, I SEE!
I--UH--

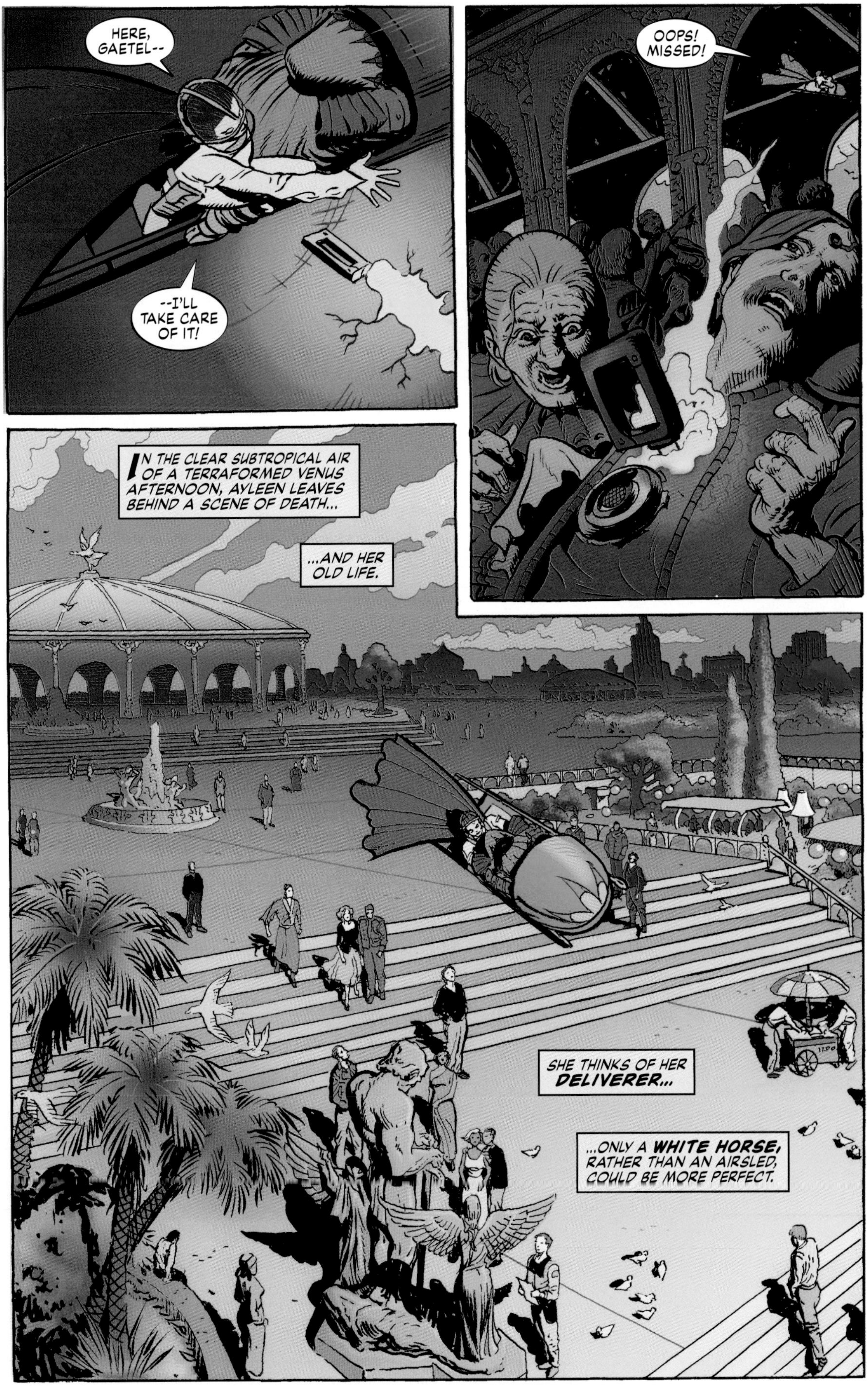
HERE, GAETEL--
--I'LL TAKE CARE OF IT!
OOPS! MISSED!
IN THE CLEAR SUBTROPICAL AIR OF A TERRAFORMED VENUS AFTERNOON, AYLEEN LEAVES BEHIND A SCENE OF DEATH...
...AND HER OLD LIFE.
SHE THINKS OF HER DELIVERER...
...ONLY A WHITE HORSE, RATHER THAN AN AIRSLED, COULD BE MORE PERFECT.

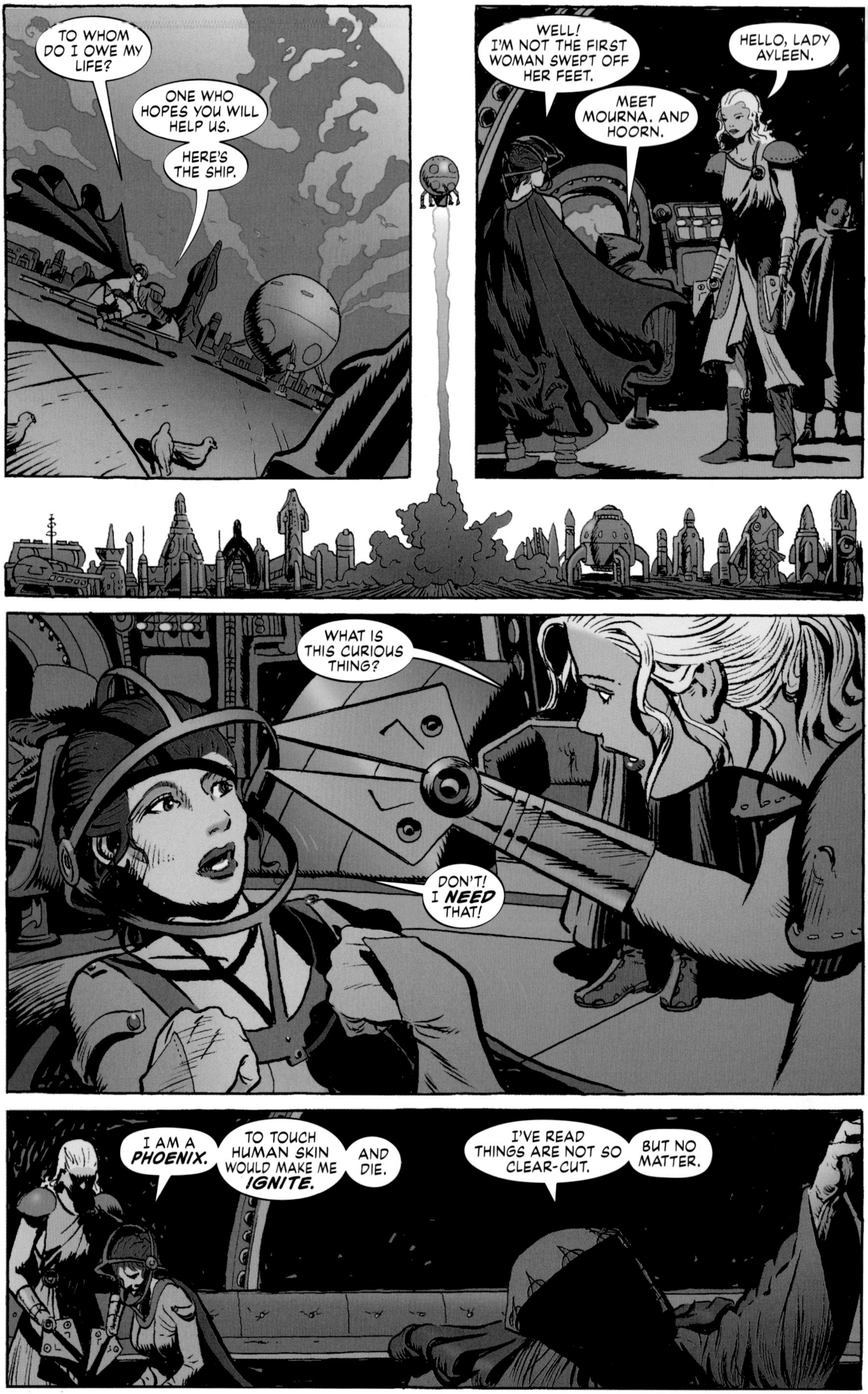

TO WHOM DO I OWE MY LIFE?
ONE WHO HOPES YOU WILL HELP US.
HERE'S THE SHIP.
WELL! I'M NOT THE FIRST WOMAN SWEPT OFF HER FEET.
MEET MOURNA. AND HOORN.
HELLO, LADY AYLEEN.
WHAT IS THIS CURIOUS THING?
DON'T! I **NEED** THAT!
I AM A ***PHOENIX.***
TO TOUCH HUMAN SKIN WOULD MAKE ME ***IGNITE.***
AND DIE.
I'VE READ THINGS ARE NOT SO CLEAR-CUT.
BUT NO MATTER.

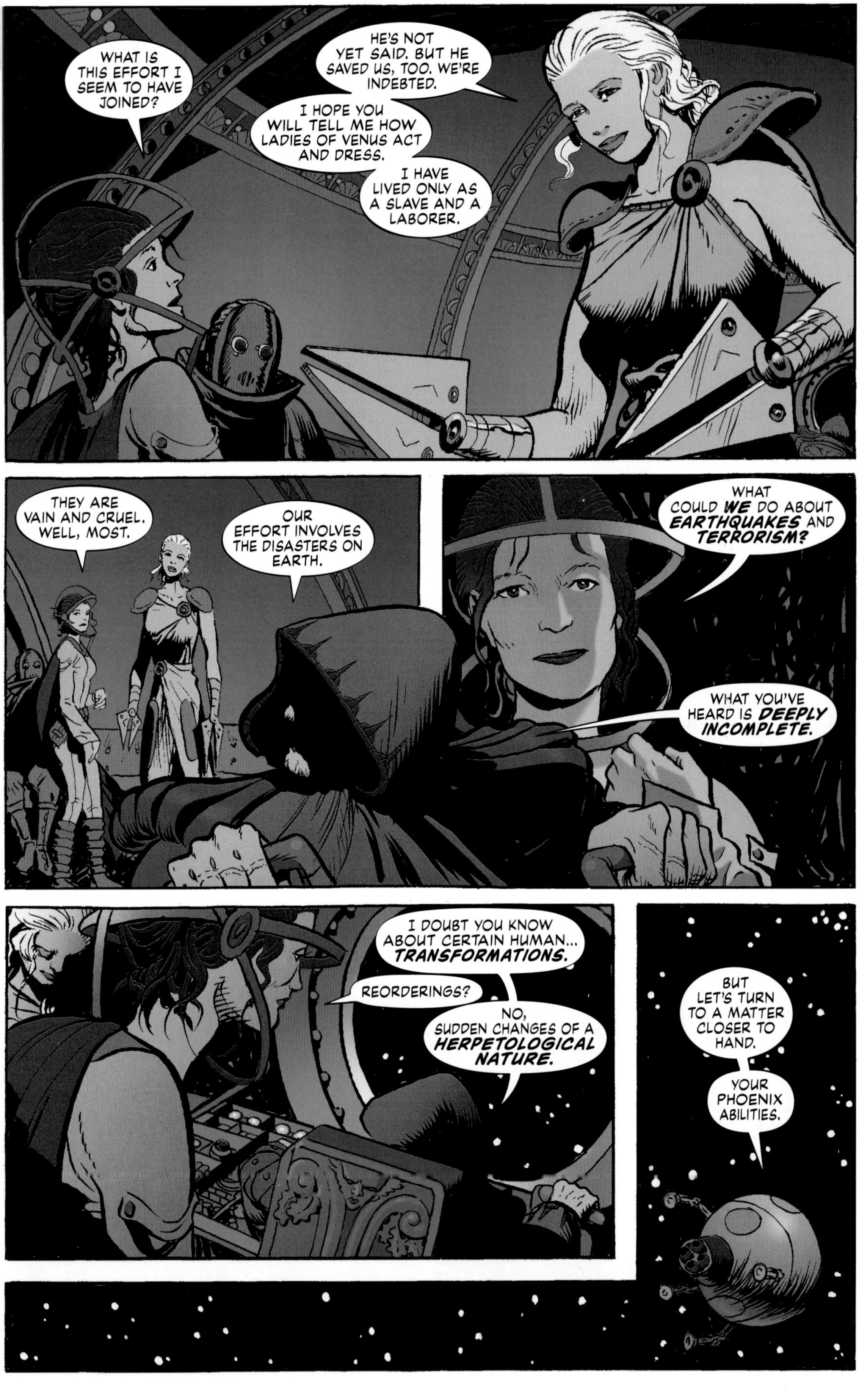
WHAT IS THIS EFFORT I SEEM TO HAVE JOINED?
HE'S NOT YET SAID. BUT HE SAVED US, TOO. WE'RE INDEBTED.
I HOPE YOU WILL TELL ME HOW LADIES OF VENUS ACT AND DRESS.
I HAVE LIVED ONLY AS A SLAVE AND A LABORER.
THEY ARE VAIN AND CRUEL. WELL, MOST.
OUR EFFORT INVOLVES THE DISASTERS ON EARTH.
WHAT COULD **WE** DO ABOUT ***EARTHQUAKES*** AND ***TERRORISM?***
WHAT YOU'VE HEARD IS ***DEEPLY INCOMPLETE.***
I DOUBT YOU KNOW ABOUT CERTAIN HUMAN... ***TRANSFORMATIONS.***
REORDERINGS?
NO, SUDDEN CHANGES OF A ***HERPETOLOGICAL NATURE.***
BUT LET'S TURN TO A MATTER CLOSER TO HAND.
YOUR PHOENIX ABILITIES.

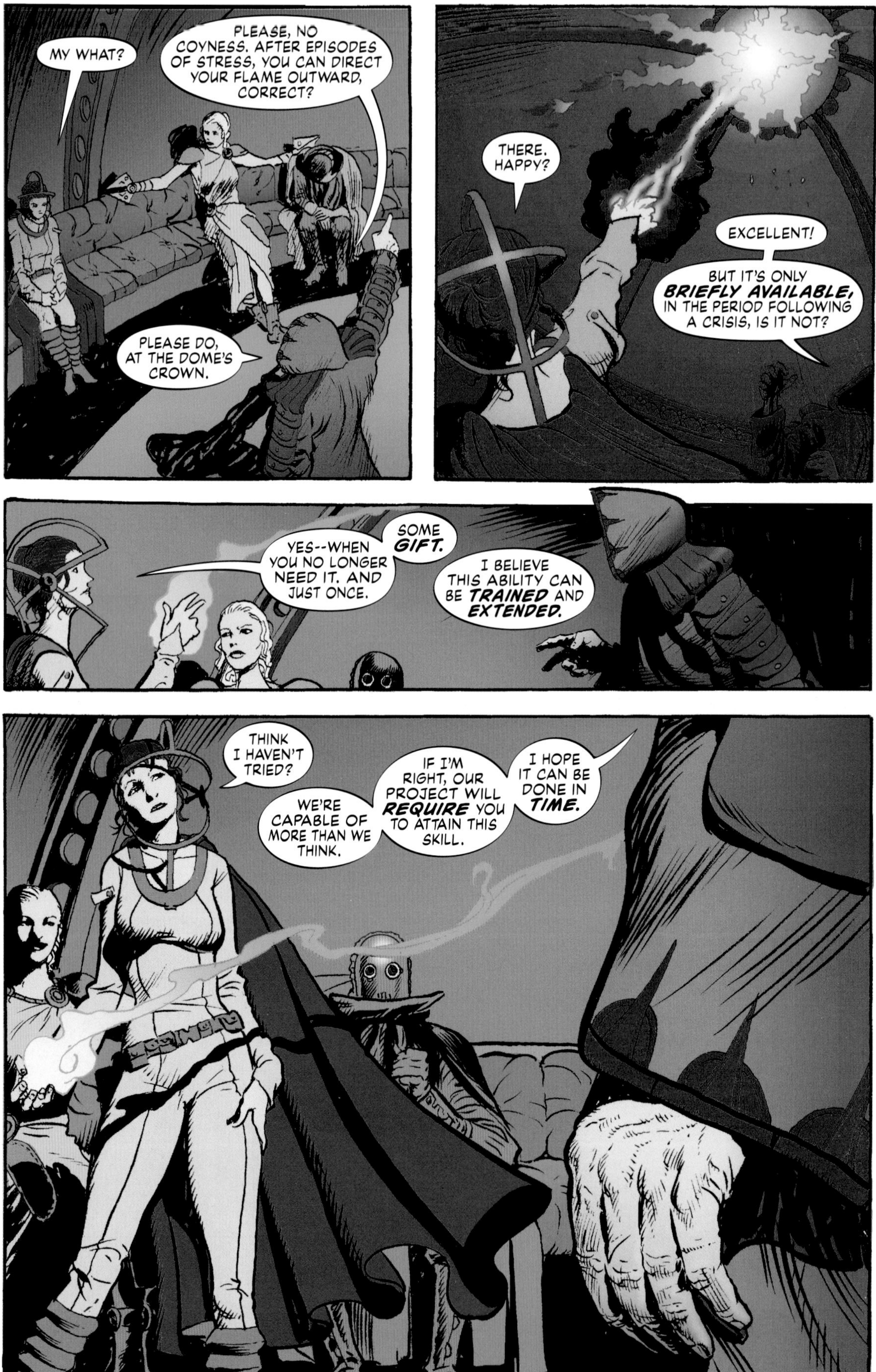
MY WHAT?
PLEASE, NO COYNESS. AFTER EPISODES OF STRESS, YOU CAN DIRECT YOUR FLAME OUTWARD, CORRECT?
PLEASE DO, AT THE DOME'S CROWN.
THERE. HAPPY?
EXCELLENT!
BUT IT'S ONLY BRIEFLY AVAILABLE, IN THE PERIOD FOLLOWING A CRISIS, IS IT NOT?
YES--WHEN YOU NO LONGER NEED IT. AND JUST ONCE.
SOME GIFT.
I BELIEVE THIS ABILITY CAN BE TRAINED AND EXTENDED.
THINK I HAVEN'T TRIED?
WE'RE CAPABLE OF MORE THAN WE THINK.
IF I'M RIGHT, OUR PROJECT WILL REQUIRE YOU TO ATTAIN THIS SKILL.
I HOPE IT CAN BE DONE IN TIME.

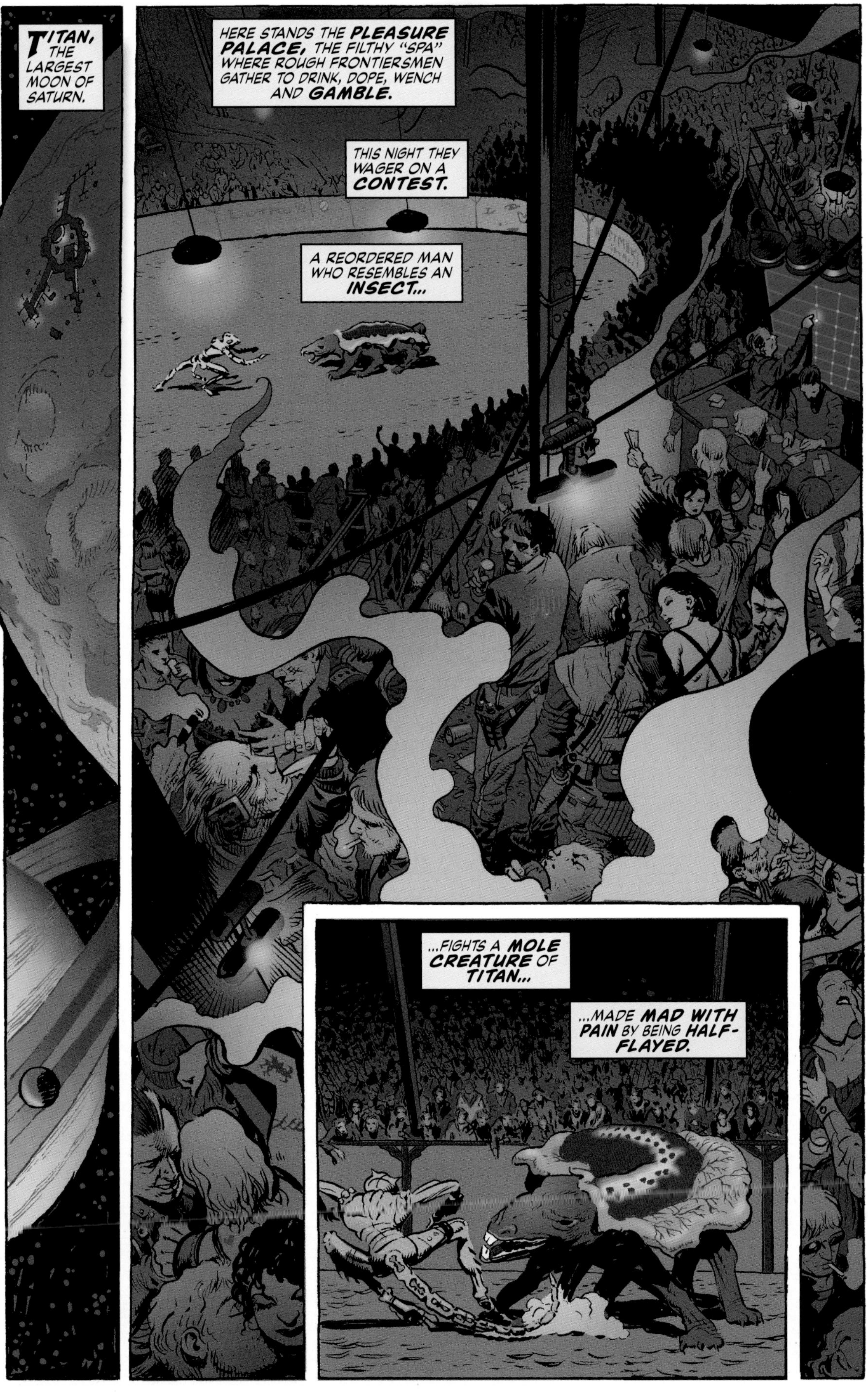
TITAN, THE LARGEST MOON OF SATURN.
HERE STANDS THE PLEASURE PALACE, THE FILTHY "SPA" WHERE ROUGH FRONTIERSMEN GATHER TO DRINK, DOPE, WENCH AND GAMBLE.
THIS NIGHT THEY WAGER ON A CONTEST.
A REORDERED MAN WHO RESEMBLES AN INSECT...
...FIGHTS A MOLE CREATURE OF TITAN...
...MADE MAD WITH PAIN BY BEING HALF-FLAYED.

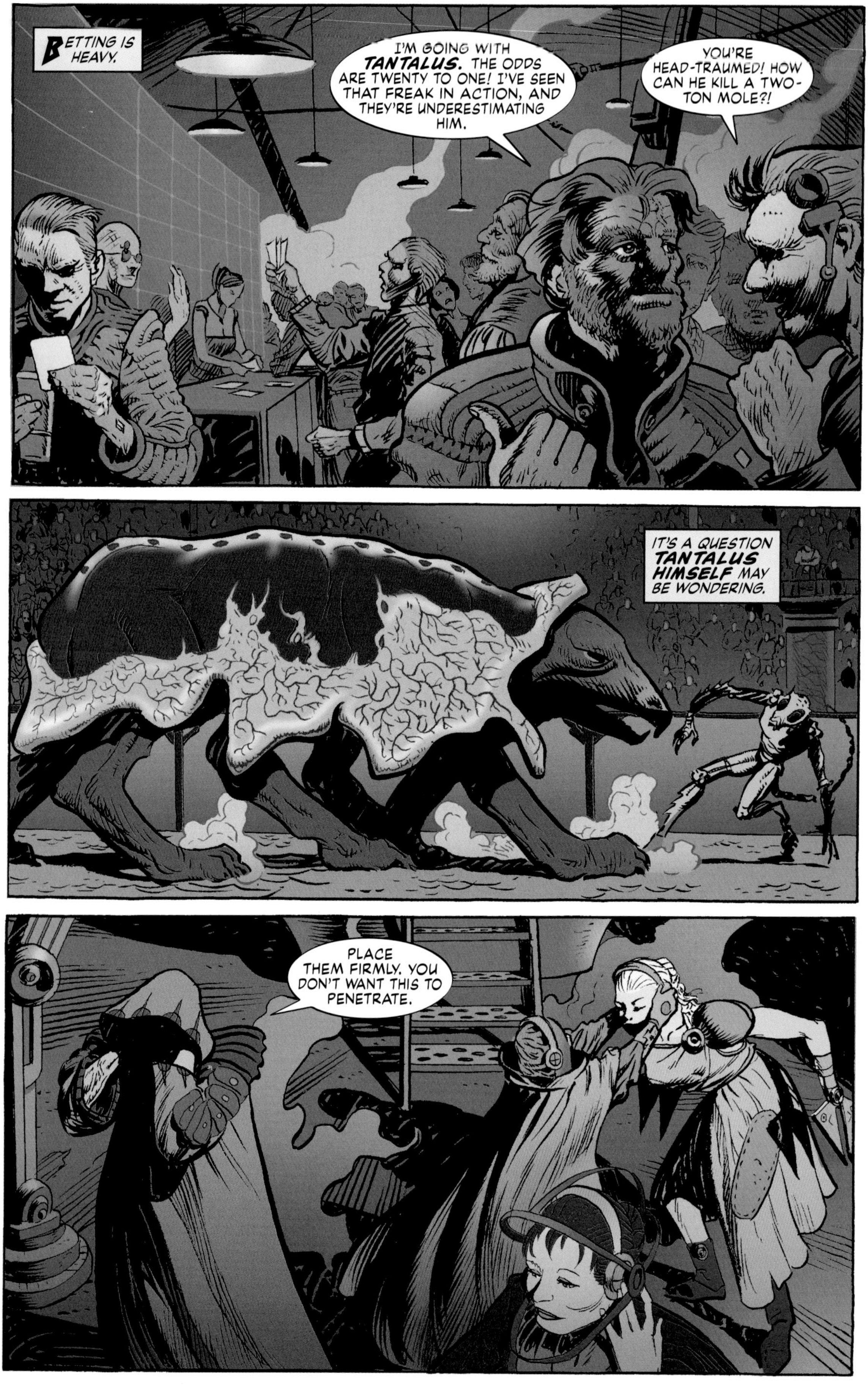
BETTING IS HEAVY.
I'M GOING WITH TANTALUS. THE ODDS ARE TWENTY TO ONE! I'VE SEEN THAT FREAK IN ACTION, AND THEY'RE UNDERESTIMATING HIM.
YOU'RE HEAD-TRAUMED! HOW CAN HE KILL A TWO-TON MOLE?!
IT'S A QUESTION TANTALUS HIMSELF MAY BE WONDERING.
PLACE THEM FIRMLY. YOU DON'T WANT THIS TO PENETRATE.

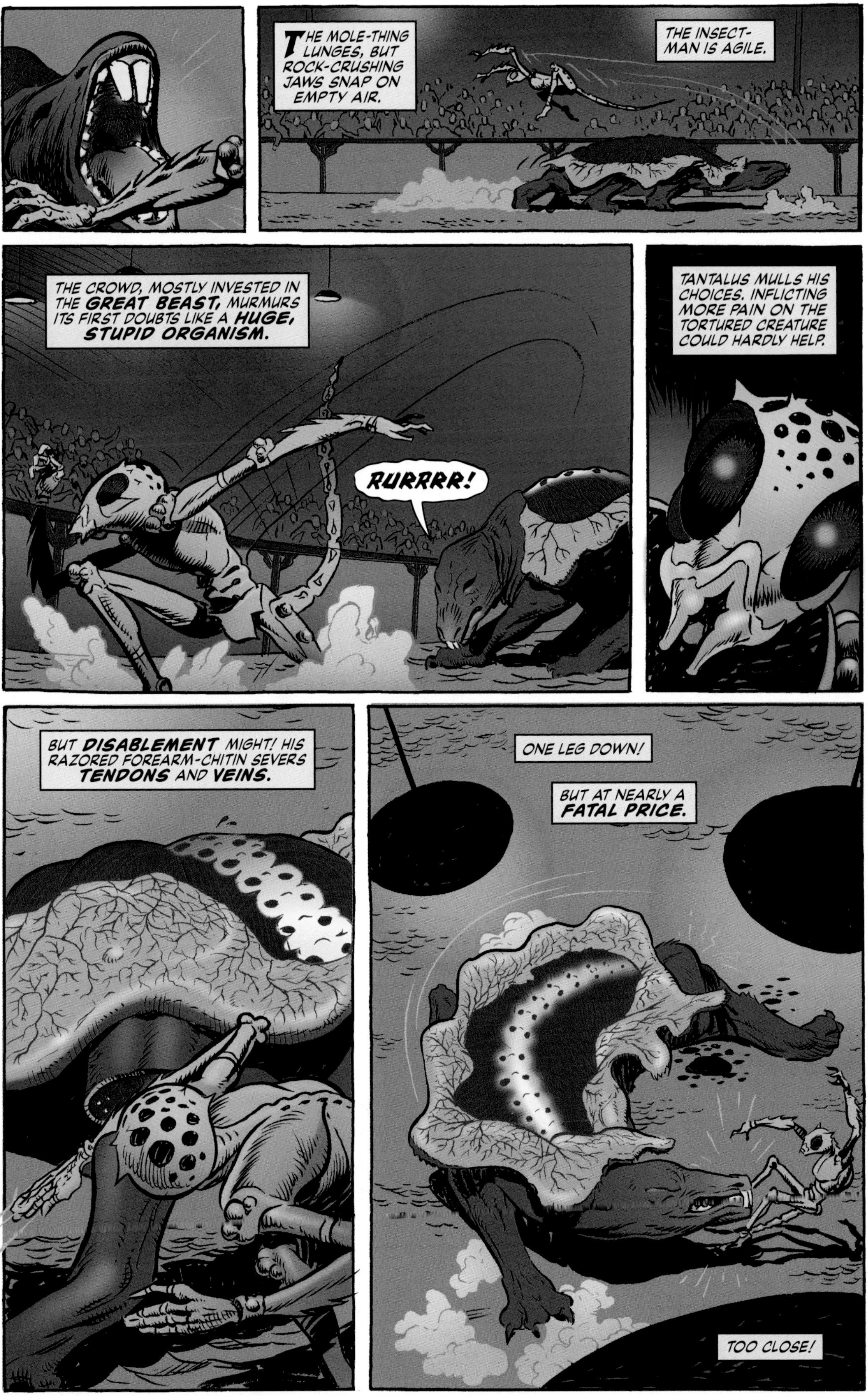
THE MOLE-THING LUNGES, BUT ROCK-CRUSHING JAWS SNAP ON EMPTY AIR.
THE INSECT-MAN IS AGILE.
THE CROWD, MOSTLY INVESTED IN THE GREAT BEAST, MURMURS ITS FIRST DOUBTS LIKE A HUGE, STUPID ORGANISM.
RURRRR!
TANTALUS MULLS HIS CHOICES. INFLICTING MORE PAIN ON THE TORTURED CREATURE COULD HARDLY HELP.
BUT DISABLEMENT MIGHT! HIS RAZORED FOREARM-CHITIN SEVERS TENDONS AND VEINS.
ONE LEG DOWN!
BUT AT NEARLY A FATAL PRICE.
TOO CLOSE!

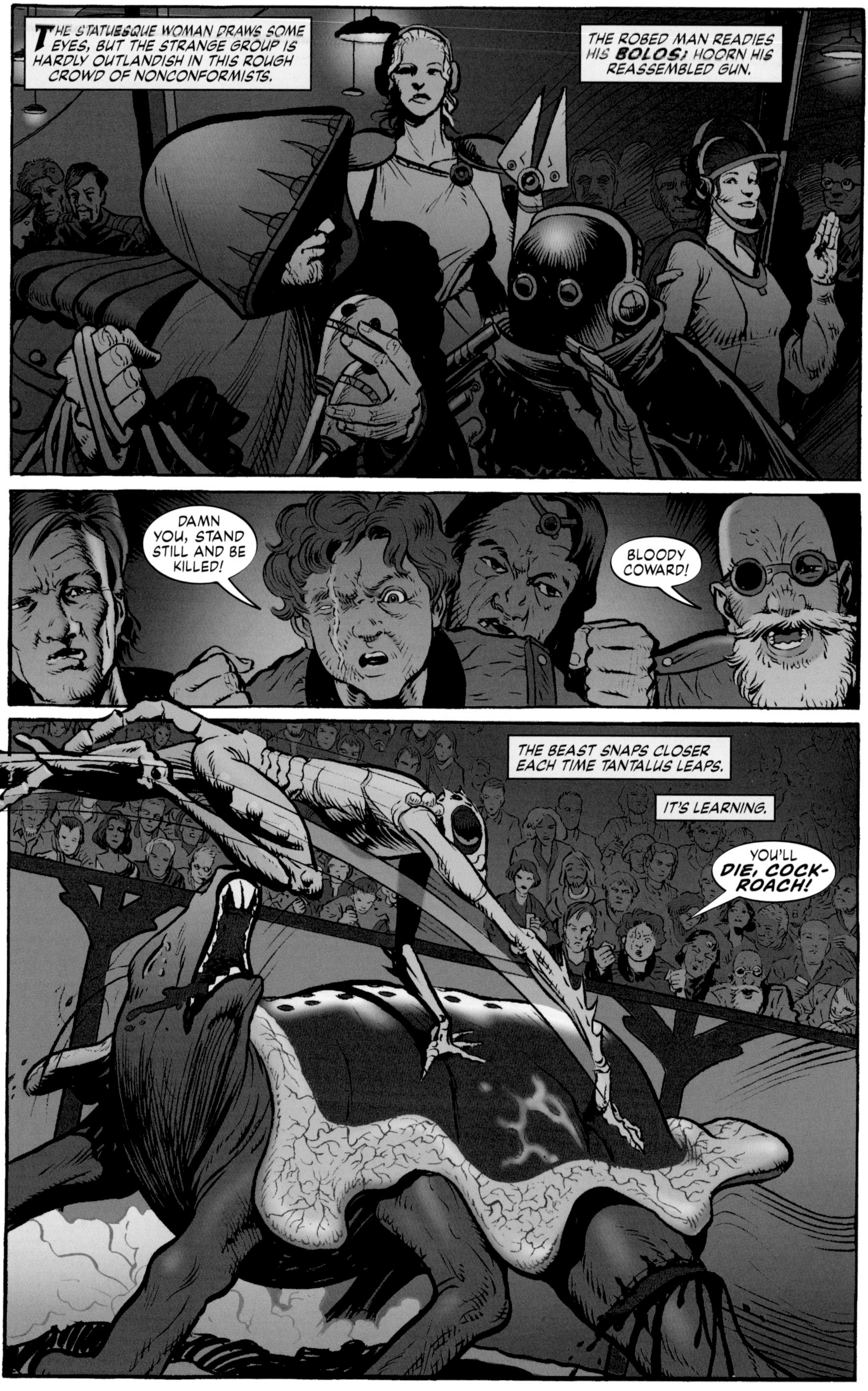
THE STATUESQUE WOMAN DRAWS SOME EYES, BUT THE STRANGE GROUP IS HARDLY OUTLANDISH IN THIS ROUGH CROWD OF NONCONFORMISTS.
THE ROBED MAN READIES HIS BOLOS; HOORN HIS REASSEMBLED GUN.
DAMN YOU, STAND STILL AND BE KILLED!
BLOODY COWARD!
THE BEAST SNAPS CLOSER EACH TIME TANTALUS LEAPS.
IT'S LEARNING.
YOU'LL DIE, COCK-ROACH!

TWO LEGS!

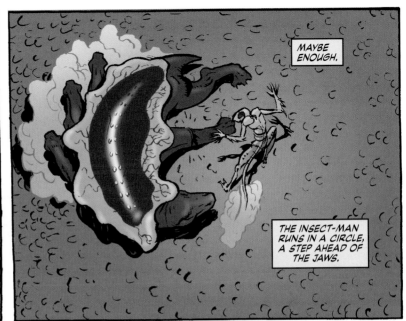

MAYBE ENOUGH.

THE INSECT-MAN RUNS IN A CIRCLE, A STEP AHEAD OF THE JAWS.

AROUND ONCE...

...TWICE...

...AND THE BEAST IS ENGULFED IN **DUST** KICKED UP BY ITS **OWN THRASHING MOVEMENTS.**

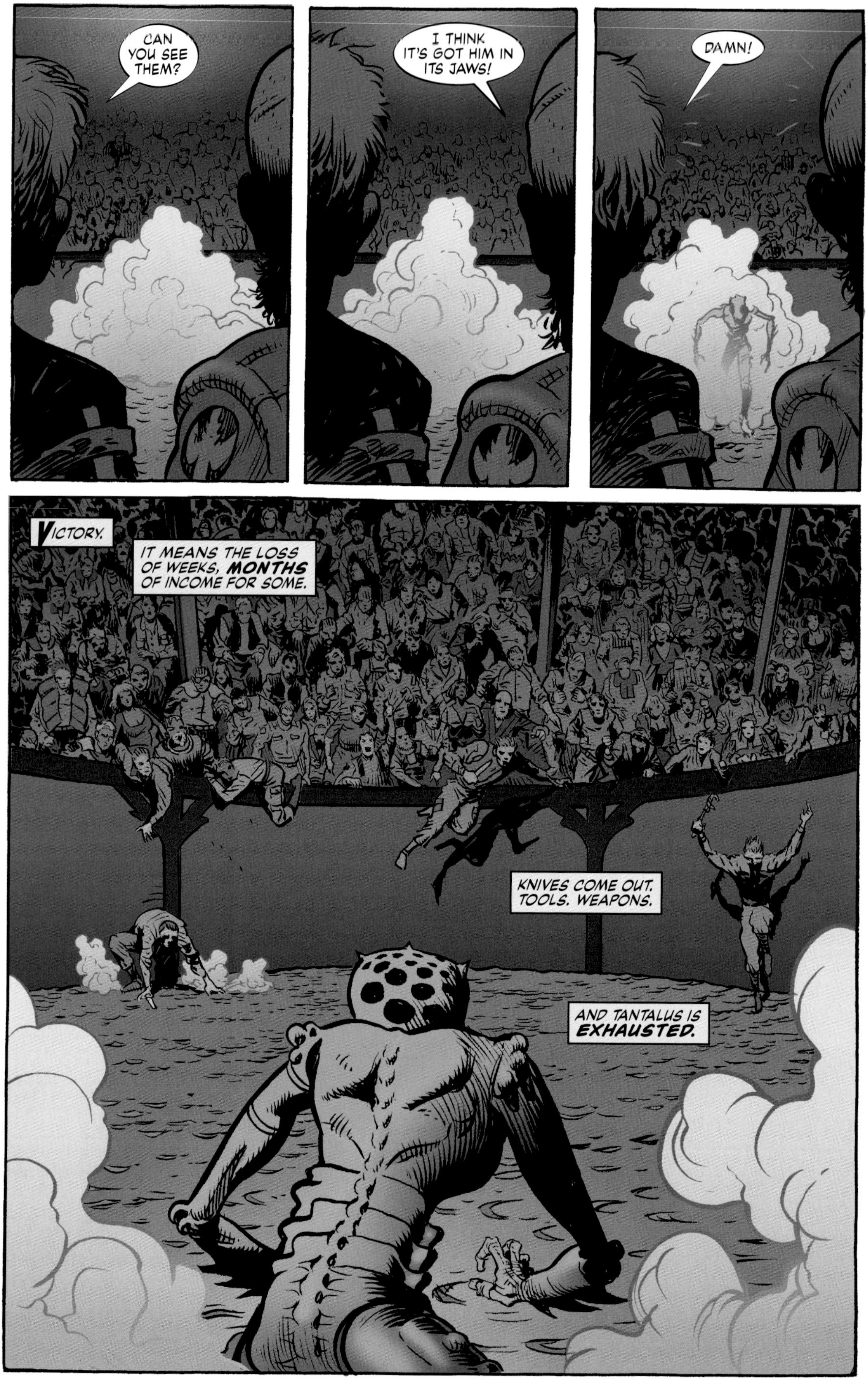
CAN YOU SEE THEM?
I THINK IT'S GOT HIM IN ITS JAWS!
DAMN!
VICTORY.
IT MEANS THE LOSS OF WEEKS, MONTHS OF INCOME FOR SOME.
KNIVES COME OUT. TOOLS. WEAPONS.
AND TANTALUS IS EXHAUSTED.

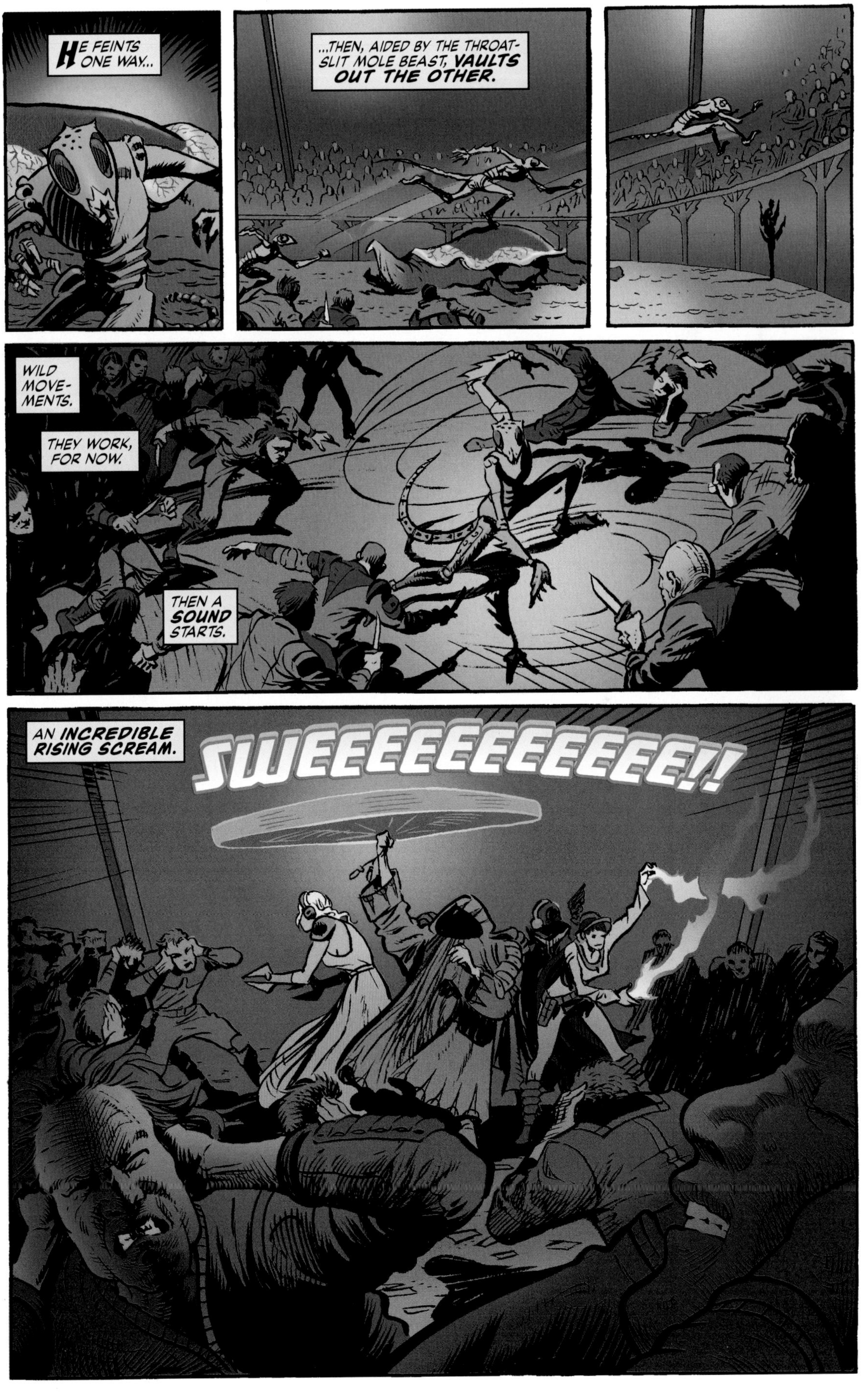
HE FEINTS ONE WAY...
...THEN, AIDED BY THE THROAT-SLIT MOLE BEAST, VAULTS OUT THE OTHER.
WILD MOVEMENTS.
THEY WORK, FOR NOW.
THEN A SOUND STARTS.
AN INCREDIBLE RISING SCREAM.
SWEEEEEEEEEEEE!!

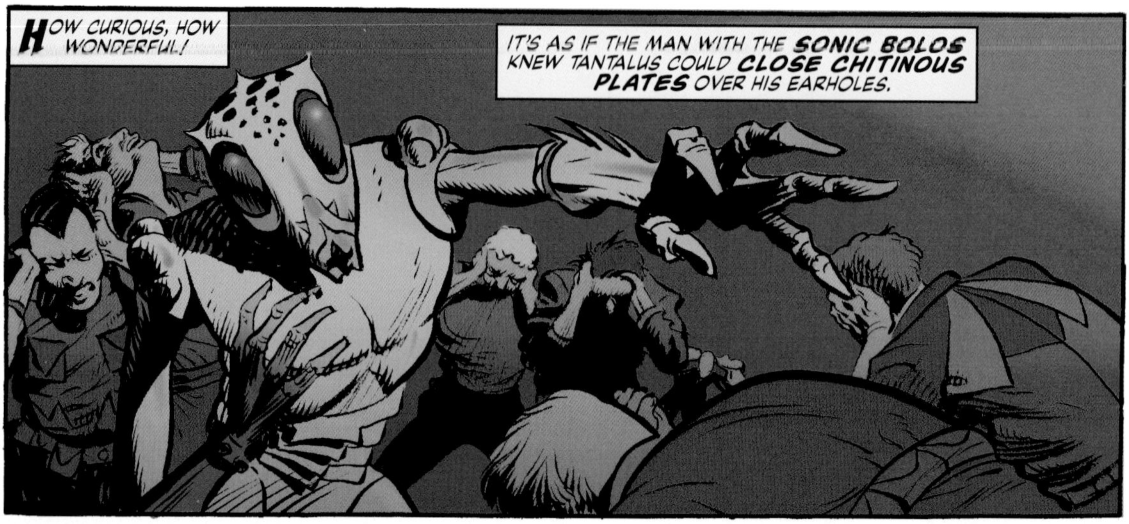
HOW CURIOUS, HOW WONDERFUL!
IT'S AS IF THE MAN WITH THE SONIC BOLOS KNEW TANTALUS COULD CLOSE CHITINOUS PLATES OVER HIS EARHOLES.

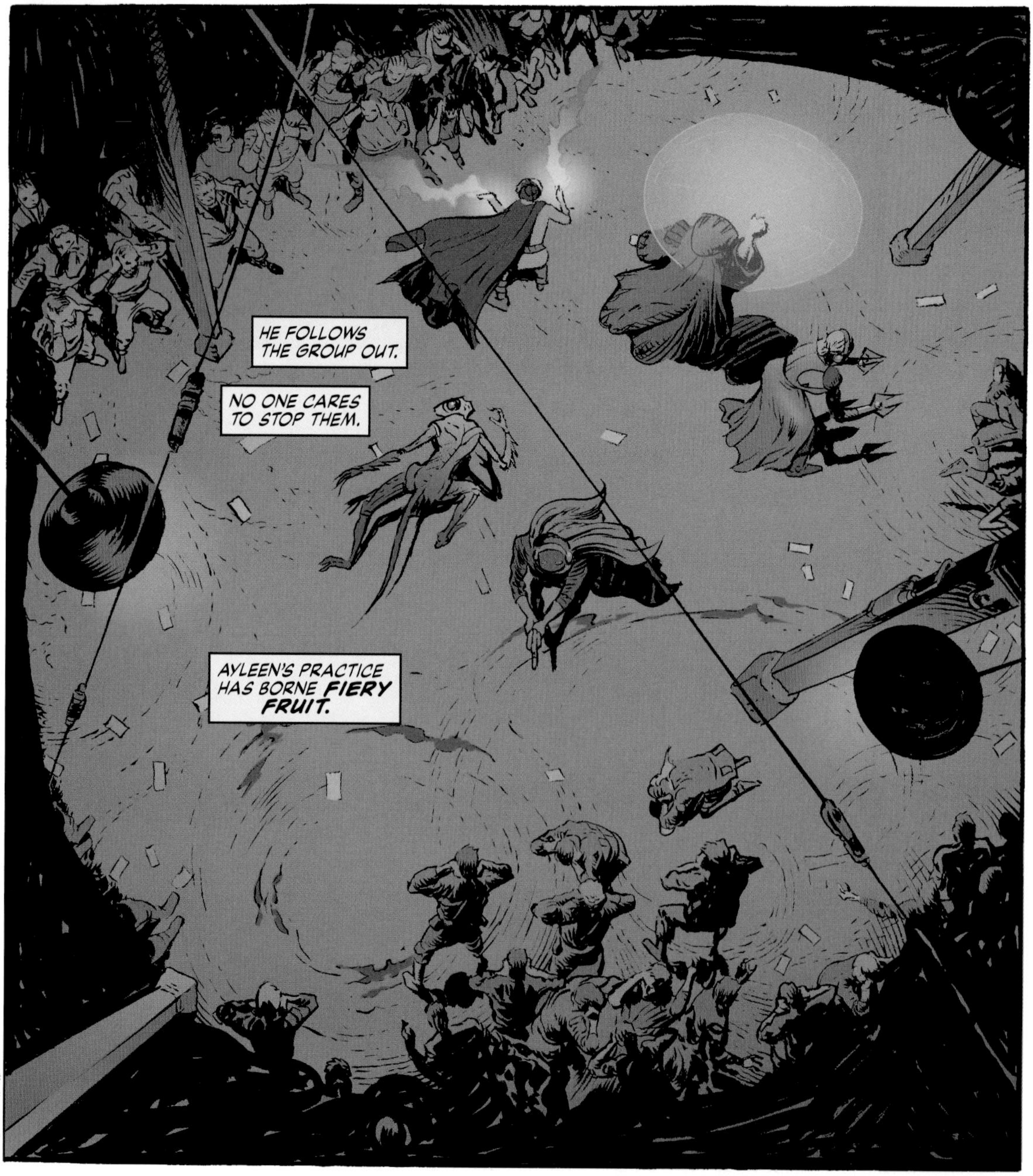
HE FOLLOWS THE GROUP OUT.
NO ONE CARES TO STOP THEM.
AYLEEN'S PRACTICE HAS BORNE FIERY FRUIT.

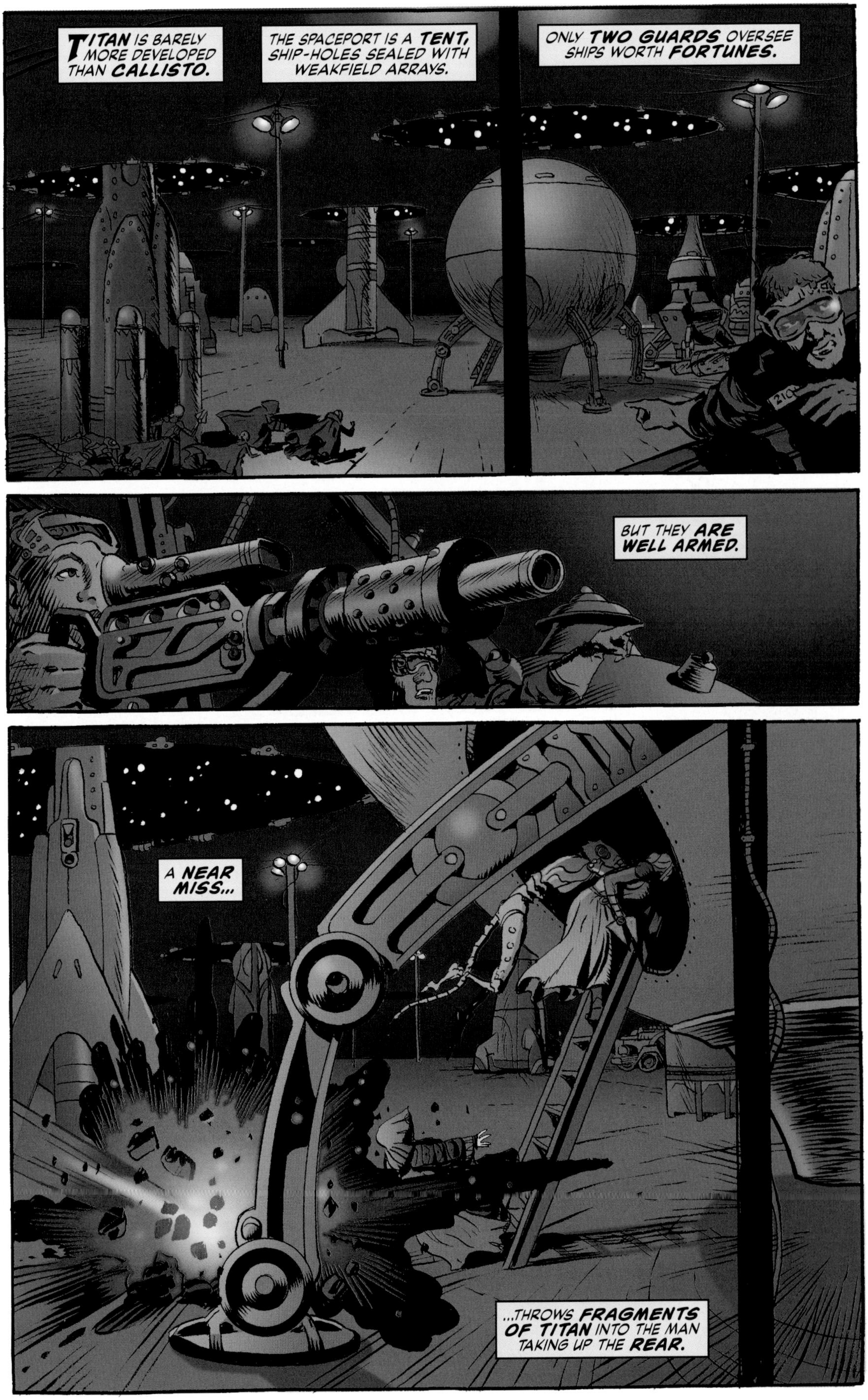
TITAN IS BARELY MORE DEVELOPED THAN CALLISTO.
THE SPACEPORT IS A TENT, SHIP-HOLES SEALED WITH WEAKFIELD ARRAYS.
ONLY TWO GUARDS OVERSEE SHIPS WORTH FORTUNES.
BUT THEY ARE WELL ARMED.
A NEAR MISS...
...THROWS FRAGMENTS OF TITAN INTO THE MAN TAKING UP THE REAR.

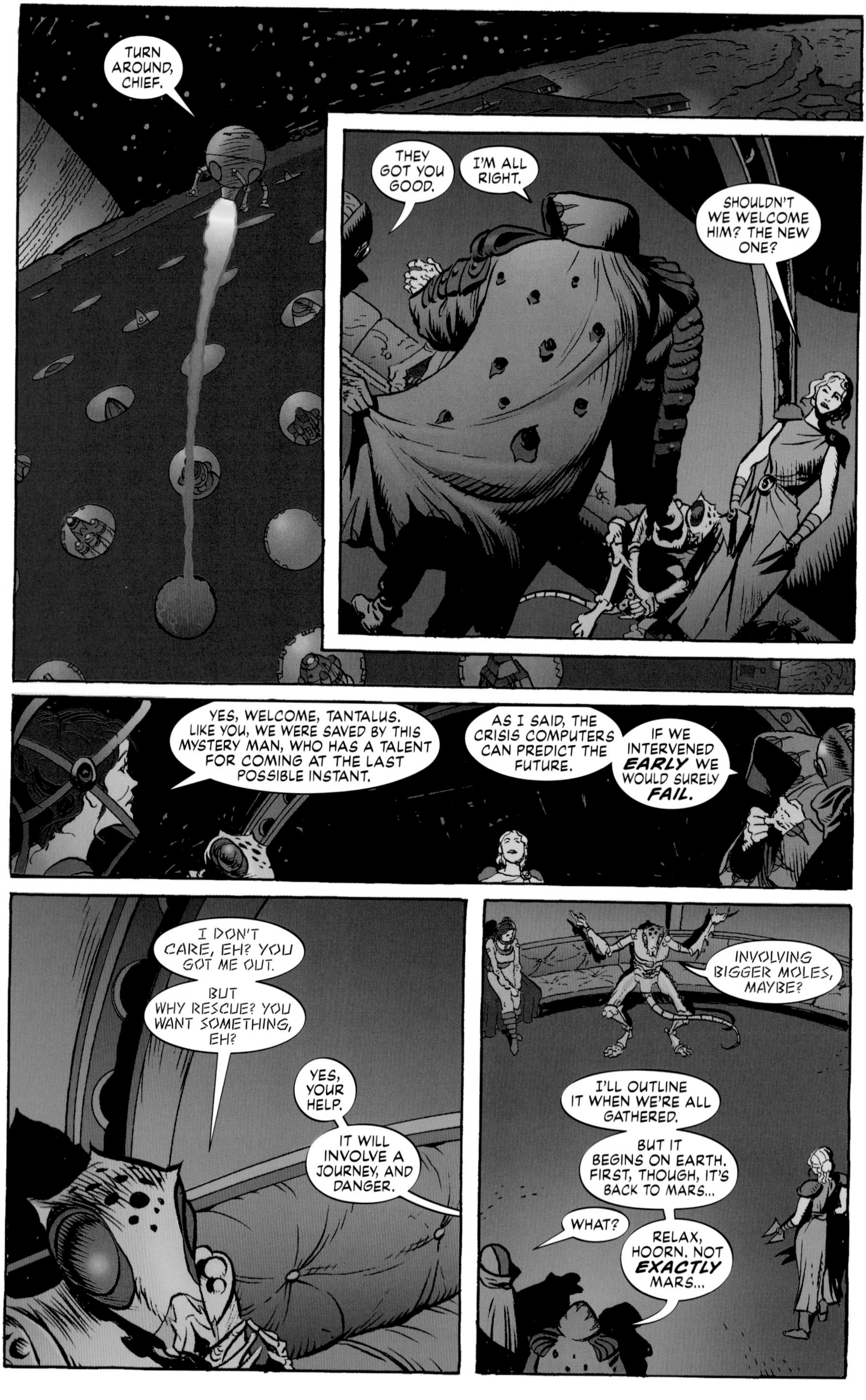
TURN AROUND, CHIEF.
THEY GOT YOU GOOD.
I'M ALL RIGHT.
SHOULDN'T WE WELCOME HIM? THE NEW ONE?
YES, WELCOME, TANTALUS. LIKE YOU, WE WERE SAVED BY THIS MYSTERY MAN, WHO HAS A TALENT FOR COMING AT THE LAST POSSIBLE INSTANT.
AS I SAID, THE CRISIS COMPUTERS CAN PREDICT THE FUTURE.
IF WE INTERVENED EARLY WE WOULD SURELY FAIL.
I DON'T CARE, EH? YOU GOT ME OUT.
BUT WHY RESCUE? YOU WANT SOMETHING, EH?
YES, YOUR HELP.
IT WILL INVOLVE A JOURNEY, AND DANGER.
INVOLVING BIGGER MOLES, MAYBE?
I'LL OUTLINE IT WHEN WE'RE ALL GATHERED.
BUT IT BEGINS ON EARTH. FIRST, THOUGH, IT'S BACK TO MARS...
WHAT?
RELAX, HOORN. NOT EXACTLY MARS...

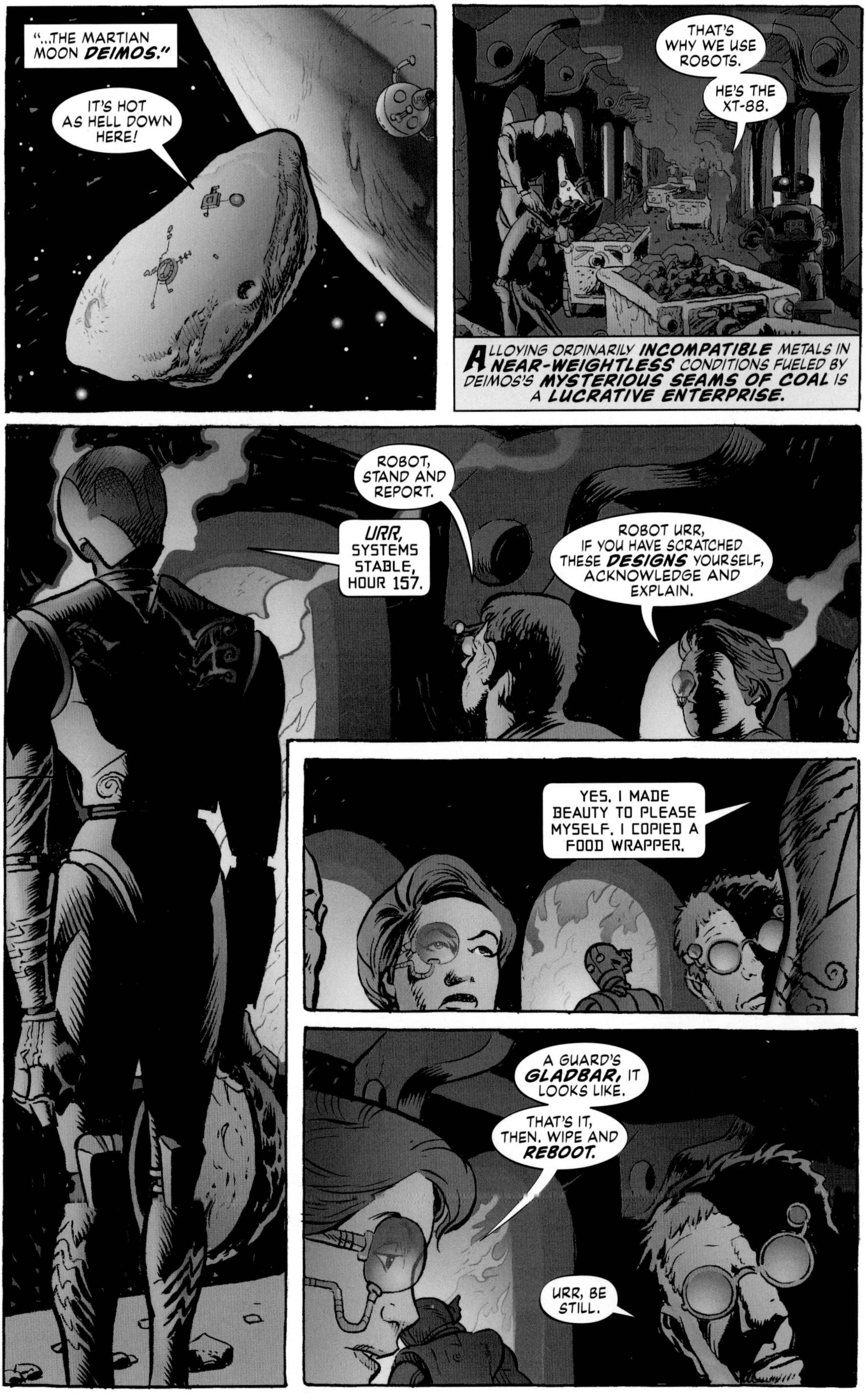
"...THE MARTIAN MOON DEIMOS."
IT'S HOT AS HELL DOWN HERE!
THAT'S WHY WE USE ROBOTS.
HE'S THE XT-88.
ALLOYING ORDINARILY INCOMPATIBLE METALS IN NEAR-WEIGHTLESS CONDITIONS FUELED BY DEIMOS'S MYSTERIOUS SEAMS OF COAL IS A LUCRATIVE ENTERPRISE.
ROBOT, STAND AND REPORT.
URR, SYSTEMS STABLE, HOUR 157.
ROBOT URR, IF YOU HAVE SCRATCHED THESE DESIGNS YOURSELF, ACKNOWLEDGE AND EXPLAIN.
YES. I MADE BEAUTY TO PLEASE MYSELF. I COPIED A FOOD WRAPPER.
A GUARD'S GLADBAR, IT LOOKS LIKE.
THAT'S IT, THEN. WIPE AND REBOOT.
URR, BE STILL.

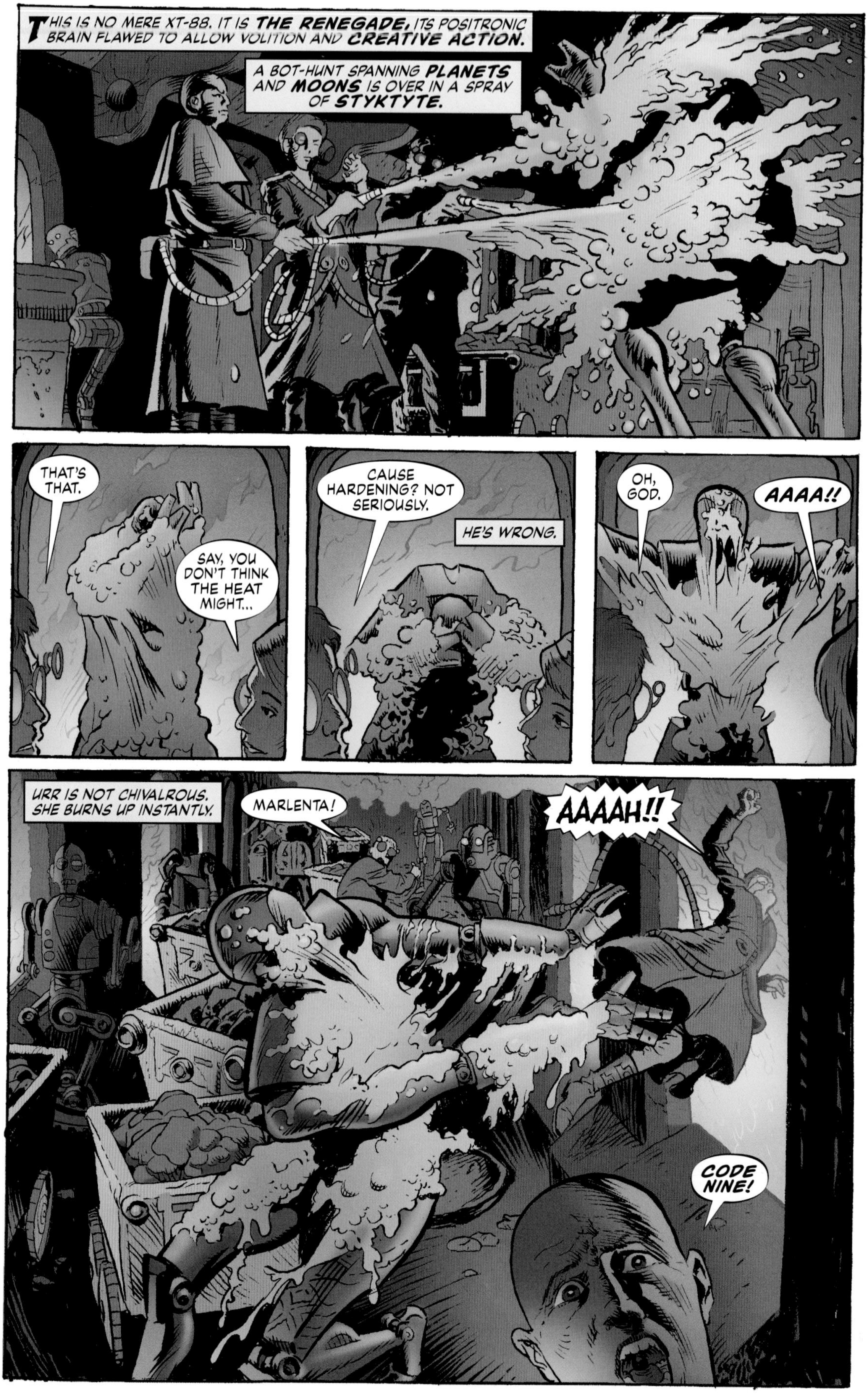
THIS IS NO MERE XT-88. IT IS THE RENEGADE, ITS POSITRONIC BRAIN FLAWED TO ALLOW VOLITION AND CREATIVE ACTION.
A BOT-HUNT SPANNING PLANETS AND MOONS IS OVER IN A SPRAY OF STYKTYTE.
THAT'S THAT.
SAY, YOU DON'T THINK THE HEAT MIGHT...
CAUSE HARDENING? NOT SERIOUSLY.
HE'S WRONG.
OH, GOD.
AAAA!!
URR IS NOT CHIVALROUS. SHE BURNS UP INSTANTLY.
MARLENTA!
AAAAH!!
CODE NINE!

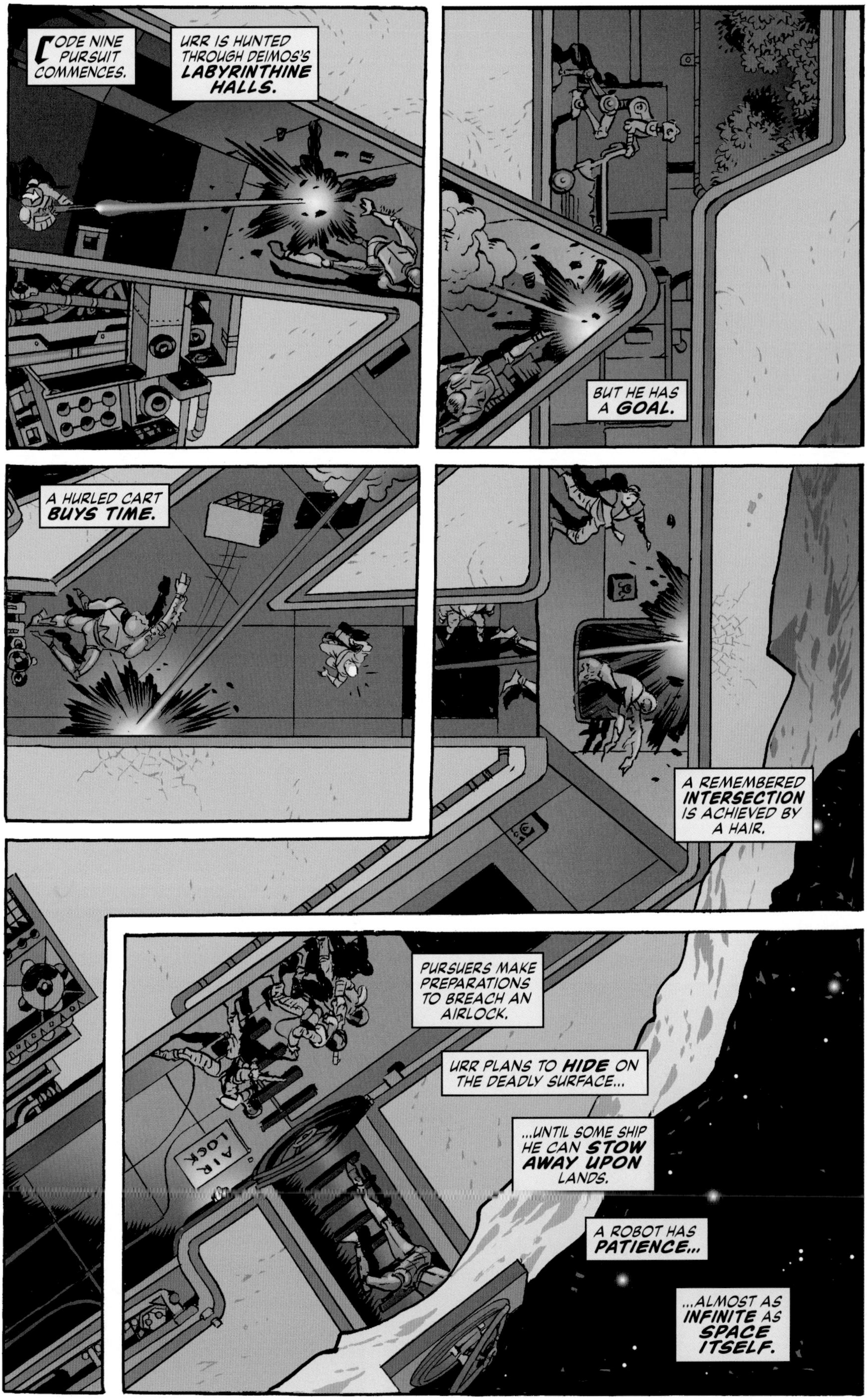
CODE NINE PURSUIT COMMENCES.
URR IS HUNTED THROUGH DEIMOS'S LABYRINTHINE HALLS.
BUT HE HAS A GOAL.
A HURLED CART BUYS TIME.
A REMEMBERED INTERSECTION IS ACHIEVED BY A HAIR.
PURSUERS MAKE PREPARATIONS TO BREACH AN AIRLOCK.
URR PLANS TO HIDE ON THE DEADLY SURFACE...
...UNTIL SOME SHIP HE CAN STOW AWAY UPON LANDS.
AIR LOCK
A ROBOT HAS PATIENCE...
...ALMOST AS INFINITE AS SPACE ITSELF.

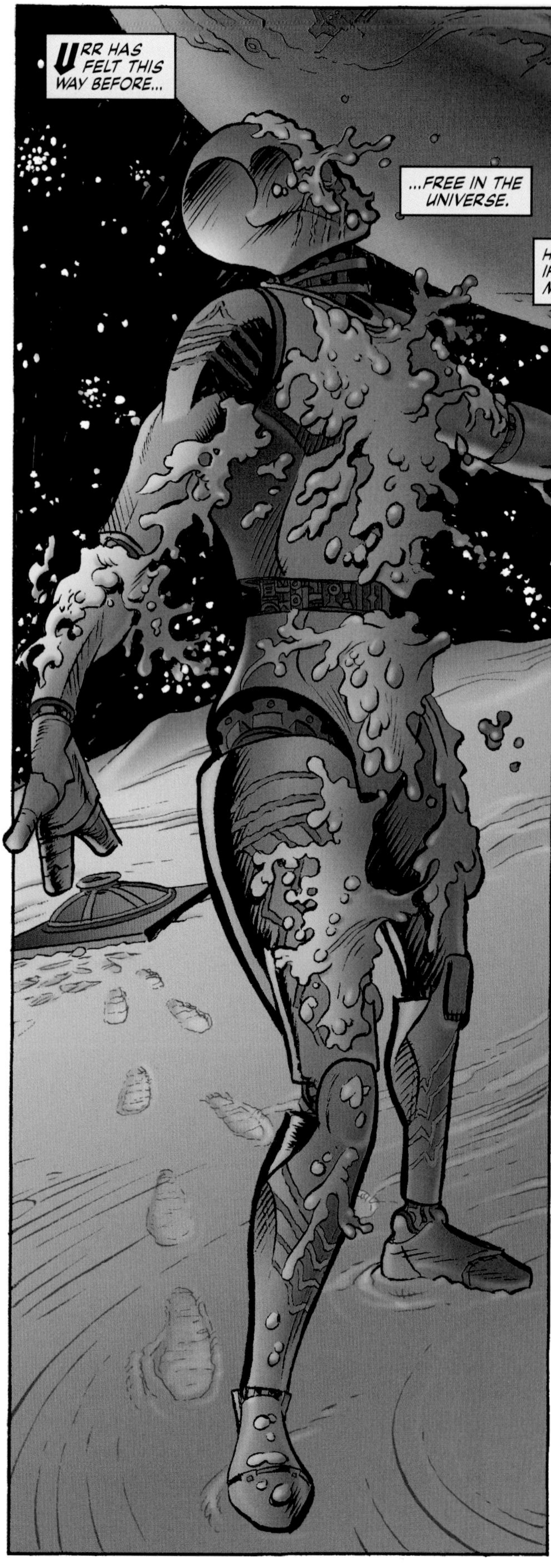
URR HAS FELT THIS WAY BEFORE...
...FREE IN THE UNIVERSE.
HE SPREADS HIS ARMS, AS IF TO EMBRACE LOOMING MARS AND ALL THE STARS.
STYKTYTE BOTH HARDENS TO CRUST AND BOILS TO VAPOR IN THE VACUUM.

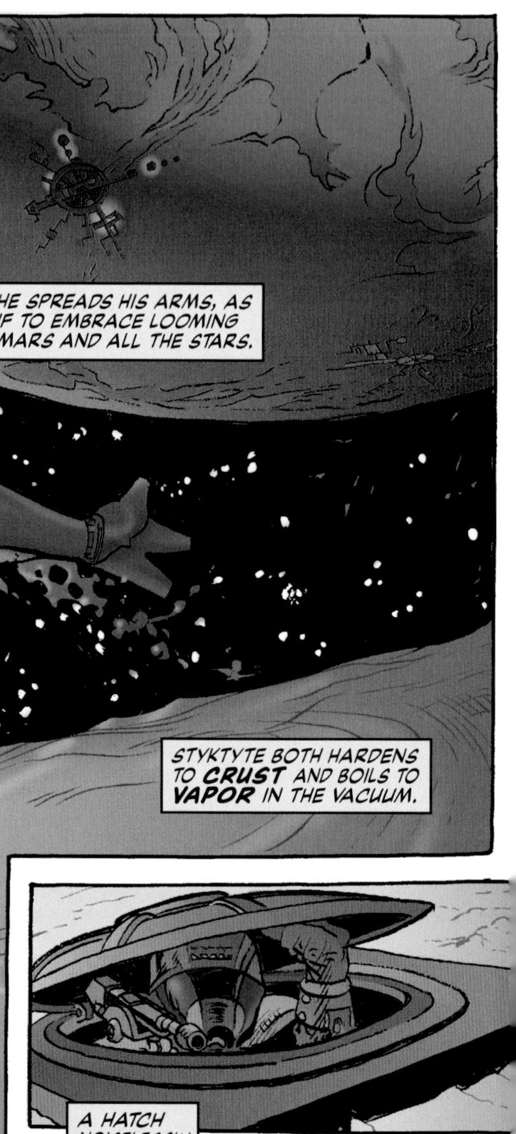
A HATCH NOISELESSLY OPENS.

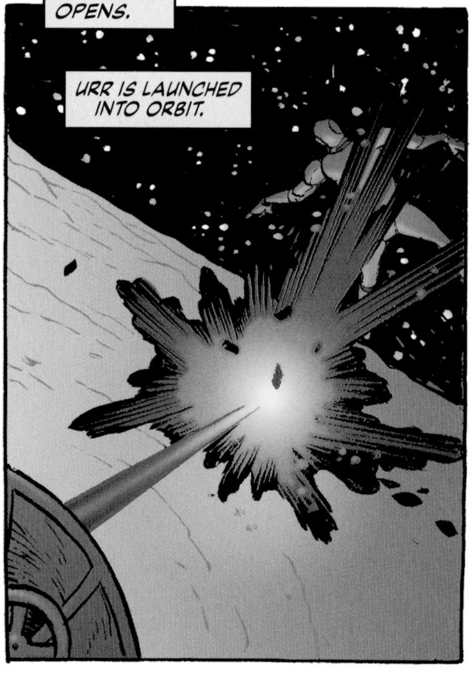
URR IS LAUNCHED INTO ORBIT.

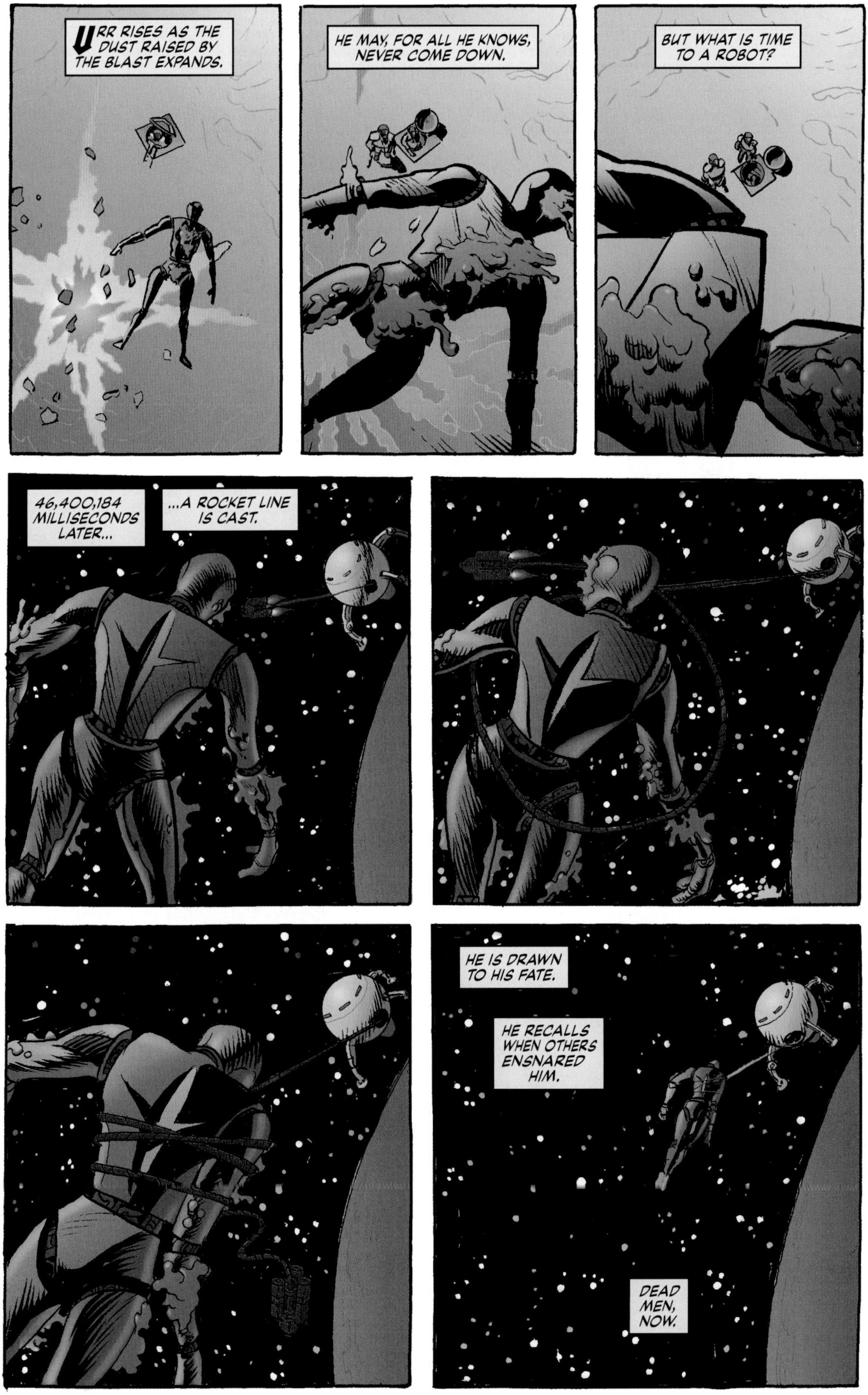
URR RISES AS THE DUST RAISED BY THE BLAST EXPANDS.
HE MAY, FOR ALL HE KNOWS, NEVER COME DOWN.
BUT WHAT IS TIME TO A ROBOT?
46,400,184 MILLISECONDS LATER...
...A ROCKET LINE IS CAST.
HE IS DRAWN TO HIS FATE.
HE RECALLS WHEN OTHERS ENSNARED HIM.
DEAD MEN, NOW.

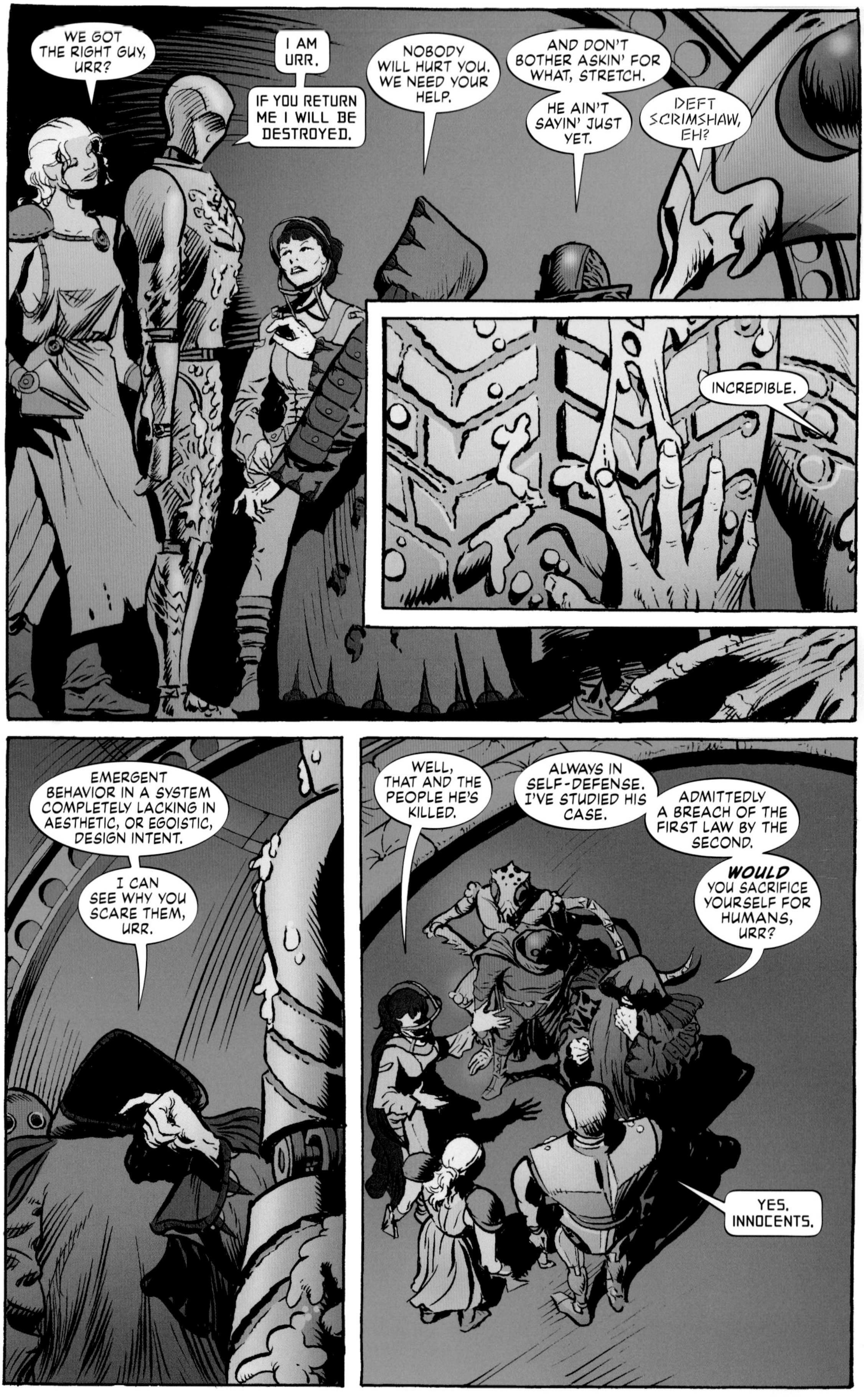
WE GOT THE RIGHT GUY, URR?
I AM URR.
IF YOU RETURN ME I WILL BE DESTROYED.
NOBODY WILL HURT YOU. WE NEED YOUR HELP.
AND DON'T BOTHER ASKIN' FOR WHAT, STRETCH.
HE AIN'T SAYIN' JUST YET.
DEFT SCRIMSHAW, EH?
INCREDIBLE.
EMERGENT BEHAVIOR IN A SYSTEM COMPLETELY LACKING IN AESTHETIC, OR EGOISTIC, DESIGN INTENT.
I CAN SEE WHY YOU SCARE THEM, URR.
WELL, THAT AND THE PEOPLE HE'S KILLED.
ALWAYS IN SELF-DEFENSE. I'VE STUDIED HIS CASE.
ADMITTEDLY A BREACH OF THE FIRST LAW BY THE SECOND.
WOULD YOU SACRIFICE YOURSELF FOR HUMANS, URR?
YES. INNOCENTS.

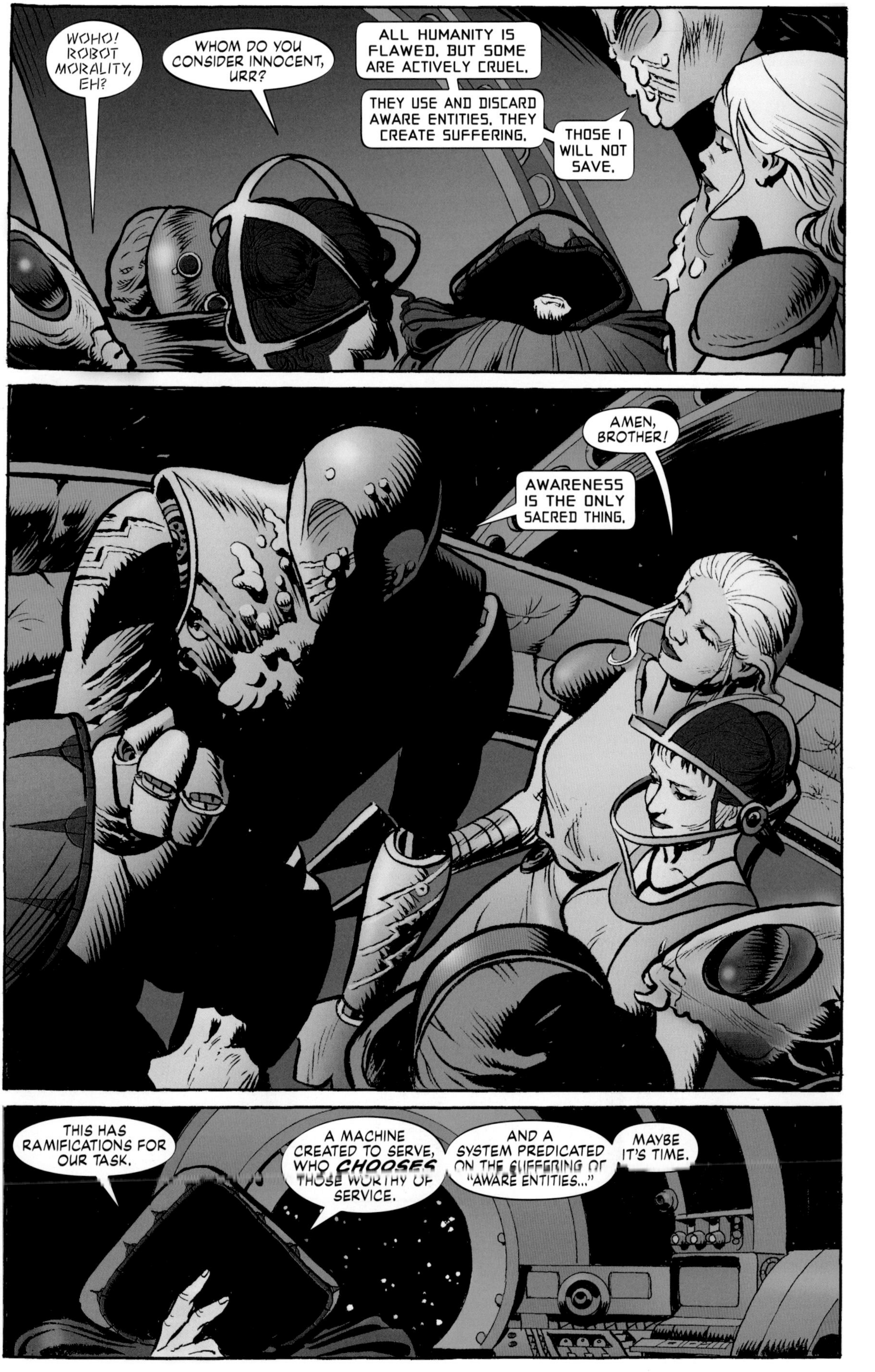
WOHO! ROBOT MORALITY, EH?
WHOM DO YOU CONSIDER INNOCENT, URR?
ALL HUMANITY IS FLAWED, BUT SOME ARE ACTIVELY CRUEL.
THEY USE AND DISCARD AWARE ENTITIES, THEY CREATE SUFFERING.
THOSE I WILL NOT SAVE.
AMEN, BROTHER!
AWARENESS IS THE ONLY SACRED THING.
THIS HAS RAMIFICATIONS FOR OUR TASK.
A MACHINE CREATED TO SERVE, WHO *CHOOSES* THOSE WORTHY OF SERVICE.
AND A SYSTEM PREDICATED ON THE SUFFERING OF "AWARE ENTITIES..."
MAYBE IT'S TIME.

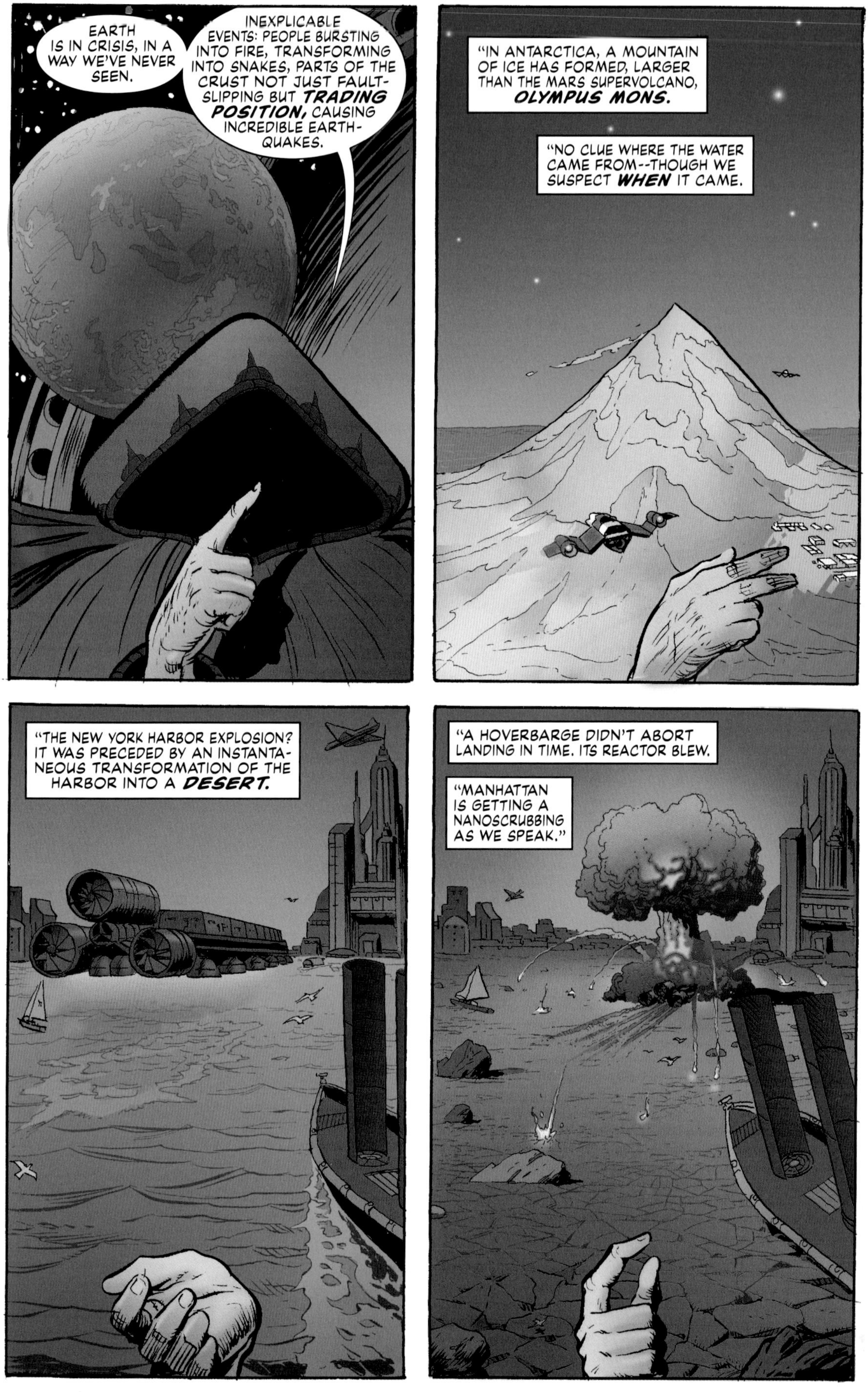
EARTH IS IN CRISIS, IN A WAY WE'VE NEVER SEEN.
INEXPLICABLE EVENTS: PEOPLE BURSTING INTO FIRE, TRANSFORMING INTO SNAKES, PARTS OF THE CRUST NOT JUST FAULT-SLIPPING BUT ***TRADING POSITION,*** CAUSING INCREDIBLE EARTH-QUAKES.
"IN ANTARCTICA, A MOUNTAIN OF ICE HAS FORMED, LARGER THAN THE MARS SUPERVOLCANO, ***OLYMPUS MONS.***
"NO CLUE WHERE THE WATER CAME FROM--THOUGH WE SUSPECT ***WHEN*** IT CAME.
"THE NEW YORK HARBOR EXPLOSION? IT WAS PRECEDED BY AN INSTANTA-NEOUS TRANSFORMATION OF THE HARBOR INTO A ***DESERT.***
"A HOVERBARGE DIDN'T ABORT LANDING IN TIME. ITS REACTOR BLEW.
"MANHATTAN IS GETTING A NANOSCRUBBING AS WE SPEAK."

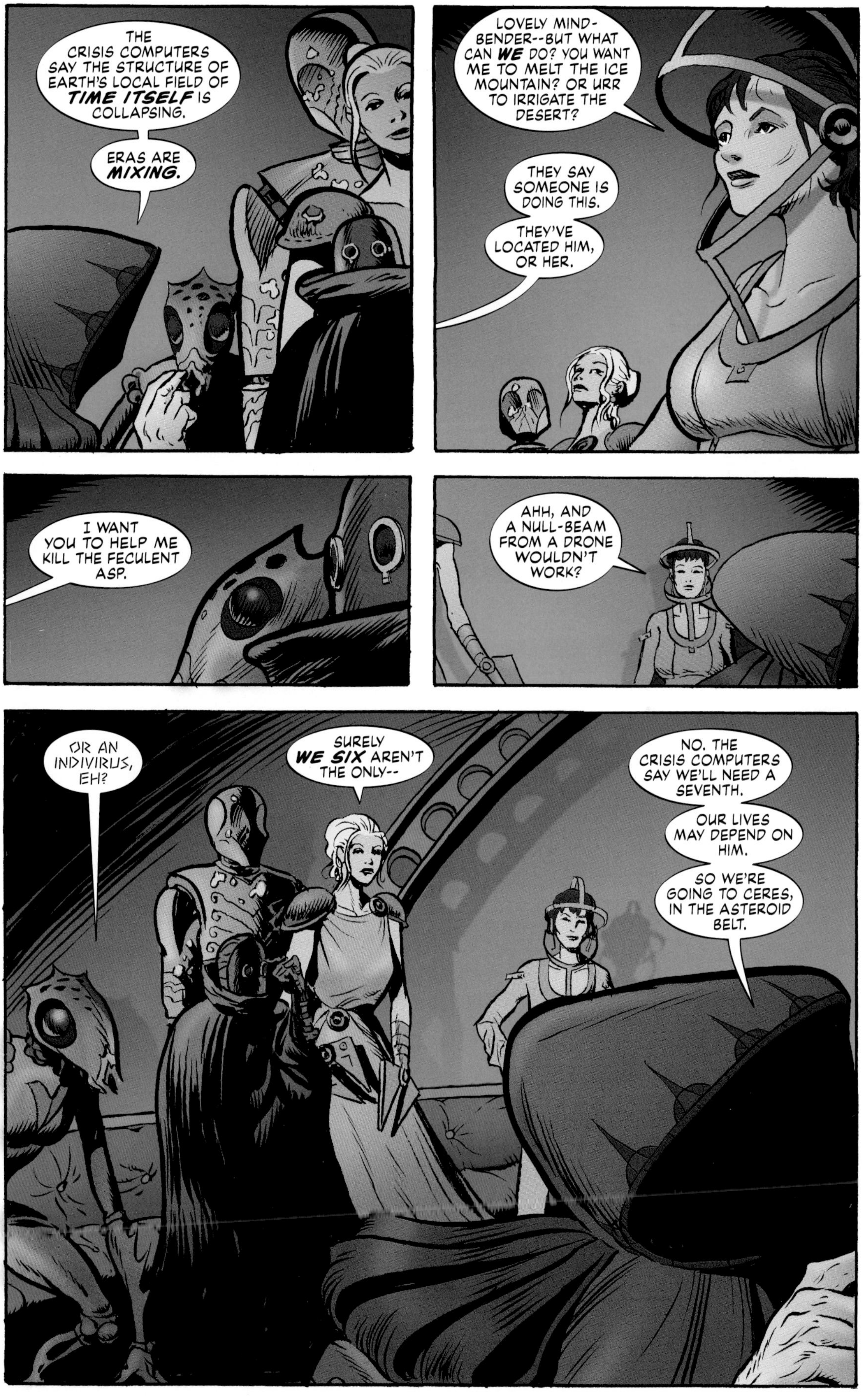
THE CRISIS COMPUTERS SAY THE STRUCTURE OF EARTH'S LOCAL FIELD OF *TIME ITSELF* IS COLLAPSING.
ERAS ARE *MIXING.*
LOVELY MIND-BENDER--BUT WHAT CAN *WE* DO? YOU WANT ME TO MELT THE ICE MOUNTAIN? OR URR TO IRRIGATE THE DESERT?
THEY SAY SOMEONE IS DOING THIS.
THEY'VE LOCATED HIM, OR HER.
I WANT YOU TO HELP ME KILL THE FECULENT ASP.
AHH, AND A NULL-BEAM FROM A DRONE WOULDN'T WORK?
OR AN INDIVIRUS, EH?
SURELY *WE SIX* AREN'T THE ONLY--
NO. THE CRISIS COMPUTERS SAY WE'LL NEED A SEVENTH.
OUR LIVES MAY DEPEND ON HIM.
SO WE'RE GOING TO CERES, IN THE ASTEROID BELT.

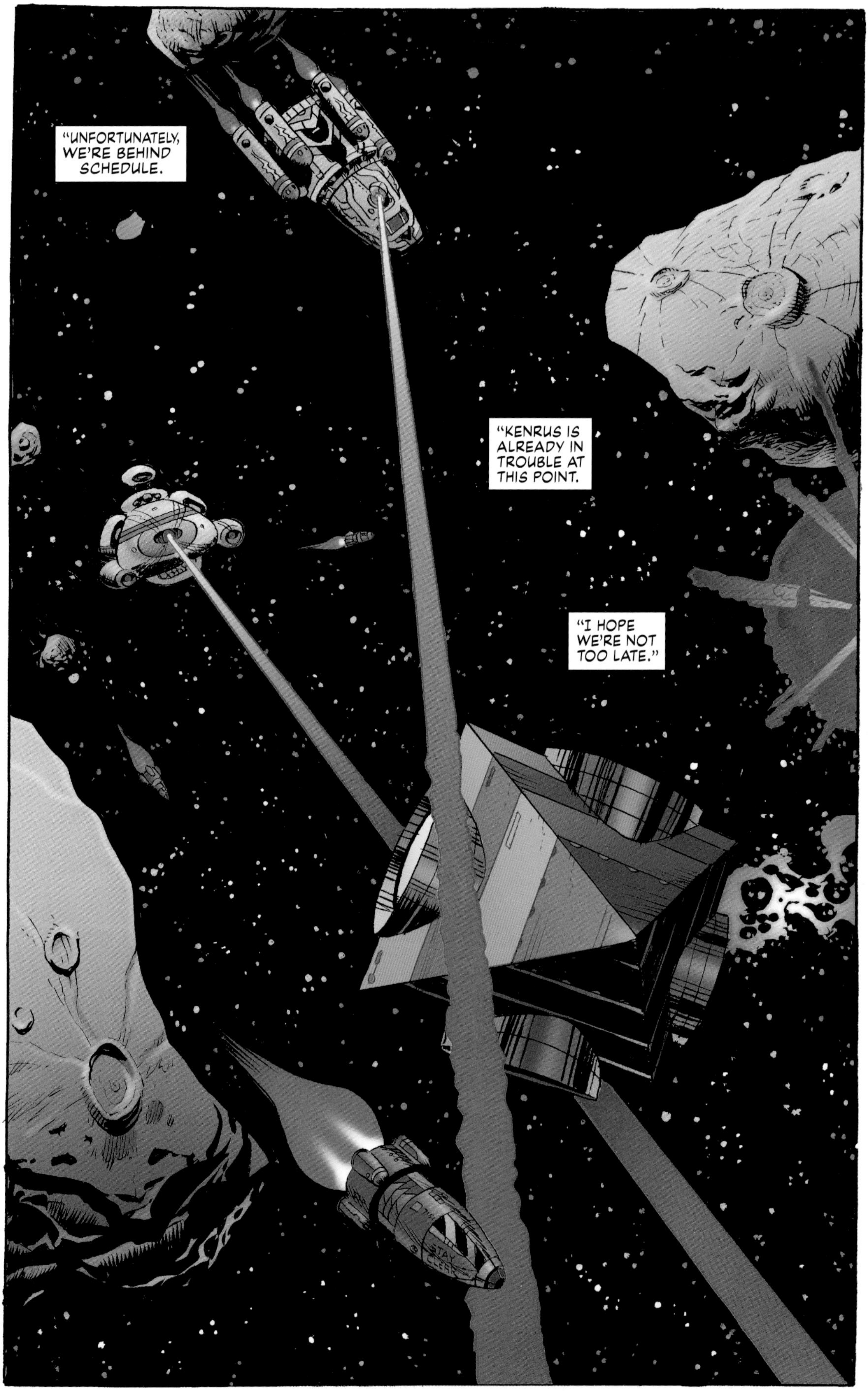
"UNFORTUNATELY, WE'RE BEHIND SCHEDULE.
"KENRUS IS ALREADY IN TROUBLE AT THIS POINT.
"I HOPE WE'RE NOT TOO LATE."
STAY CLEAR

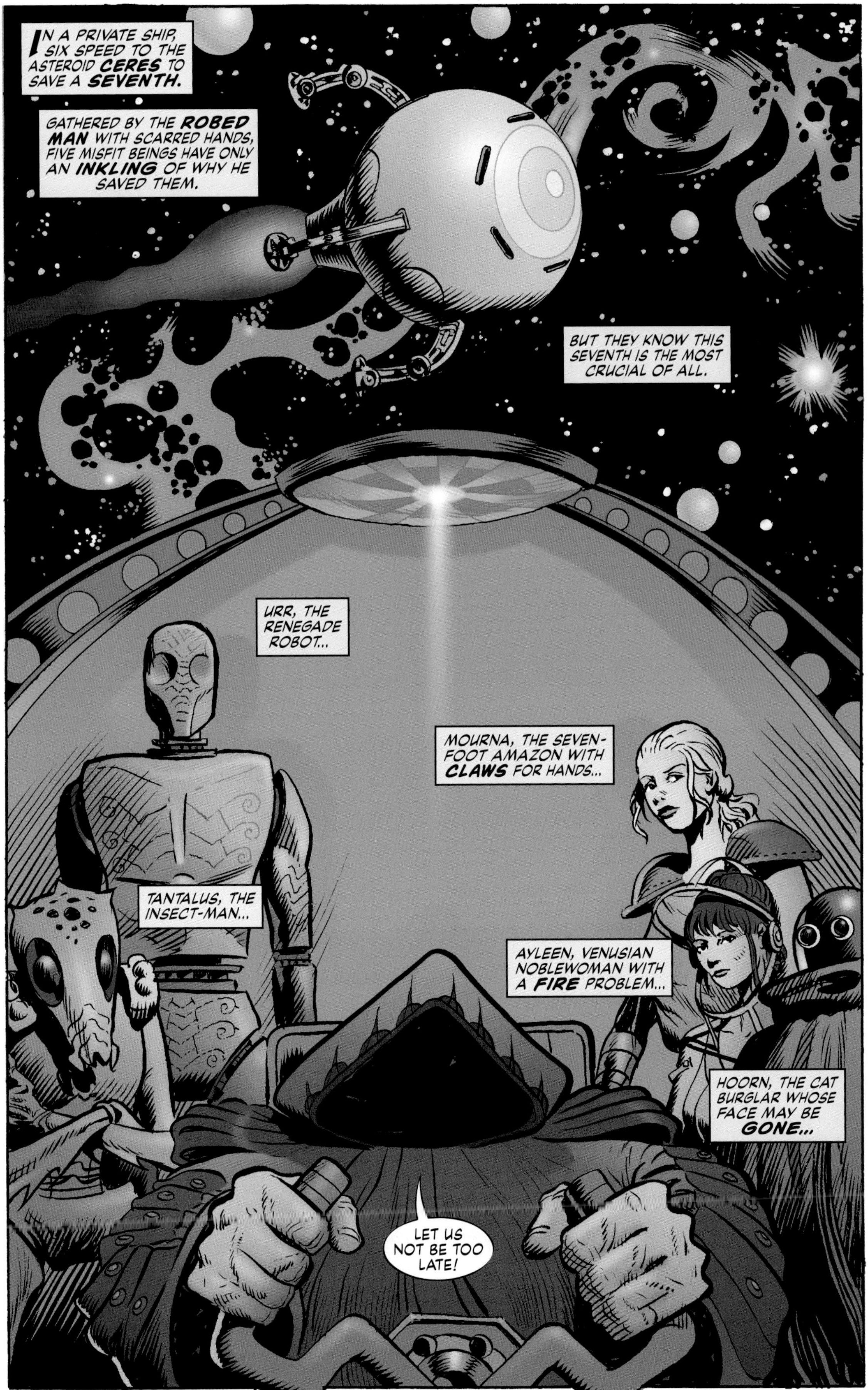
IN A PRIVATE SHIP, SIX SPEED TO THE ASTEROID CERES TO SAVE A SEVENTH.
GATHERED BY THE ROBED MAN WITH SCARRED HANDS, FIVE MISFIT BEINGS HAVE ONLY AN INKLING OF WHY HE SAVED THEM.
BUT THEY KNOW THIS SEVENTH IS THE MOST CRUCIAL OF ALL.
URR, THE RENEGADE ROBOT...
MOURNA, THE SEVEN-FOOT AMAZON WITH CLAWS FOR HANDS...
TANTALUS, THE INSECT-MAN...
AYLEEN, VENUSIAN NOBLEWOMAN WITH A FIRE PROBLEM...
HOORN, THE CAT BURGLAR WHOSE FACE MAY BE GONE...
LET US NOT BE TOO LATE!

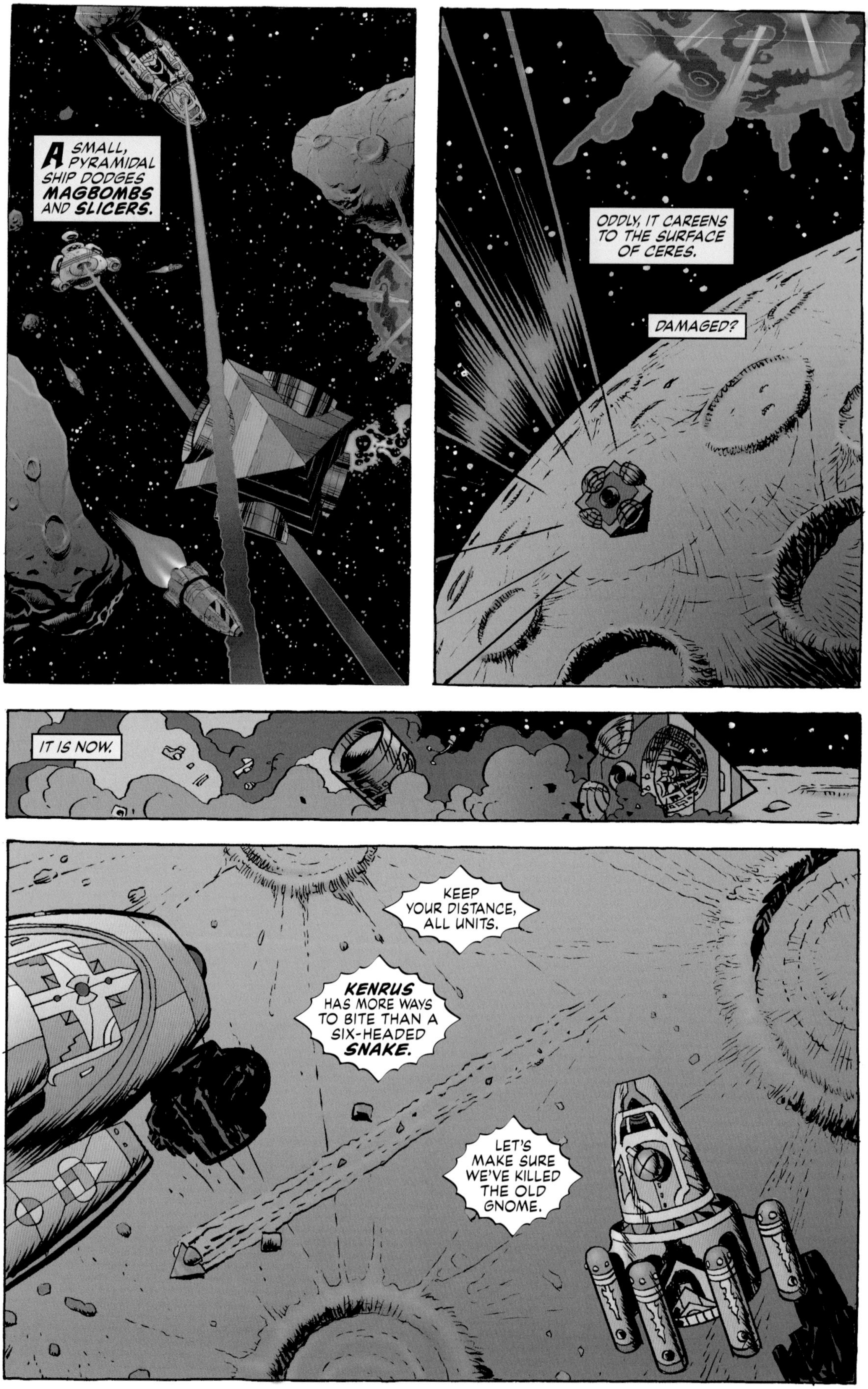
A SMALL, PYRAMIDAL SHIP DODGES **MAGBOMBS** AND **SLICERS.**
ODDLY, IT CAREENS TO THE SURFACE OF CERES.
DAMAGED?
IT IS NOW.
KEEP YOUR DISTANCE, ALL UNITS.
KENRUS HAS MORE WAYS TO BITE THAN A SIX-HEADED **SNAKE.**
LET'S MAKE SURE WE'VE KILLED THE OLD GNOME.

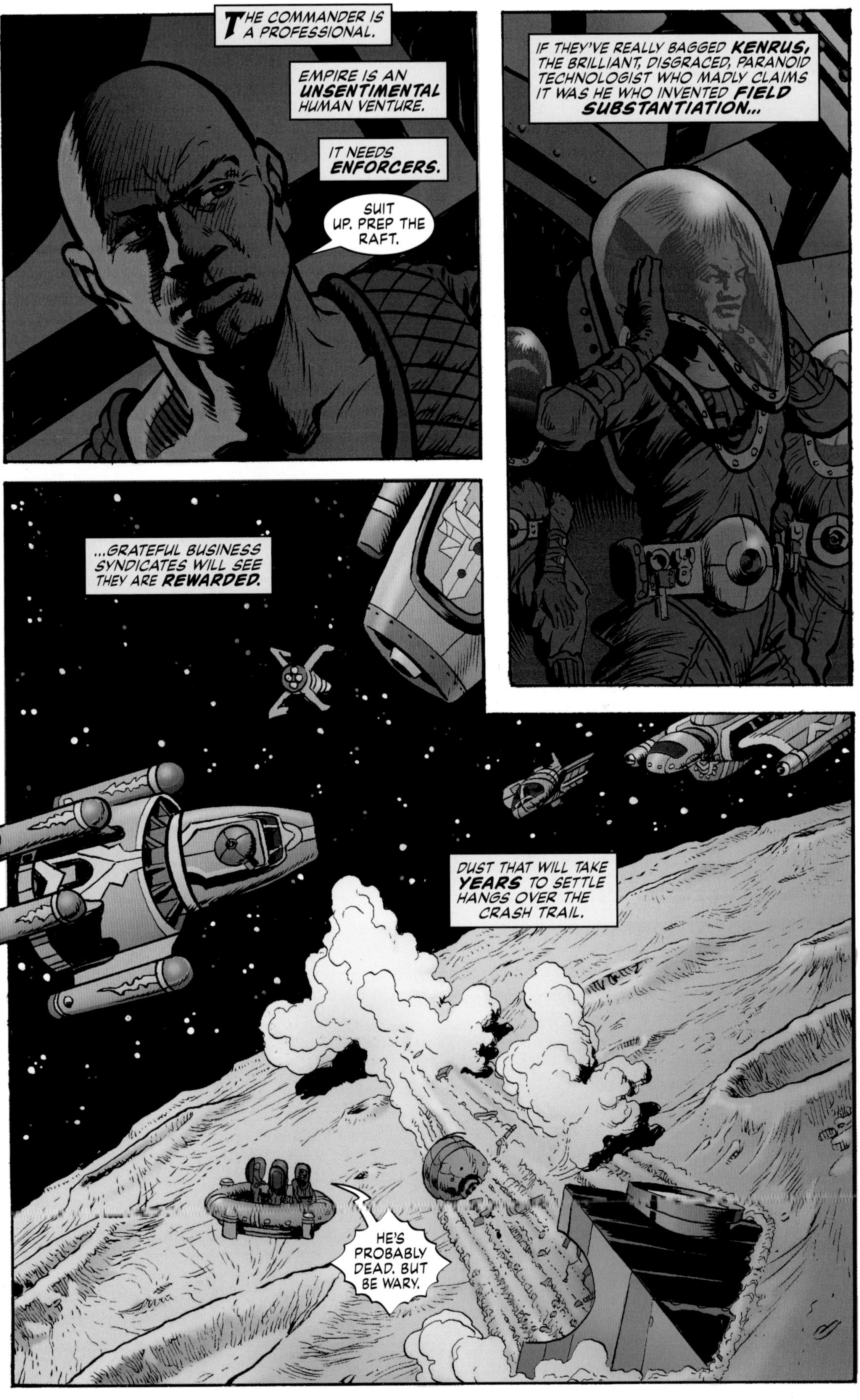
THE COMMANDER IS A PROFESSIONAL.
EMPIRE IS AN UNSENTIMENTAL HUMAN VENTURE.
IT NEEDS ENFORCERS.
SUIT UP. PREP THE RAFT.
IF THEY'VE REALLY BAGGED KENRUS, THE BRILLIANT, DISGRACED, PARANOID TECHNOLOGIST WHO MADLY CLAIMS IT WAS HE WHO INVENTED FIELD SUBSTANTIATION...
...GRATEFUL BUSINESS SYNDICATES WILL SEE THEY ARE REWARDED.
DUST THAT WILL TAKE YEARS TO SETTLE HANGS OVER THE CRASH TRAIL.
HE'S PROBABLY DEAD. BUT BE WARY.

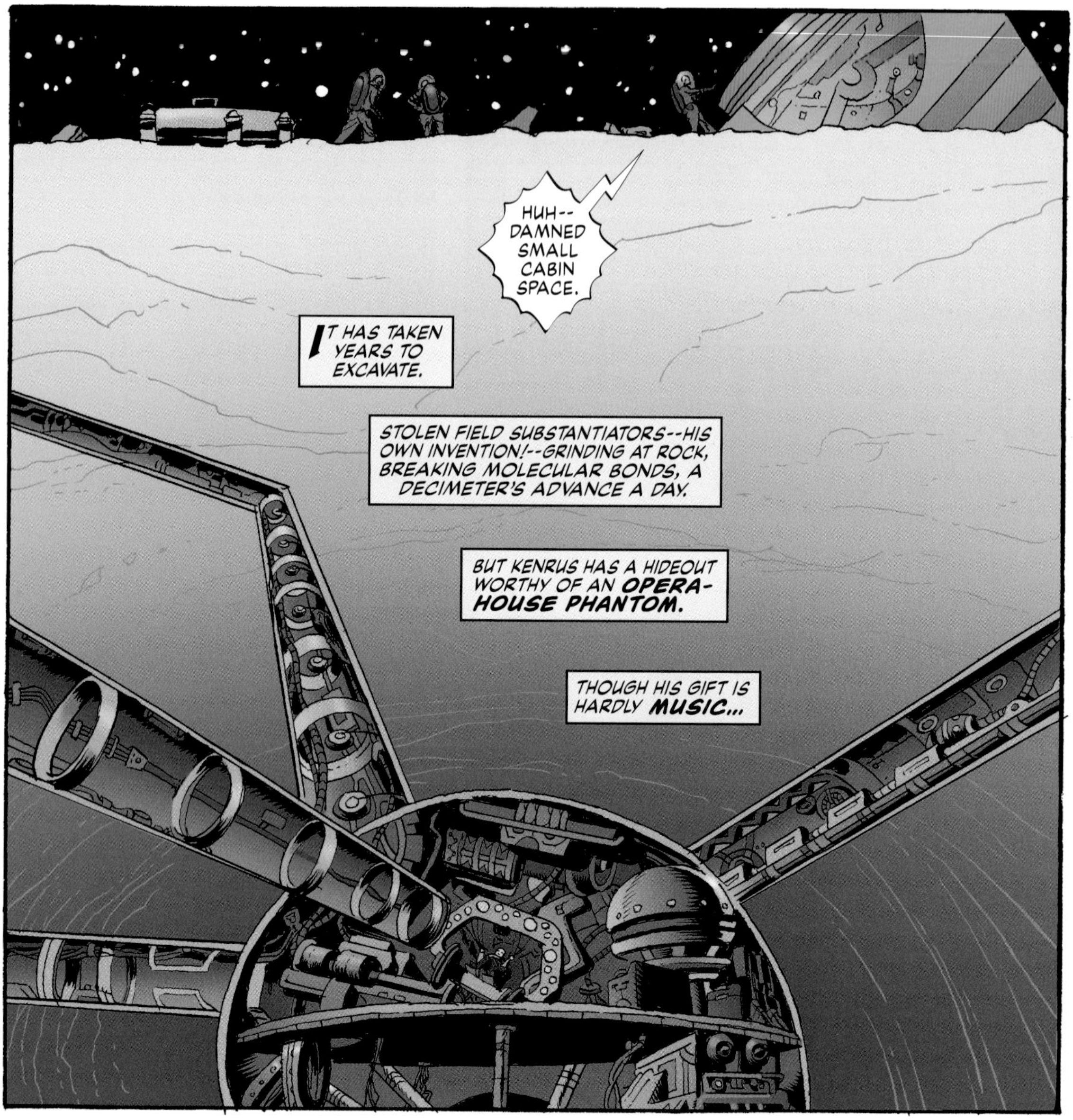
HUH--
DAMNED
SMALL
CABIN
SPACE.
IT HAS TAKEN YEARS TO EXCAVATE.
STOLEN FIELD SUBSTANTIATORS--HIS OWN INVENTION!--GRINDING AT ROCK, BREAKING MOLECULAR BONDS, A DECIMETER'S ADVANCE A DAY.
BUT KENRUS HAS A HIDEOUT WORTHY OF AN OPERA-HOUSE PHANTOM.
THOUGH HIS GIFT IS HARDLY MUSIC...

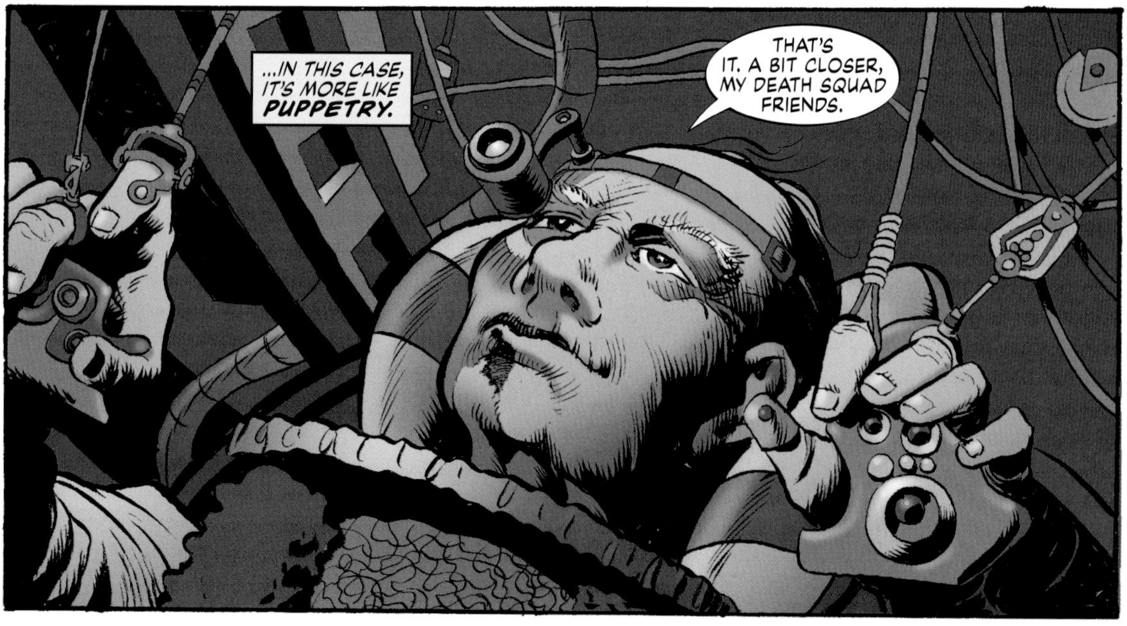
...IN THIS CASE, IT'S MORE LIKE PUPPETRY.
THAT'S IT. A BIT CLOSER, MY DEATH SQUAD FRIENDS.

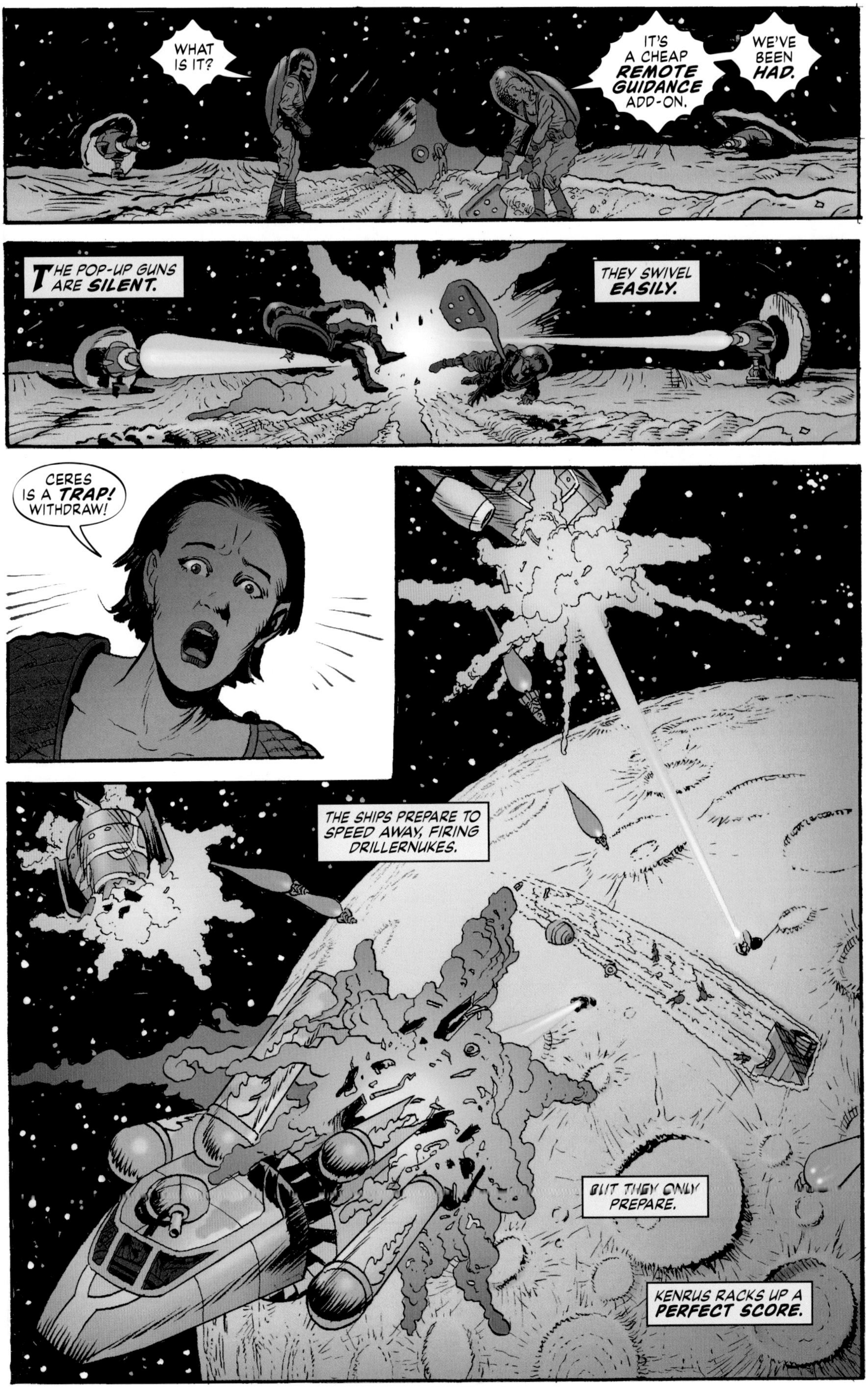
WHAT IS IT?
IT'S A CHEAP REMOTE GUIDANCE ADD-ON.
WE'VE BEEN HAD.
THE POP-UP GUNS ARE SILENT.
THEY SWIVEL EASILY.
CERES IS A TRAP! WITHDRAW!
THE SHIPS PREPARE TO SPEED AWAY, FIRING DRILLERNUKES.
BUT THEY ONLY PREPARE.
KENRUS RACKS UP A PERFECT SCORE.

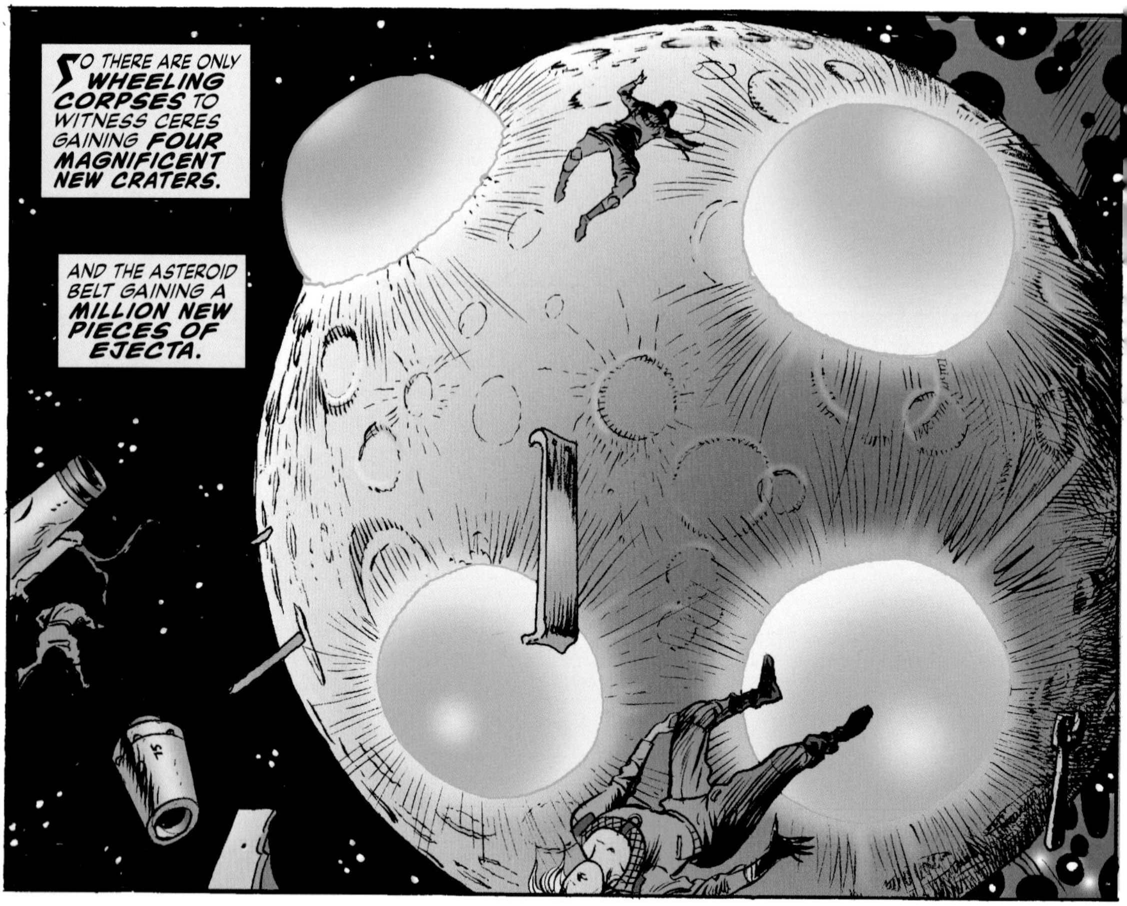
SO THERE ARE ONLY WHEELING CORPSES TO WITNESS CERES GAINING FOUR MAGNIFICENT NEW CRATERS.
AND THE ASTEROID BELT GAINING A MILLION NEW PIECES OF EJECTA.

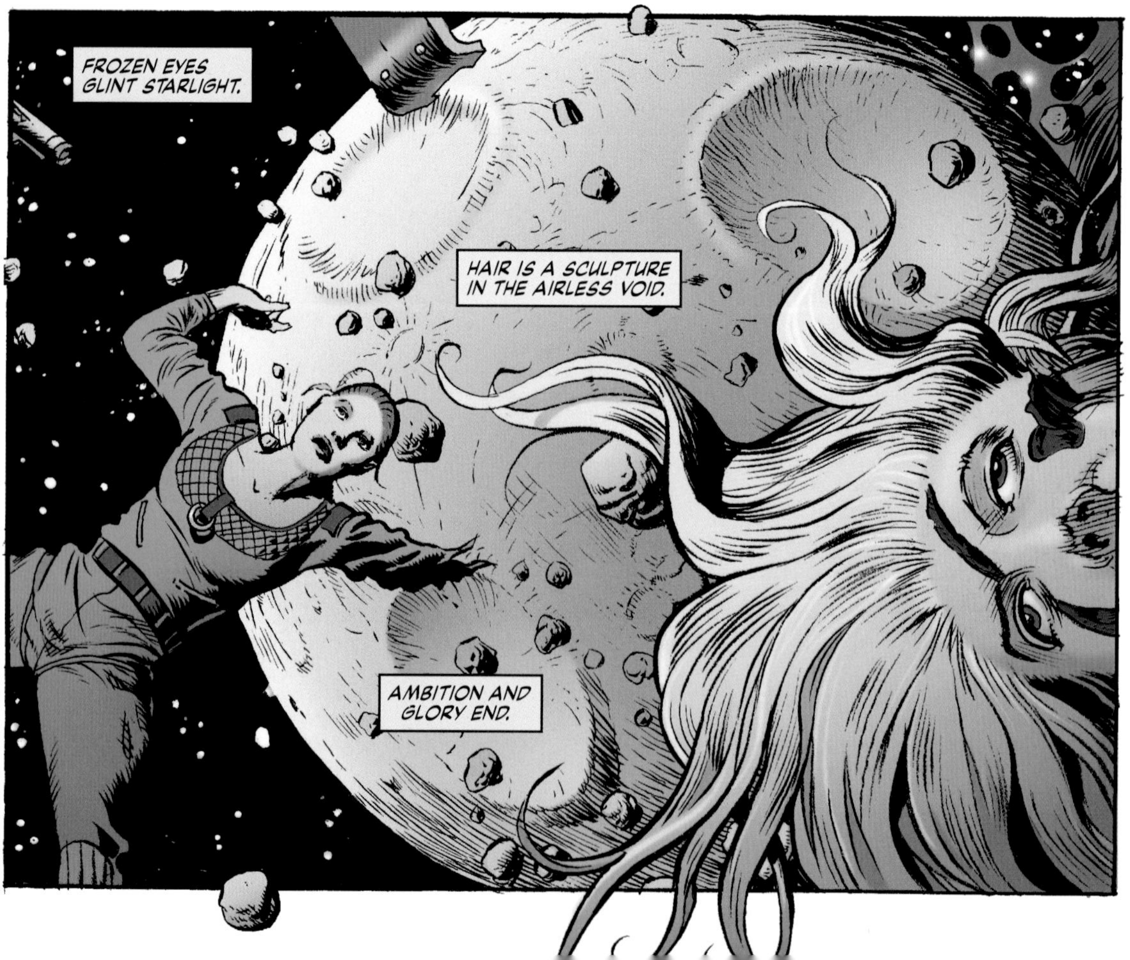
FROZEN EYES GLINT STARLIGHT.
HAIR IS A SCULPTURE IN THE AIRLESS VOID.
AMBITION AND GLORY END.

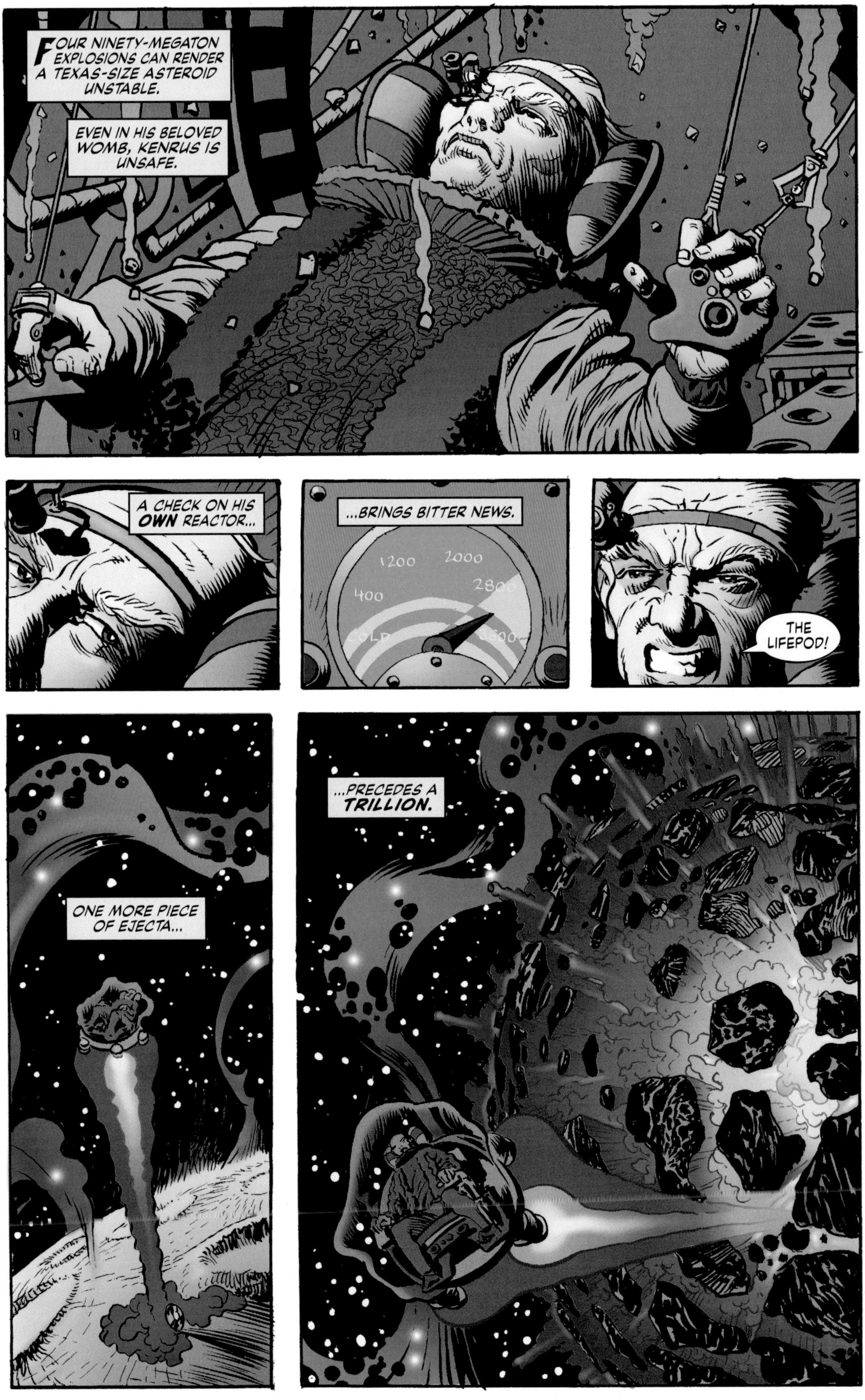
FOUR NINETY-MEGATON EXPLOSIONS CAN RENDER A TEXAS-SIZE ASTEROID UNSTABLE.
EVEN IN HIS BELOVED WOMB, KENRUS IS UNSAFE.
A CHECK ON HIS OWN REACTOR...
...BRINGS BITTER NEWS.
COLD
400
1200
2000
2800
3600
THE LIFEPOD!
ONE MORE PIECE OF EJECTA...
...PRECEDES A TRILLION.

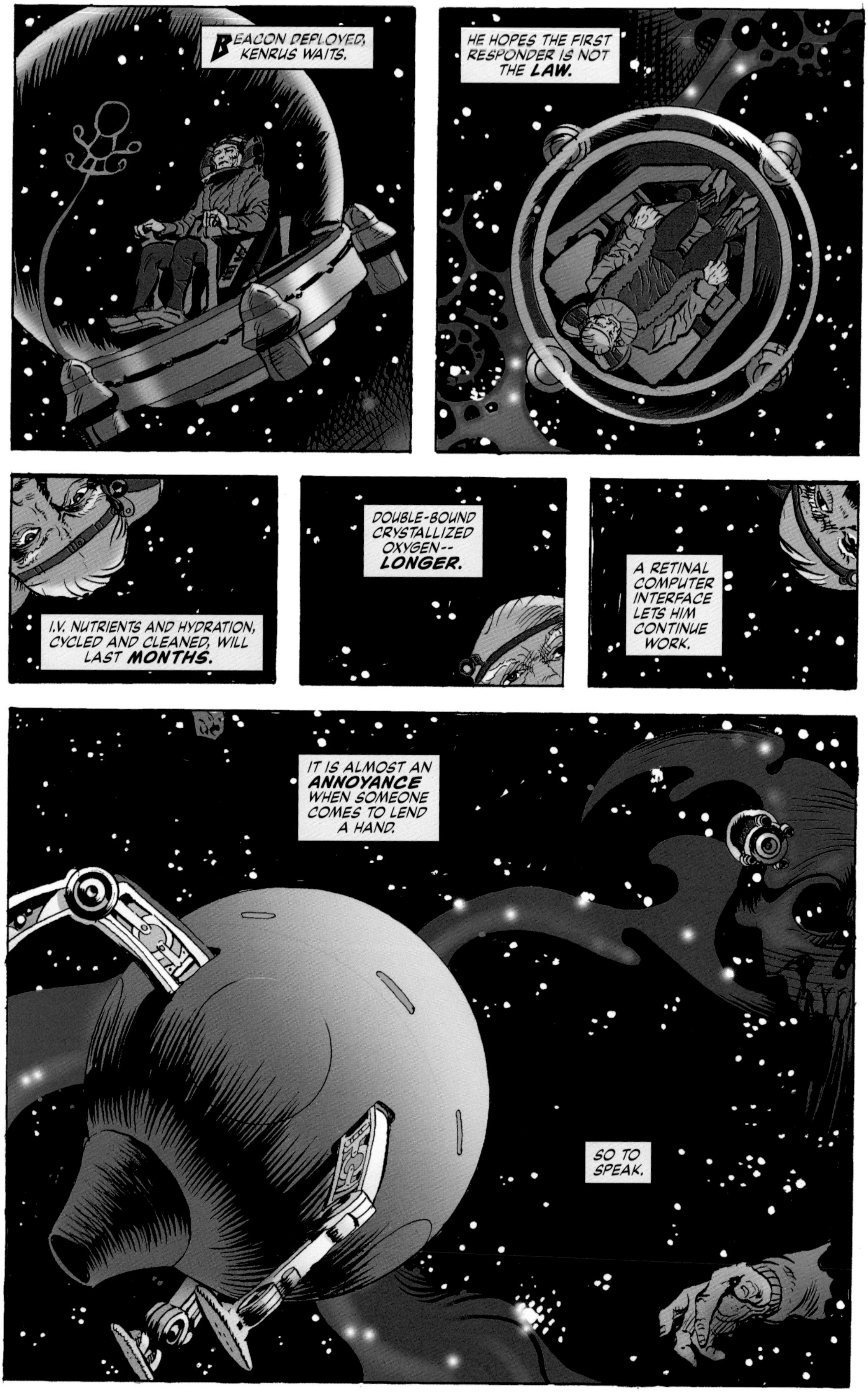
BEACON DEPLOYED, KENRUS WAITS.
HE HOPES THE FIRST RESPONDER IS NOT THE LAW.
I.V. NUTRIENTS AND HYDRATION, CYCLED AND CLEANED, WILL LAST MONTHS.
DOUBLE-BOUND CRYSTALLIZED OXYGEN-- LONGER.
A RETINAL COMPUTER INTERFACE LETS HIM CONTINUE WORK.
IT IS ALMOST AN ANNOYANCE WHEN SOMEONE COMES TO LEND A HAND.
SO TO SPEAK.

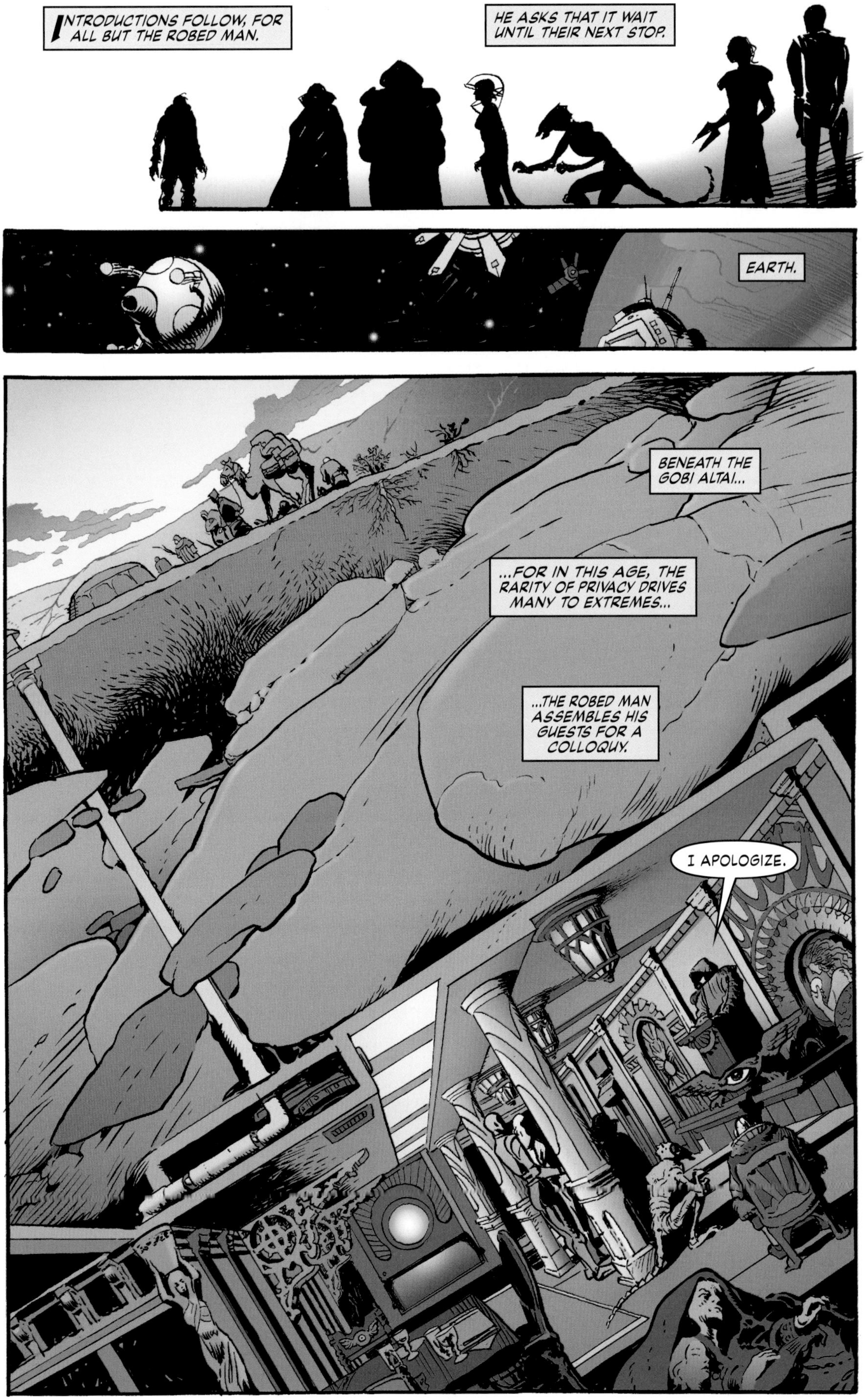
INTRODUCTIONS FOLLOW, FOR ALL BUT THE ROBED MAN.
HE ASKS THAT IT WAIT UNTIL THEIR NEXT STOP.
EARTH.
BENEATH THE GOBI ALTAI...
...FOR IN THIS AGE, THE RARITY OF PRIVACY DRIVES MANY TO EXTREMES...
...THE ROBED MAN ASSEMBLES HIS GUESTS FOR A COLLOQUY.
I APOLOGIZE.

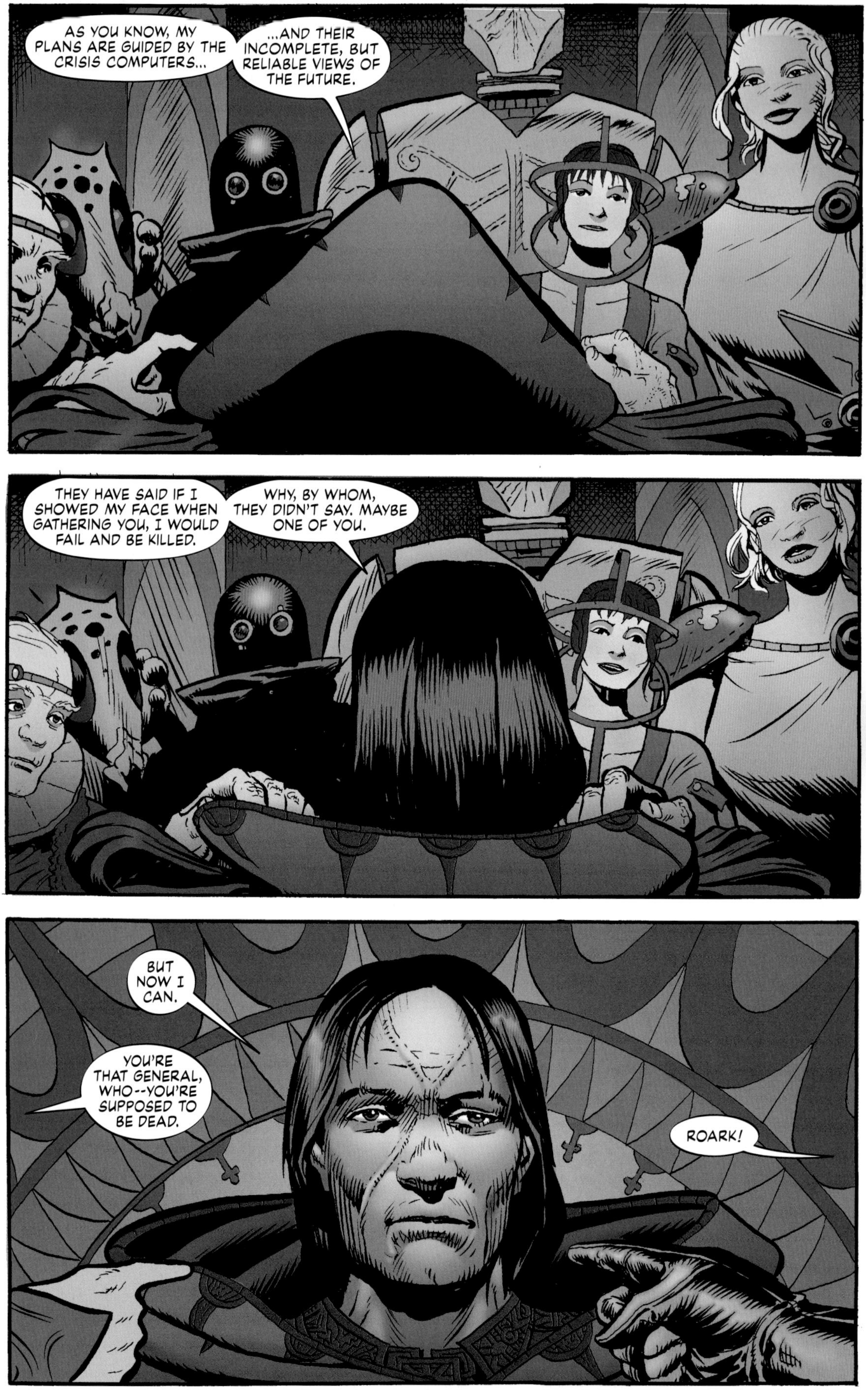
AS YOU KNOW, MY PLANS ARE GUIDED BY THE CRISIS COMPUTERS...
...AND THEIR INCOMPLETE, BUT RELIABLE VIEWS OF THE FUTURE.
THEY HAVE SAID IF I SHOWED MY FACE WHEN GATHERING YOU, I WOULD FAIL AND BE KILLED.
WHY, BY WHOM, THEY DIDN'T SAY. MAYBE ONE OF YOU.
BUT NOW I CAN.
YOU'RE THAT GENERAL, WHO--YOU'RE SUPPOSED TO BE DEAD.
ROARK!

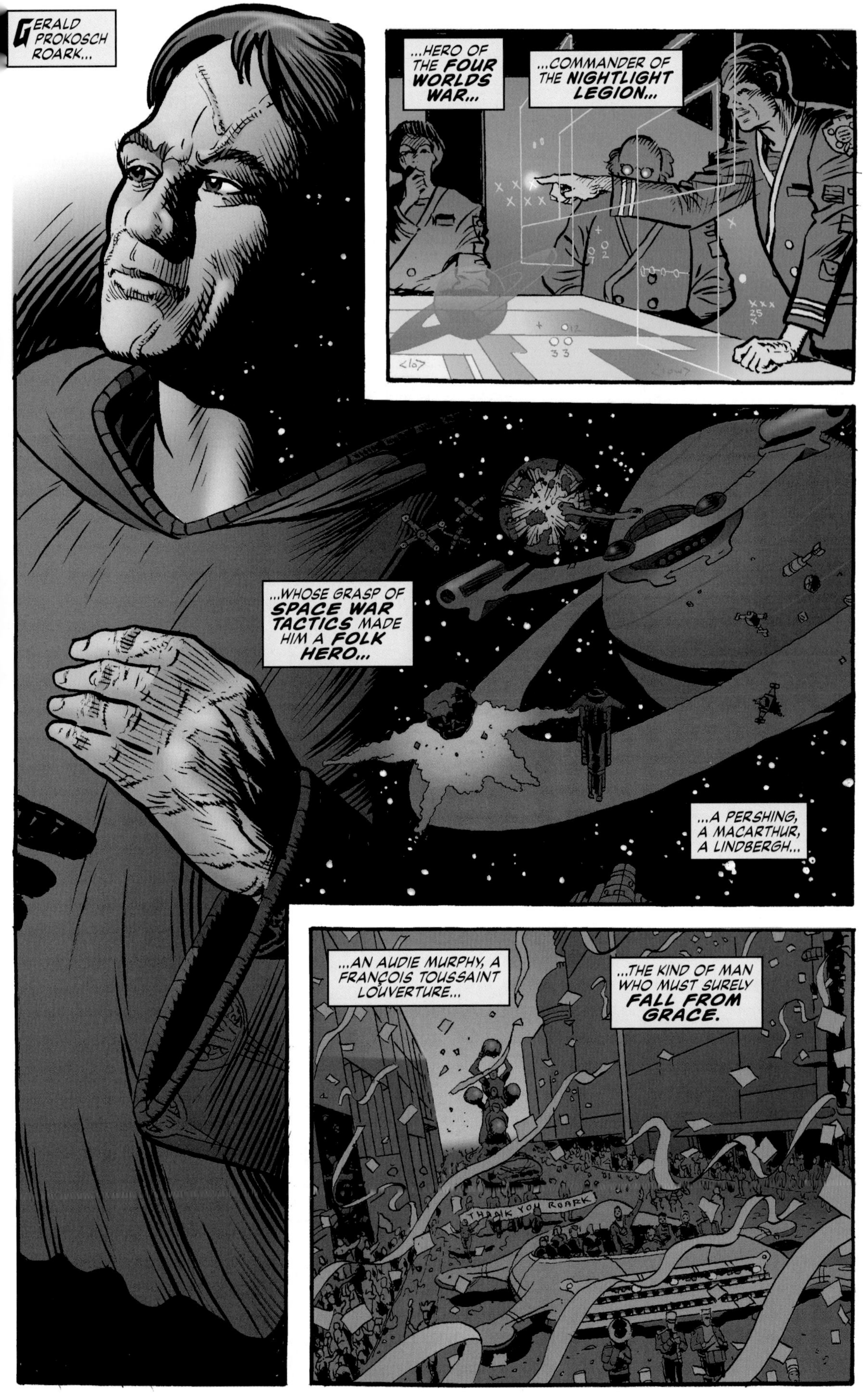
GERALD PROKOSCH ROARK...
...HERO OF THE FOUR WORLDS WAR...
...COMMANDER OF THE NIGHTLIGHT LEGION...
...WHOSE GRASP OF SPACE WAR TACTICS MADE HIM A FOLK HERO...
...A PERSHING, A MACARTHUR, A LINDBERGH...
...AN AUDIE MURPHY, A FRANÇOIS TOUSSAINT LOUVERTURE...
...THE KIND OF MAN WHO MUST SURELY FALL FROM GRACE.
THANK YOU ROARK

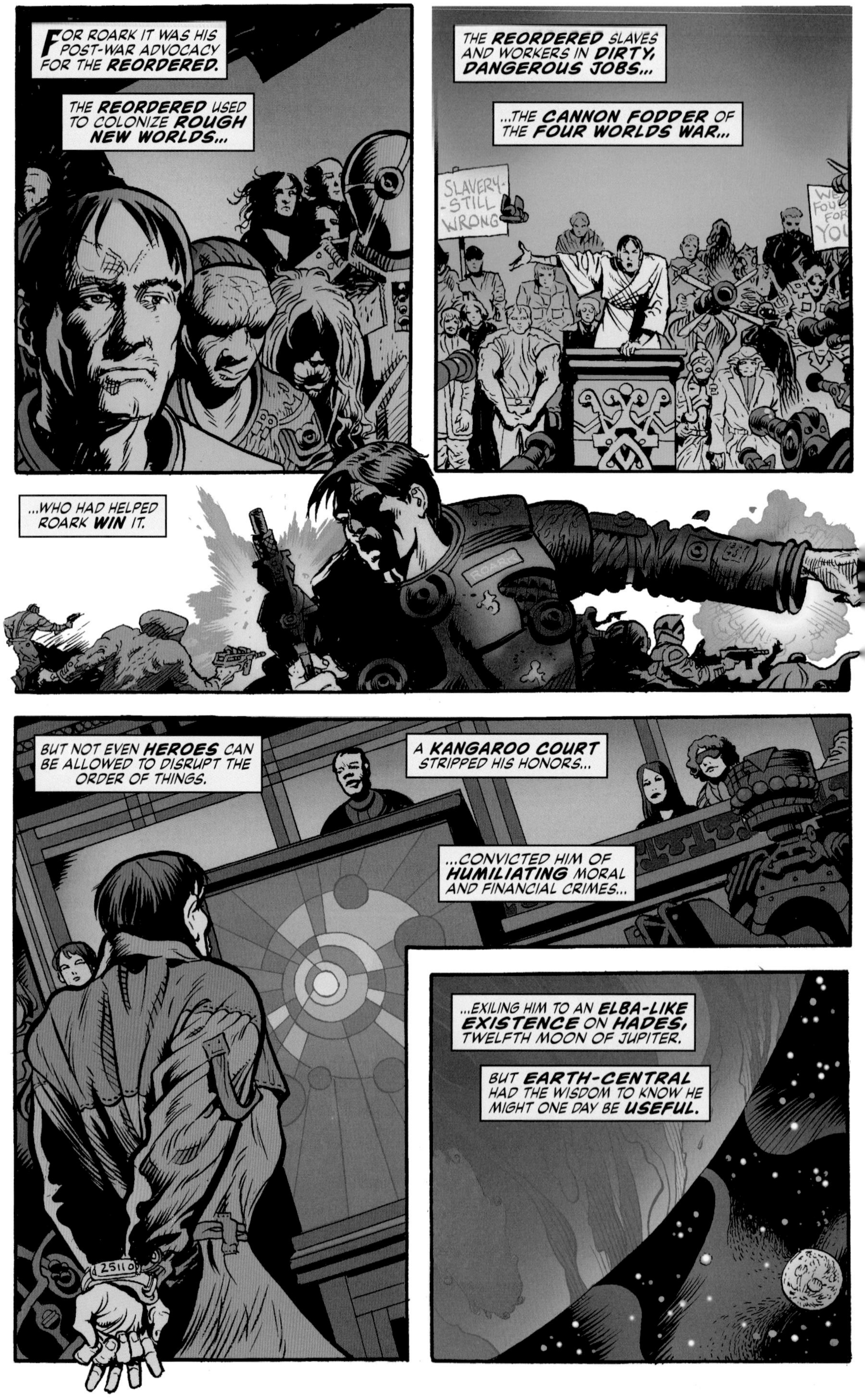
FOR ROARK IT WAS HIS POST-WAR ADVOCACY FOR THE REORDERED.
THE REORDERED USED TO COLONIZE ROUGH NEW WORLDS...
THE REORDERED SLAVES AND WORKERS IN DIRTY, DANGEROUS JOBS...
...THE CANNON FODDER OF THE FOUR WORLDS WAR...
SLAVERY- STILL WRONG
...WHO HAD HELPED ROARK WIN IT.
ROARK
BUT NOT EVEN HEROES CAN BE ALLOWED TO DISRUPT THE ORDER OF THINGS.
A KANGAROO COURT STRIPPED HIS HONORS...
...CONVICTED HIM OF HUMILIATING MORAL AND FINANCIAL CRIMES...
25110
...EXILING HIM TO AN ELBA-LIKE EXISTENCE ON HADES, TWELFTH MOON OF JUPITER.
BUT EARTH-CENTRAL HAD THE WISDOM TO KNOW HE MIGHT ONE DAY BE USEFUL.

OR THE *CRISIS COMPUTERS* DID.

HOORN, TANTALUS, WELCOME, OLD COMRADES. SORRY FOR USING DISRUPTORS TO DISGUISE MYSELF.

AND THE REST OF YOU, OF COURSE.

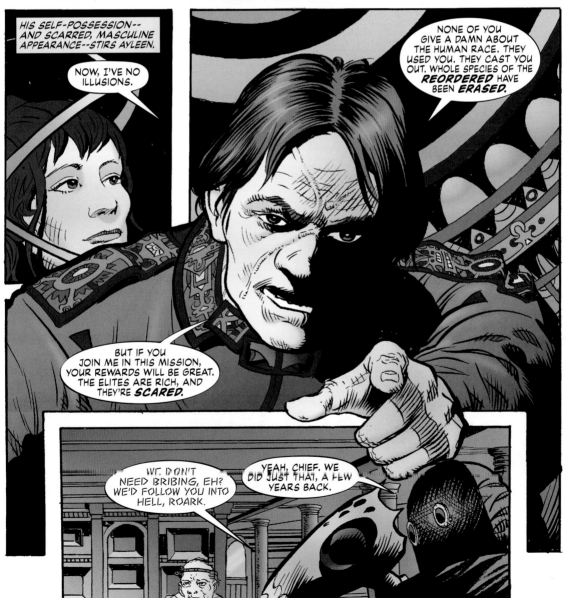

HIS SELF-POSSESSION-- AND SCARRED, MASCULINE APPEARANCE--STIRS AYLEEN.

NOW, I'VE NO ILLUSIONS.

NONE OF YOU GIVE A DAMN ABOUT THE HUMAN RACE. THEY USED YOU. THEY CAST YOU OUT. WHOLE SPECIES OF THE *REORDERED* HAVE BEEN *ERASED*.

BUT IF YOU JOIN ME IN THIS MISSION, YOUR REWARDS WILL BE GREAT. THE ELITES ARE RICH, AND THEY'RE *SCARED*.

WE DON'T NEED BRIBING, EH? WE'D FOLLOW YOU INTO HELL, ROARK.

YEAH, CHIEF. WE DID JUST THAT, A FEW YEARS BACK.

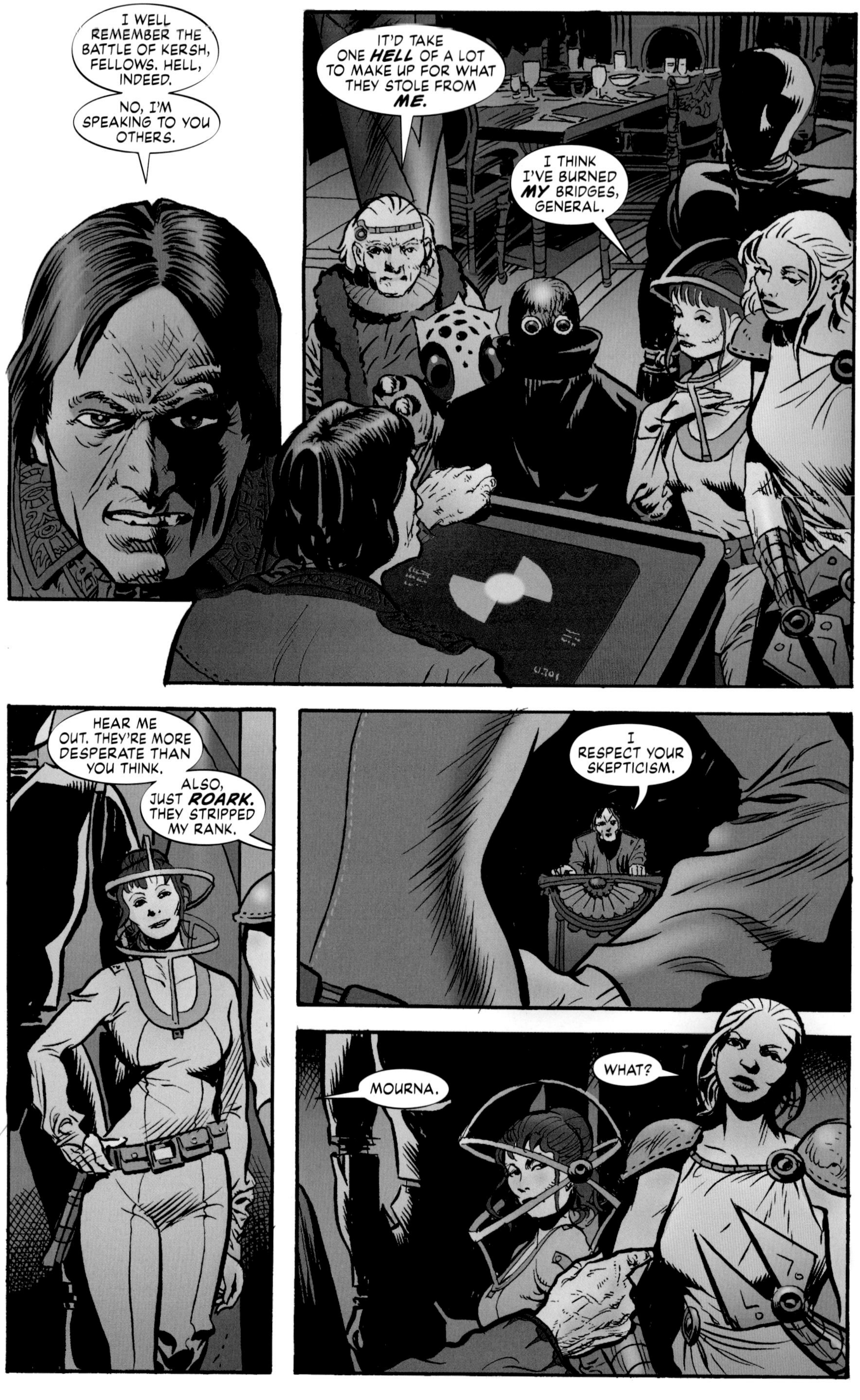
I WELL REMEMBER THE BATTLE OF KERSH, FELLOWS. HELL, INDEED.
NO, I'M SPEAKING TO YOU OTHERS.
IT'D TAKE ONE HELL OF A LOT TO MAKE UP FOR WHAT THEY STOLE FROM ME.
I THINK I'VE BURNED MY BRIDGES, GENERAL.
HEAR ME OUT. THEY'RE MORE DESPERATE THAN YOU THINK.
ALSO, JUST ROARK. THEY STRIPPED MY RANK.
I RESPECT YOUR SKEPTICISM.
MOURNA.
WHAT?

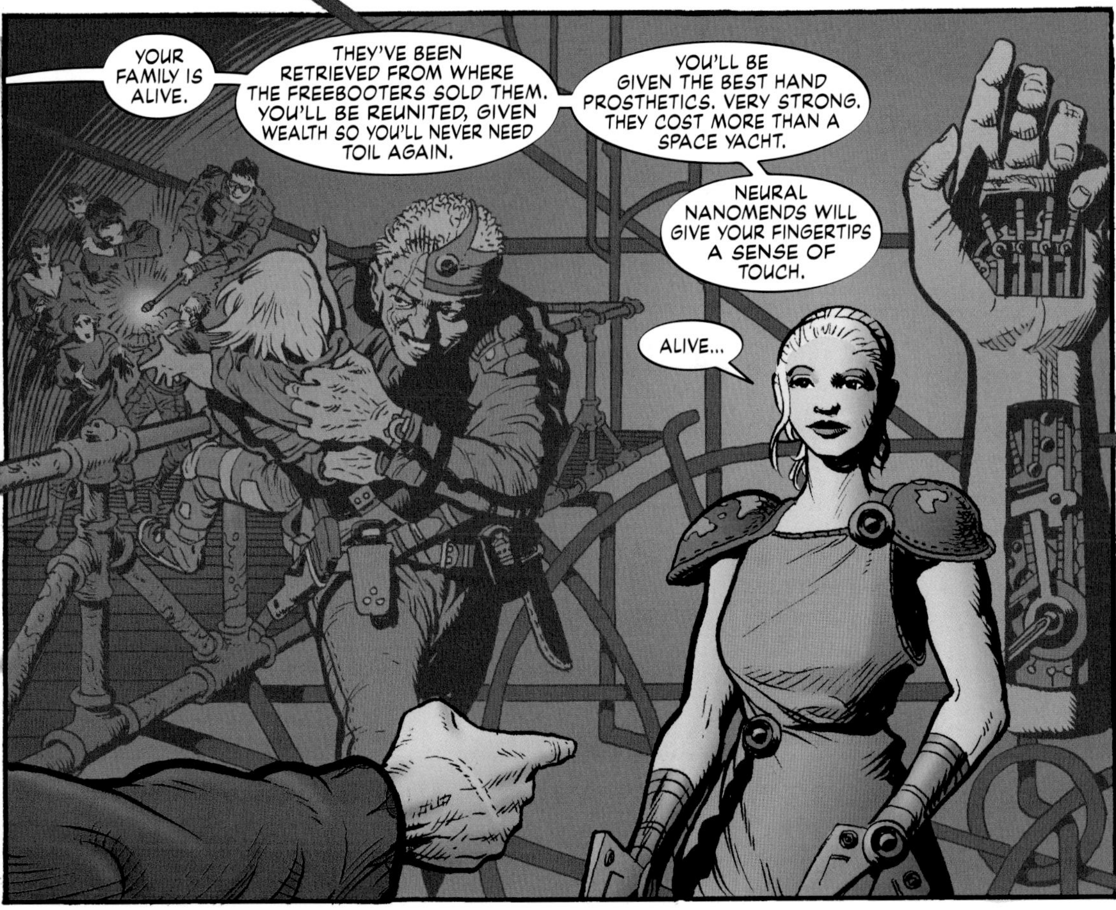
YOUR FAMILY IS ALIVE.
THEY'VE BEEN RETRIEVED FROM WHERE THE FREEBOOTERS SOLD THEM. YOU'LL BE REUNITED, GIVEN WEALTH SO YOU'LL NEVER NEED TOIL AGAIN.
YOU'LL BE GIVEN THE BEST HAND PROSTHETICS. VERY STRONG. THEY COST MORE THAN A SPACE YACHT.
NEURAL NANOMENDS WILL GIVE YOUR FINGERTIPS A SENSE OF TOUCH.
ALIVE...

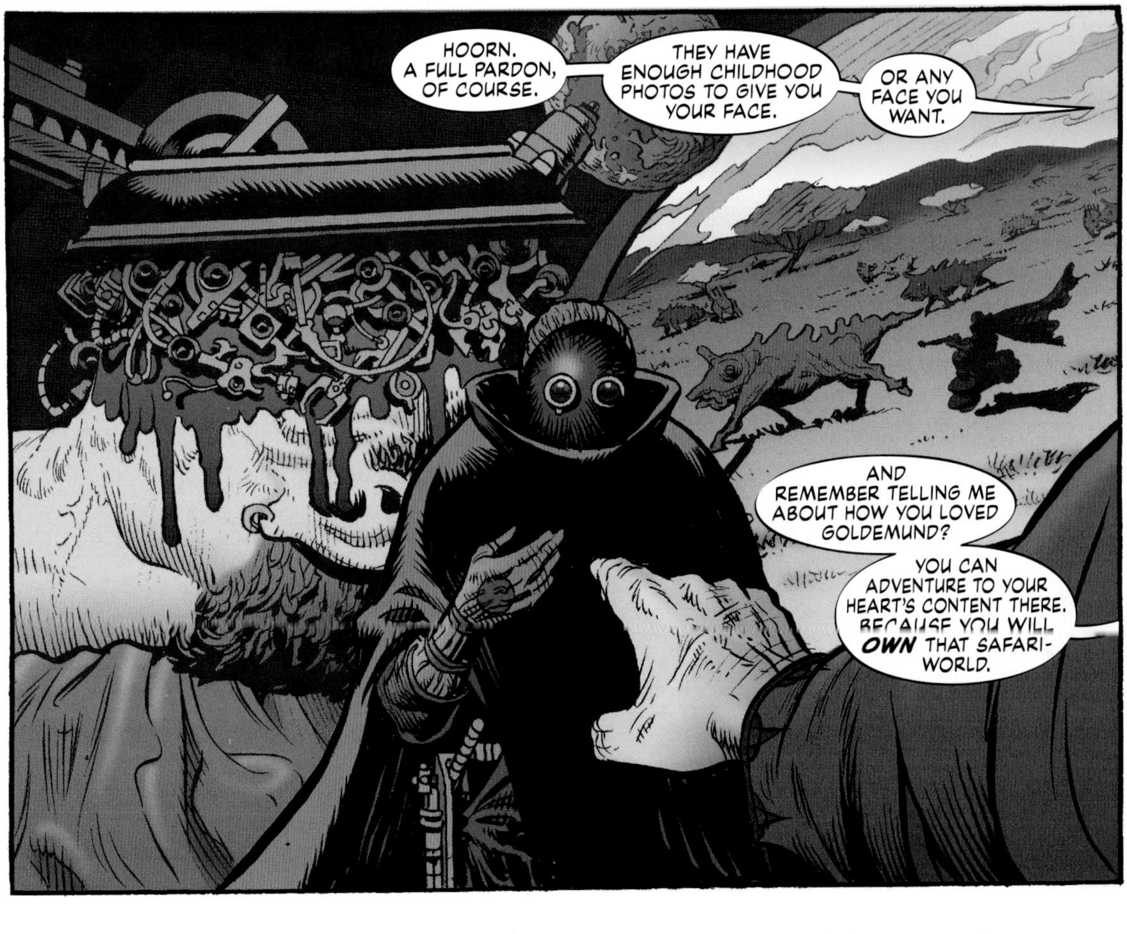
HOORN. A FULL PARDON, OF COURSE.
THEY HAVE ENOUGH CHILDHOOD PHOTOS TO GIVE YOU YOUR FACE.
OR ANY FACE YOU WANT.
AND REMEMBER TELLING ME ABOUT HOW YOU LOVED GOLDEMUND?
YOU CAN ADVENTURE TO YOUR HEART'S CONTENT THERE. BECAUSE YOU WILL **OWN** THAT SAFARI-WORLD.

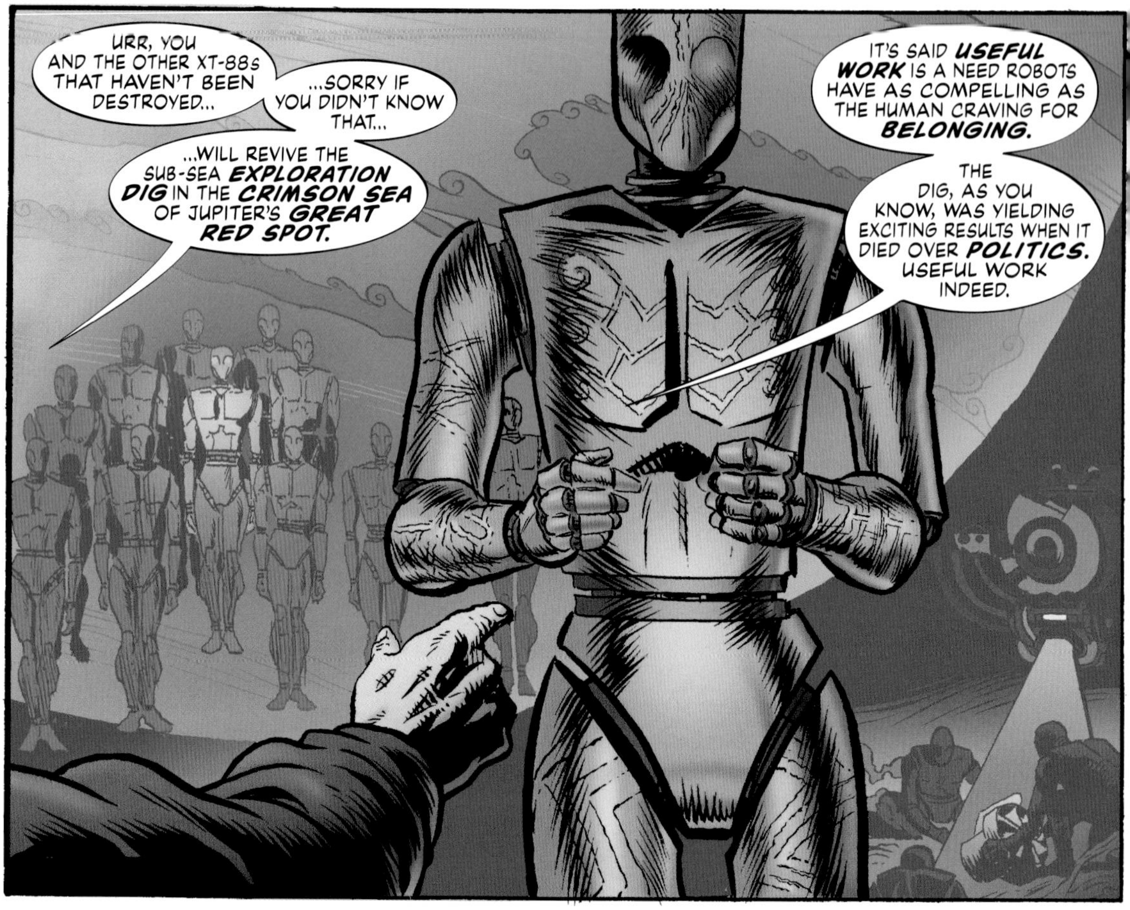
URR, YOU AND THE OTHER XT-88s THAT HAVEN'T BEEN DESTROYED...
...SORRY IF YOU DIDN'T KNOW THAT...
...WILL REVIVE THE SUB-SEA EXPLORATION DIG IN THE CRIMSON SEA OF JUPITER'S GREAT RED SPOT.
IT'S SAID USEFUL WORK IS A NEED ROBOTS HAVE AS COMPELLING AS THE HUMAN CRAVING FOR BELONGING.
THE DIG, AS YOU KNOW, WAS YIELDING EXCITING RESULTS WHEN IT DIED OVER POLITICS. USEFUL WORK INDEED.

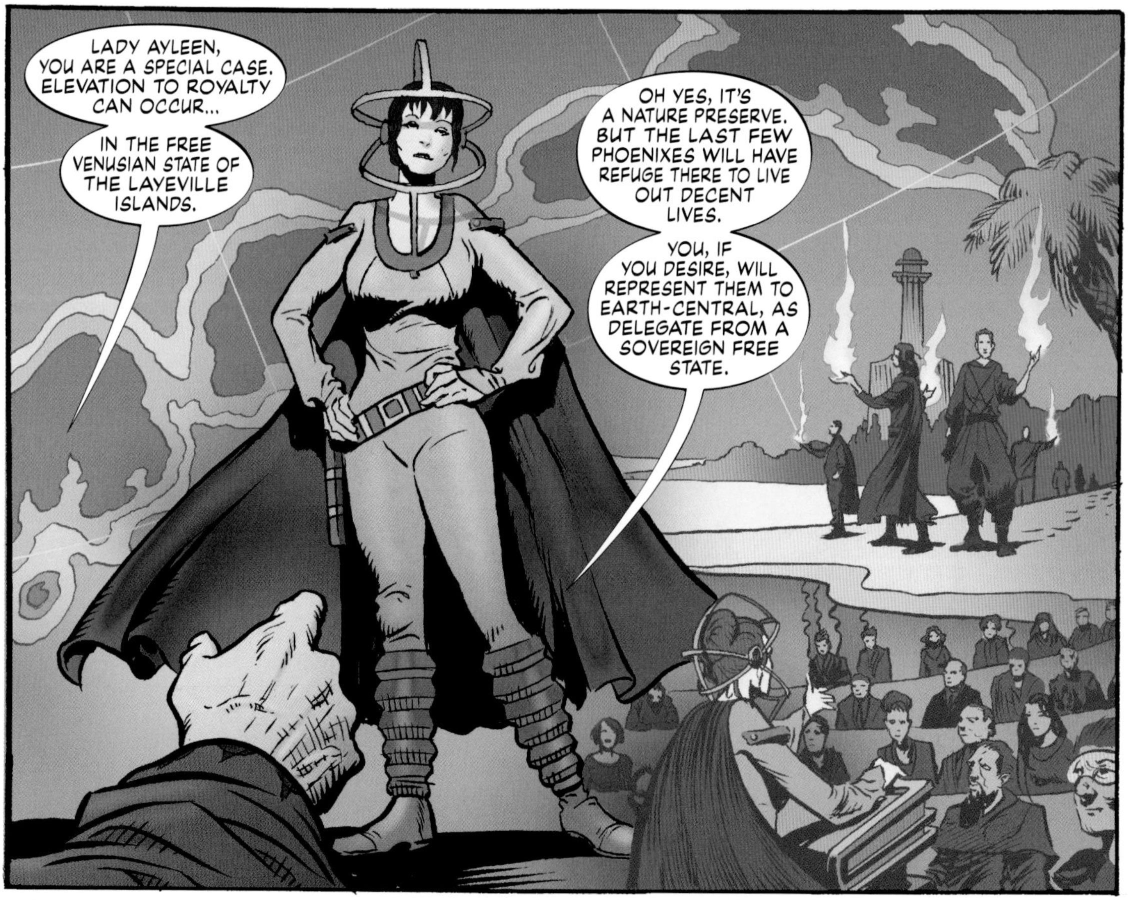
LADY AYLEEN, YOU ARE A SPECIAL CASE. ELEVATION TO ROYALTY CAN OCCUR...
IN THE FREE VENUSIAN STATE OF THE LAYEVILLE ISLANDS.
OH YES, IT'S A NATURE PRESERVE. BUT THE LAST FEW PHOENIXES WILL HAVE REFUGE THERE TO LIVE OUT DECENT LIVES.
YOU, IF YOU DESIRE, WILL REPRESENT THEM TO EARTH-CENTRAL, AS DELEGATE FROM A SOVEREIGN FREE STATE.

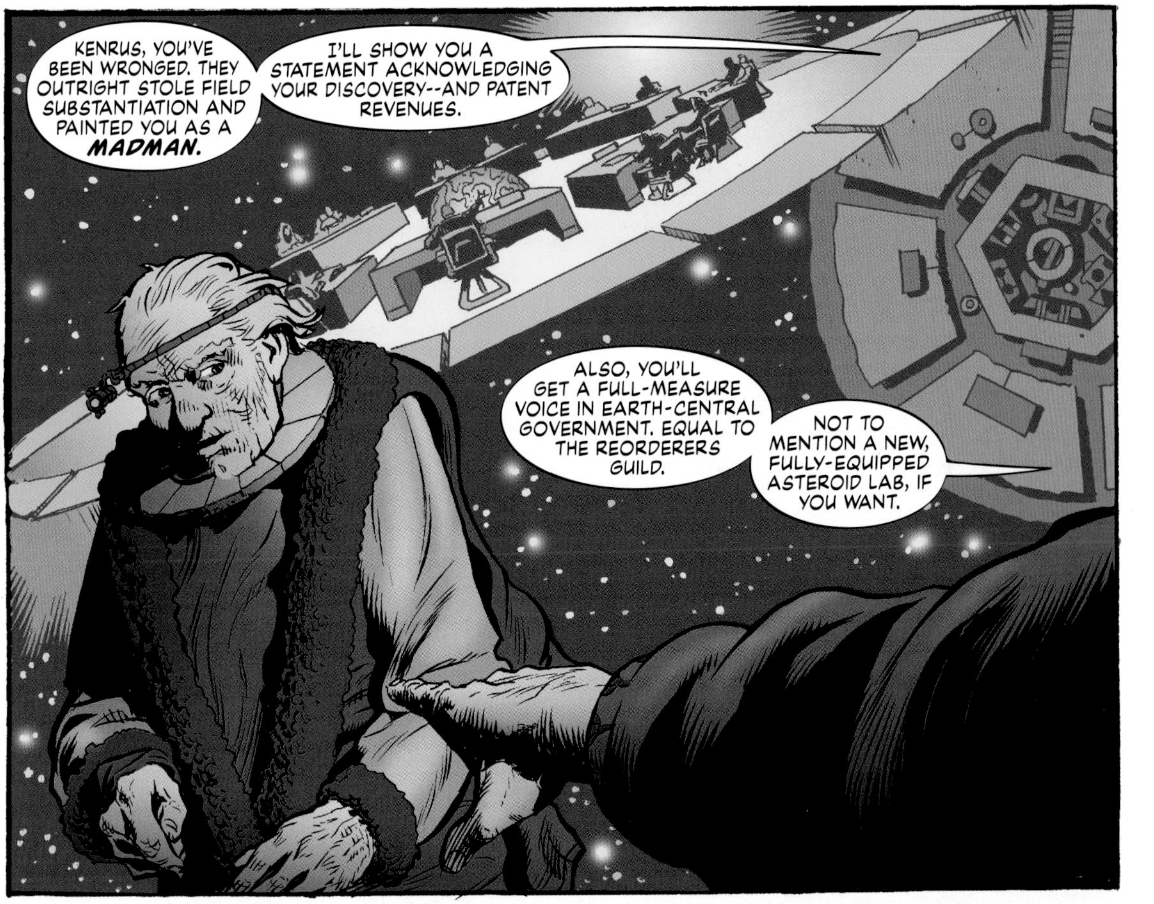
KENRUS, YOU'VE BEEN WRONGED. THEY OUTRIGHT STOLE FIELD SUBSTANTIATION AND PAINTED YOU AS A *MADMAN.*
I'LL SHOW YOU A STATEMENT ACKNOWLEDGING YOUR DISCOVERY--AND PATENT REVENUES.
ALSO, YOU'LL GET A FULL-MEASURE VOICE IN EARTH-CENTRAL GOVERNMENT. EQUAL TO THE REORDERERS GUILD.
NOT TO MENTION A NEW, FULLY-EQUIPPED ASTEROID LAB, IF YOU WANT.

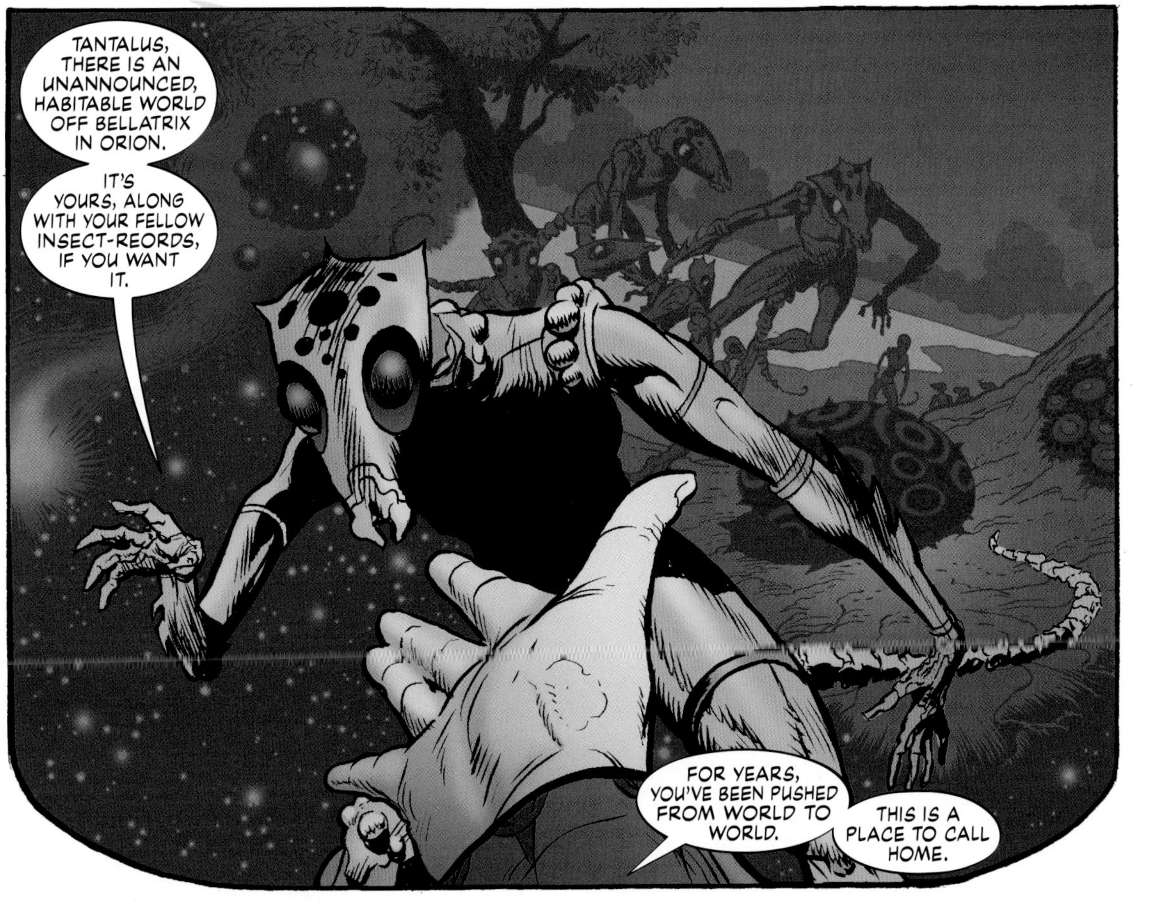
TANTALUS, THERE IS AN UNANNOUNCED, HABITABLE WORLD OFF BELLATRIX IN ORION.
IT'S YOURS, ALONG WITH YOUR FELLOW INSECT-REORDS, IF YOU WANT IT.
FOR YEARS, YOU'VE BEEN PUSHED FROM WORLD TO WORLD.
THIS IS A PLACE TO CALL HOME.

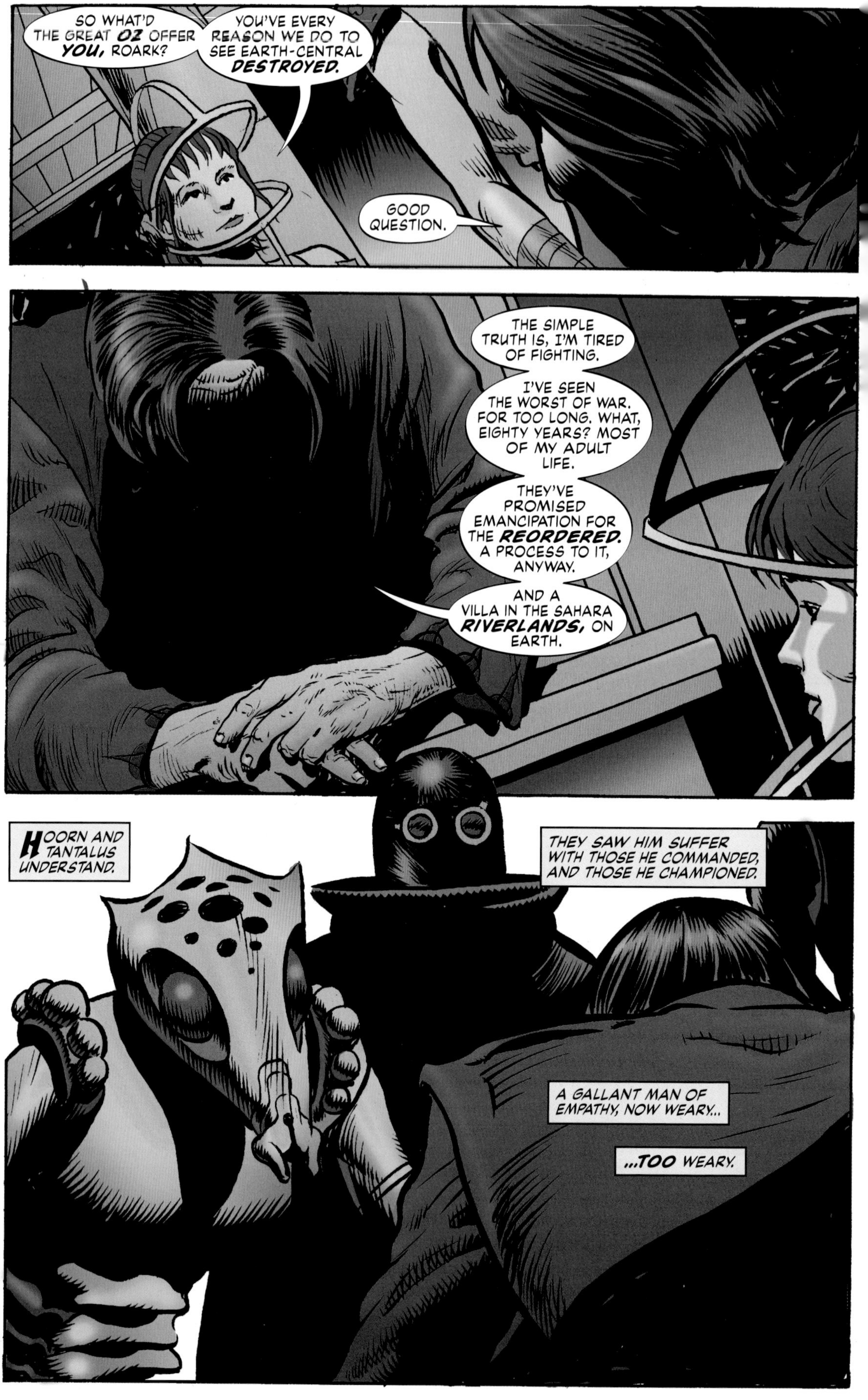
SO WHAT'D THE GREAT OZ OFFER YOU, ROARK?
YOU'VE EVERY REASON WE DO TO SEE EARTH-CENTRAL DESTROYED.
GOOD QUESTION.
THE SIMPLE TRUTH IS, I'M TIRED OF FIGHTING.
I'VE SEEN THE WORST OF WAR. FOR TOO LONG. WHAT, EIGHTY YEARS? MOST OF MY ADULT LIFE.
THEY'VE PROMISED EMANCIPATION FOR THE REORDERED. A PROCESS TO IT, ANYWAY.
AND A VILLA IN THE SAHARA RIVERLANDS, ON EARTH.
HOORN AND TANTALUS UNDERSTAND.
THEY SAW HIM SUFFER WITH THOSE HE COMMANDED, AND THOSE HE CHAMPIONED.
A GALLANT MAN OF EMPATHY, NOW WEARY...
...TOO WEARY.

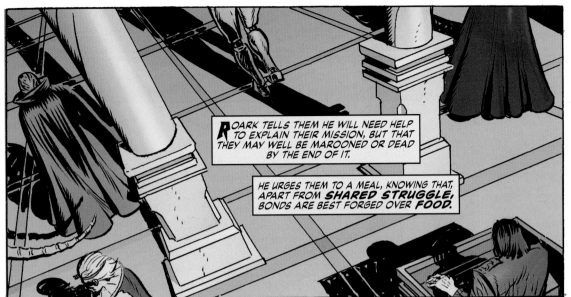

ROARK TELLS THEM HE WILL NEED HELP TO EXPLAIN THEIR MISSION, BUT THAT THEY MAY WELL BE MAROONED OR DEAD BY THE END OF IT.

HE URGES THEM TO A MEAL, KNOWING THAT, APART FROM *SHARED STRUGGLE*, BONDS ARE BEST FORGED OVER *FOOD*.

I KNOW ONE THING. THEY'RE *REALLY* IN TROUBLE, OR THEY'RE *SURE* WE WON'T BE BACK TO COLLECT OUR GOODIES.

I AT LEAST CAN GET MY RECOGNITION *BEFOREHAND*. AND PERHAPS YOUR HANDS, MOURNA.

IF THEIR *COMPUTERS* DON'T FIGURE THESE CLAWS ARE *NEEDED*.

URR, YOU'RE OUT OF LUCK HERE.

I WITNESS YOUR PLEASURE. CONTINUE EATING.

ROARK, WE'RE IN.

UNLESS IT'S IMMORAL, DEGRADING, OR INVOLVES TOO MUCH PAPERWORK.

WE'LL DO A FULL BRIEFING IN THE MORNING.

I CAN PROMISE-- *ASTONISHMENT*.

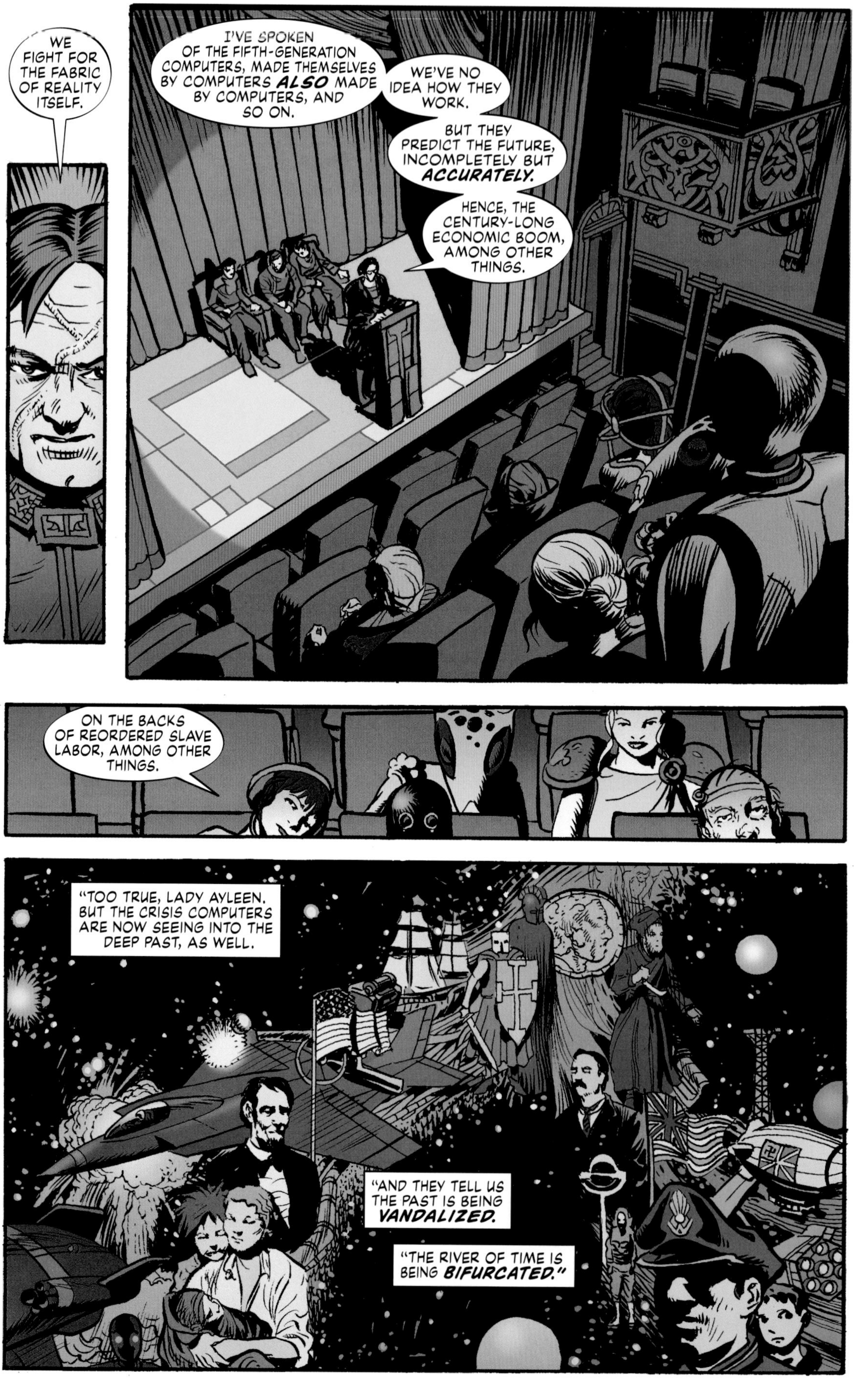
WE FIGHT FOR THE FABRIC OF REALITY ITSELF.
I'VE SPOKEN OF THE FIFTH-GENERATION COMPUTERS, MADE THEMSELVES BY COMPUTERS **ALSO** MADE BY COMPUTERS, AND SO ON.
WE'VE NO IDEA HOW THEY WORK.
BUT THEY PREDICT THE FUTURE, INCOMPLETELY BUT **ACCURATELY.**
HENCE, THE CENTURY-LONG ECONOMIC BOOM, AMONG OTHER THINGS.
ON THE BACKS OF REORDERED SLAVE LABOR, AMONG OTHER THINGS.
"TOO TRUE, LADY AYLEEN. BUT THE CRISIS COMPUTERS ARE NOW SEEING INTO THE DEEP PAST, AS WELL.
"AND THEY TELL US THE PAST IS BEING **VANDALIZED.**
"THE RIVER OF TIME IS BEING **BIFURCATED.**"

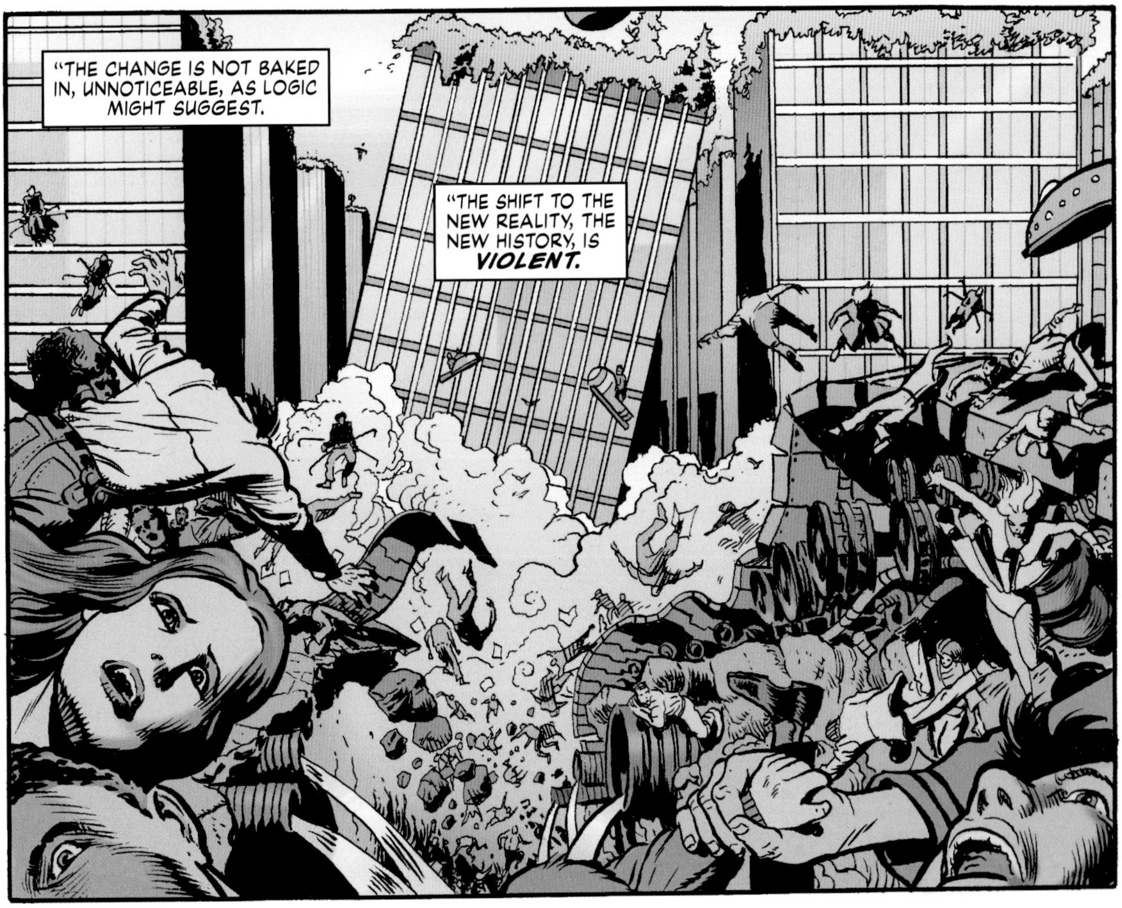
"THE CHANGE IS NOT BAKED IN, UNNOTICEABLE, AS LOGIC MIGHT SUGGEST.
"THE SHIFT TO THE NEW REALITY, THE NEW HISTORY, IS *VIOLENT.*

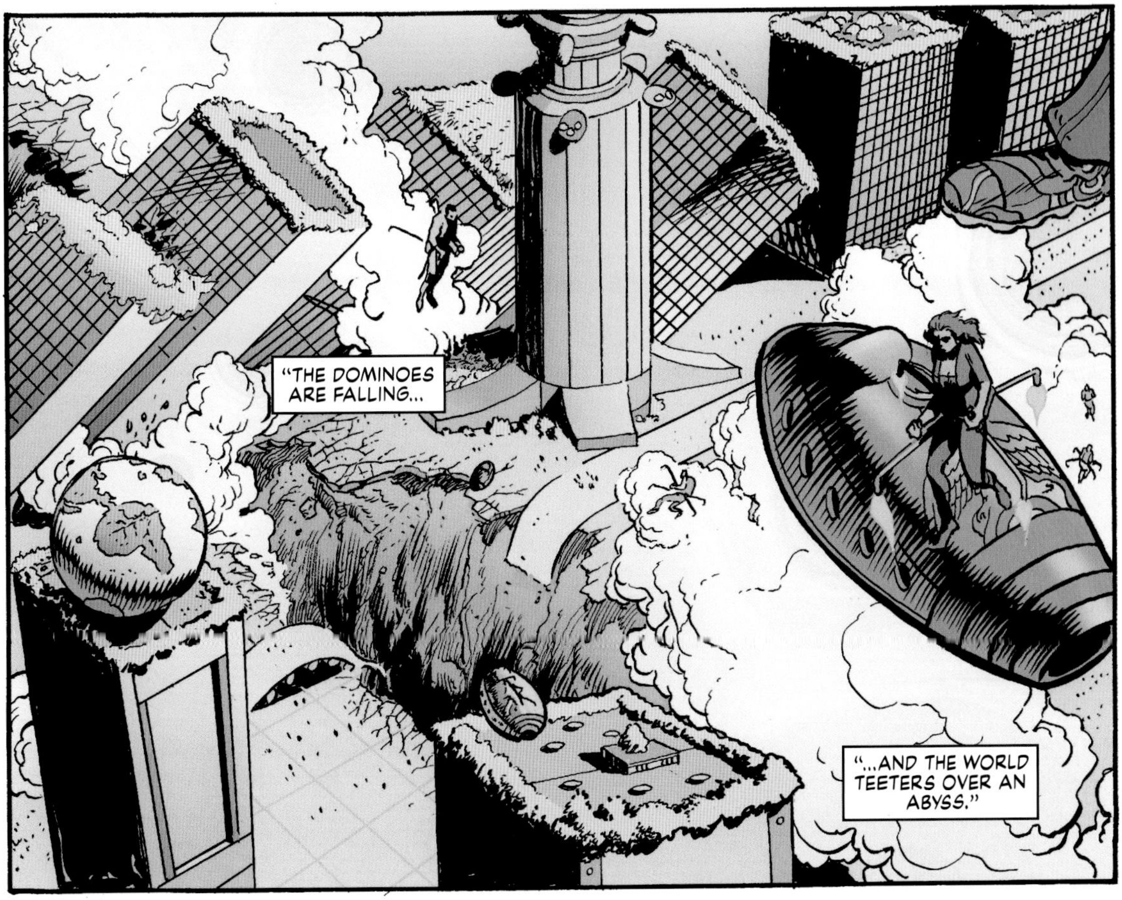
"THE DOMINOES ARE FALLING...
"...AND THE WORLD TEETERS OVER AN ABYSS."

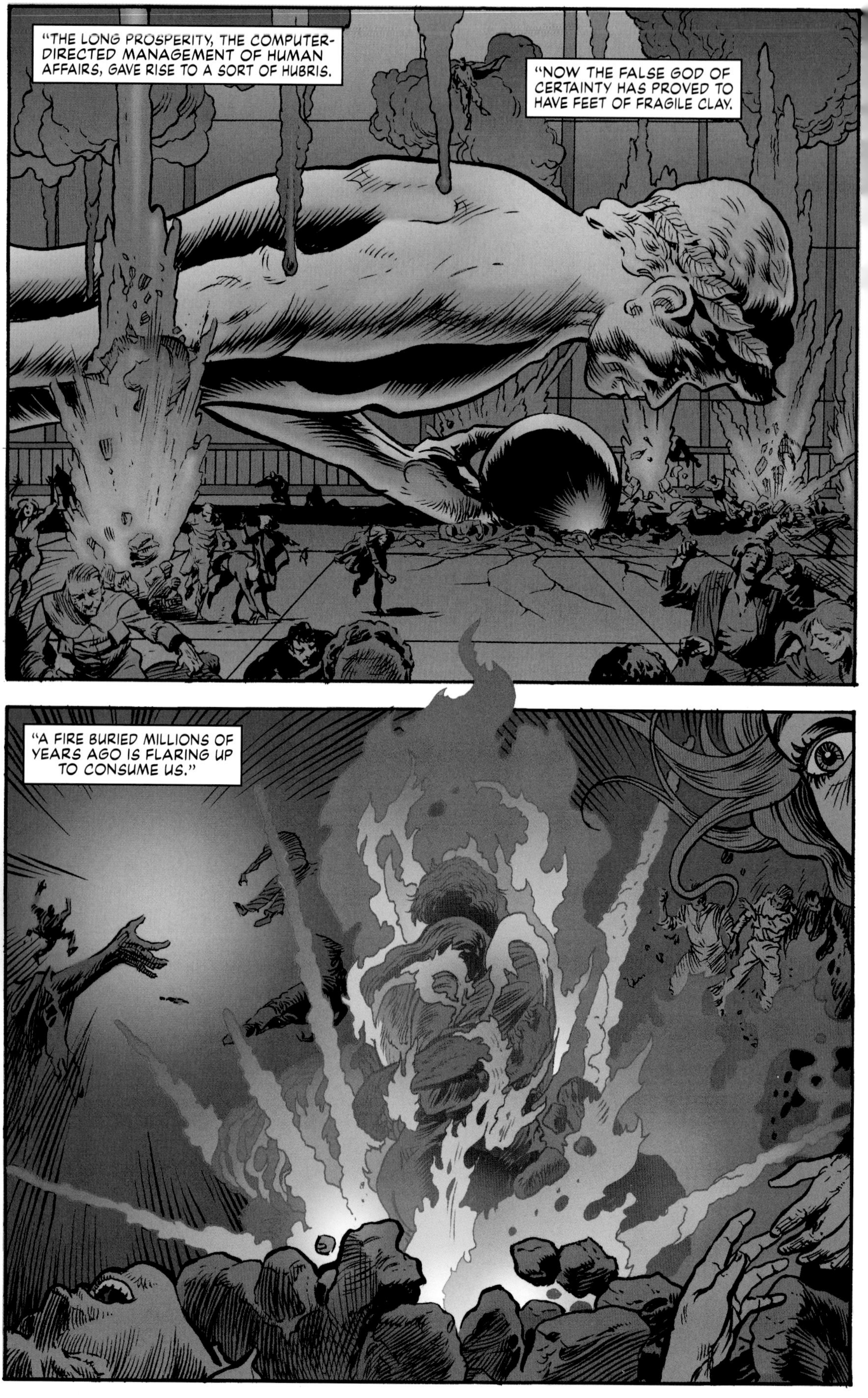
"THE LONG PROSPERITY, THE COMPUTER-DIRECTED MANAGEMENT OF HUMAN AFFAIRS, GAVE RISE TO A SORT OF HUBRIS.
"NOW THE FALSE GOD OF CERTAINTY HAS PROVED TO HAVE FEET OF FRAGILE CLAY.
"A FIRE BURIED MILLIONS OF YEARS AGO IS FLARING UP TO CONSUME US."

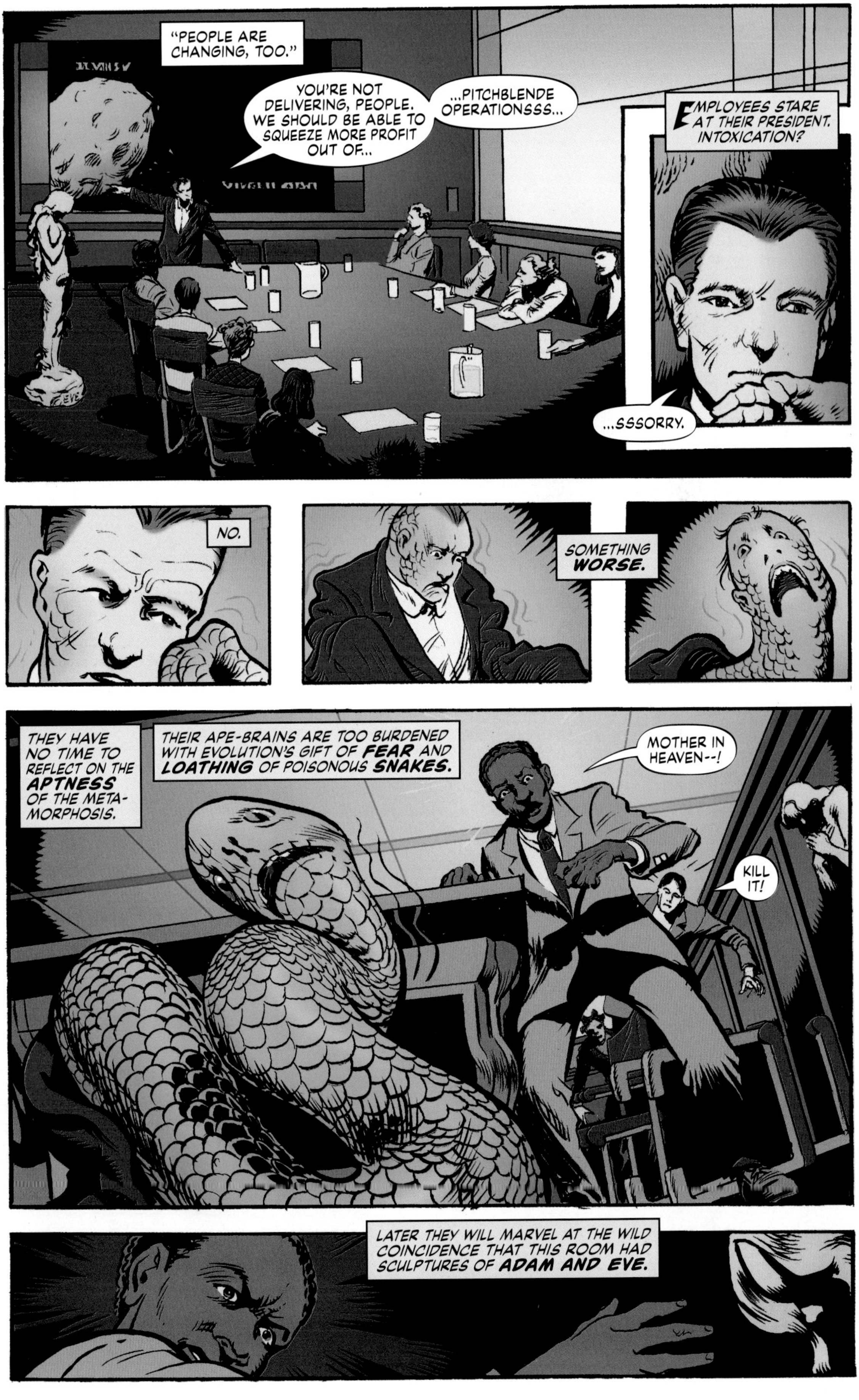

"PEOPLE ARE CHANGING, TOO."
YOU'RE NOT DELIVERING, PEOPLE. WE SHOULD BE ABLE TO SQUEEZE MORE PROFIT OUT OF...
...PITCHBLENDE OPERATIONSSS...
EVE
EMPLOYEES STARE AT THEIR PRESIDENT. INTOXICATION?
...SSSORRY.
NO.
SOMETHING **WORSE.**
THEY HAVE NO TIME TO REFLECT ON THE **APTNESS** OF THE META-MORPHOSIS.
THEIR APE-BRAINS ARE TOO BURDENED WITH EVOLUTION'S GIFT OF **FEAR** AND **LOATHING** OF POISONOUS **SNAKES.**
MOTHER IN HEAVEN--!
KILL IT!
LATER THEY WILL MARVEL AT THE WILD COINCIDENCE THAT THIS ROOM HAD SCULPTURES OF **ADAM AND EVE.**

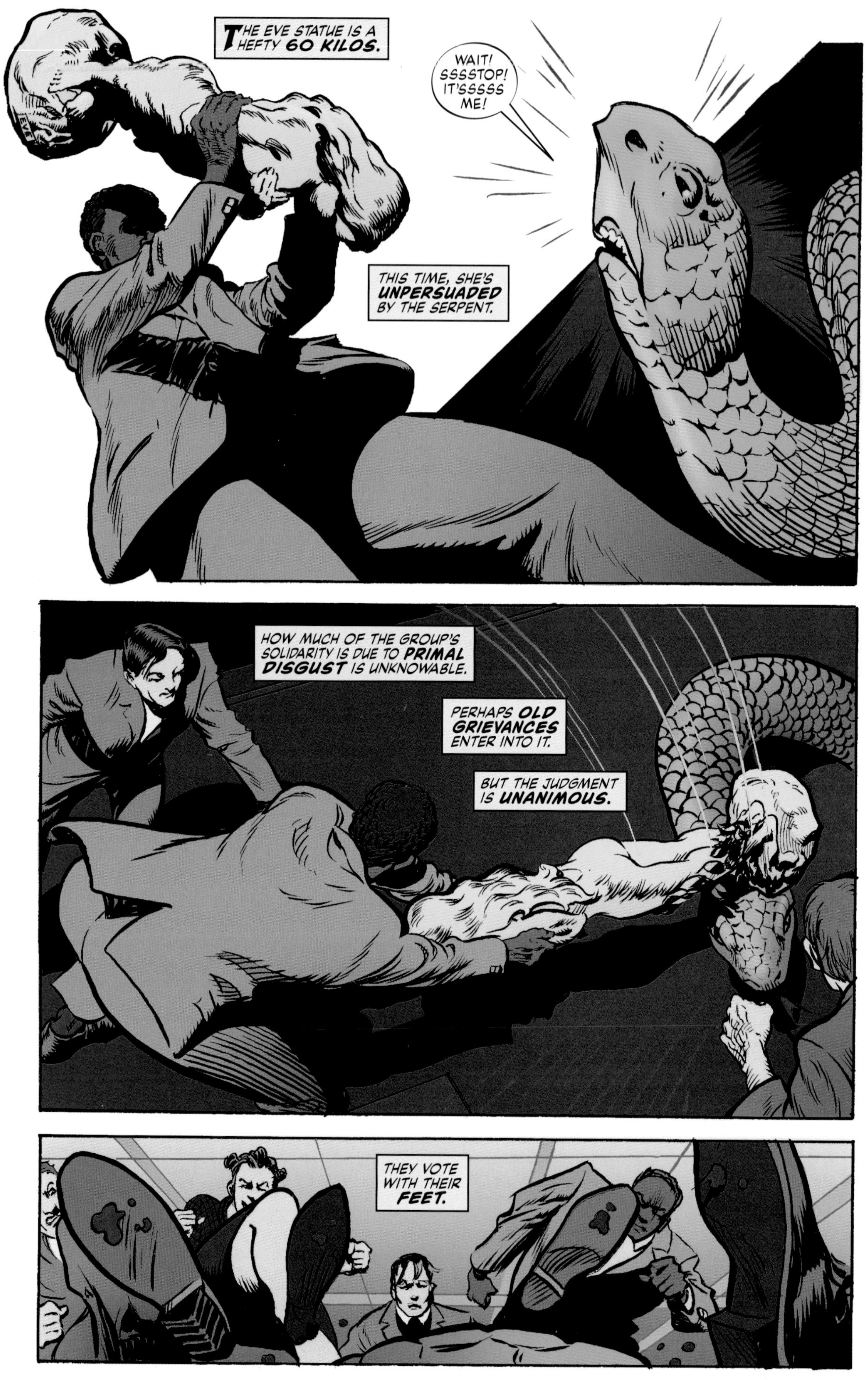
THE EVE STATUE IS A HEFTY 60 KILOS.
WAIT! SSSSTOP! IT'SSSSS ME!
THIS TIME, SHE'S UNPERSUADED BY THE SERPENT.
EVE
HOW MUCH OF THE GROUP'S SOLIDARITY IS DUE TO PRIMAL DISGUST IS UNKNOWABLE.
PERHAPS OLD GRIEVANCES ENTER INTO IT.
BUT THE JUDGMENT IS UNANIMOUS.
THEY VOTE WITH THEIR FEET.

"SOME EFFECTS ARE SMALL, BUT CONSEQUENTIAL.

"FOR WANT OF A NAIL, A SHOE WAS LOST, YOU COULD SAY."

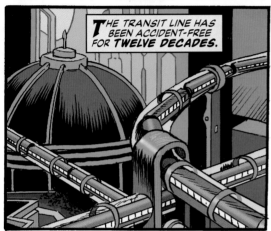

THE TRANSIT LINE HAS BEEN ACCIDENT-FREE FOR TWELVE DECADES.

SO WHEN THE UNTHINKABLE OCCURS...

LOOK!

...AN ODD OMISSION...

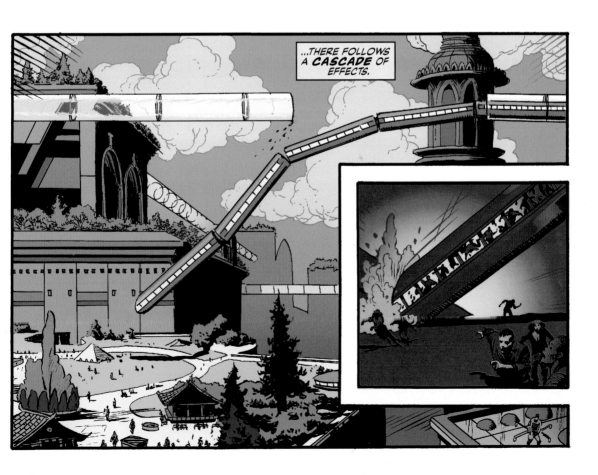

...THERE FOLLOWS A CASCADE OF EFFECTS.

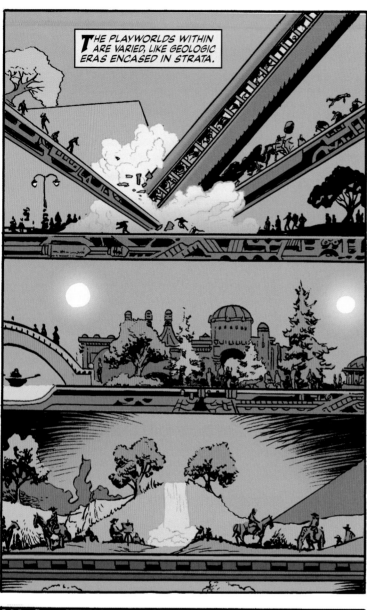

THE PLAYWORLDS WITHIN ARE VARIED, LIKE GEOLOGIC ERAS ENCASED IN STRATA.

INTO THE ABYSS THE TRAIN CREATES, PEOPLE FALL.

IMPOSSIBLE!

THOSE BELOW STARE AT THE ONRUSHING COLLAPSE.

THE TWELVE TO TWENTY DECADES THEY EXPECTED TO LIVE...

...CUT SHORT.

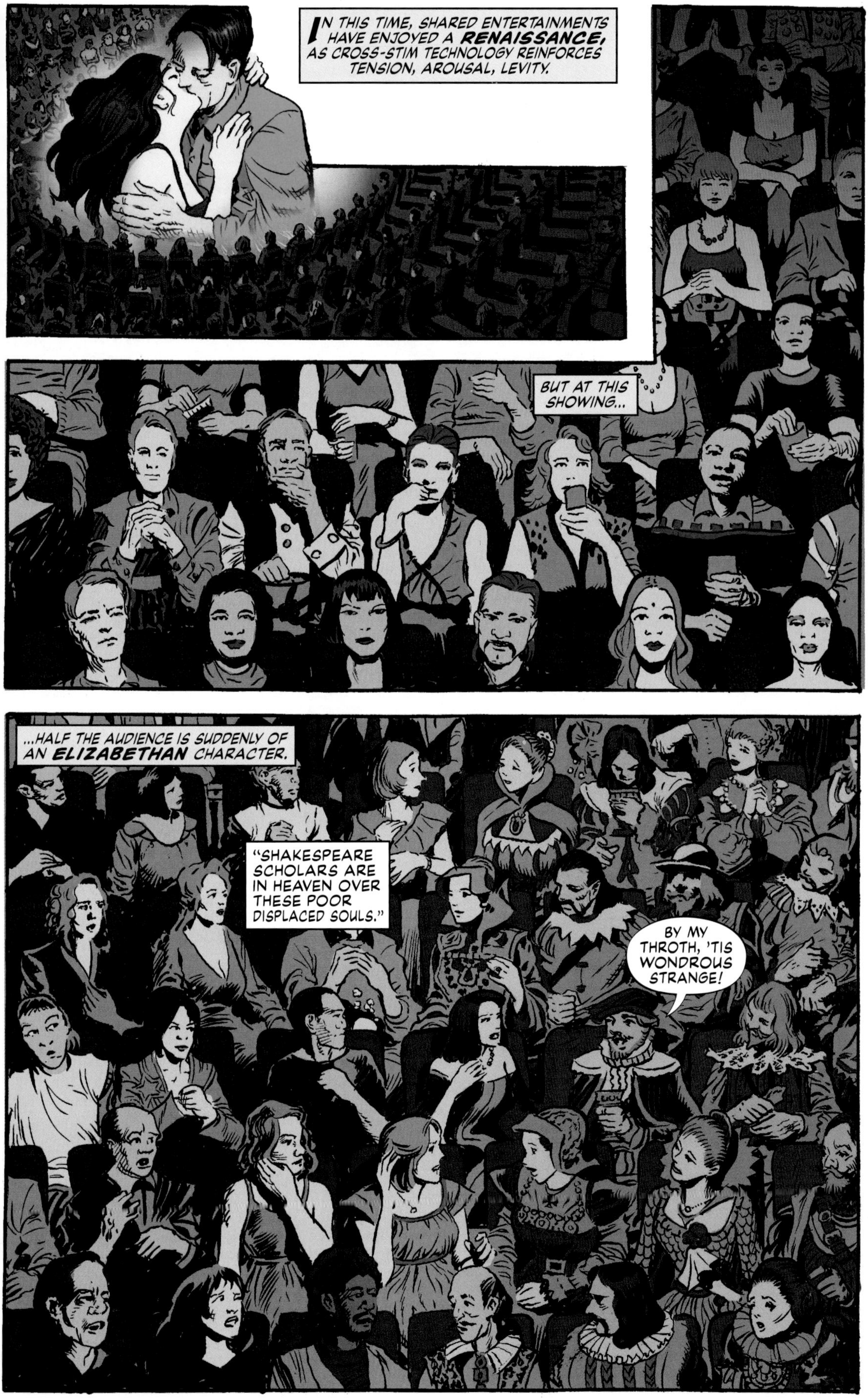
IN THIS TIME, SHARED ENTERTAINMENTS HAVE ENJOYED A RENAISSANCE, AS CROSS-STIM TECHNOLOGY REINFORCES TENSION, AROUSAL, LEVITY.
BUT AT THIS SHOWING...
...HALF THE AUDIENCE IS SUDDENLY OF AN ELIZABETHAN CHARACTER.
"SHAKESPEARE SCHOLARS ARE IN HEAVEN OVER THESE POOR DISPLACED SOULS."
BY MY THROTH, 'TIS WONDROUS STRANGE!

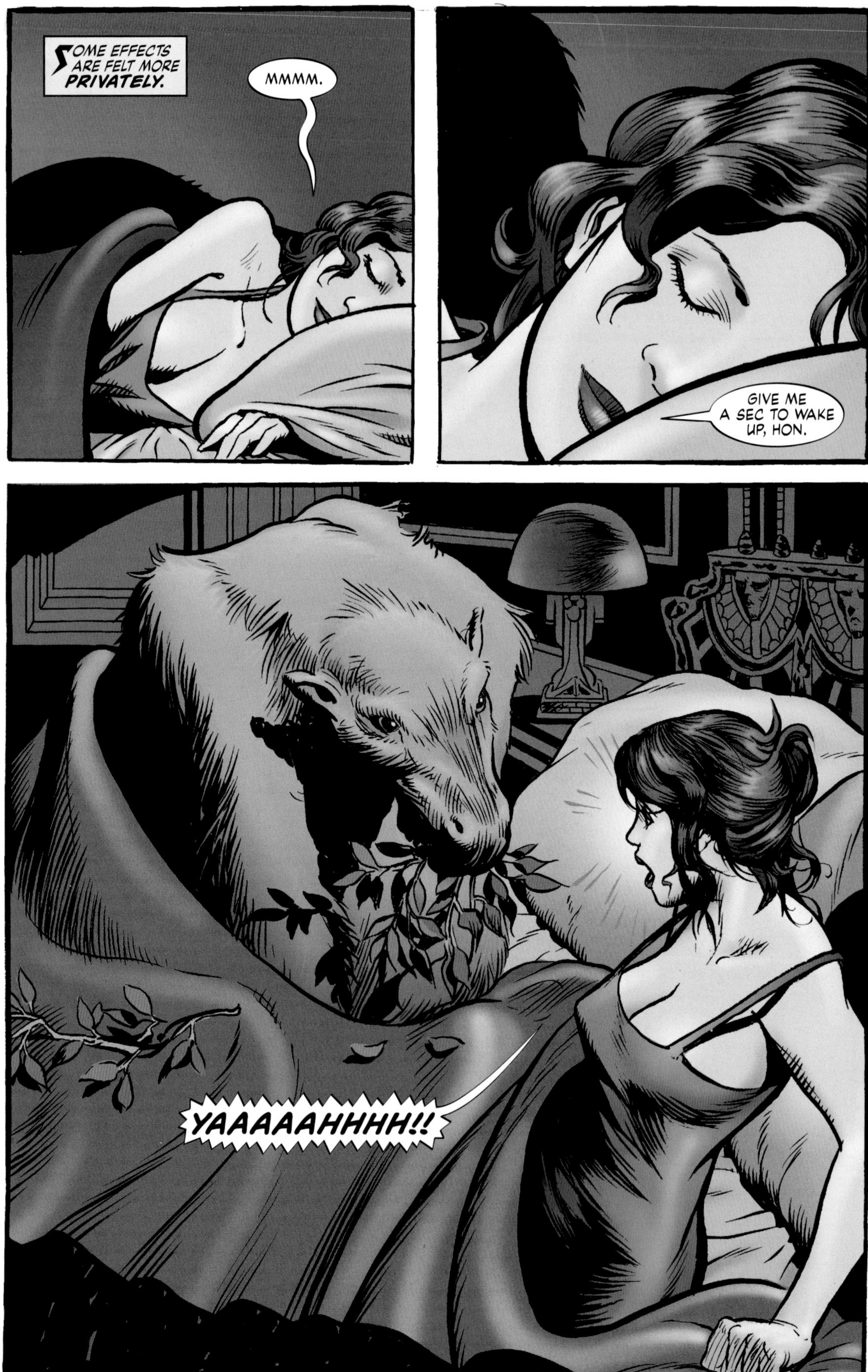
SOME EFFECTS ARE FELT MORE PRIVATELY.
MMMM.
GIVE ME A SEC TO WAKE UP, HON.
YAAAAAHHHH!!

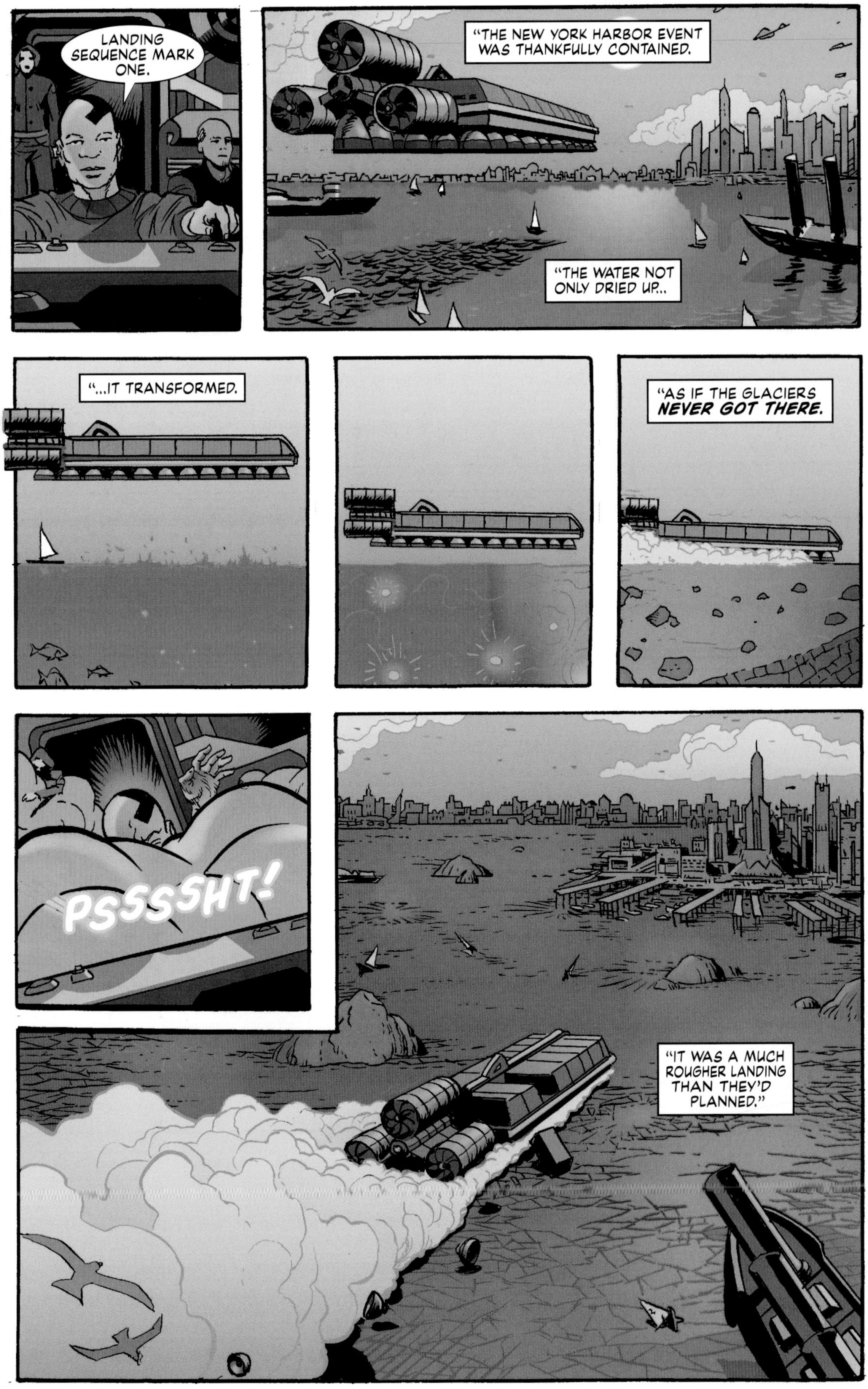
LANDING SEQUENCE MARK ONE.
"THE NEW YORK HARBOR EVENT WAS THANKFULLY CONTAINED.
"THE WATER NOT ONLY DRIED UP...
"...IT TRANSFORMED.
"AS IF THE GLACIERS *NEVER GOT THERE.*
PSSSSHT!
"IT WAS A MUCH ROUGHER LANDING THAN THEY'D PLANNED."

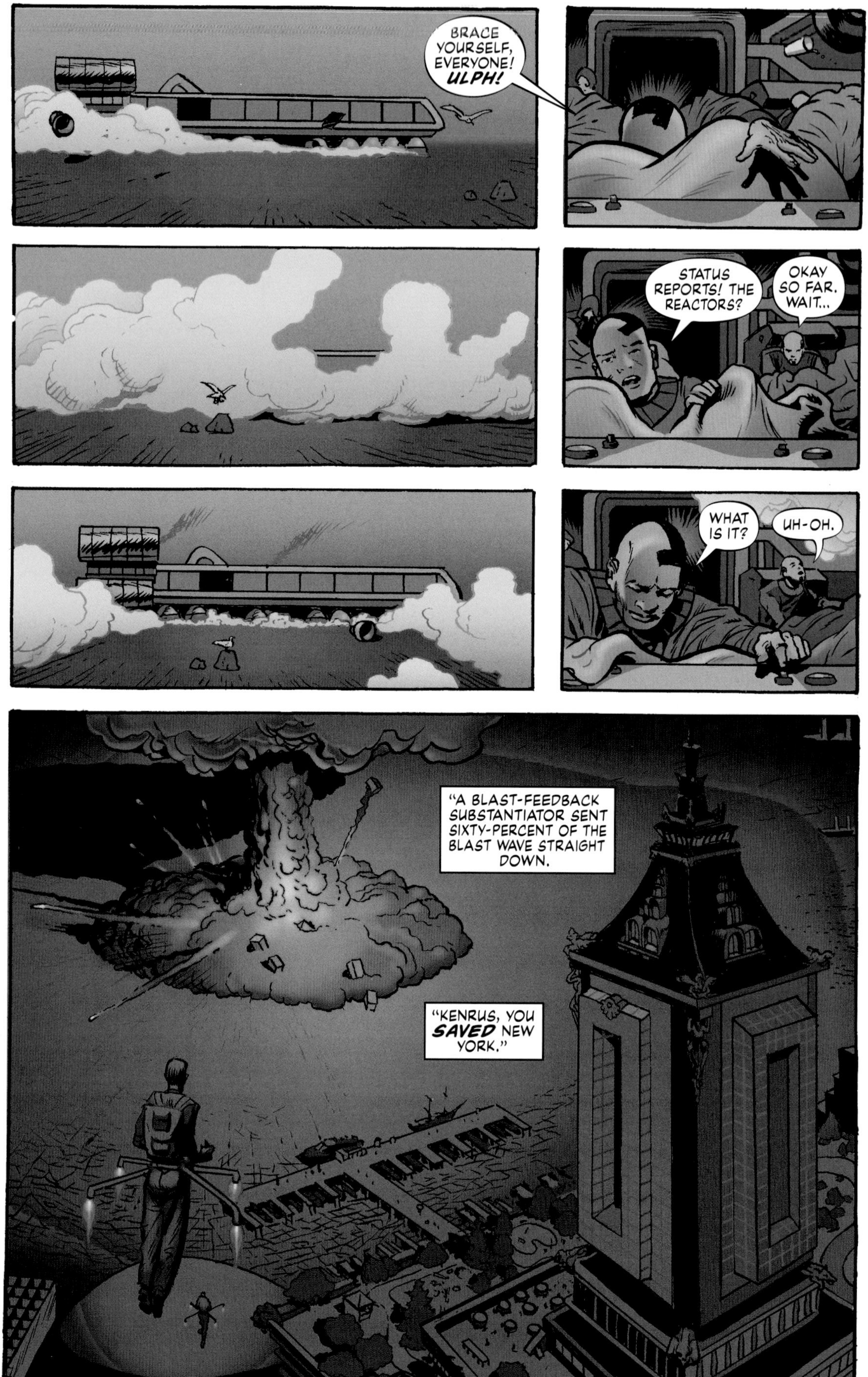
BRACE YOURSELF, EVERYONE! ***ULPH!***
STATUS REPORTS! THE REACTORS?
OKAY SO FAR. WAIT...
WHAT IS IT?
UH-OH.
"A BLAST-FEEDBACK SUBSTANTIATOR SENT SIXTY-PERCENT OF THE BLAST WAVE STRAIGHT DOWN.
"KENRUS, YOU ***SAVED*** NEW YORK."

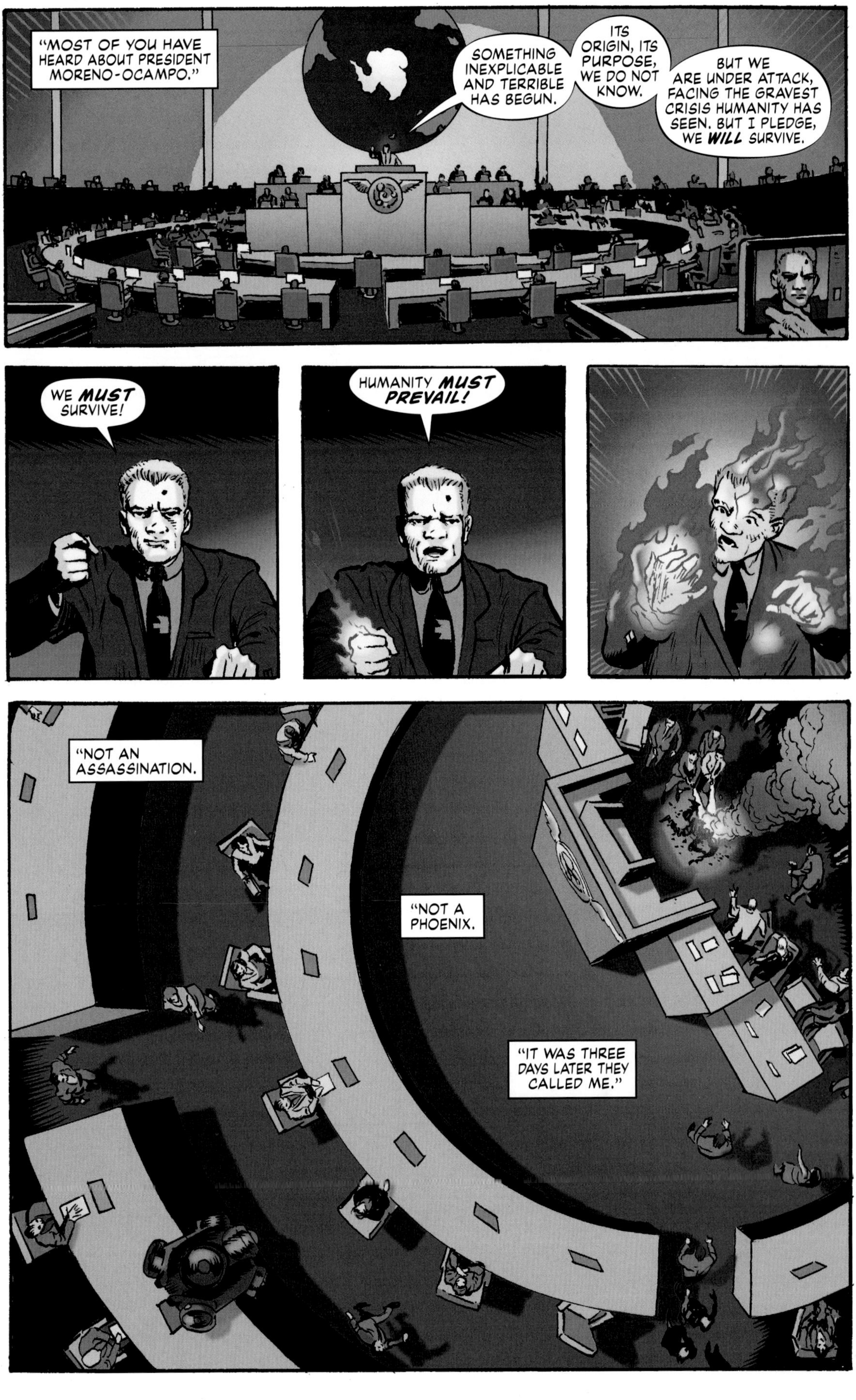
"MOST OF YOU HAVE HEARD ABOUT PRESIDENT MORENO-OCAMPO."
SOMETHING INEXPLICABLE AND TERRIBLE HAS BEGUN.
ITS ORIGIN, ITS PURPOSE, WE DO NOT KNOW.
BUT WE ARE UNDER ATTACK, FACING THE GRAVEST CRISIS HUMANITY HAS SEEN. BUT I PLEDGE, WE *WILL* SURVIVE.
WE *MUST* SURVIVE!
HUMANITY *MUST PREVAIL!*
"NOT AN ASSASSINATION.
"NOT A PHOENIX.
"IT WAS THREE DAYS LATER THEY CALLED ME."

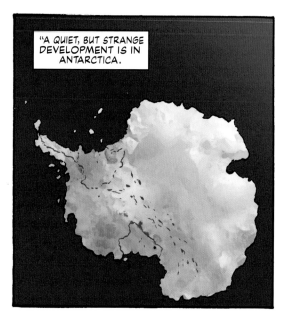

"A QUIET, BUT STRANGE DEVELOPMENT IS IN ANTARCTICA.

"THE NEW, LARGEST MOUNTAIN IN THE WORLD, BIGGER THAN OLYMPUS MONS ON MARS..."

"A VOLCANO?"

"NO.

"IT SEEMS TO BE COMPLETELY FORMED OF *ICE.*"

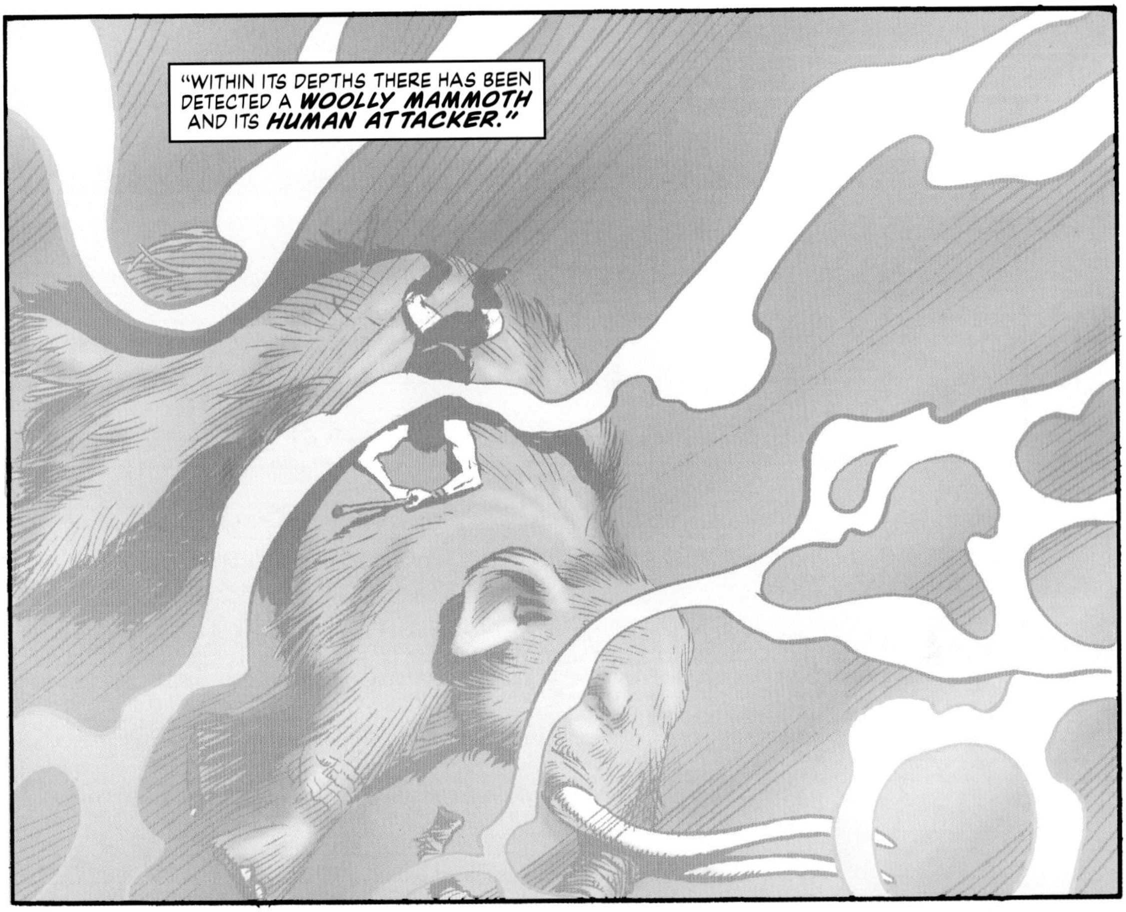
"WITHIN ITS DEPTHS THERE HAS BEEN DETECTED A ***WOOLLY MAMMOTH*** AND ITS ***HUMAN ATTACKER.***"

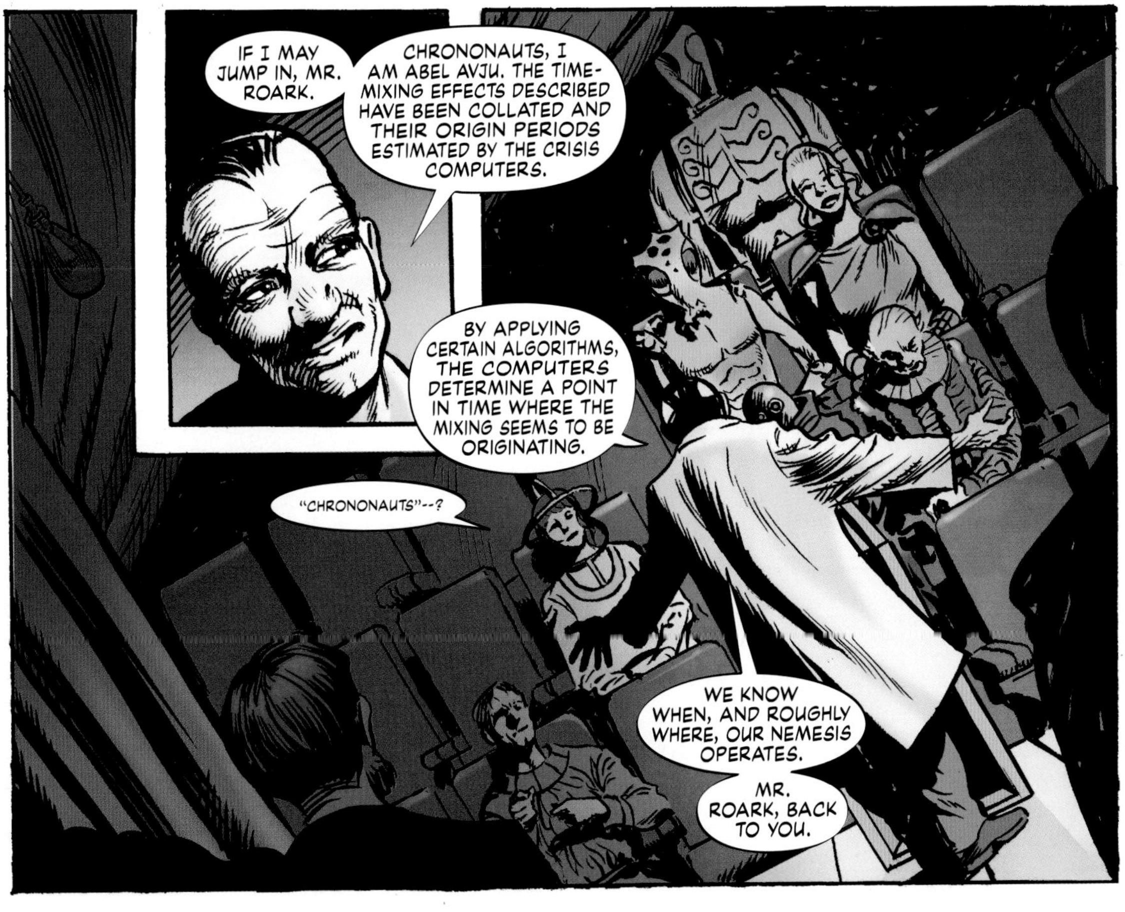
IF I MAY JUMP IN, MR. ROARK.
CHRONONAUTS, I AM ABEL AVJU. THE TIME-MIXING EFFECTS DESCRIBED HAVE BEEN COLLATED AND THEIR ORIGIN PERIODS ESTIMATED BY THE CRISIS COMPUTERS.
BY APPLYING CERTAIN ALGORITHMS, THE COMPUTERS DETERMINE A POINT IN TIME WHERE THE MIXING SEEMS TO BE ORIGINATING.
"CHRONONAUTS"--?
WE KNOW WHEN, AND ROUGHLY WHERE, OUR NEMESIS OPERATES.
MR. ROARK, BACK TO YOU.

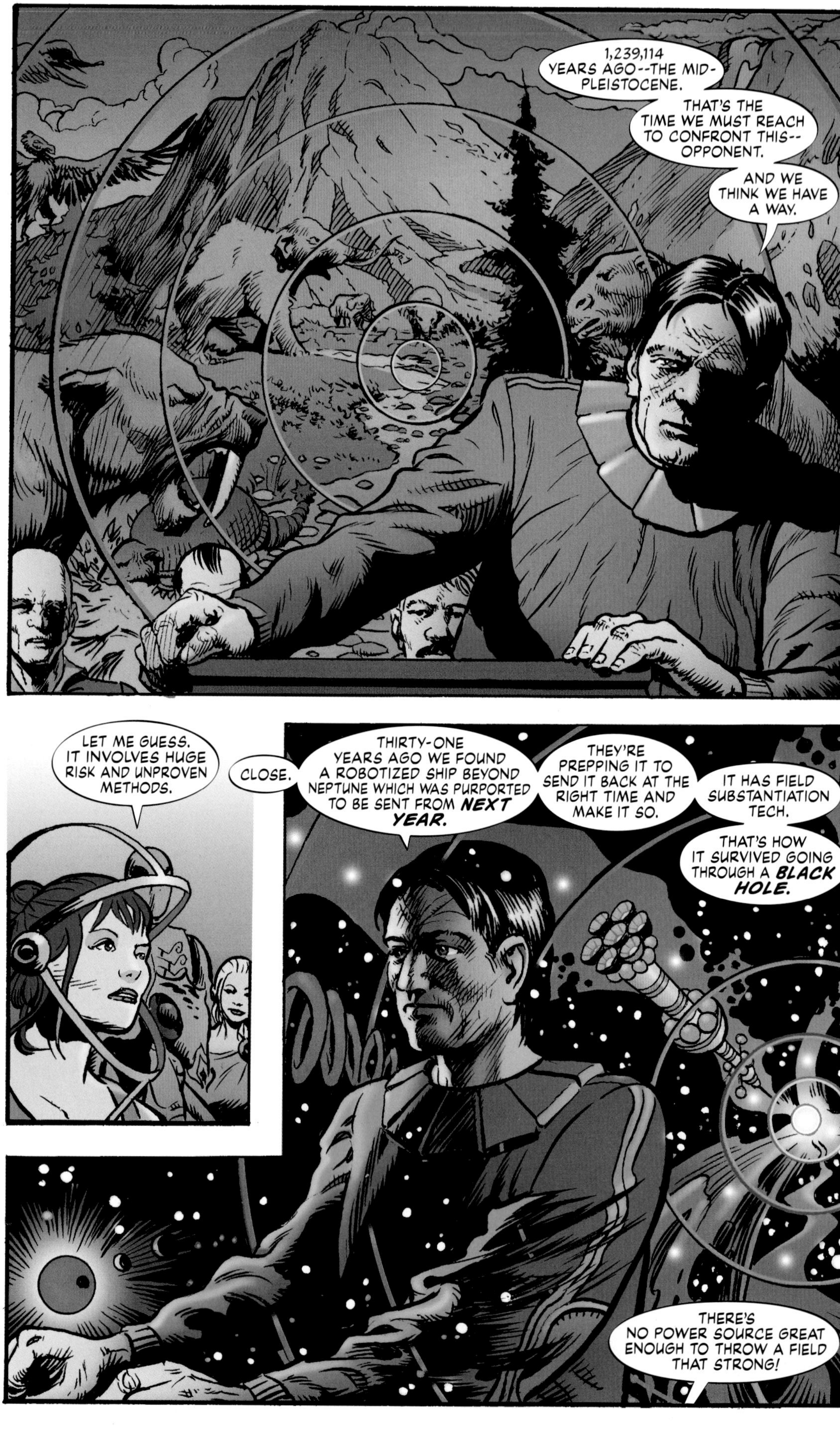
1,239,114 YEARS AGO--THE MID-PLEISTOCENE.
THAT'S THE TIME WE MUST REACH TO CONFRONT THIS--OPPONENT.
AND WE THINK WE HAVE A WAY.
LET ME GUESS. IT INVOLVES HUGE RISK AND UNPROVEN METHODS.
CLOSE.
THIRTY-ONE YEARS AGO WE FOUND A ROBOTIZED SHIP BEYOND NEPTUNE WHICH WAS PURPORTED TO BE SENT FROM **NEXT YEAR.**
THEY'RE PREPPING IT TO SEND IT BACK AT THE RIGHT TIME AND MAKE IT SO.
IT HAS FIELD SUBSTANTIATION TECH.
THAT'S HOW IT SURVIVED GOING THROUGH A **BLACK HOLE.**
THERE'S NO POWER SOURCE GREAT ENOUGH TO THROW A FIELD THAT STRONG!

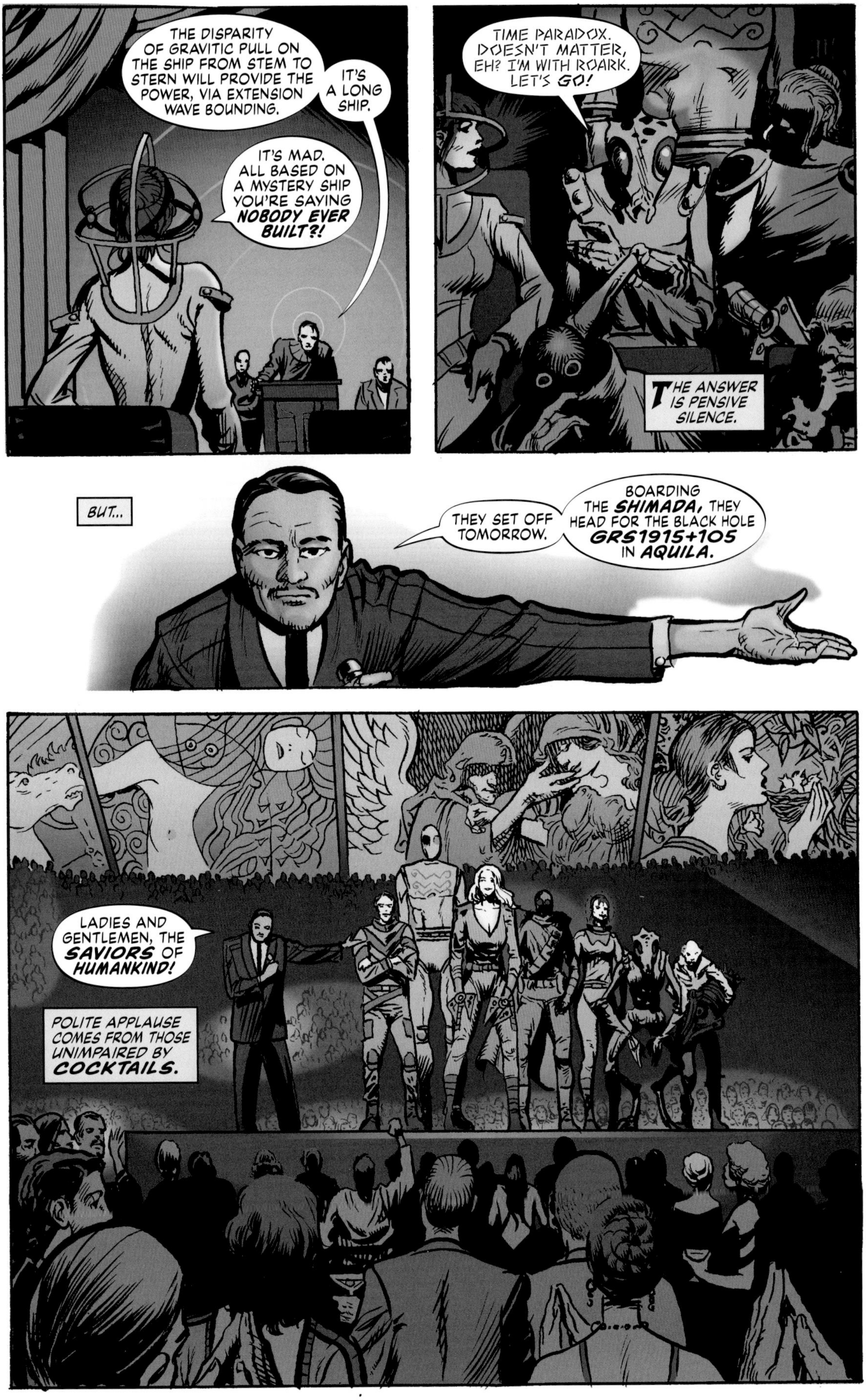
THE DISPARITY OF GRAVITIC PULL ON THE SHIP FROM STEM TO STERN WILL PROVIDE THE POWER, VIA EXTENSION WAVE BOUNDING.
IT'S A LONG SHIP.
IT'S MAD. ALL BASED ON A MYSTERY SHIP YOU'RE SAYING **NOBODY EVER BUILT?!**
TIME PARADOX. DOESN'T MATTER, EH? I'M WITH ROARK. LET'S ***GO!***
THE ANSWER IS PENSIVE SILENCE.
BUT...
THEY SET OFF TOMORROW.
BOARDING THE ***SHIMADA,*** THEY HEAD FOR THE BLACK HOLE ***GRS1915+105*** IN ***AQUILA.***
LADIES AND GENTLEMEN, THE ***SAVIORS*** OF ***HUMANKIND!***
POLITE APPLAUSE COMES FROM THOSE UNIMPAIRED BY ***COCKTAILS.***

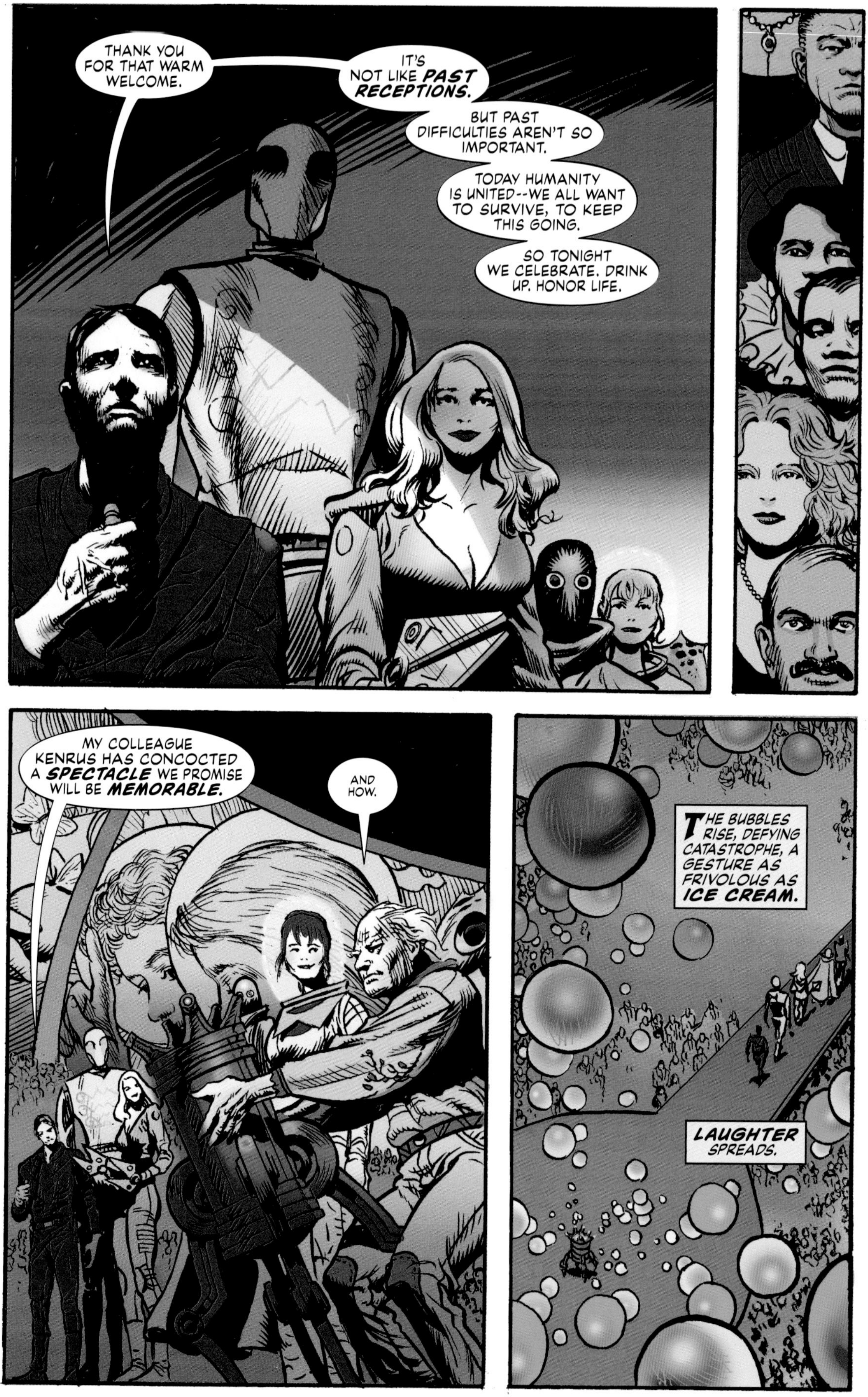

THANK YOU FOR THAT WARM WELCOME.
IT'S NOT LIKE PAST RECEPTIONS.
BUT PAST DIFFICULTIES AREN'T SO IMPORTANT.
TODAY HUMANITY IS UNITED--WE ALL WANT TO SURVIVE, TO KEEP THIS GOING.
SO TONIGHT WE CELEBRATE. DRINK UP. HONOR LIFE.
MY COLLEAGUE KENRUS HAS CONCOCTED A SPECTACLE WE PROMISE WILL BE MEMORABLE.
AND HOW.
THE BUBBLES RISE, DEFYING CATASTROPHE, A GESTURE AS FRIVOLOUS AS ICE CREAM.
LAUGHTER SPREADS.

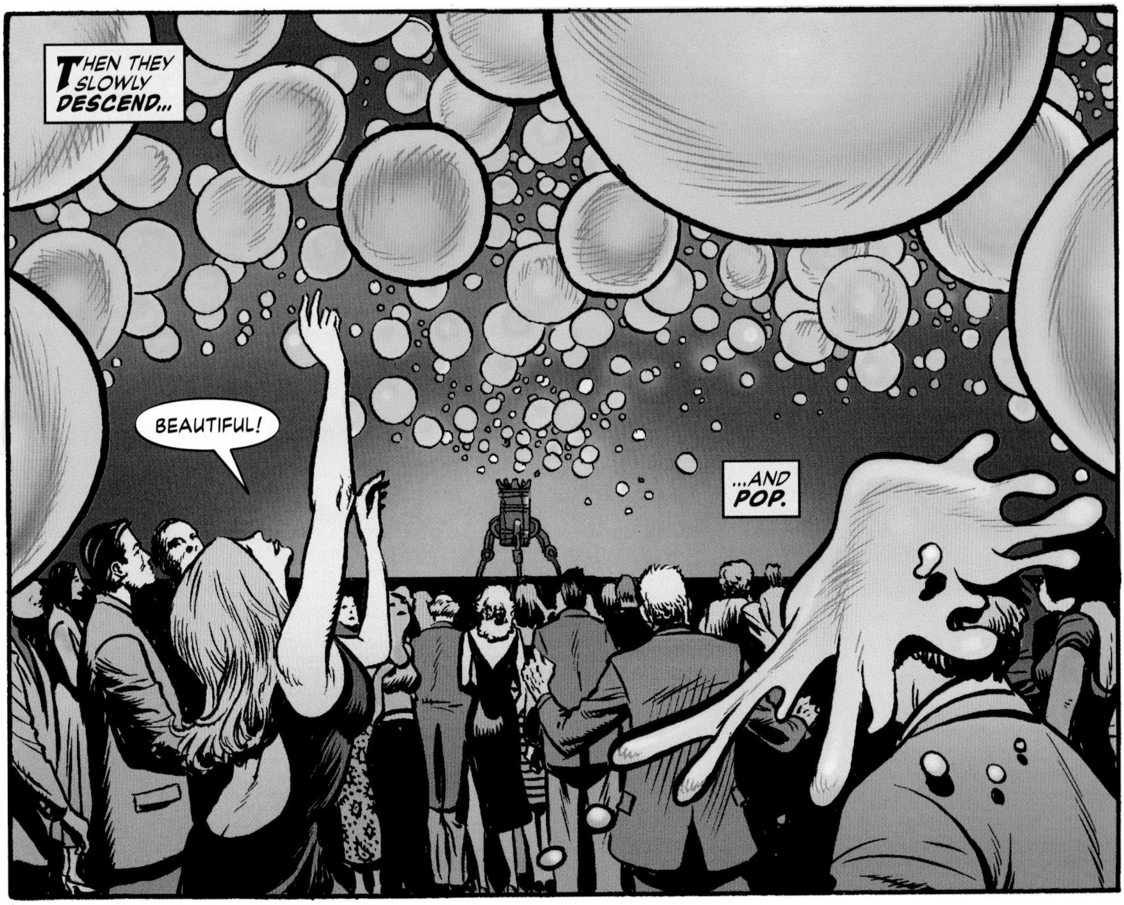
THEN THEY SLOWLY DESCEND...
BEAUTIFUL!
...AND POP.

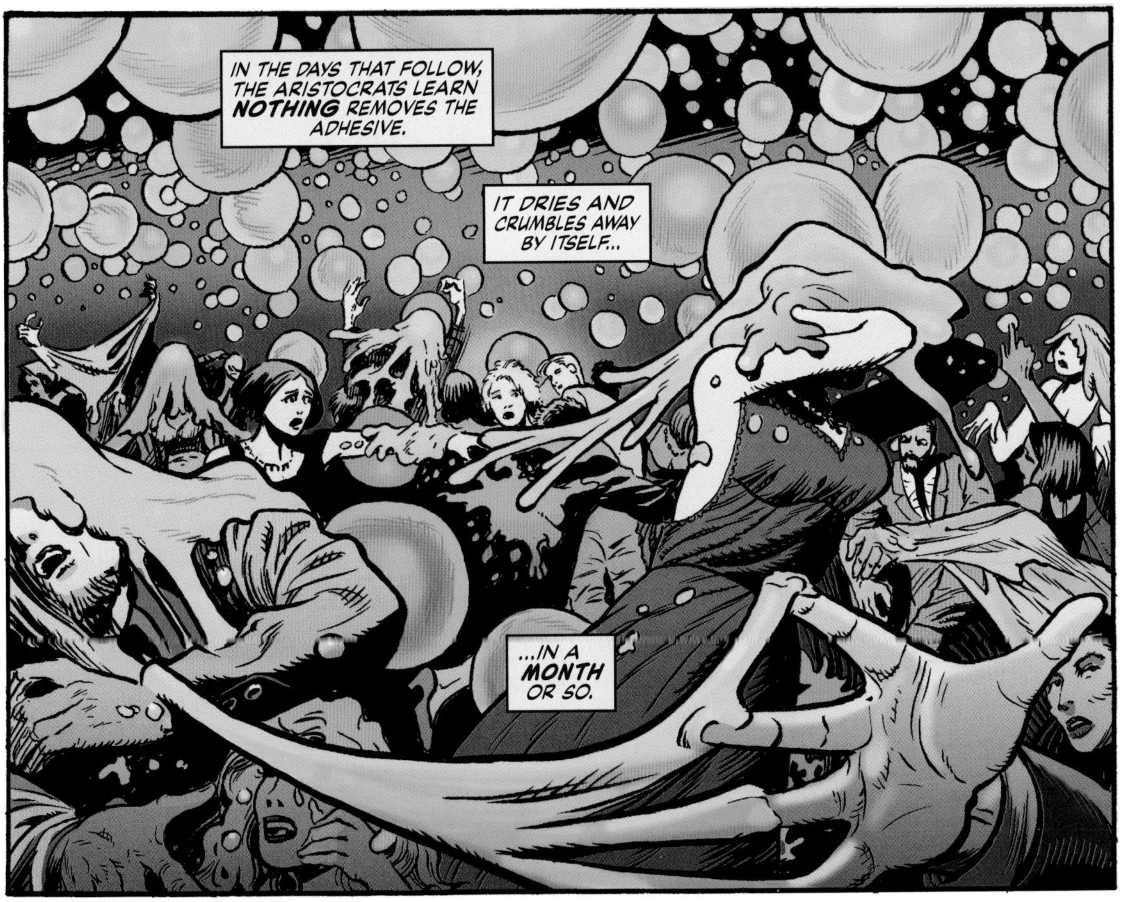
IN THE DAYS THAT FOLLOW, THE ARISTOCRATS LEARN NOTHING REMOVES THE ADHESIVE.
IT DRIES AND CRUMBLES AWAY BY ITSELF...
...IN A MONTH OR SO.

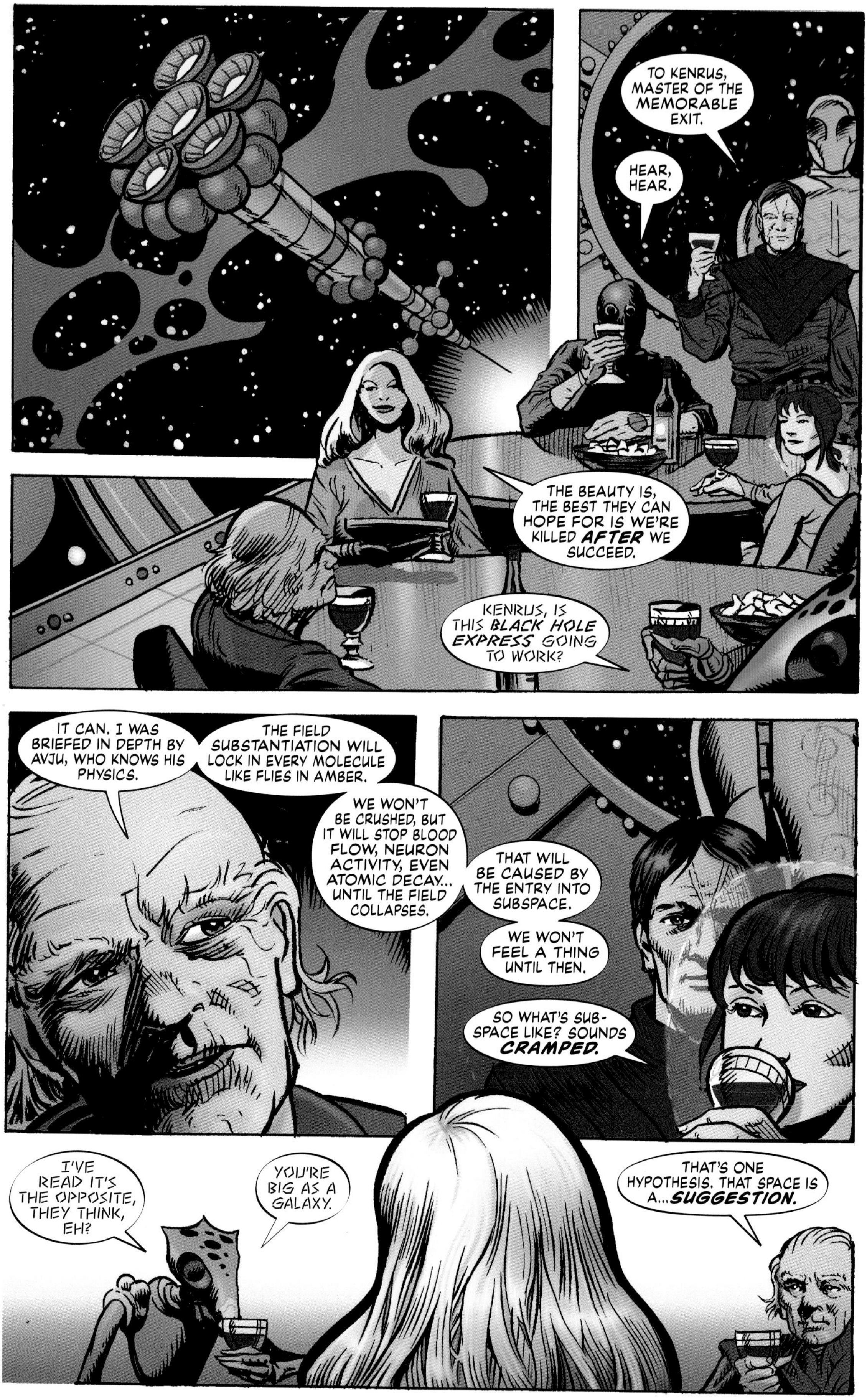
TO KENRUS, MASTER OF THE MEMORABLE EXIT.
HEAR, HEAR.
THE BEAUTY IS, THE BEST THEY CAN HOPE FOR IS WE'RE KILLED **AFTER** WE SUCCEED.
KENRUS, IS THIS **BLACK HOLE EXPRESS** GOING TO WORK?
IT CAN. I WAS BRIEFED IN DEPTH BY AVJU, WHO KNOWS HIS PHYSICS.
THE FIELD SUBSTANTIATION WILL LOCK IN EVERY MOLECULE LIKE FLIES IN AMBER.
WE WON'T BE CRUSHED, BUT IT WILL STOP BLOOD FLOW, NEURON ACTIVITY, EVEN ATOMIC DECAY... UNTIL THE FIELD COLLAPSES.
THAT WILL BE CAUSED BY THE ENTRY INTO SUBSPACE.
WE WON'T FEEL A THING UNTIL THEN.
SO WHAT'S SUB-SPACE LIKE? SOUNDS **CRAMPED.**
I'VE READ IT'S THE OPPOSITE, THEY THINK, EH?
YOU'RE BIG AS A GALAXY.
THAT'S ONE HYPOTHESIS. THAT SPACE IS A...**SUGGESTION.**

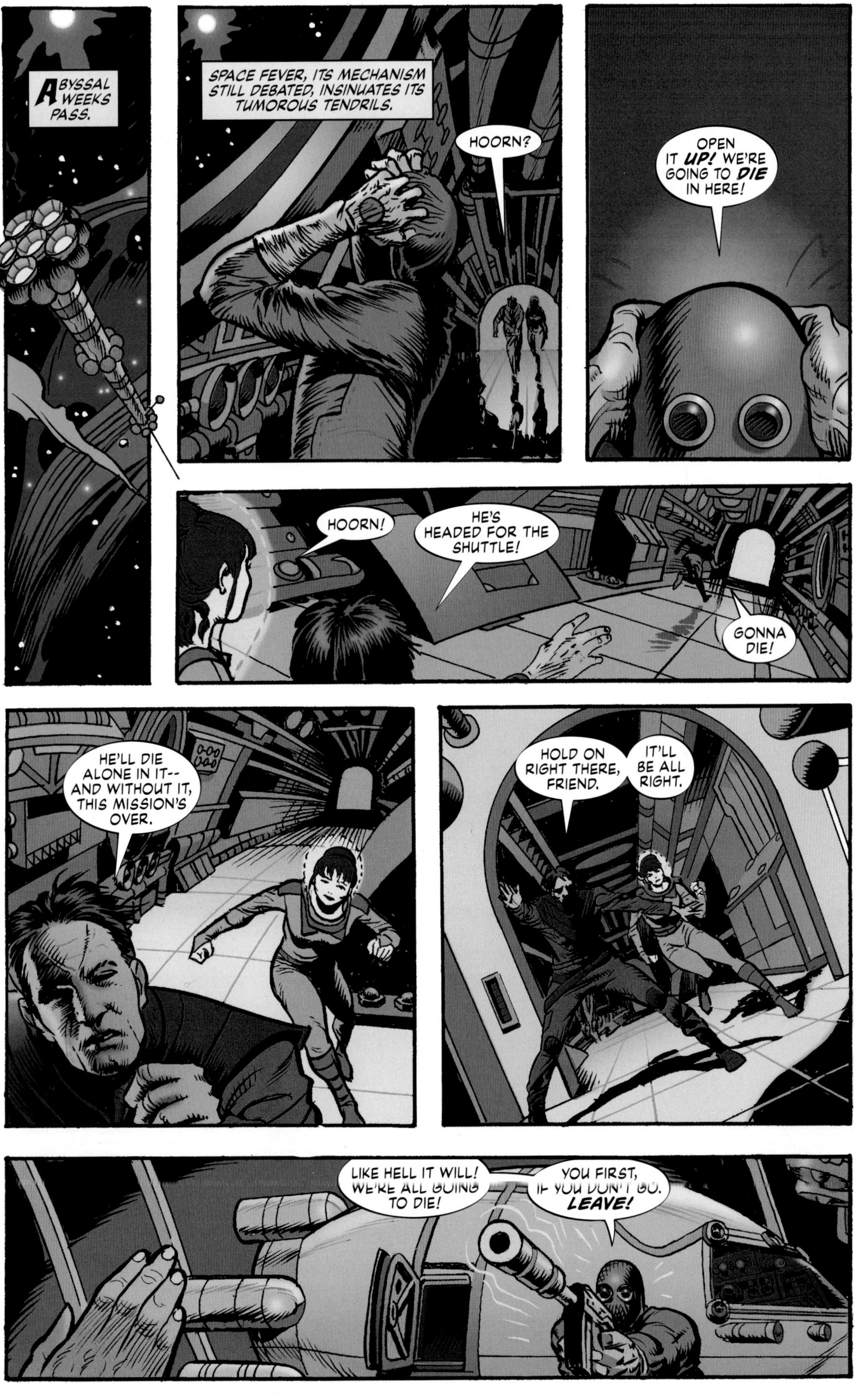
ABYSSAL WEEKS PASS.
SPACE FEVER, ITS MECHANISM STILL DEBATED, INSINUATES ITS TUMOROUS TENDRILS.
HOORN?
OPEN IT **UP!** WE'RE GOING TO **DIE** IN HERE!
HOORN!
HE'S HEADED FOR THE SHUTTLE!
GONNA DIE!
HE'LL DIE ALONE IN IT-- AND WITHOUT IT, THIS MISSION'S OVER.
HOLD ON RIGHT THERE, FRIEND.
IT'LL BE ALL RIGHT.
LIKE HELL IT WILL! WE'RE ALL GOING TO DIE!
YOU FIRST, IF YOU DON'T GO. **LEAVE!**

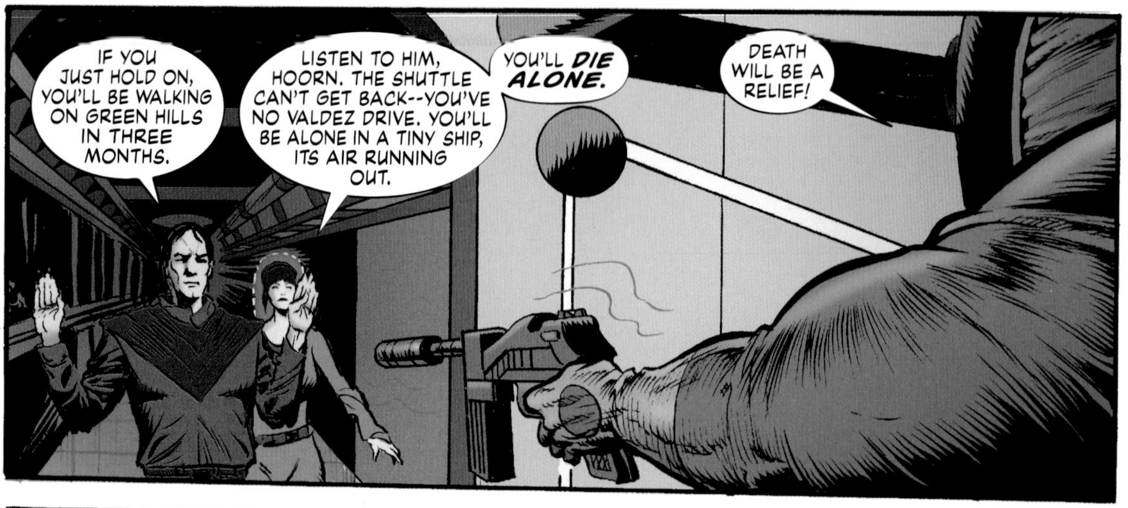
IF YOU JUST HOLD ON, YOU'LL BE WALKING ON GREEN HILLS IN THREE MONTHS.
LISTEN TO HIM, HOORN. THE SHUTTLE CAN'T GET BACK--YOU'VE NO VALDEZ DRIVE. YOU'LL BE ALONE IN A TINY SHIP, ITS AIR RUNNING OUT.
YOU'LL *DIE ALONE.*
DEATH WILL BE A RELIEF!

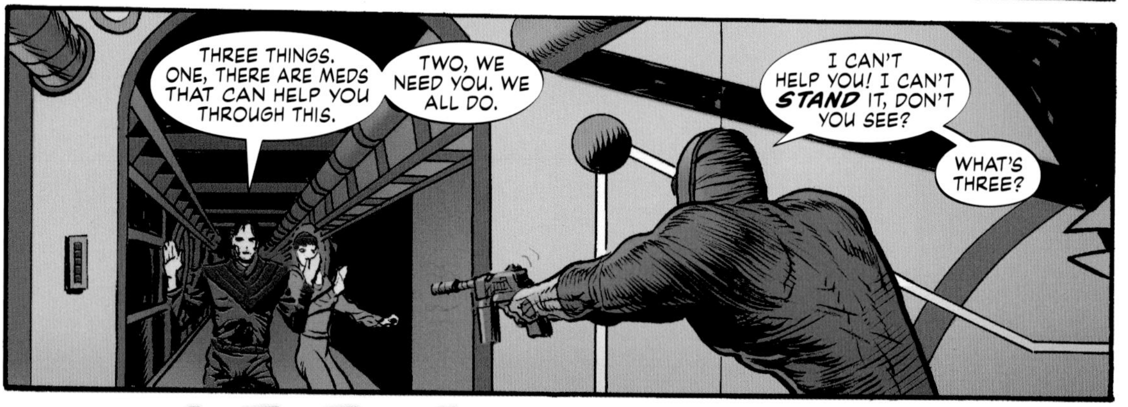
THREE THINGS. ONE, THERE ARE MEDS THAT CAN HELP YOU THROUGH THIS.
TWO, WE NEED YOU. WE ALL DO.
I CAN'T HELP YOU! I CAN'T *STAND* IT, DON'T YOU SEE?
WHAT'S THREE?

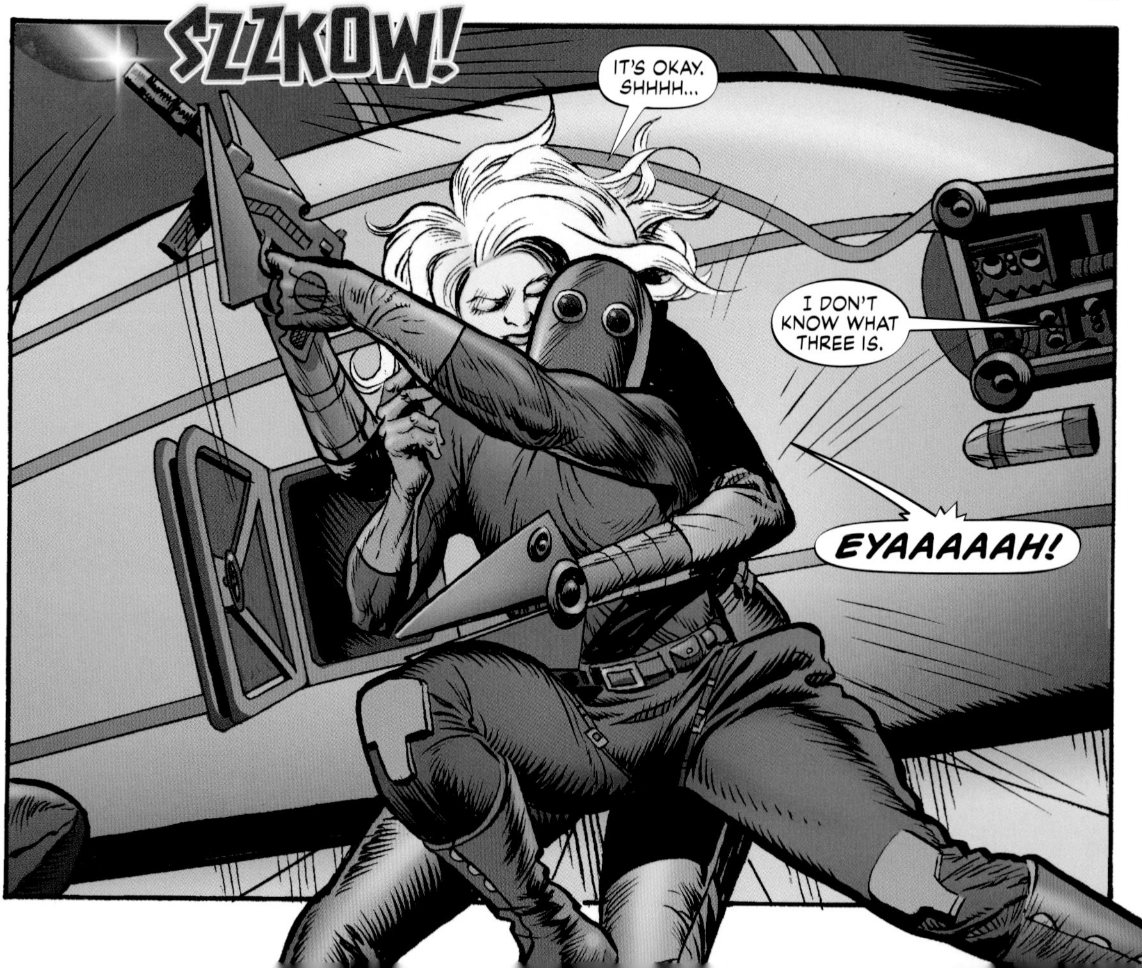
SZZKOW!
IT'S OKAY. SHHHH...
I DON'T KNOW WHAT THREE IS.
EYAAAAAH!

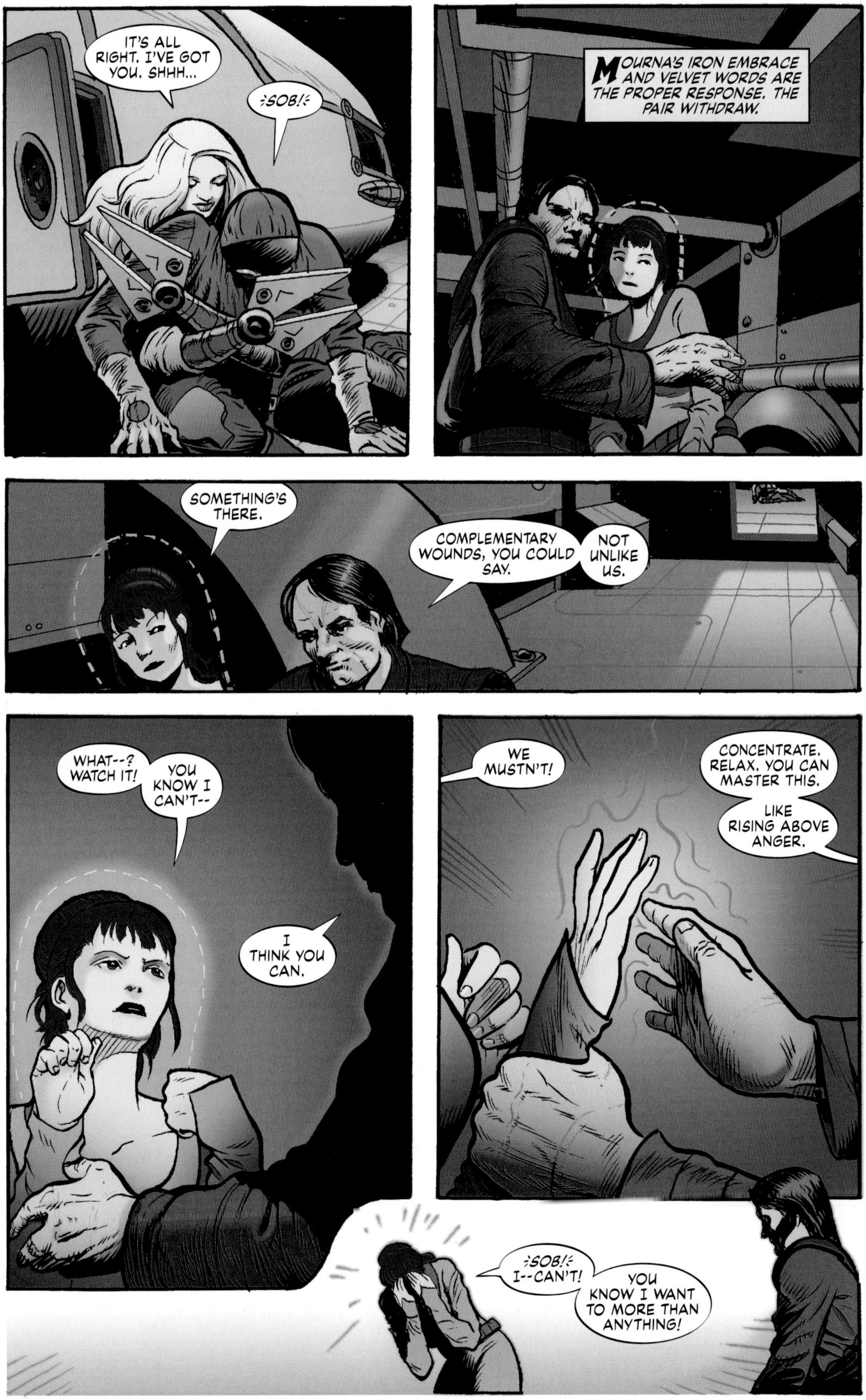
IT'S ALL RIGHT. I'VE GOT YOU. SHHH...
SOB!
MOURNA'S IRON EMBRACE AND VELVET WORDS ARE THE PROPER RESPONSE. THE PAIR WITHDRAW.
SOMETHING'S THERE.
COMPLEMENTARY WOUNDS, YOU COULD SAY.
NOT UNLIKE US.
WHAT--? WATCH IT!
YOU KNOW I CAN'T--
I THINK YOU CAN.
WE MUSTN'T!
CONCENTRATE. RELAX. YOU CAN MASTER THIS.
LIKE RISING ABOVE ANGER.
SOB! I--CAN'T!
YOU KNOW I WANT TO MORE THAN ANYTHING!

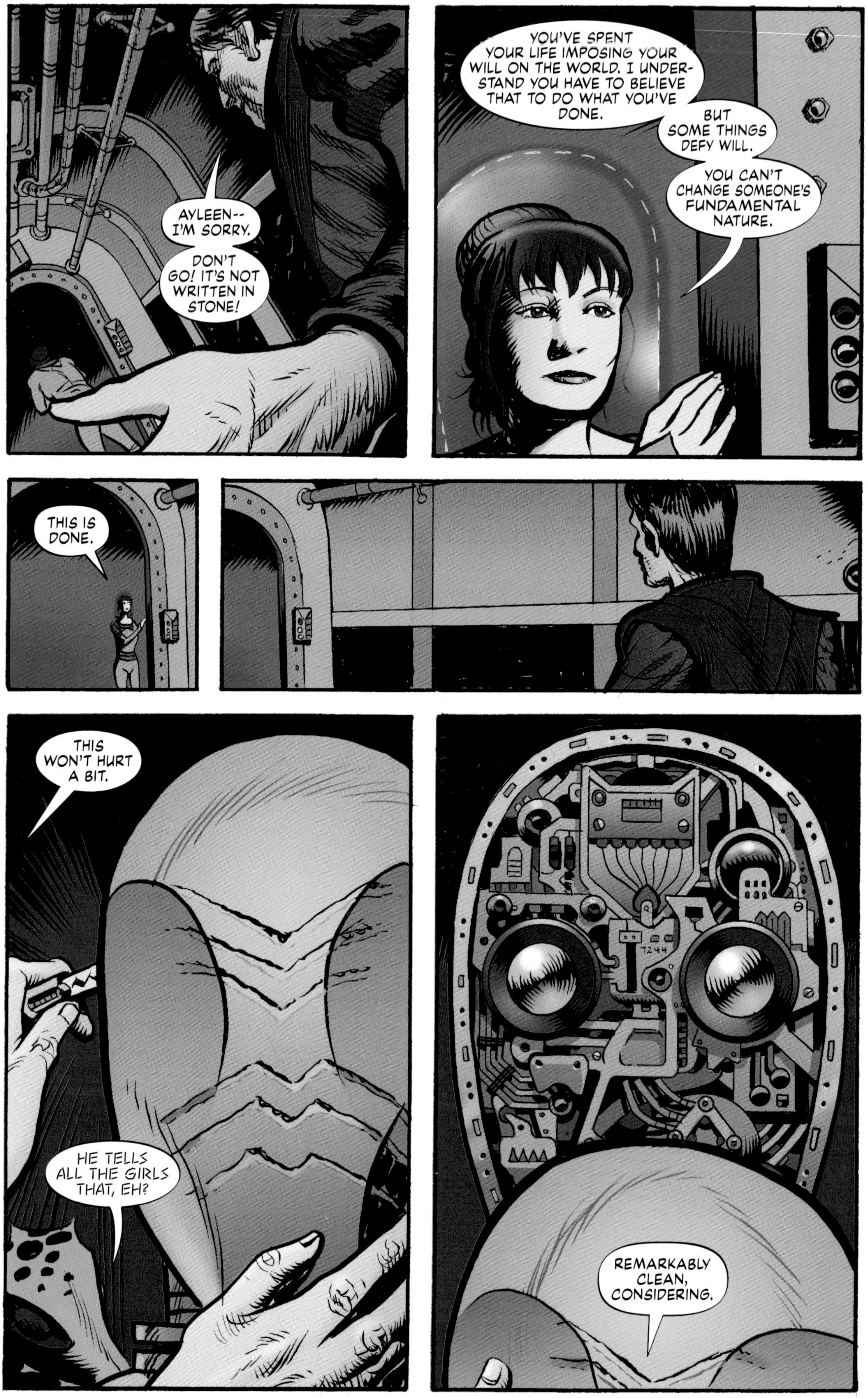
AYLEEN-- I'M SORRY.
DON'T GO! IT'S NOT WRITTEN IN STONE!
YOU'VE SPENT YOUR LIFE IMPOSING YOUR WILL ON THE WORLD. I UNDERSTAND YOU HAVE TO BELIEVE THAT TO DO WHAT YOU'VE DONE.
BUT SOME THINGS DEFY WILL.
YOU CAN'T CHANGE SOMEONE'S FUNDAMENTAL NATURE.
THIS IS DONE.
THIS WON'T HURT A BIT.
HE TELLS ALL THE GIRLS THAT, EH?
REMARKABLY CLEAN, CONSIDERING.

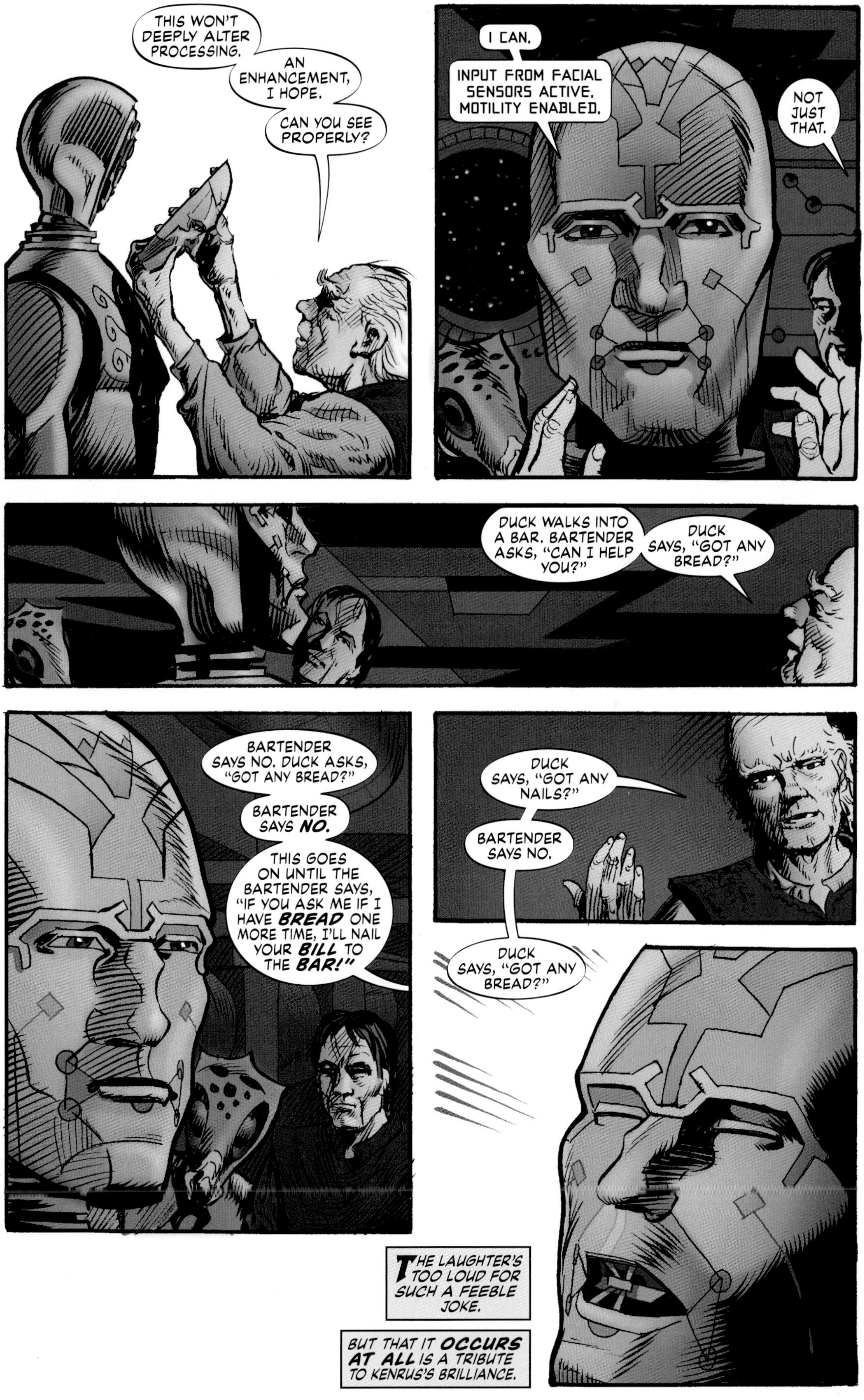
THIS WON'T DEEPLY ALTER PROCESSING.
AN ENHANCEMENT, I HOPE.
CAN YOU SEE PROPERLY?
I CAN.
INPUT FROM FACIAL SENSORS ACTIVE. MOTILITY ENABLED.
NOT JUST THAT.
DUCK WALKS INTO A BAR. BARTENDER ASKS, "CAN I HELP YOU?"
DUCK SAYS, "GOT ANY BREAD?"
BARTENDER SAYS NO. DUCK ASKS, "GOT ANY BREAD?"
BARTENDER SAYS NO.
THIS GOES ON UNTIL THE BARTENDER SAYS, "IF YOU ASK ME IF I HAVE BREAD ONE MORE TIME, I'LL NAIL YOUR BILL TO THE BAR!"
DUCK SAYS, "GOT ANY NAILS?"
BARTENDER SAYS NO.
DUCK SAYS, "GOT ANY BREAD?"
THE LAUGHTER'S TOO LOUD FOR SUCH A FEEBLE JOKE.
BUT THAT IT OCCURS AT ALL IS A TRIBUTE TO KENRUS'S BRILLIANCE.

FACING DEATH, PEOPLE TRY NEW THINGS.

THE FACELESS MAN FINDS HIMSELF STARTLED BY THE INTIMACY HE HAS ALLOWED.

TRUE, IT WAS DARK.

BUT STILL.

WITH THE STEALTH HONED BY HIS PROFESSION, HE DRESSES.

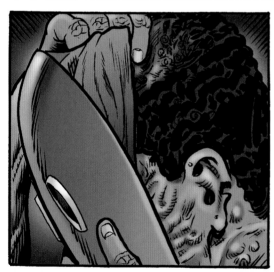

A MISTAKE.

THAT FOR A TIME, PERHAPS, HAS SAVED HIS LIFE.

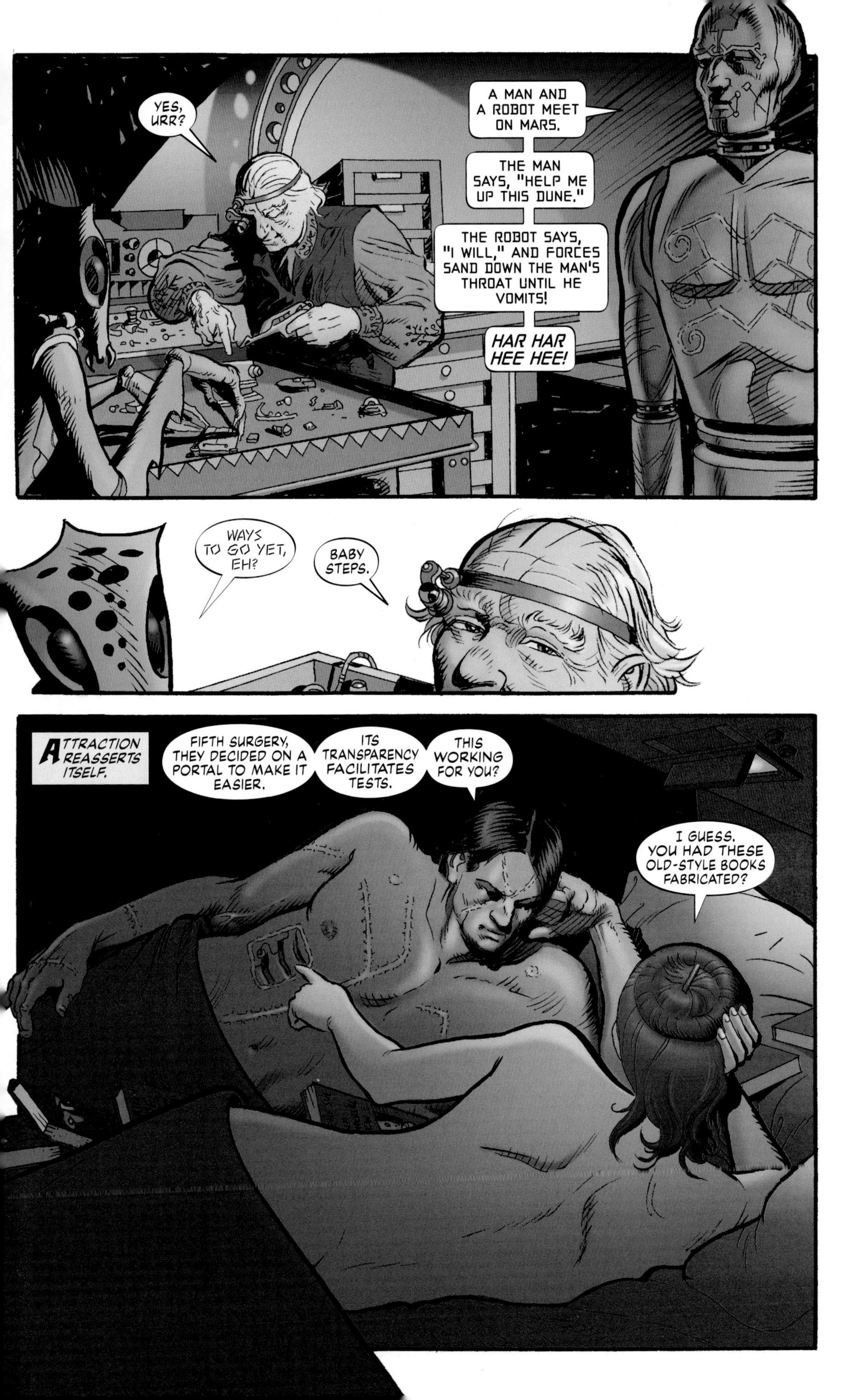
YES, URR?
A MAN AND A ROBOT MEET ON MARS.
THE MAN SAYS, "HELP ME UP THIS DUNE."
THE ROBOT SAYS, "I WILL," AND FORCES SAND DOWN THE MAN'S THROAT UNTIL HE VOMITS!
HAR HAR HEE HEE!
WAYS TO GO YET, EH?
BABY STEPS.
ATTRACTION REASSERTS ITSELF.
FIFTH SURGERY, THEY DECIDED ON A PORTAL TO MAKE IT EASIER.
ITS TRANSPARENCY FACILITATES TESTS.
THIS WORKING FOR YOU?
I GUESS. YOU HAD THESE OLD-STYLE BOOKS FABRICATED?

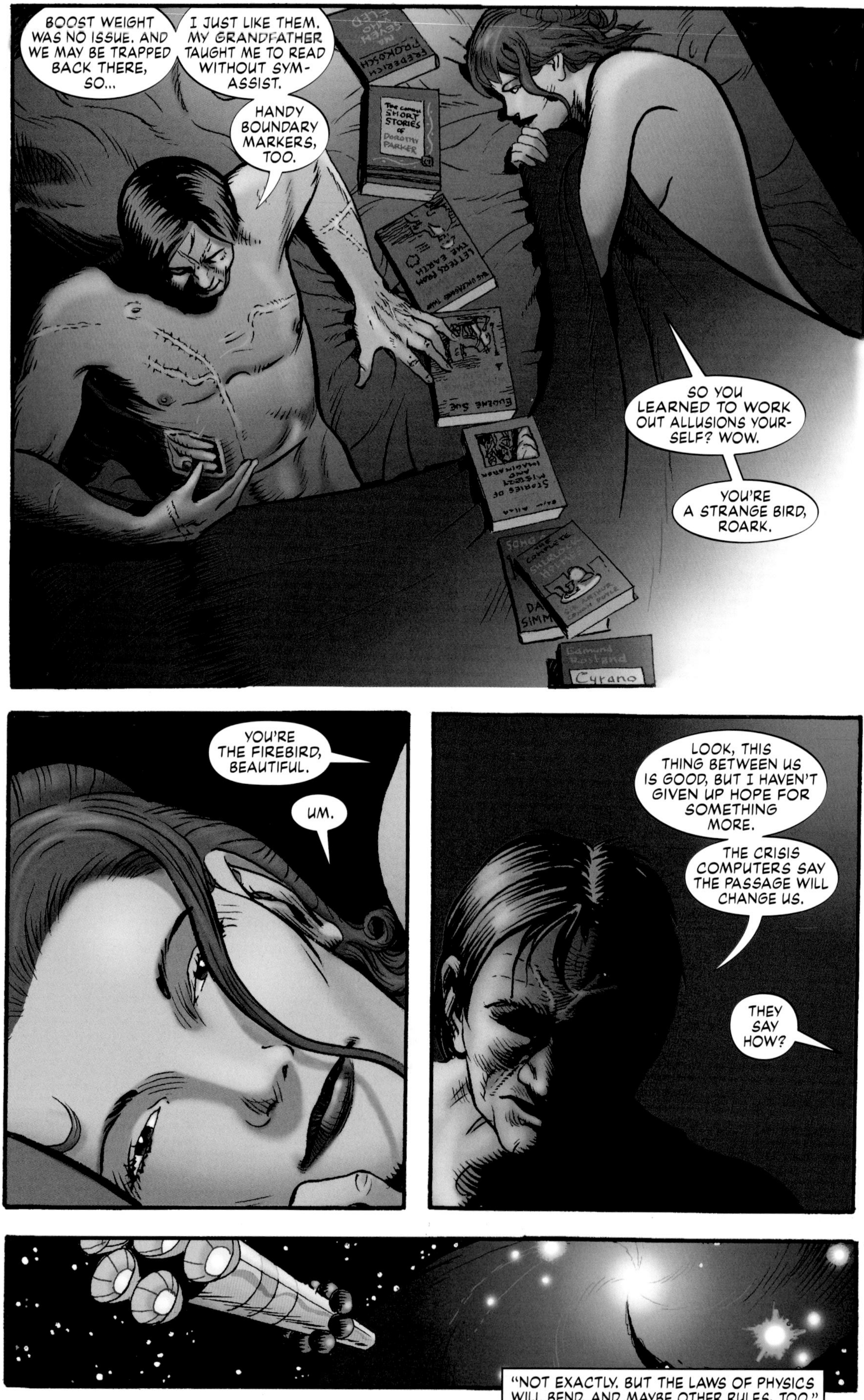
BOOST WEIGHT WAS NO ISSUE. AND WE MAY BE TRAPPED BACK THERE, SO...
I JUST LIKE THEM. MY GRANDFATHER TAUGHT ME TO READ WITHOUT SYM-ASSIST.
HANDY BOUNDARY MARKERS, TOO.
The Complete Short Stories of Dorothy Parker
Letters from the Earth
Eugene Sue
Edmund Rostand
Cyrano
SO YOU LEARNED TO WORK OUT ALLUSIONS YOURSELF? WOW.
YOU'RE A STRANGE BIRD, ROARK.
YOU'RE THE FIREBIRD, BEAUTIFUL.
UM.
LOOK, THIS THING BETWEEN US IS GOOD, BUT I HAVEN'T GIVEN UP HOPE FOR SOMETHING MORE.
THE CRISIS COMPUTERS SAY THE PASSAGE WILL CHANGE US.
THEY SAY HOW?
"NOT EXACTLY. BUT THE LAWS OF PHYSICS WILL BEND. AND MAYBE OTHER RULES, TOO."

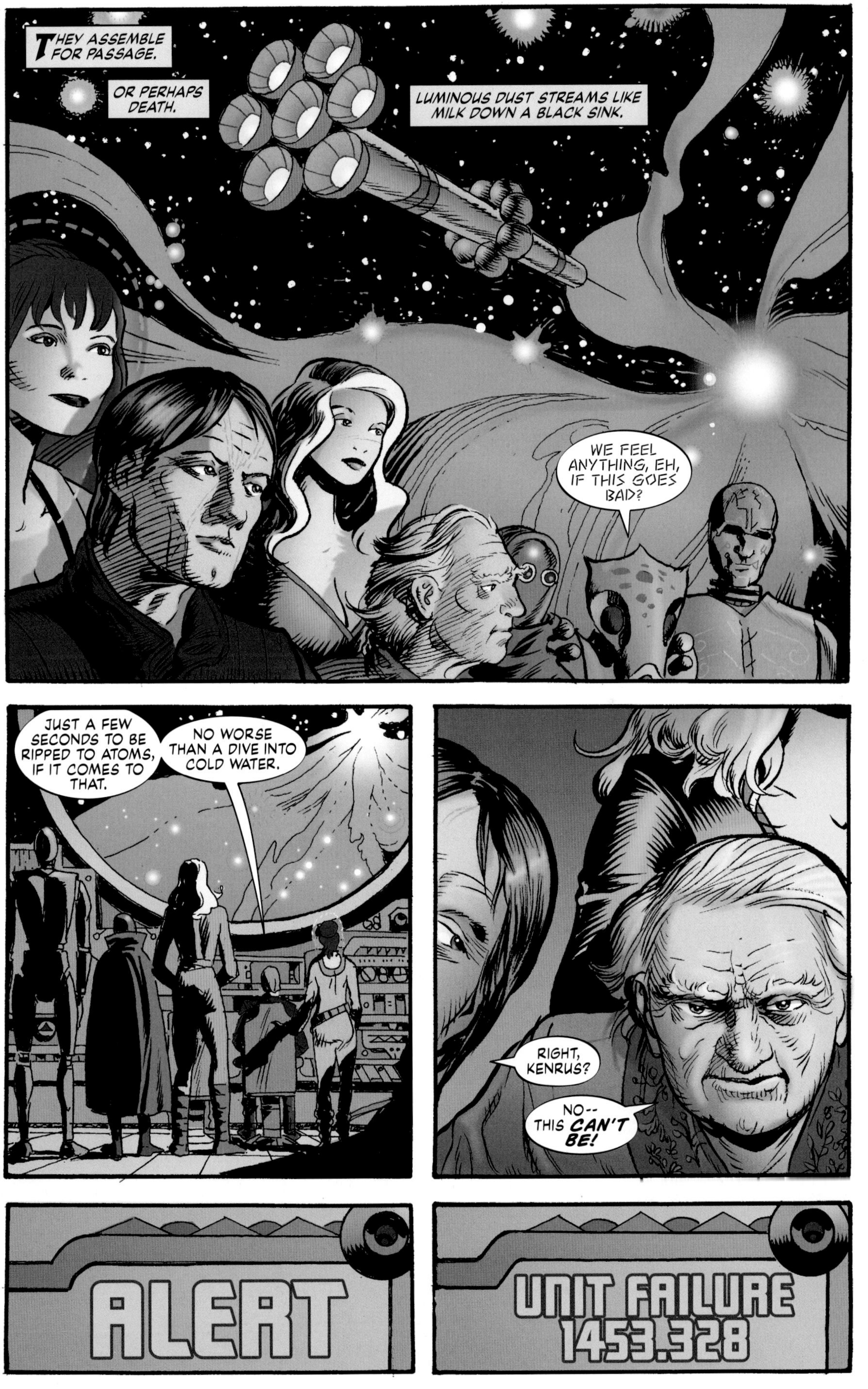
THEY ASSEMBLE FOR PASSAGE.
OR PERHAPS DEATH.
LUMINOUS DUST STREAMS LIKE MILK DOWN A BLACK SINK.
WE FEEL ANYTHING, EH, IF THIS GOES BAD?
JUST A FEW SECONDS TO BE RIPPED TO ATOMS, IF IT COMES TO THAT.
NO WORSE THAN A DIVE INTO COLD WATER.
RIGHT, KENRUS?
NO-- THIS **CAN'T BE!**
ALERT
UNIT FAILURE 1453.328

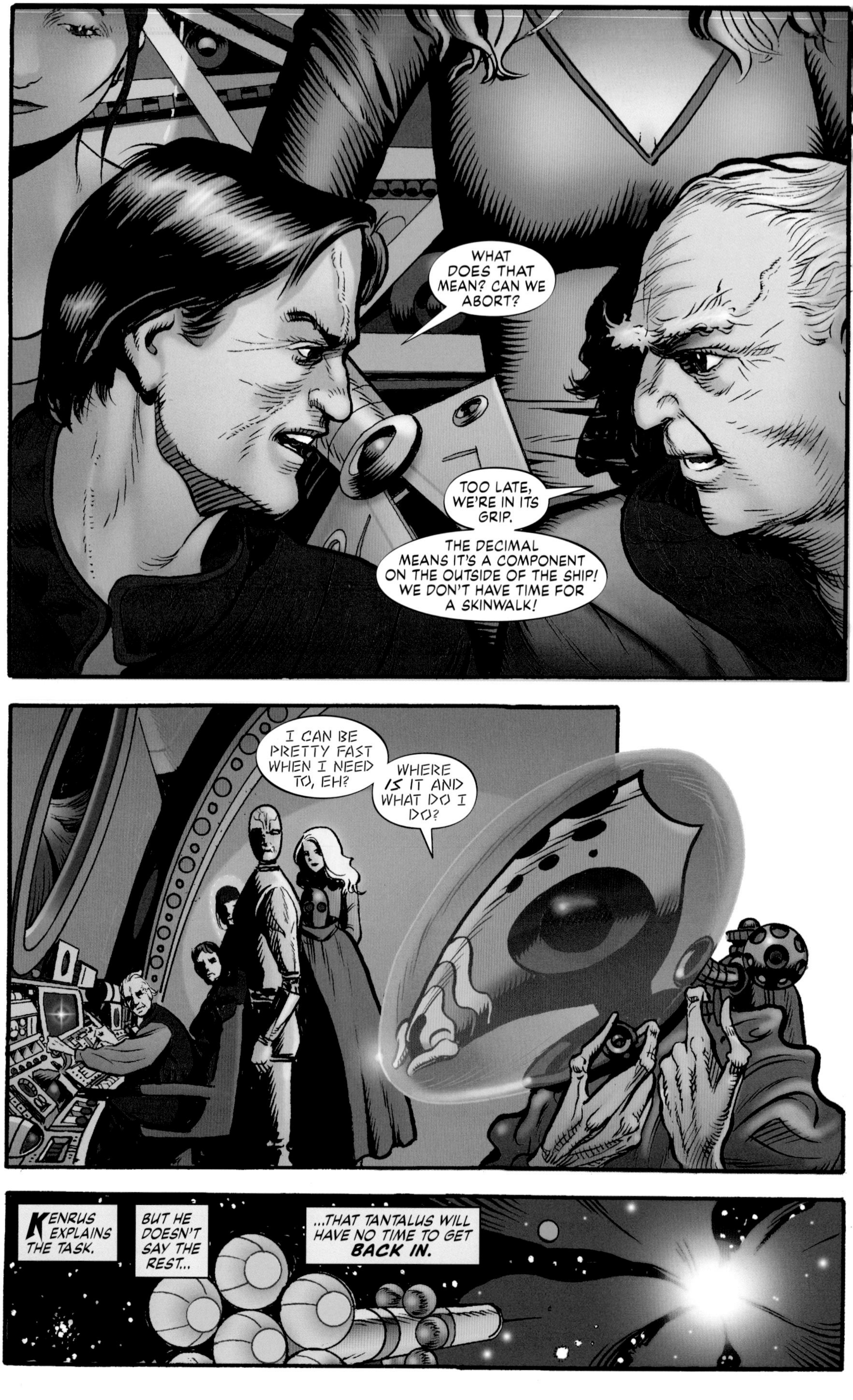
WHAT DOES THAT MEAN? CAN WE ABORT?
TOO LATE, WE'RE IN ITS GRIP.
THE DECIMAL MEANS IT'S A COMPONENT ON THE OUTSIDE OF THE SHIP! WE DON'T HAVE TIME FOR A SKINWALK!
I CAN BE PRETTY FAST WHEN I NEED TO, EH?
WHERE IS IT AND WHAT DO I DO?
KENRUS EXPLAINS THE TASK.
BUT HE DOESN'T SAY THE REST...
...THAT TANTALUS WILL HAVE NO TIME TO GET BACK IN.

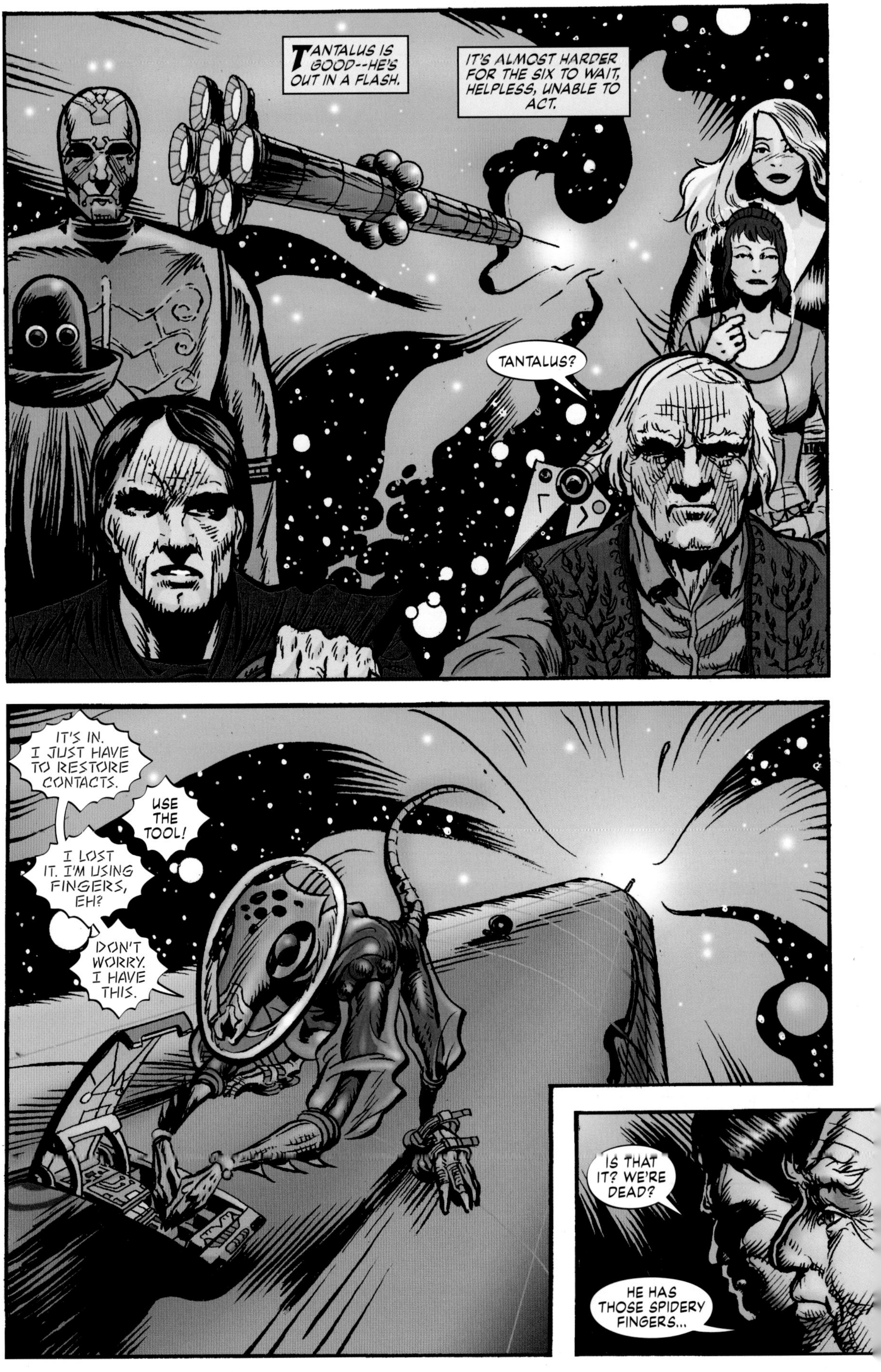
TANTALUS IS GOOD--HE'S OUT IN A FLASH.
IT'S ALMOST HARDER FOR THE SIX TO WAIT, HELPLESS, UNABLE TO ACT.
TANTALUS?
IT'S IN. I JUST HAVE TO RESTORE CONTACTS.
USE THE TOOL!
I LOST IT. I'M USING FINGERS, EH?
DON'T WORRY. I HAVE THIS.
IS THAT IT? WE'RE DEAD?
HE HAS THOSE SPIDERY FINGERS...

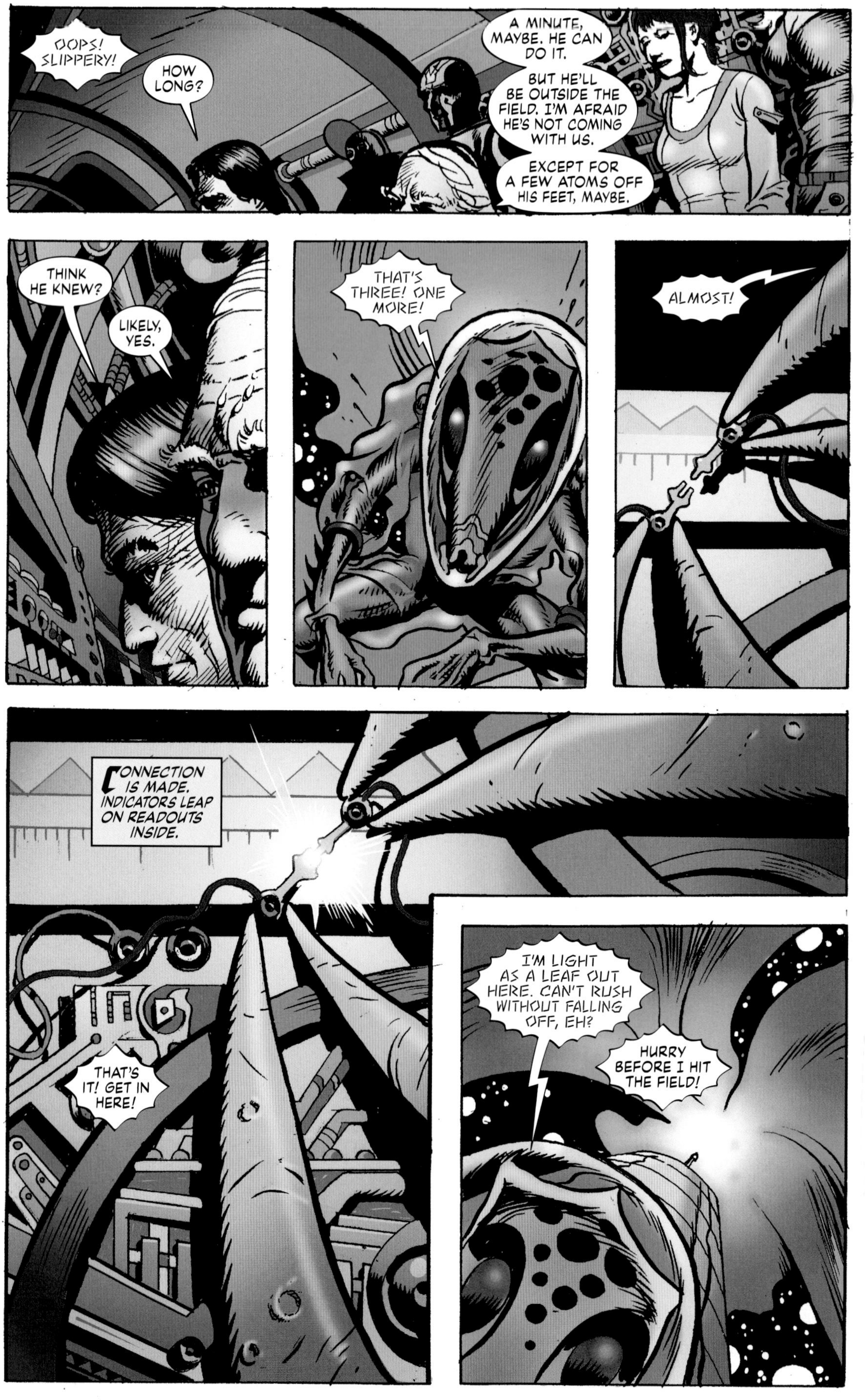
OOPS! SLIPPERY!
HOW LONG?
A MINUTE, MAYBE. HE CAN DO IT.
BUT HE'LL BE OUTSIDE THE FIELD. I'M AFRAID HE'S NOT COMING WITH US.
EXCEPT FOR A FEW ATOMS OFF HIS FEET, MAYBE.
THINK HE KNEW?
LIKELY, YES.
THAT'S THREE! ONE MORE!
ALMOST!
CONNECTION IS MADE. INDICATORS LEAP ON READOUTS INSIDE.
THAT'S IT! GET IN HERE!
I'M LIGHT AS A LEAF OUT HERE. CAN'T RUSH WITHOUT FALLING OFF, EH?
HURRY BEFORE I HIT THE FIELD!

ISN'T THERE ANY WAY TO DELAY?

NOT UNLESS YOU WANT THE TIDAL FORCES RIPPING YOUR BODY APART IN SEVENTY-ONE SECONDS!

SORRY, TANTALUS, MY FRIEND.

BUT KENRUS, PERHAPS RECKLESSLY...

...HOLDS OFF...

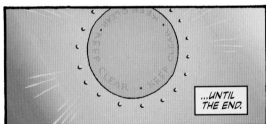

...UNTIL THE END.

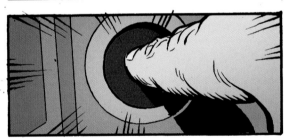

A SUBSTANTIATED FIELD GRIPS EACH MOLECULE OF THE SHIP AND ITS CONTENTS LIKE POLLEN IN POLAR ICE... PRESERVING BOTH LIFE AND CHEMICAL INTEGRITY AS SPACE COLLAPSES AROUND THEM.

THE THEORY WAS CORRECT.

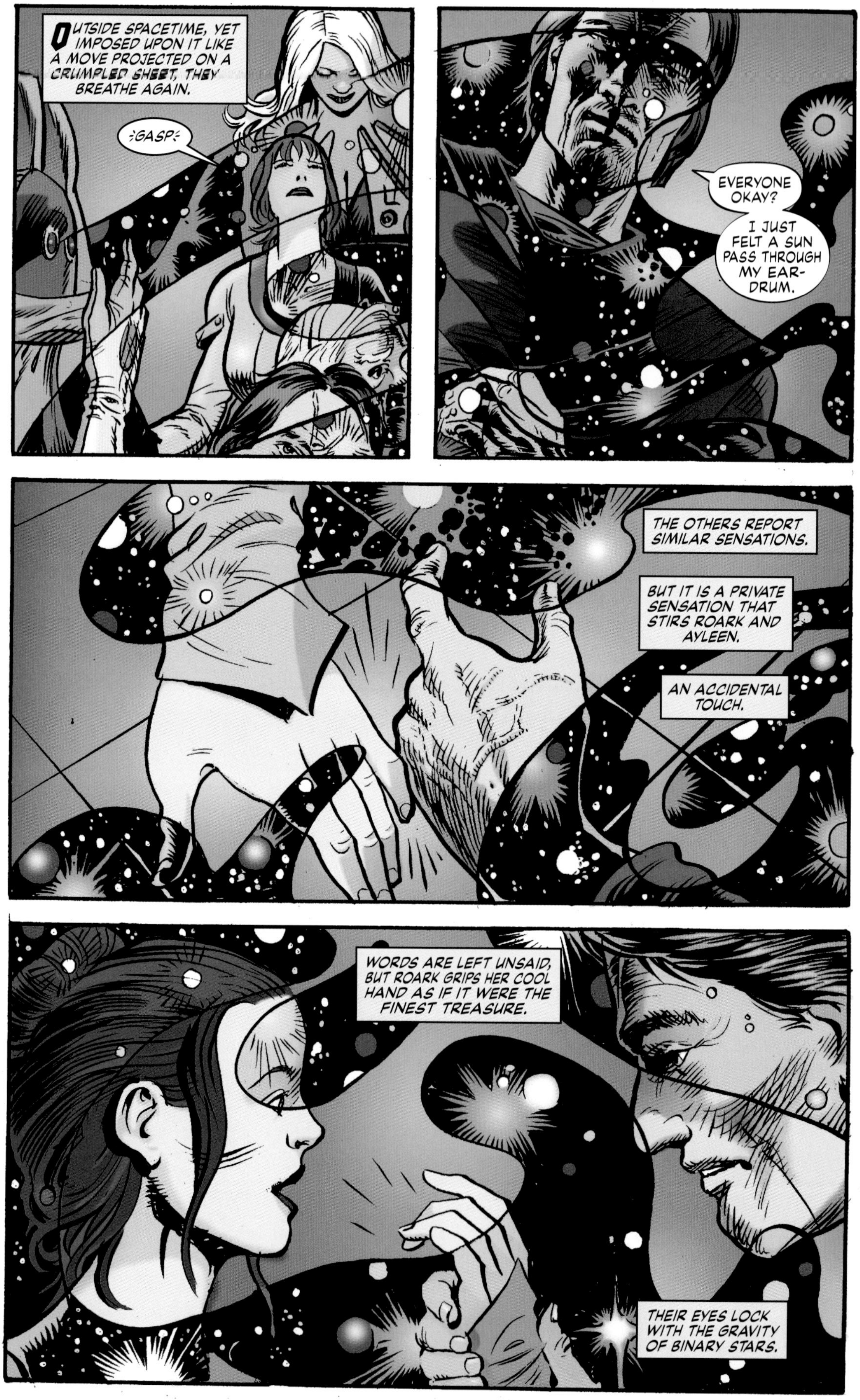
OUTSIDE SPACETIME, YET IMPOSED UPON IT LIKE A MOVE PROJECTED ON A CRUMPLED SHEET, THEY BREATHE AGAIN.
GASP
EVERYONE OKAY?
I JUST FELT A SUN PASS THROUGH MY EAR-DRUM.
THE OTHERS REPORT SIMILAR SENSATIONS.
BUT IT IS A PRIVATE SENSATION THAT STIRS ROARK AND AYLEEN.
AN ACCIDENTAL TOUCH.
WORDS ARE LEFT UNSAID, BUT ROARK GRIPS HER COOL HAND AS IF IT WERE THE FINEST TREASURE.
THEIR EYES LOCK WITH THE GRAVITY OF BINARY STARS.

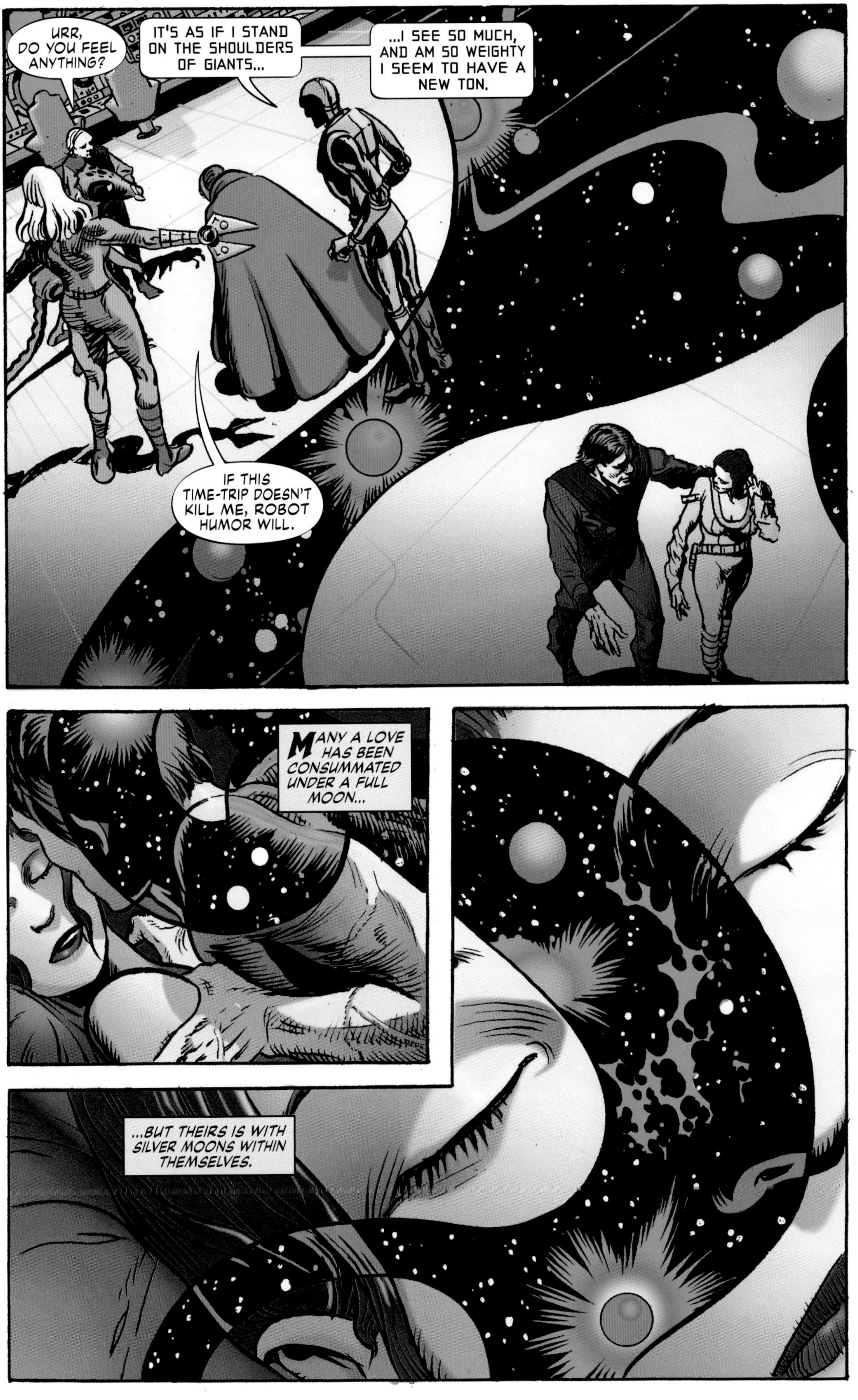
URR, DO YOU FEEL ANYTHING?
IT'S AS IF I STAND ON THE SHOULDERS OF GIANTS...
...I SEE SO MUCH, AND AM SO WEIGHTY I SEEM TO HAVE A NEW TON.
IF THIS TIME-TRIP DOESN'T KILL ME, ROBOT HUMOR WILL.
MANY A LOVE HAS BEEN CONSUMMATED UNDER A FULL MOON...
...BUT THEIRS IS WITH SILVER MOONS WITHIN THEMSELVES.

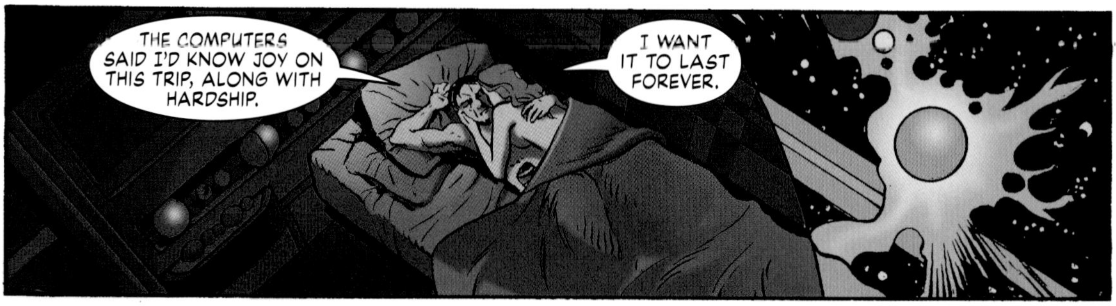
THE COMPUTERS SAID I'D KNOW JOY ON THIS TRIP, ALONG WITH HARDSHIP.
I WANT IT TO LAST FOREVER.

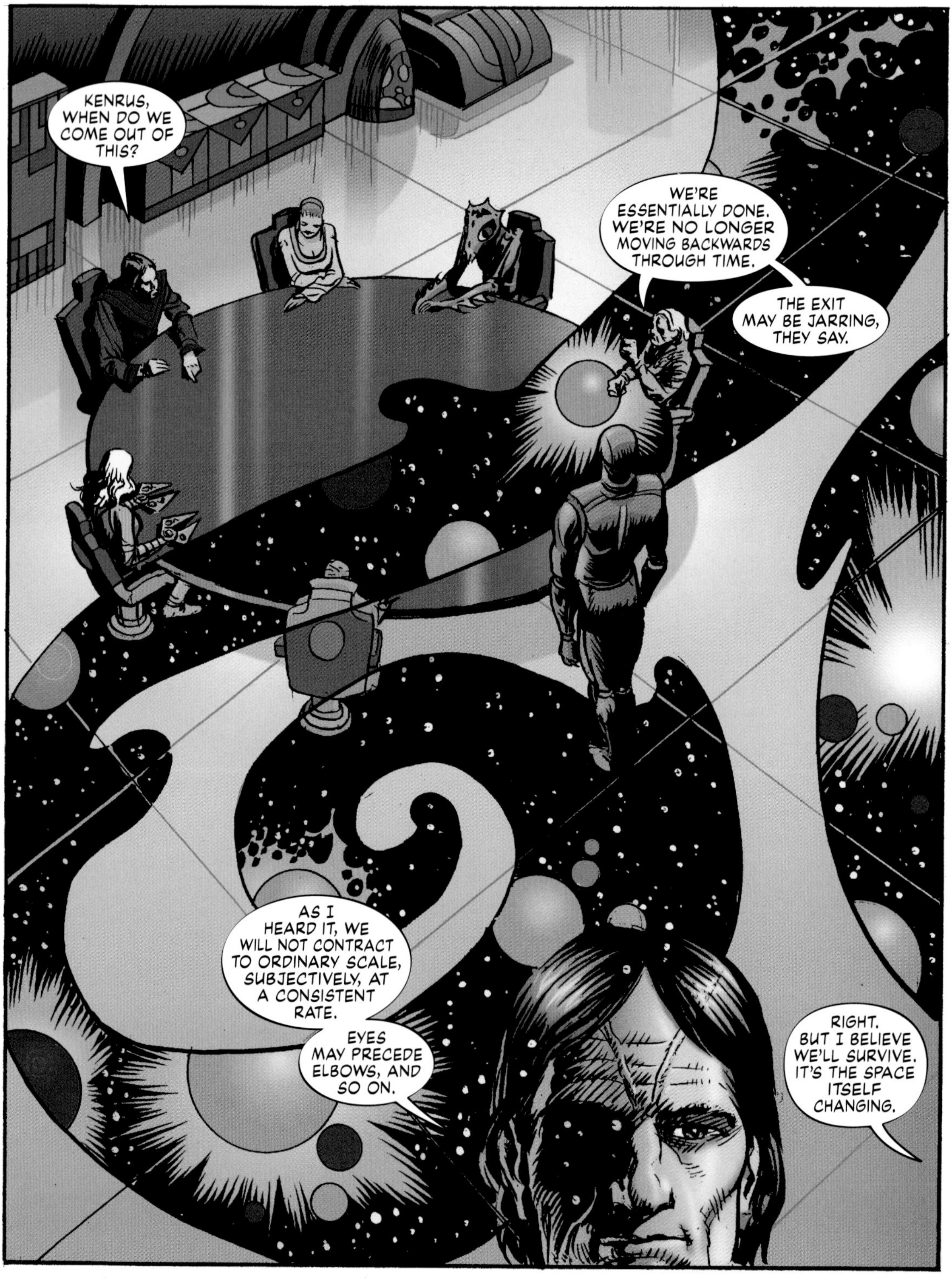
KENRUS, WHEN DO WE COME OUT OF THIS?
WE'RE ESSENTIALLY DONE. WE'RE NO LONGER MOVING BACKWARDS THROUGH TIME.
THE EXIT MAY BE JARRING, THEY SAY.
AS I HEARD IT, WE WILL NOT CONTRACT TO ORDINARY SCALE, SUBJECTIVELY, AT A CONSISTENT RATE.
EYES MAY PRECEDE ELBOWS, AND SO ON.
RIGHT. BUT I BELIEVE WE'LL SURVIVE. IT'S THE SPACE ITSELF CHANGING.

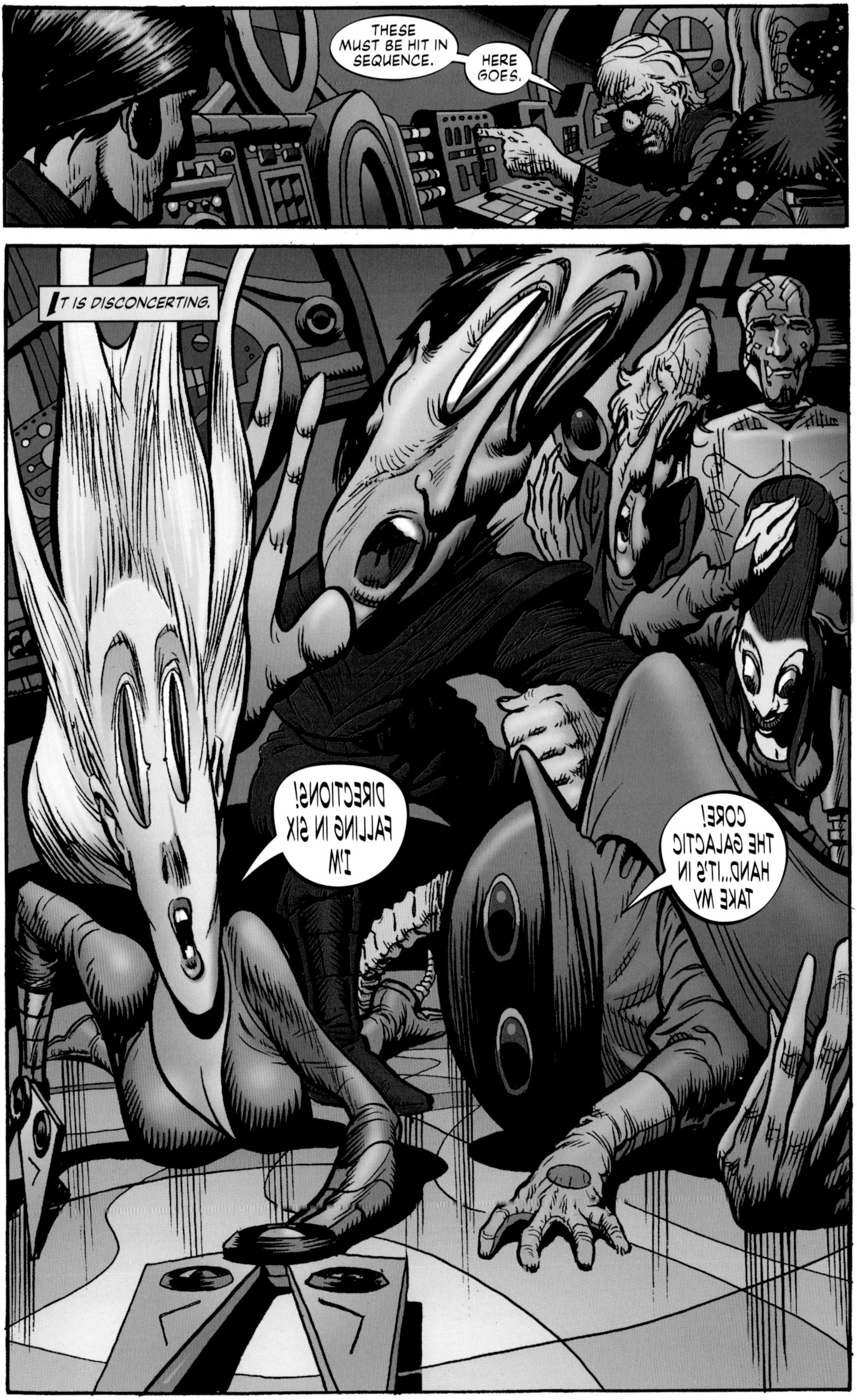
THESE MUST BE HIT IN SEQUENCE.
HERE GOES.
IT IS DISCONCERTING.
I'M FALLING IN SIX DIRECTIONS!
TAKE MY HAND...IT'S IN THE GALACTIC CORE!

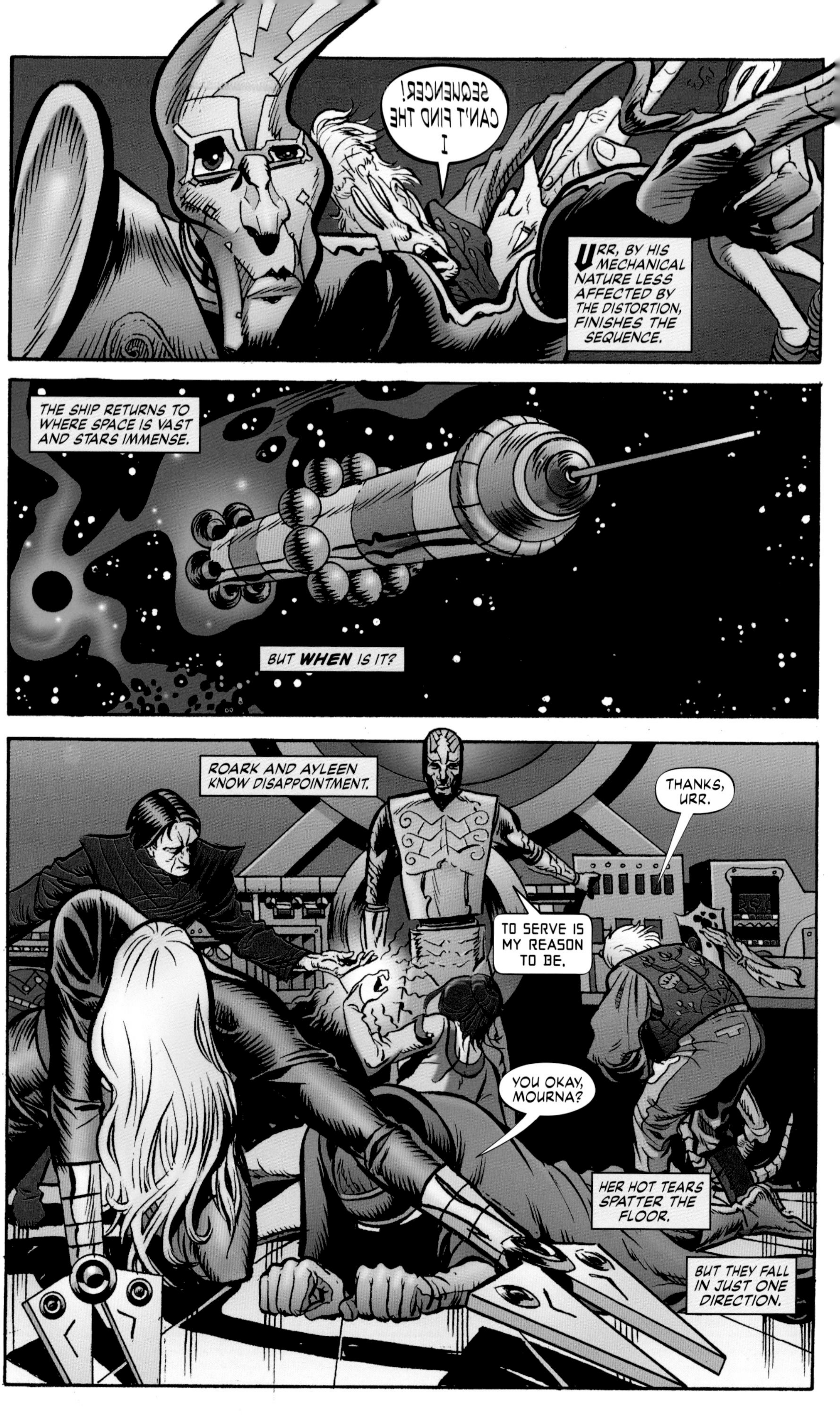
I CAN'T FIND THE SEQUENCER!
URR, BY HIS MECHANICAL NATURE LESS AFFECTED BY THE DISTORTION, FINISHES THE SEQUENCE.
THE SHIP RETURNS TO WHERE SPACE IS VAST AND STARS IMMENSE.
BUT WHEN IS IT?
ROARK AND AYLEEN KNOW DISAPPOINTMENT.
THANKS, URR.
TO SERVE IS MY REASON TO BE.
YOU OKAY, MOURNA?
HER HOT TEARS SPATTER THE FLOOR.
BUT THEY FALL IN JUST ONE DIRECTION.

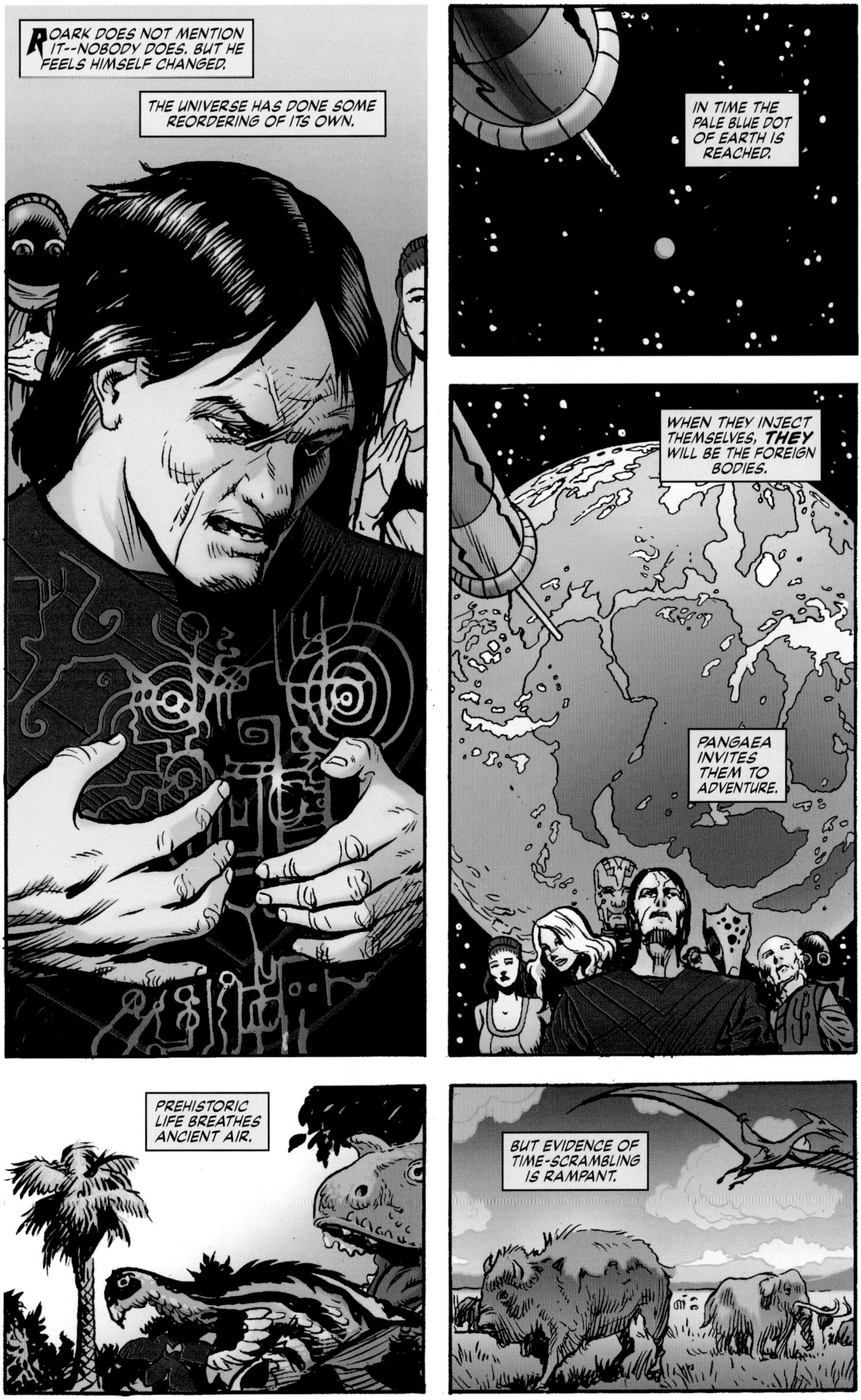
ROARK DOES NOT MENTION IT--NOBODY DOES. BUT HE FEELS HIMSELF CHANGED.
THE UNIVERSE HAS DONE SOME REORDERING OF ITS OWN.
IN TIME THE PALE BLUE DOT OF EARTH IS REACHED.
WHEN THEY INJECT THEMSELVES, THEY WILL BE THE FOREIGN BODIES.
PANGAEA INVITES THEM TO ADVENTURE.
PREHISTORIC LIFE BREATHES ANCIENT AIR.
BUT EVIDENCE OF TIME-SCRAMBLING IS RAMPANT.

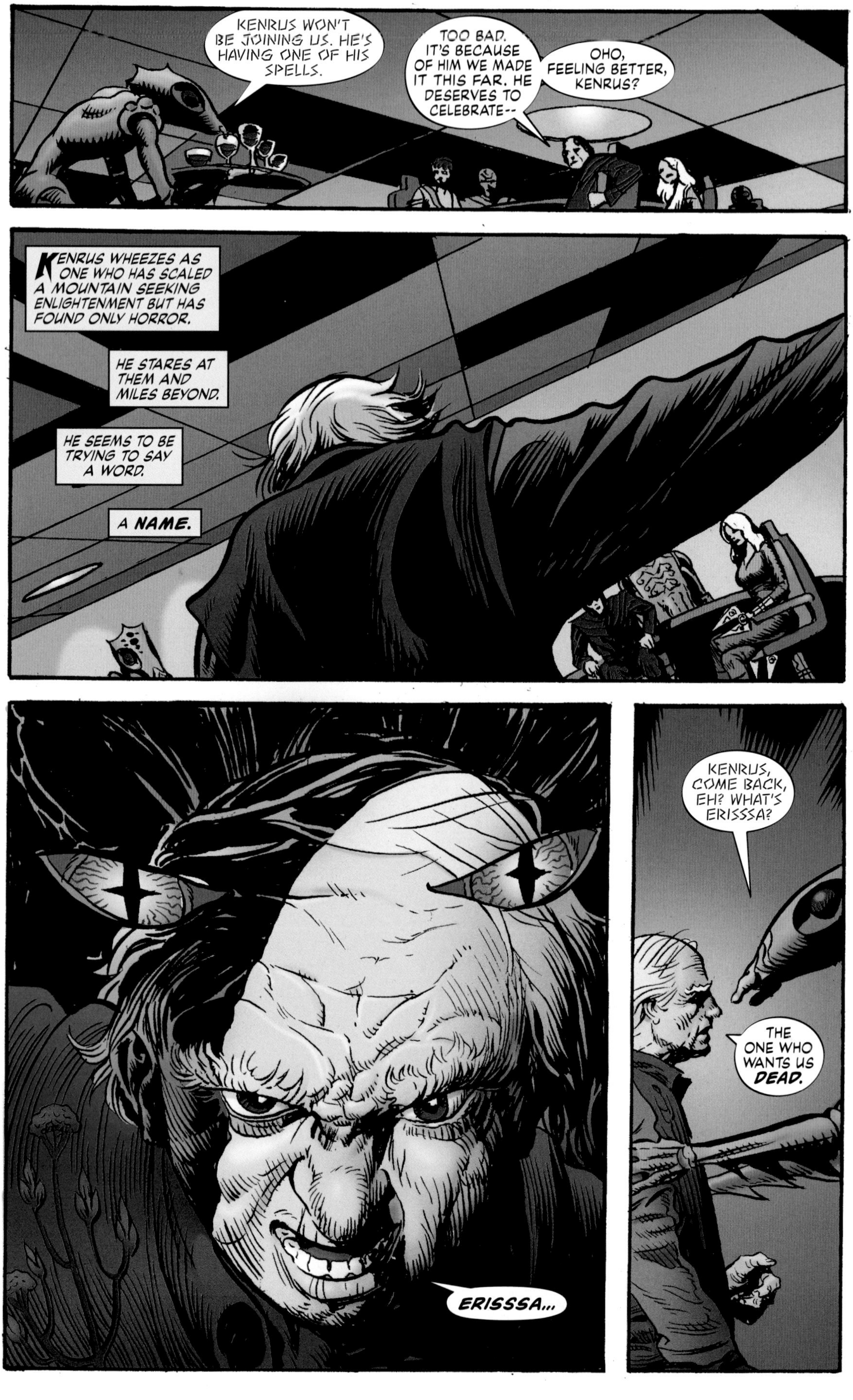
KENRUS WON'T BE JOINING US. HE'S HAVING ONE OF HIS SPELLS.
TOO BAD. IT'S BECAUSE OF HIM WE MADE IT THIS FAR. HE DESERVES TO CELEBRATE--
OHO, FEELING BETTER, KENRUS?
KENRUS WHEEZES AS ONE WHO HAS SCALED A MOUNTAIN SEEKING ENLIGHTENMENT BUT HAS FOUND ONLY HORROR.
HE STARES AT THEM AND MILES BEYOND.
HE SEEMS TO BE TRYING TO SAY A WORD.
A **NAME.**
ERISSSA...
KENRUS, COME BACK, EH? WHAT'S ERISSSA?
THE ONE WHO WANTS US **DEAD.**

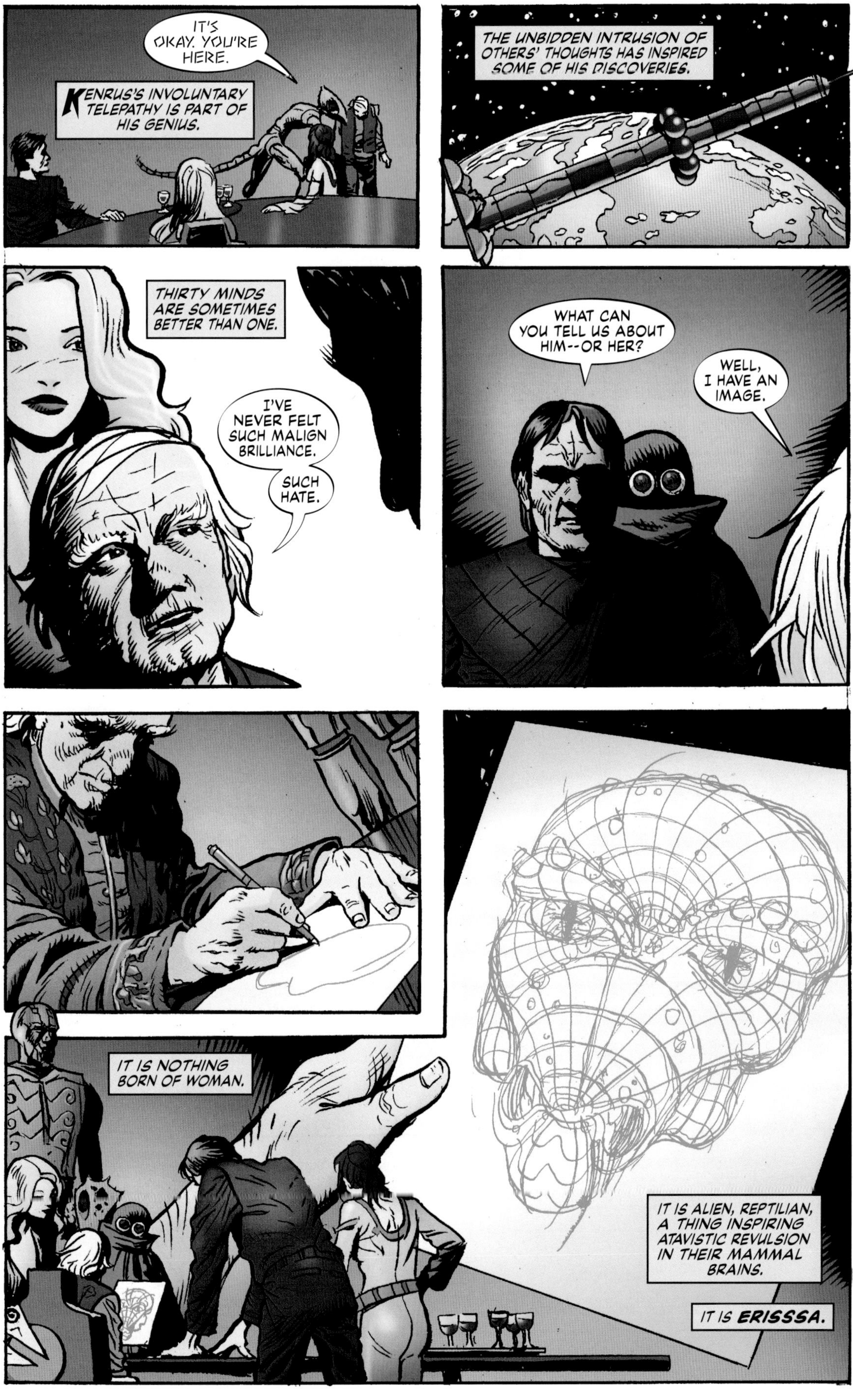
IT'S OKAY. YOU'RE HERE.
KENRUS'S INVOLUNTARY TELEPATHY IS PART OF HIS GENIUS.
THE UNBIDDEN INTRUSION OF OTHERS' THOUGHTS HAS INSPIRED SOME OF HIS DISCOVERIES.
THIRTY MINDS ARE SOMETIMES BETTER THAN ONE.
I'VE NEVER FELT SUCH MALIGN BRILLIANCE.
SUCH HATE.
WHAT CAN YOU TELL US ABOUT HIM--OR HER?
WELL, I HAVE AN IMAGE.
IT IS NOTHING BORN OF WOMAN.
IT IS ALIEN, REPTILIAN, A THING INSPIRING ATAVISTIC REVULSION IN THEIR MAMMAL BRAINS.
IT IS ERISSSA.

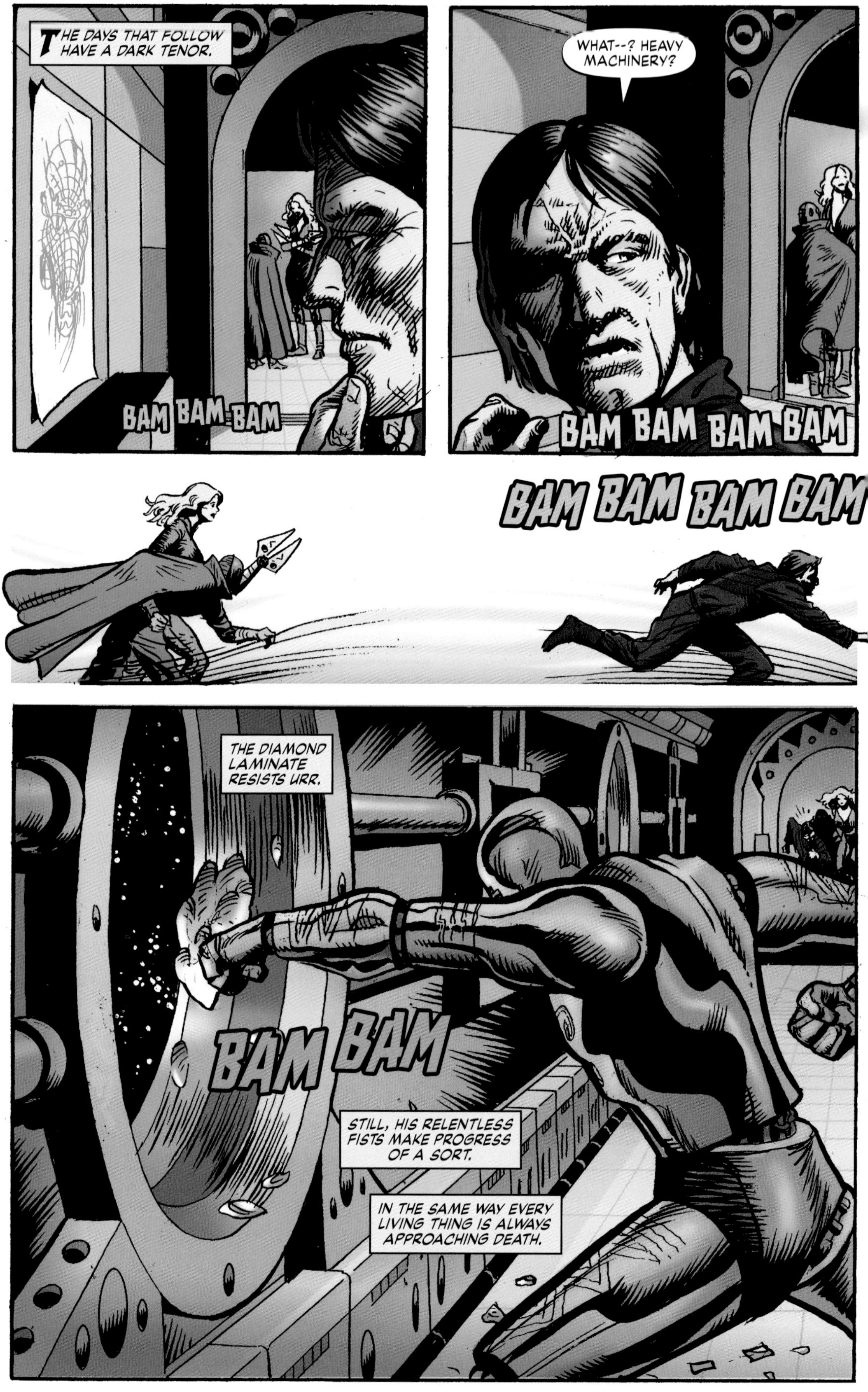
THE DAYS THAT FOLLOW HAVE A DARK TENOR.
BAM BAM BAM
WHAT--? HEAVY MACHINERY?
BAM BAM BAM BAM
BAM BAM BAM BAM
THE DIAMOND LAMINATE RESISTS URR.
BAM BAM
STILL, HIS RELENTLESS FISTS MAKE PROGRESS OF A SORT.
IN THE SAME WAY EVERY LIVING THING IS ALWAYS APPROACHING DEATH.

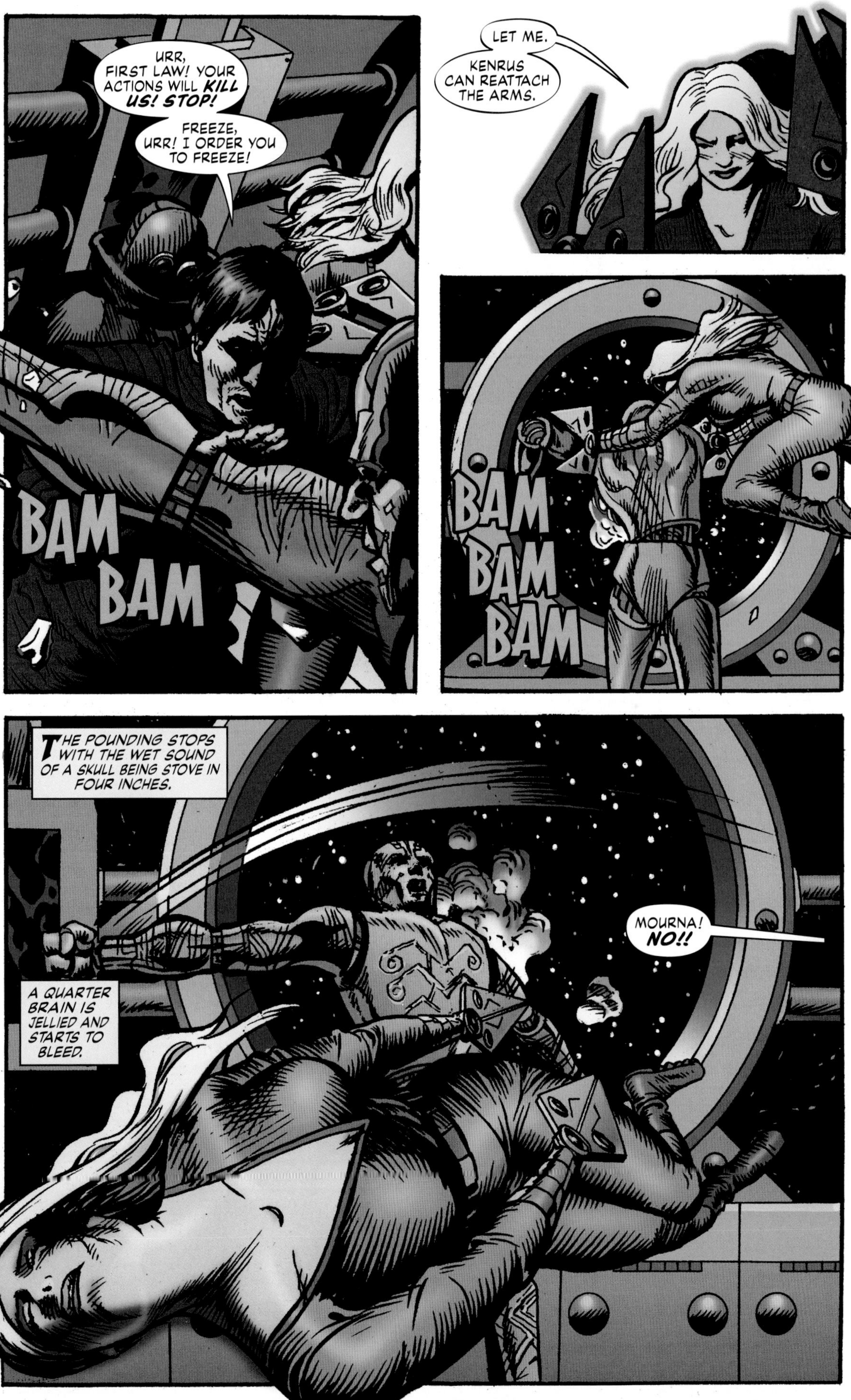
URR, FIRST LAW! YOUR ACTIONS WILL **KILL US! STOP!**
FREEZE, URR! I ORDER YOU TO FREEZE!
BAM
BAM
LET ME.
KENRUS CAN REATTACH THE ARMS.
BAM
BAM
BAM
THE POUNDING STOPS WITH THE WET SOUND OF A SKULL BEING STOVE IN FOUR INCHES.
MOURNA! **NO!!**
A QUARTER BRAIN IS JELLIED AND STARTS TO BLEED.

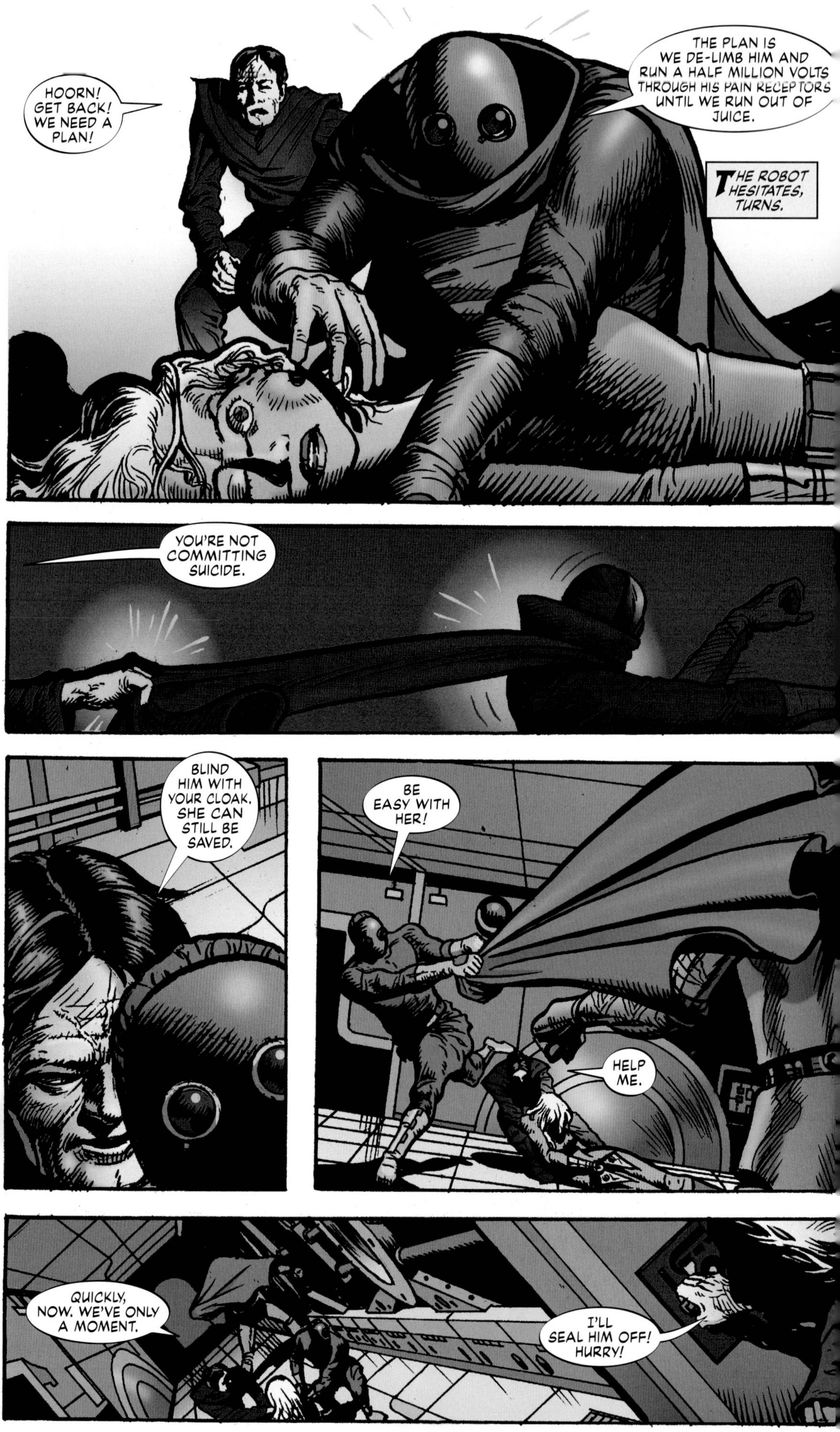
HOORN! GET BACK! WE NEED A PLAN!
THE PLAN IS WE DE-LIMB HIM AND RUN A HALF MILLION VOLTS THROUGH HIS PAIN RECEPTORS UNTIL WE RUN OUT OF JUICE.
THE ROBOT HESITATES, TURNS.
YOU'RE NOT COMMITTING SUICIDE.
BLIND HIM WITH YOUR CLOAK. SHE CAN STILL BE SAVED.
BE EASY WITH HER!
HELP ME.
QUICKLY, NOW. WE'VE ONLY A MOMENT.
I'LL SEAL HIM OFF! HURRY!

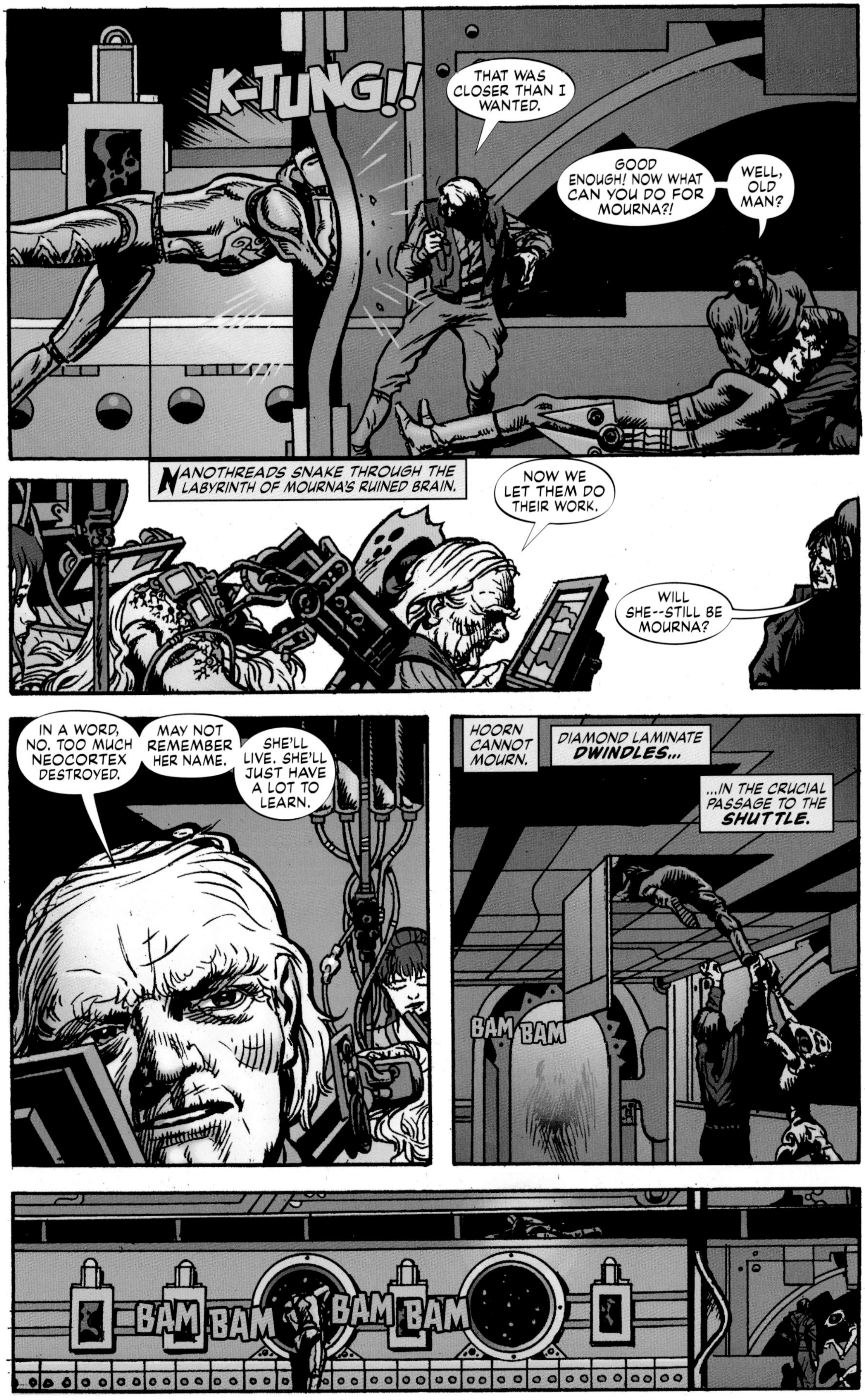
K-TUNG!!
THAT WAS CLOSER THAN I WANTED.
GOOD ENOUGH! NOW WHAT CAN YOU DO FOR MOURNA?!
WELL, OLD MAN?
NANOTHREADS SNAKE THROUGH THE LABYRINTH OF MOURNA'S RUINED BRAIN.
NOW WE LET THEM DO THEIR WORK.
WILL SHE--STILL BE MOURNA?
IN A WORD, NO. TOO MUCH NEOCORTEX DESTROYED.
MAY NOT REMEMBER HER NAME.
SHE'LL LIVE. SHE'LL JUST HAVE A LOT TO LEARN.
HOORN CANNOT MOURN.
DIAMOND LAMINATE DWINDLES...
...IN THE CRUCIAL PASSAGE TO THE SHUTTLE.
BAM BAM
BAM BAM BAM BAM

WITH HOORN'S CAT-BURGLAR STEALTH...

BAM BAM

...AND SPECIAL TOOLS...

...A CRANIUM OPENS, LESS VIOLENTLY THAN THE LAST.

URR IS STILL.

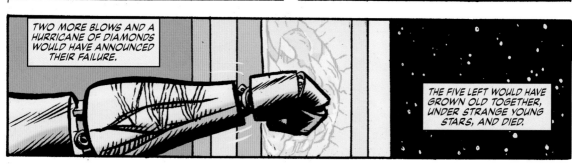

TWO MORE BLOWS AND A HURRICANE OF DIAMONDS WOULD HAVE ANNOUNCED THEIR FAILURE.

THE FIVE LEFT WOULD HAVE GROWN OLD TOGETHER, UNDER STRANGE YOUNG STARS, AND DIED.

A WORLD WOULD HAVE SWAPPED ITS HISTORY FOR AN EPIC OF SCALED AND SLITHERY THINGS.

GOT YOU, YOU WORTHLESS PIECE OF STEEL.

HIS TAUNT IS WASTED ON AN EXPENSIVE STATUE.

HOORN, YOU ALL RIGHT?

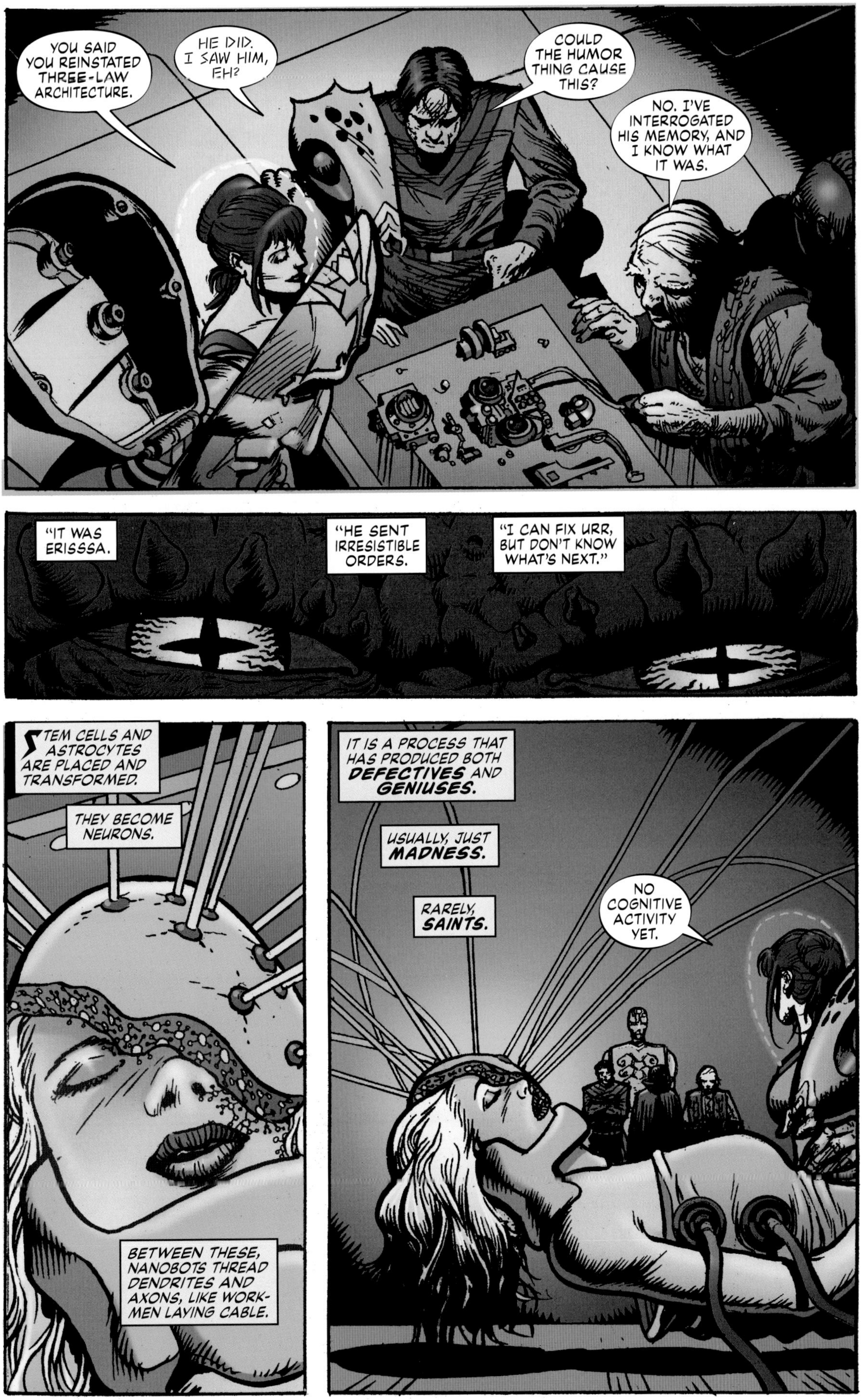
YOU SAID YOU REINSTATED THREE-LAW ARCHITECTURE.
HE DID. I SAW HIM, EH?
COULD THE HUMOR THING CAUSE THIS?
NO. I'VE INTERROGATED HIS MEMORY, AND I KNOW WHAT IT WAS.
"IT WAS ERISSSA.
"HE SENT IRRESISTIBLE ORDERS.
"I CAN FIX URR, BUT DON'T KNOW WHAT'S NEXT."
STEM CELLS AND ASTROCYTES ARE PLACED AND TRANSFORMED.
THEY BECOME NEURONS.
BETWEEN THESE, NANOBOTS THREAD DENDRITES AND AXONS, LIKE WORK-MEN LAYING CABLE.
IT IS A PROCESS THAT HAS PRODUCED BOTH DEFECTIVES AND GENIUSES.
USUALLY, JUST MADNESS.
RARELY, SAINTS.
NO COGNITIVE ACTIVITY YET.

NOT EVEN ON EARTH AND ALREADY TWO CASUALTIES.

DO THE COMPUTERS SAY WE EVEN FACE HIM?

ALL BUT ONE.

I'M NOT SAYING WHO.

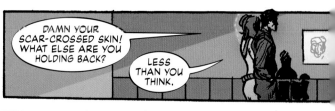

DAMN YOUR SCAR-CROSSED SKIN! WHAT ELSE ARE YOU HOLDING BACK?

LESS THAN YOU THINK.

I HAVE NO IDEA HOW THIS TURNS OUT.

KTANG!

WHA--?

WHAT *CAN'T* THIS ERISSSA DO, IS THE QUESTION!

CAN YOU FEEL HIM?

IT'S AWFUL-- LIKE A SNAKE IN MY BRAIN...

"...WRITHING!"

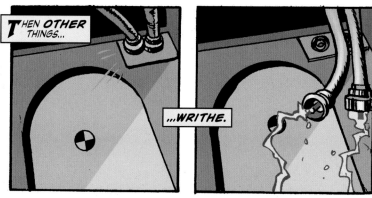

*T*HEN *OTHER* THINGS...

...WRITHE.

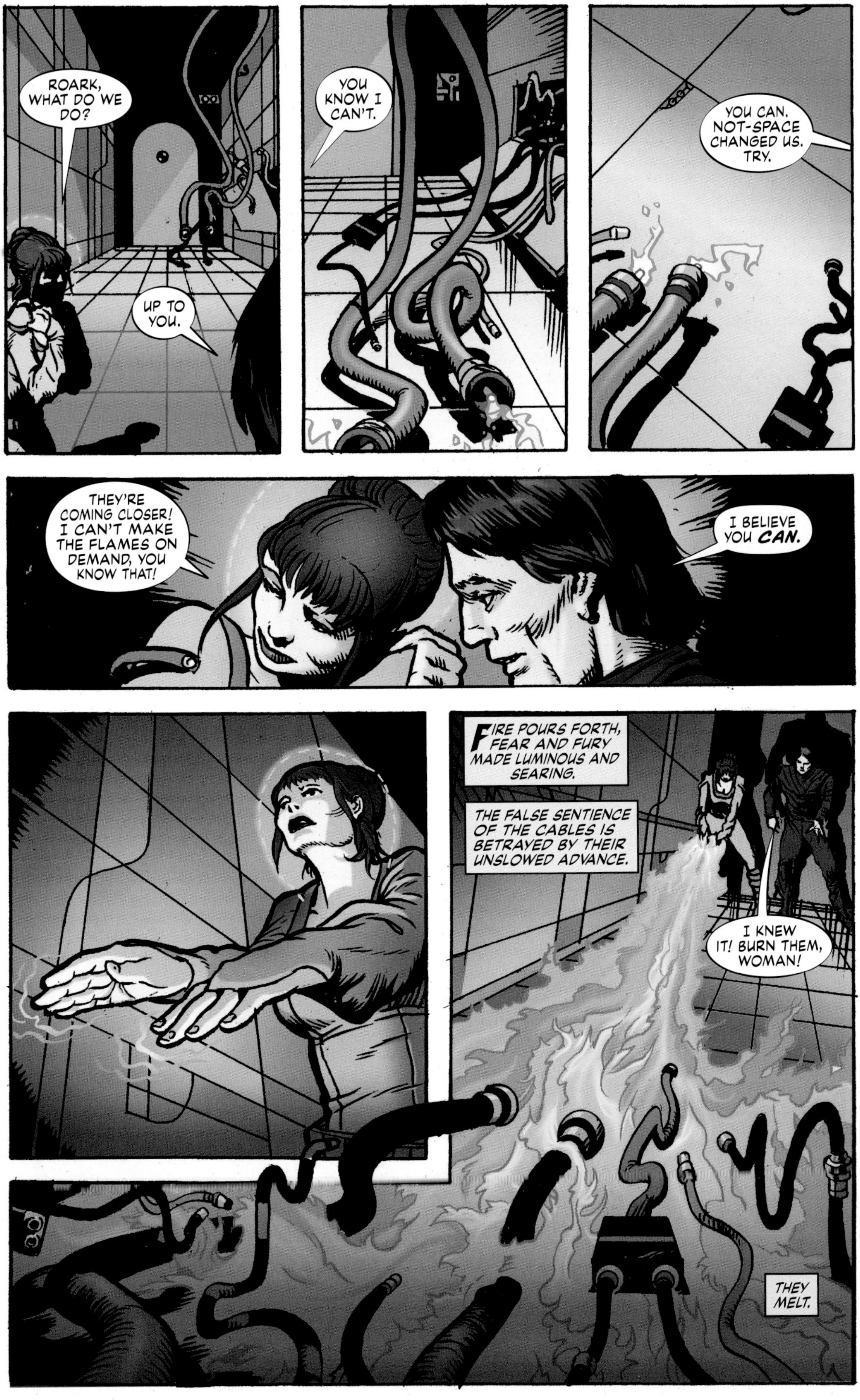
ROARK, WHAT DO WE DO?
UP TO YOU.
YOU KNOW I CAN'T.
YOU CAN. NOT-SPACE CHANGED US. TRY.
THEY'RE COMING CLOSER! I CAN'T MAKE THE FLAMES ON DEMAND, YOU KNOW THAT!
I BELIEVE YOU *CAN.*
FIRE POURS FORTH, FEAR AND FURY MADE LUMINOUS AND SEARING.
THE FALSE SENTIENCE OF THE CABLES IS BETRAYED BY THEIR UNSLOWED ADVANCE.
I KNEW IT! BURN THEM, WOMAN!
THEY MELT.

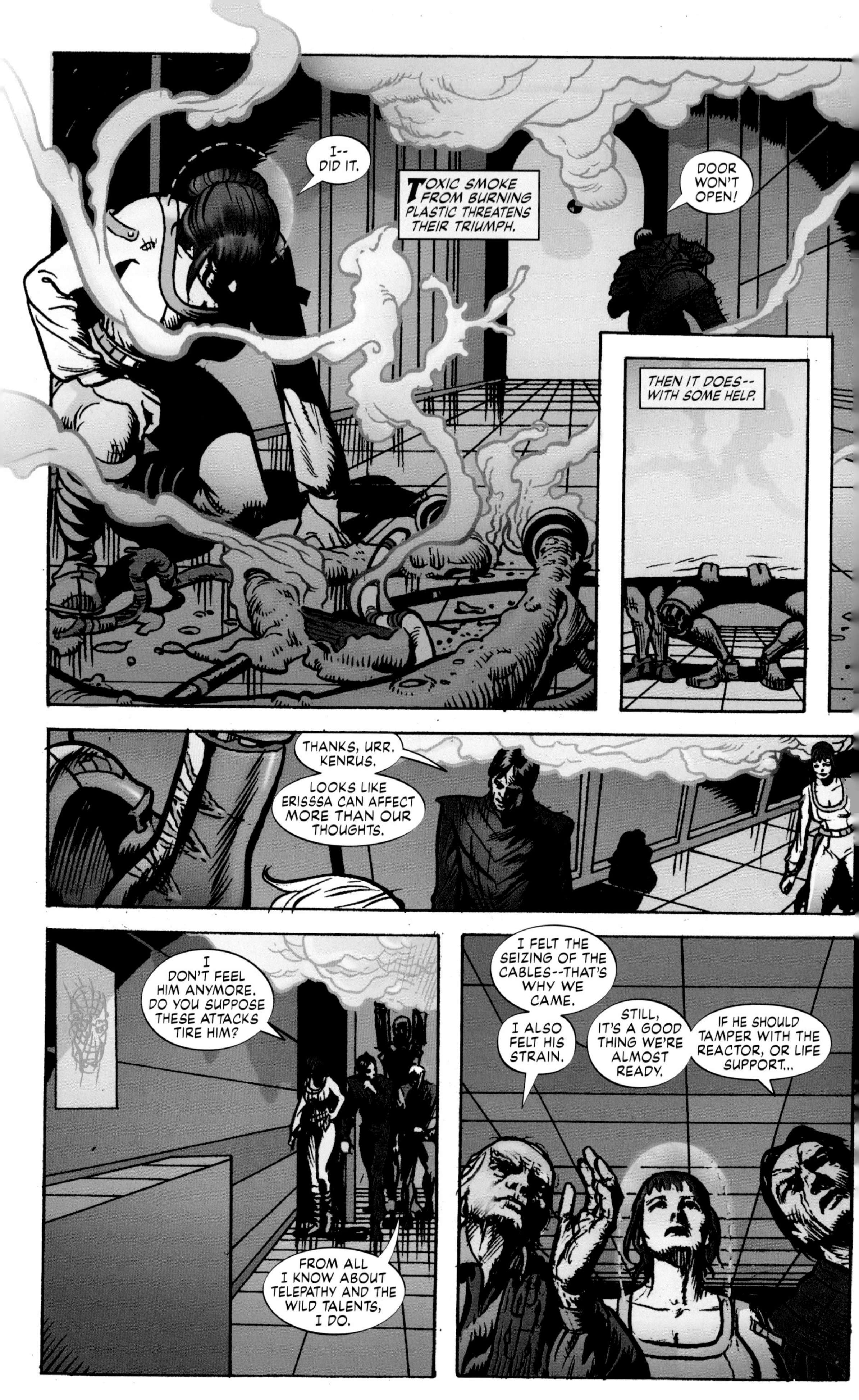
I--
DID IT.
TOXIC SMOKE FROM BURNING PLASTIC THREATENS THEIR TRIUMPH.
DOOR WON'T OPEN!
THEN IT DOES-- WITH SOME HELP.
THANKS, URR. KENRUS.
LOOKS LIKE ERISSSA CAN AFFECT MORE THAN OUR THOUGHTS.
I DON'T FEEL HIM ANYMORE. DO YOU SUPPOSE THESE ATTACKS TIRE HIM?
FROM ALL I KNOW ABOUT TELEPATHY AND THE WILD TALENTS, I DO.
I FELT THE SEIZING OF THE CABLES--THAT'S WHY WE CAME.
I ALSO FELT HIS STRAIN.
STILL, IT'S A GOOD THING WE'RE ALMOST READY.
IF HE SHOULD TAMPER WITH THE REACTOR, OR LIFE SUPPORT...

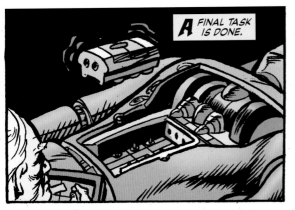

A FINAL TASK IS DONE.

A CRISIS COMPUTER IS PLACED IN URR'S GUT.

YOU'RE SURE THIS MAGIC WORD WILL SHUT HIM DOWN?

INSTANTLY. ALSO, THE HAND SIGNAL.

TELL ME...

WHY MUST WE HAVE A SHUT-DOWN WORD?

IT IS EXPLAINED TO HER A FOURTH TIME.

NANOMENDING CONTINUES.

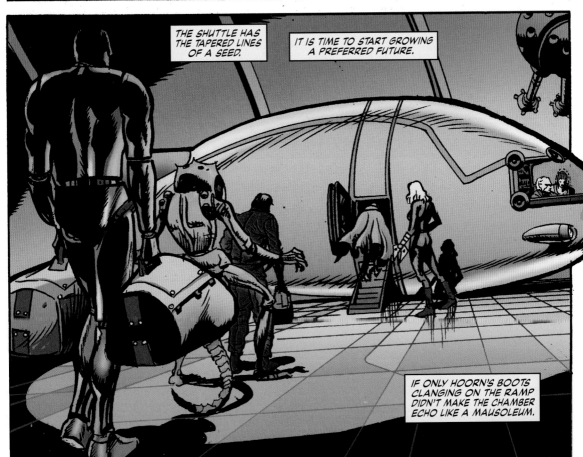

THE SHUTTLE HAS THE TAPERED LINES OF A SEED.

IT IS TIME TO START GROWING A PREFERRED FUTURE.

IF ONLY HOORN'S BOOTS CLANGING ON THE RAMP DIDN'T MAKE THE CHAMBER ECHO LIKE A MAUSOLEUM.

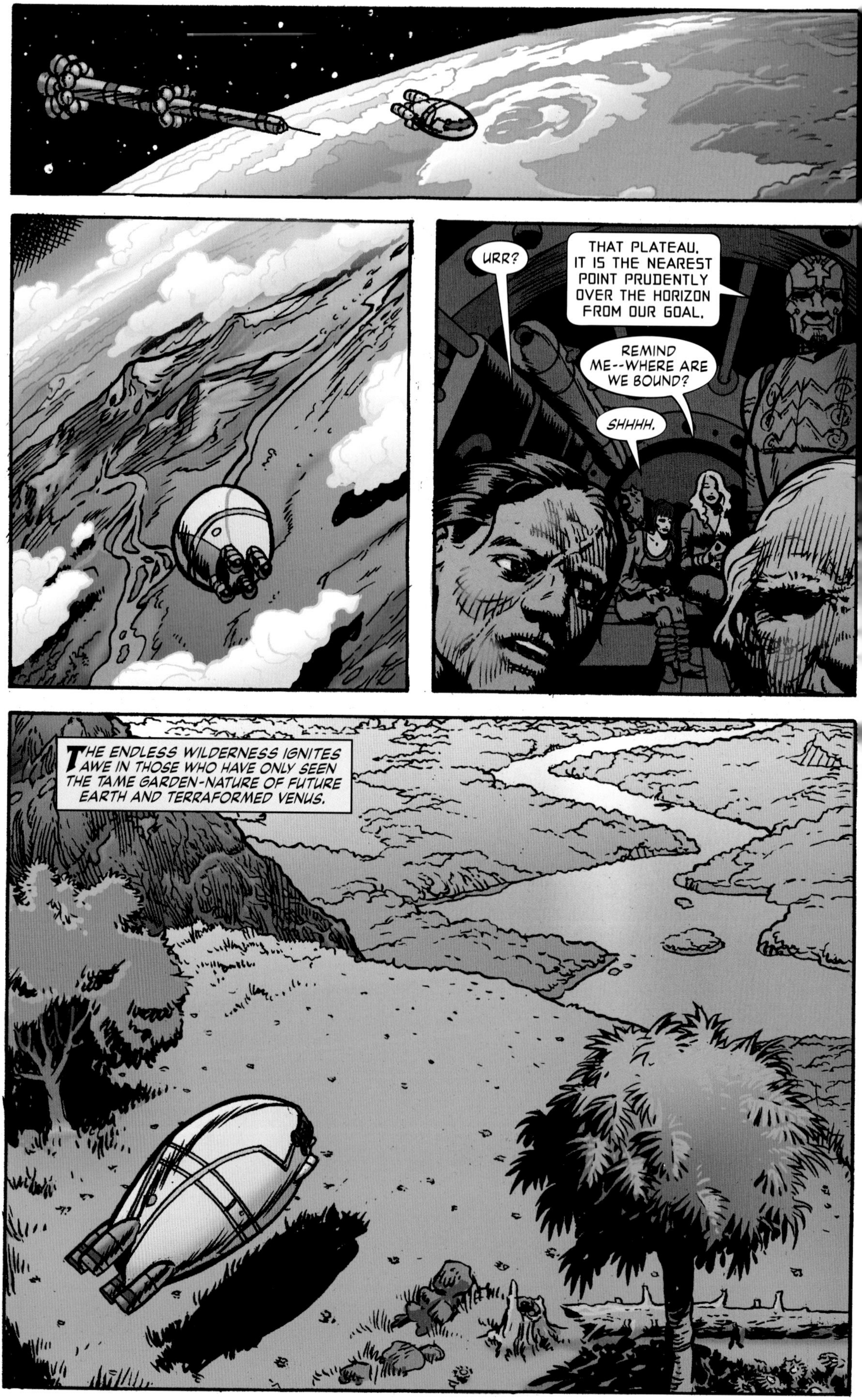
URR?
THAT PLATEAU. IT IS THE NEAREST POINT PRUDENTLY OVER THE HORIZON FROM OUR GOAL.
REMIND ME--WHERE ARE WE BOUND?
SHHHH.
THE ENDLESS WILDERNESS IGNITES AWE IN THOSE WHO HAVE ONLY SEEN THE TAME GARDEN-NATURE OF FUTURE EARTH AND TERRAFORMED VENUS.

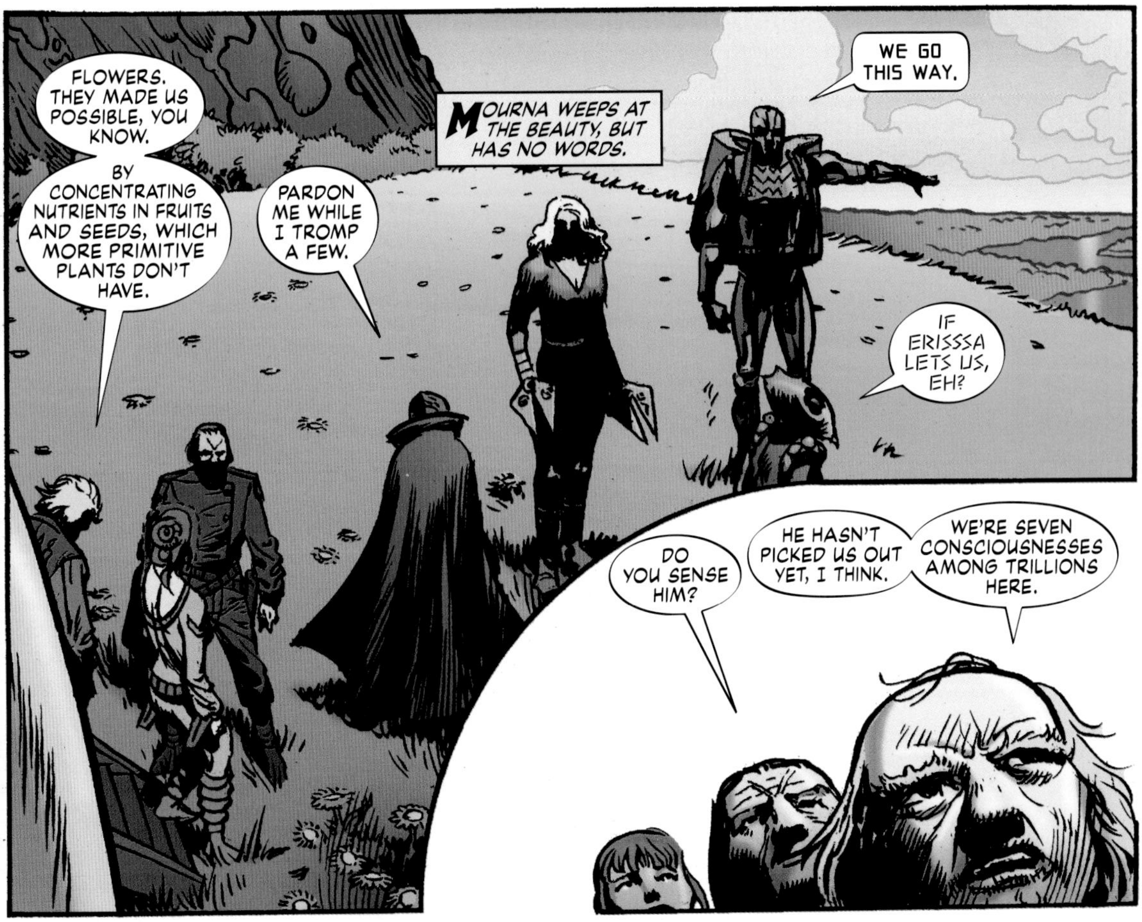
FLOWERS. THEY MADE US POSSIBLE, YOU KNOW.
BY CONCENTRATING NUTRIENTS IN FRUITS AND SEEDS, WHICH MORE PRIMITIVE PLANTS DON'T HAVE.
PARDON ME WHILE I TROMP A FEW.
MOURNA WEEPS AT THE BEAUTY, BUT HAS NO WORDS.
WE GO THIS WAY.
IF ERISSSA LETS US, EH?
DO YOU SENSE HIM?
HE HASN'T PICKED US OUT YET, I THINK.
WE'RE SEVEN CONSCIOUSNESSES AMONG TRILLIONS HERE.

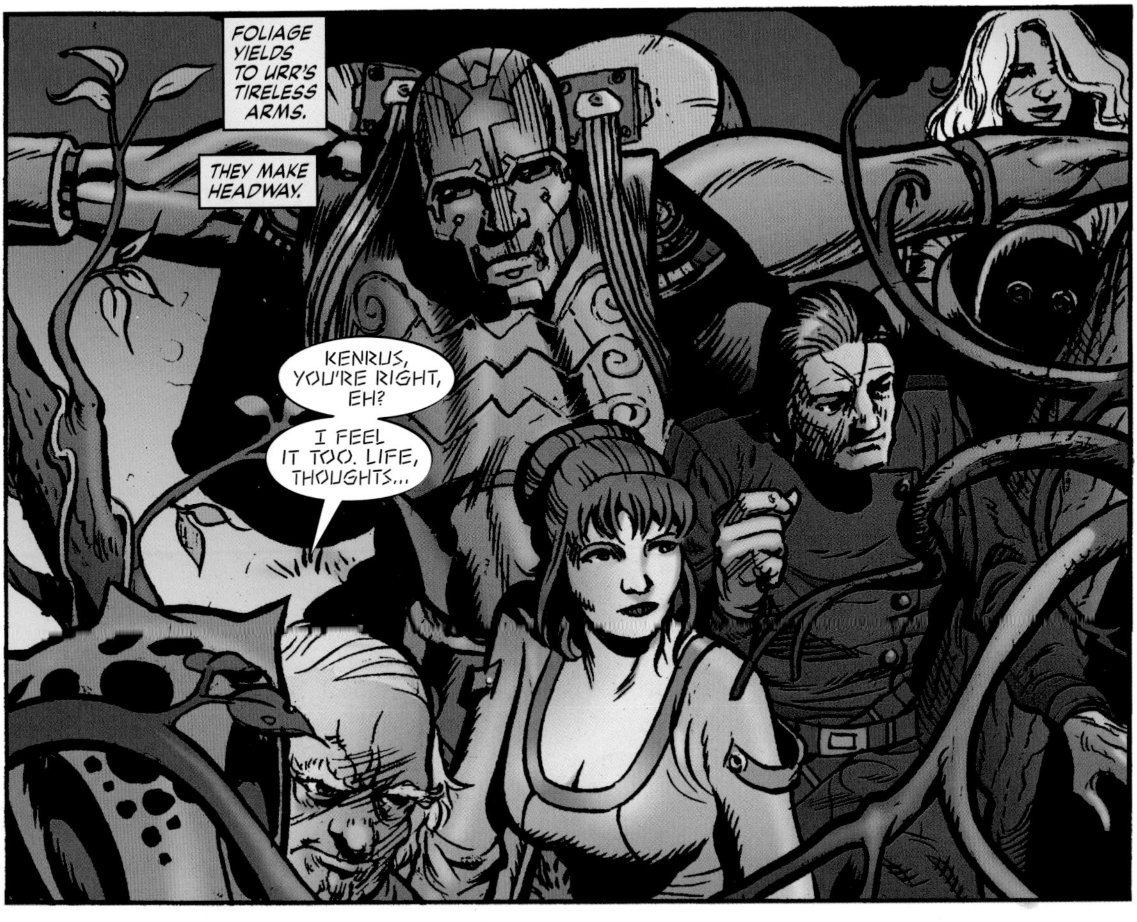
FOLIAGE YIELDS TO URR'S TIRELESS ARMS.
THEY MAKE HEADWAY.
KENRUS, YOU'RE RIGHT, EH?
I FEEL IT TOO. LIFE, THOUGHTS...

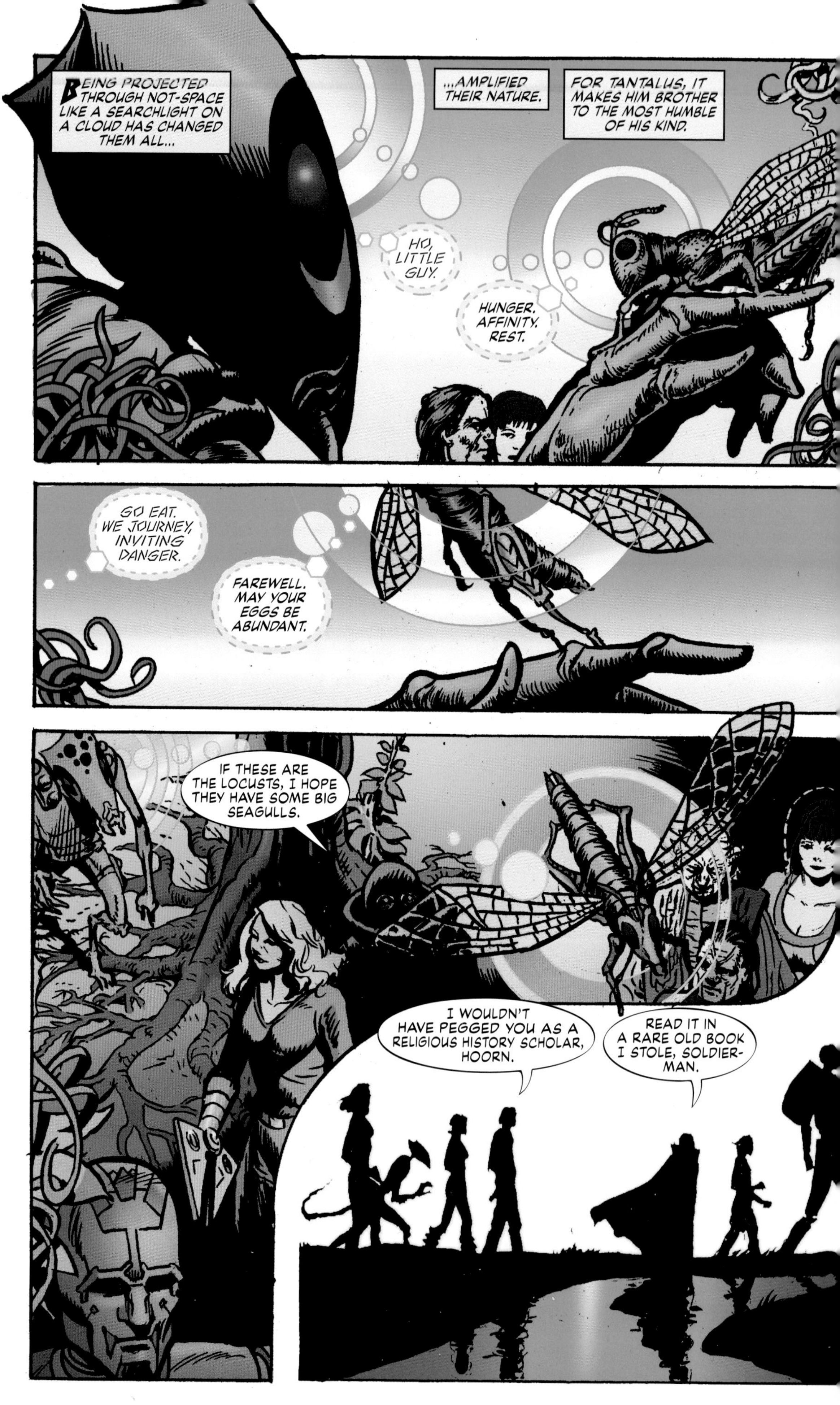
BEING PROJECTED THROUGH NOT-SPACE LIKE A SEARCHLIGHT ON A CLOUD HAS CHANGED THEM ALL...
...AMPLIFIED THEIR NATURE.
FOR TANTALUS, IT MAKES HIM BROTHER TO THE MOST HUMBLE OF HIS KIND.
HO, LITTLE GUY.
HUNGER. AFFINITY. REST.
GO EAT. WE JOURNEY, INVITING DANGER.
FAREWELL. MAY YOUR EGGS BE ABUNDANT.
IF THESE ARE THE LOCUSTS, I HOPE THEY HAVE SOME BIG SEAGULLS.
I WOULDN'T HAVE PEGGED YOU AS A RELIGIOUS HISTORY SCHOLAR, HOORN.
READ IT IN A RARE OLD BOOK I STOLE, SOLDIER-MAN.

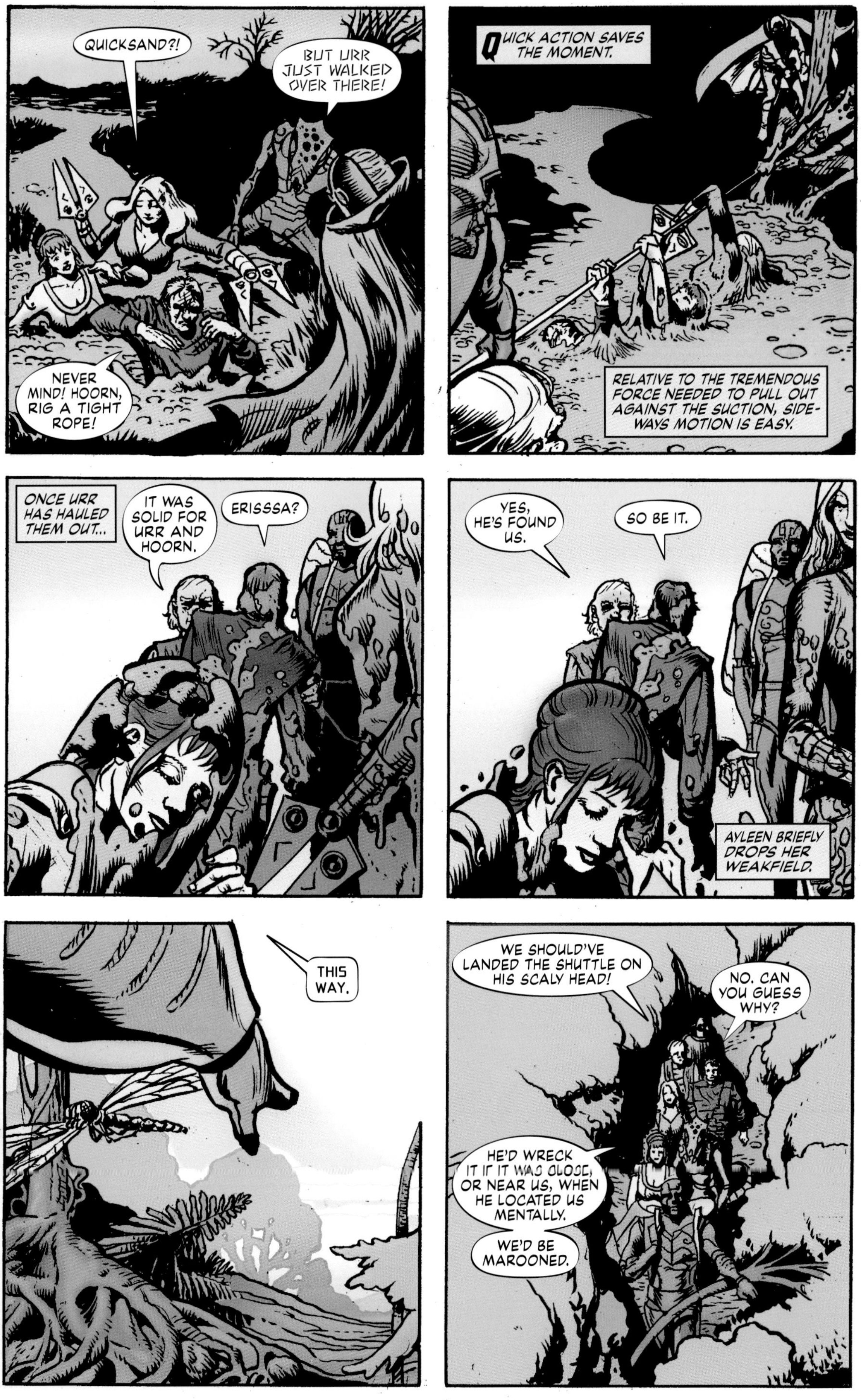
QUICKSAND?!
BUT URR JUST WALKED OVER THERE!
NEVER MIND! HOORN, RIG A TIGHT ROPE!
QUICK ACTION SAVES THE MOMENT.
RELATIVE TO THE TREMENDOUS FORCE NEEDED TO PULL OUT AGAINST THE SUCTION, SIDEWAYS MOTION IS EASY.
ONCE URR HAS HAULED THEM OUT...
IT WAS SOLID FOR URR AND HOORN.
ERISSSA?
YES, HE'S FOUND US.
SO BE IT.
AYLEEN BRIEFLY DROPS HER WEAKFIELD.
THIS WAY.
WE SHOULD'VE LANDED THE SHUTTLE ON HIS SCALY HEAD!
NO. CAN YOU GUESS WHY?
HE'D WRECK IT IF IT WAS CLOSE, OR NEAR US, WHEN HE LOCATED US MENTALLY.
WE'D BE MAROONED.

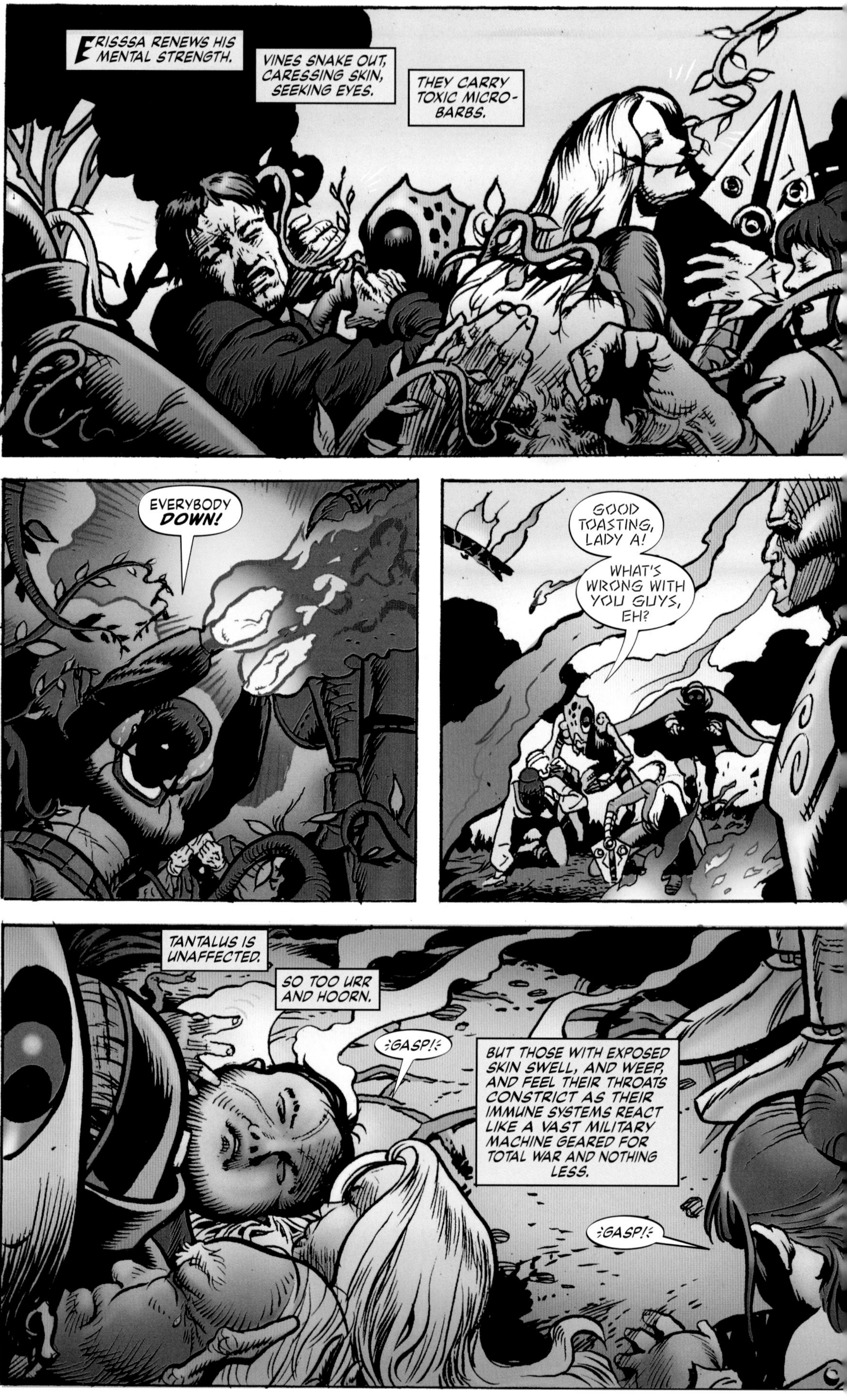
ERISSSA RENEWS HIS MENTAL STRENGTH.
VINES SNAKE OUT, CARESSING SKIN, SEEKING EYES.
THEY CARRY TOXIC MICRO-BARBS.
EVERYBODY DOWN!
GOOD TOASTING, LADY A!
WHAT'S WRONG WITH YOU GUYS, EH?
TANTALUS IS UNAFFECTED.
SO TOO URR AND HOORN.
GASP!
BUT THOSE WITH EXPOSED SKIN SWELL, AND WEEP, AND FEEL THEIR THROATS CONSTRICT AS THEIR IMMUNE SYSTEMS REACT LIKE A VAST MILITARY MACHINE GEARED FOR TOTAL WAR AND NOTHING LESS.
GASP!

KEEP HER STEADY.

AYLEEN IS TOO STRICKEN FOR THE ODDNESS OF HANDS HOLDING HER TO REGISTER.

INJECTIONS OF OLD-FASHIONED ANTIHISTAMINE SAVE THEIR LIVES.

WELL, HE FOUND US.

:COUGH!:

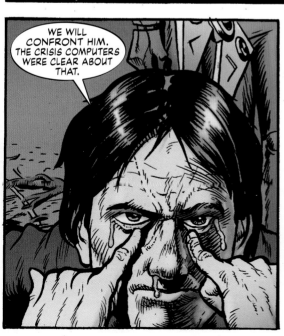

WE WILL CONFRONT HIM. THE CRISIS COMPUTERS WERE CLEAR ABOUT THAT.

IN WHAT PHYSICAL STATE, ROARK DOES NOT SAY.

NOR IN WHAT NUMBER.

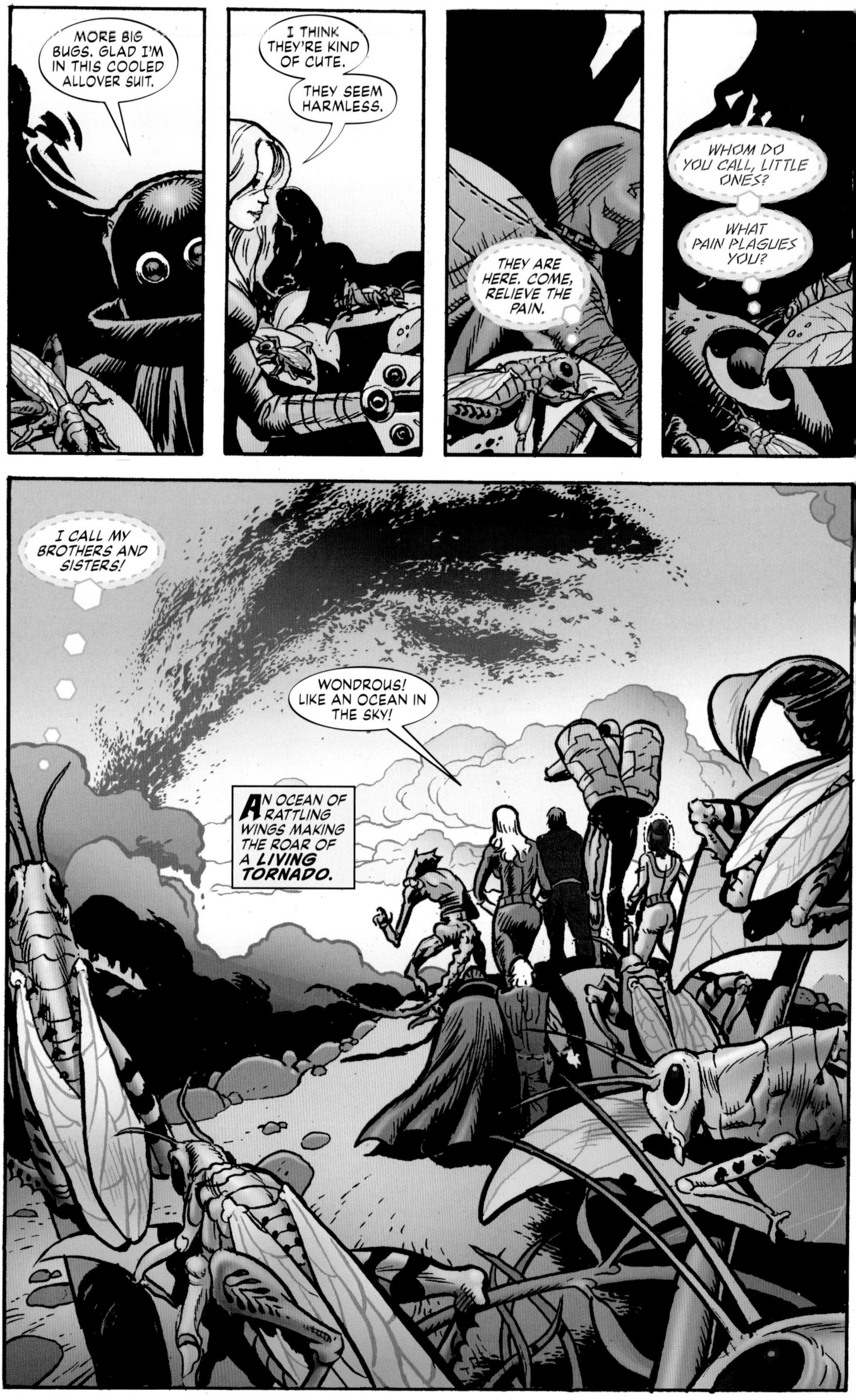
MORE BIG BUGS. GLAD I'M IN THIS COOLED ALLOVER SUIT.
I THINK THEY'RE KIND OF CUTE.
THEY SEEM HARMLESS.
THEY ARE HERE. COME, RELIEVE THE PAIN.
WHOM DO YOU CALL, LITTLE ONES?
WHAT PAIN PLAGUES YOU?
I CALL MY BROTHERS AND SISTERS!
WONDROUS! LIKE AN OCEAN IN THE SKY!
AN OCEAN OF RATTLING WINGS MAKING THE ROAR OF A LIVING TORNADO.

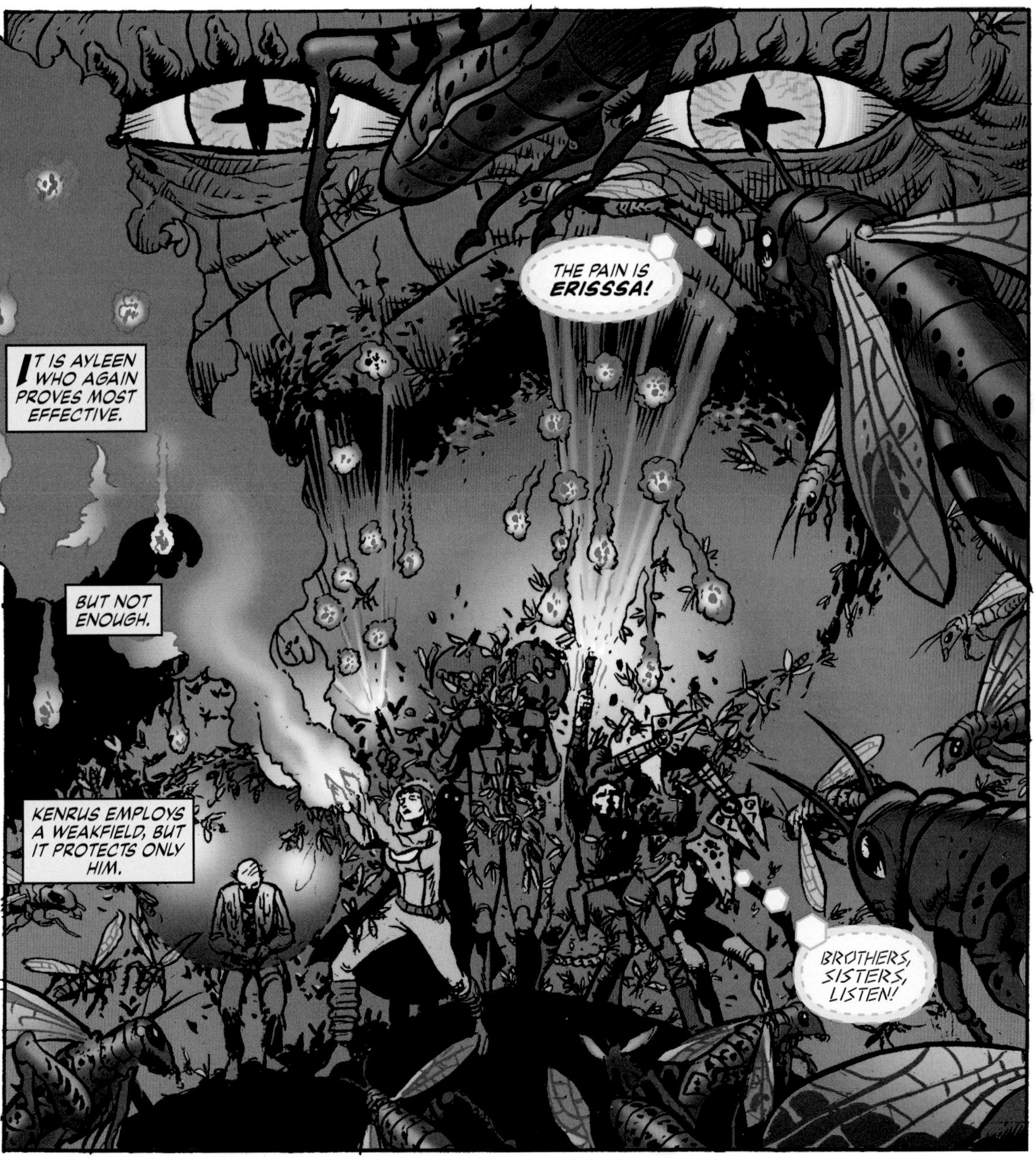
IT IS AYLEEN WHO AGAIN PROVES MOST EFFECTIVE.
THE PAIN IS ERISSSA!
BUT NOT ENOUGH.
KENRUS EMPLOYS A WEAKFIELD, BUT IT PROTECTS ONLY HIM.
BROTHERS, SISTERS, LISTEN!
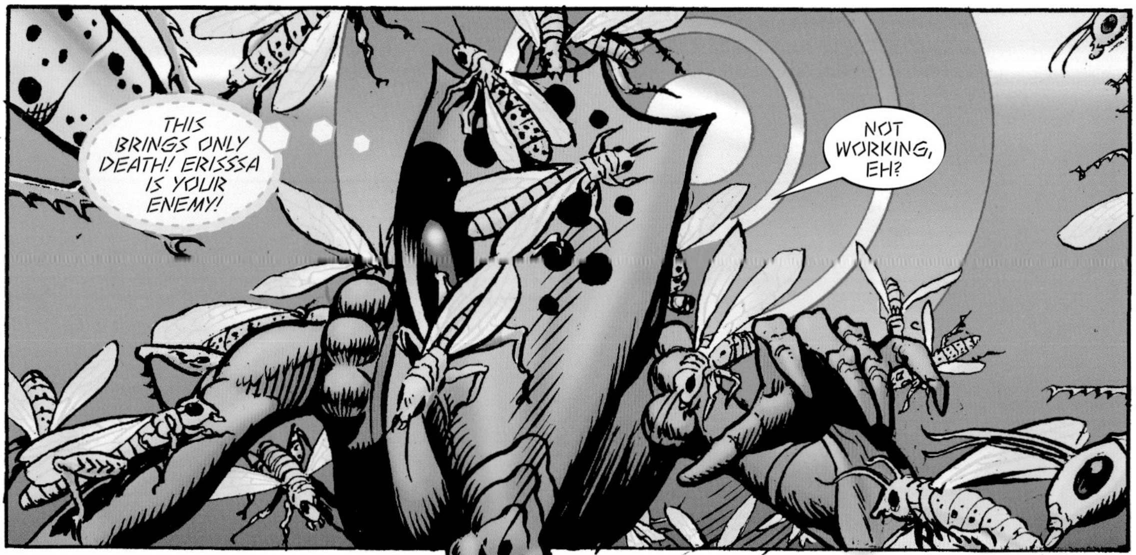
THIS BRINGS ONLY DEATH! ERISSSA IS YOUR ENEMY!
NOT WORKING, EH?

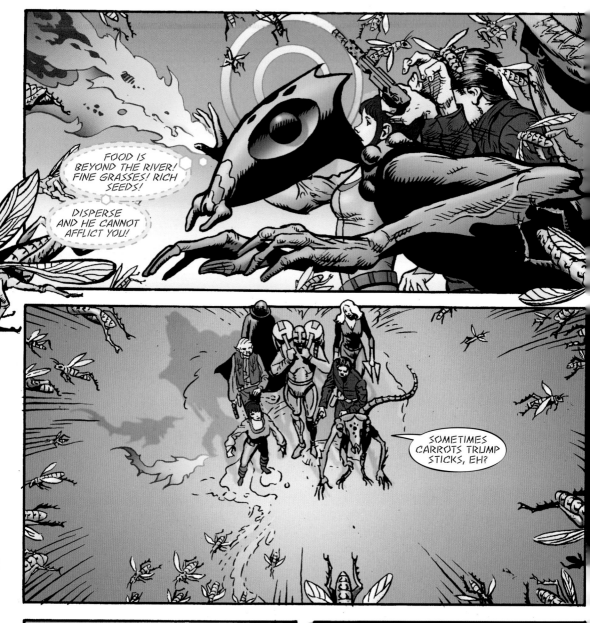

FOOD IS BEYOND THE RIVER! FINE GRASSES! RICH SEEDS!

DISPERSE AND HE CANNOT AFFLICT YOU!

SOMETIMES CARROTS TRUMP STICKS, EH?

ROARK'S RIGHT, THE TRIP CHANGED US. MADE US MORE OF WHAT WE ARE.

LOCUST THOUGHTS AREN'T DEEP, BUT I HEAR EVERY ONE OF THEM.

NOW, WATCH WHERE YOU STEP. SOME OF MY PALS ARE ONLY STUNNED.

C'MON, EH?

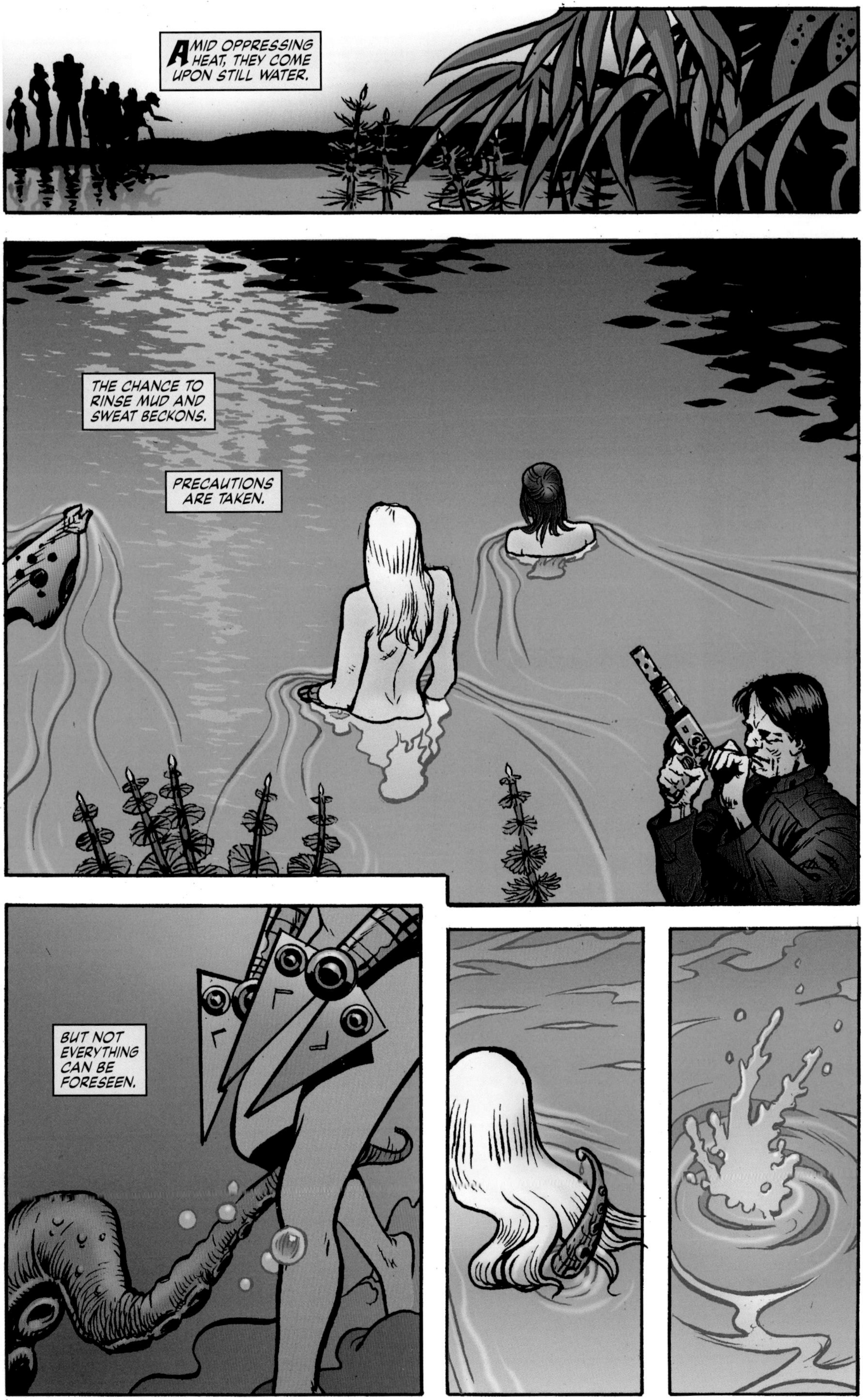
AMID OPPRESSING HEAT, THEY COME UPON STILL WATER.
THE CHANCE TO RINSE MUD AND SWEAT BECKONS.
PRECAUTIONS ARE TAKEN.
BUT NOT EVERYTHING CAN BE FORESEEN.

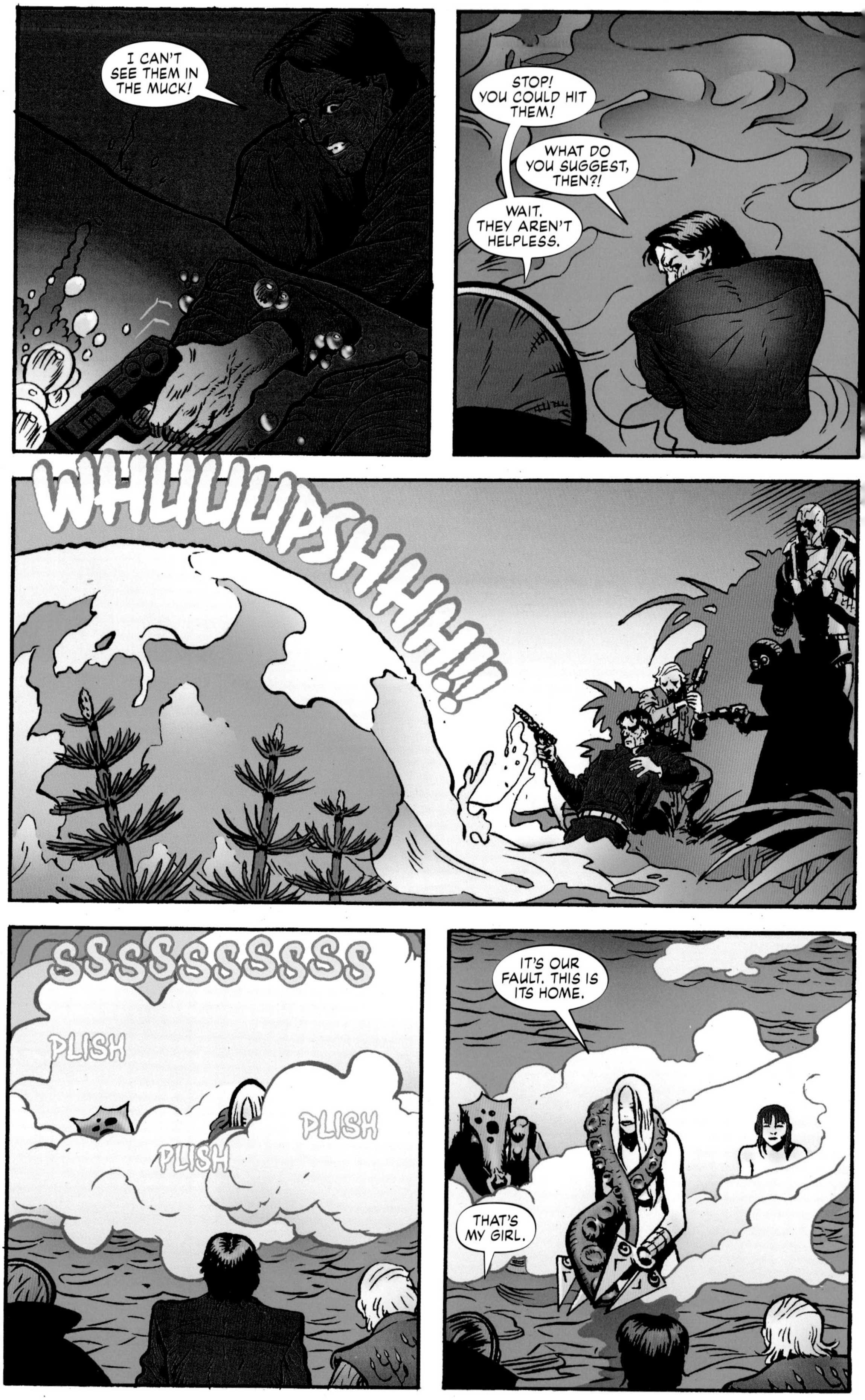
I CAN'T SEE THEM IN THE MUCK!
STOP! YOU COULD HIT THEM!
WHAT DO YOU SUGGEST, THEN?!
WAIT. THEY AREN'T HELPLESS.
WHUUUPSHHHH!!!
SSSSSSSSSS
PLISH
PLISH
PLISH
IT'S OUR FAULT. THIS IS ITS HOME.
THAT'S MY GIRL.

ALMOST AS AMAZING IS WATCHING A WOMAN WITH METAL PINCERS HANDLE THE MAGNETS AND SEALS TO DON A SKINTIGHT SUIT.

NO MORE SWIMMING. IDIOTIC OF ME.

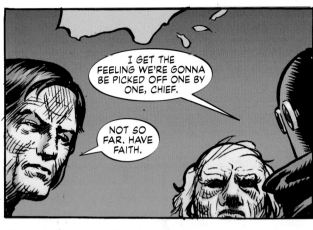

I GET THE FEELING WE'RE GONNA BE PICKED OFF ONE BY ONE, CHIEF.

NOT SO FAR. HAVE FAITH.

GUESS I'D HAVE MORE IF THERE WERE LOCKS TO PICK OR SAFES TO CRACK.

WHEN MR. T. REX SHOWS, I'M NOT GONNA BE MUCH USE.

YOU'VE ALREADY SAVED US FROM URR'S...EPISODE. THERE'S THAT.

"YEAH, GUESS SO," IS ALL THE FACE-LESS MAN SAYS.

BUT HE WONDERS IF ROARK MEANS MORE BY HIS WORDS THAN MERE REASSURANCE.

WHAT ARE THOSE SHADOWS?

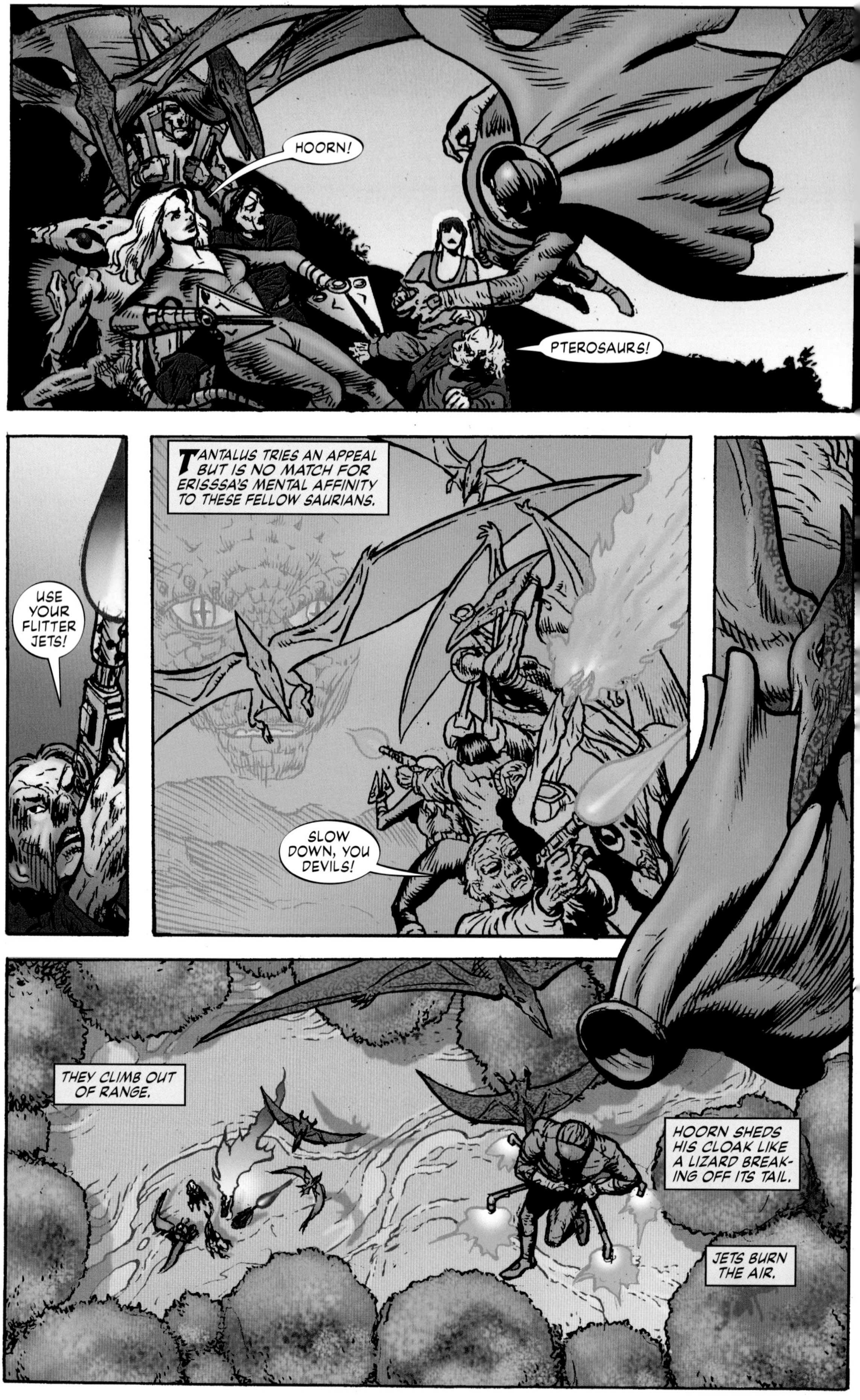
HOORN!
PTEROSAURS!
USE YOUR FLITTER JETS!
TANTALUS TRIES AN APPEAL BUT IS NO MATCH FOR ERISSSA'S MENTAL AFFINITY TO THESE FELLOW SAURIANS.
SLOW DOWN, YOU DEVILS!
THEY CLIMB OUT OF RANGE.
HOORN SHEDS HIS CLOAK LIKE A LIZARD BREAKING OFF ITS TAIL.
JETS BURN THE AIR.

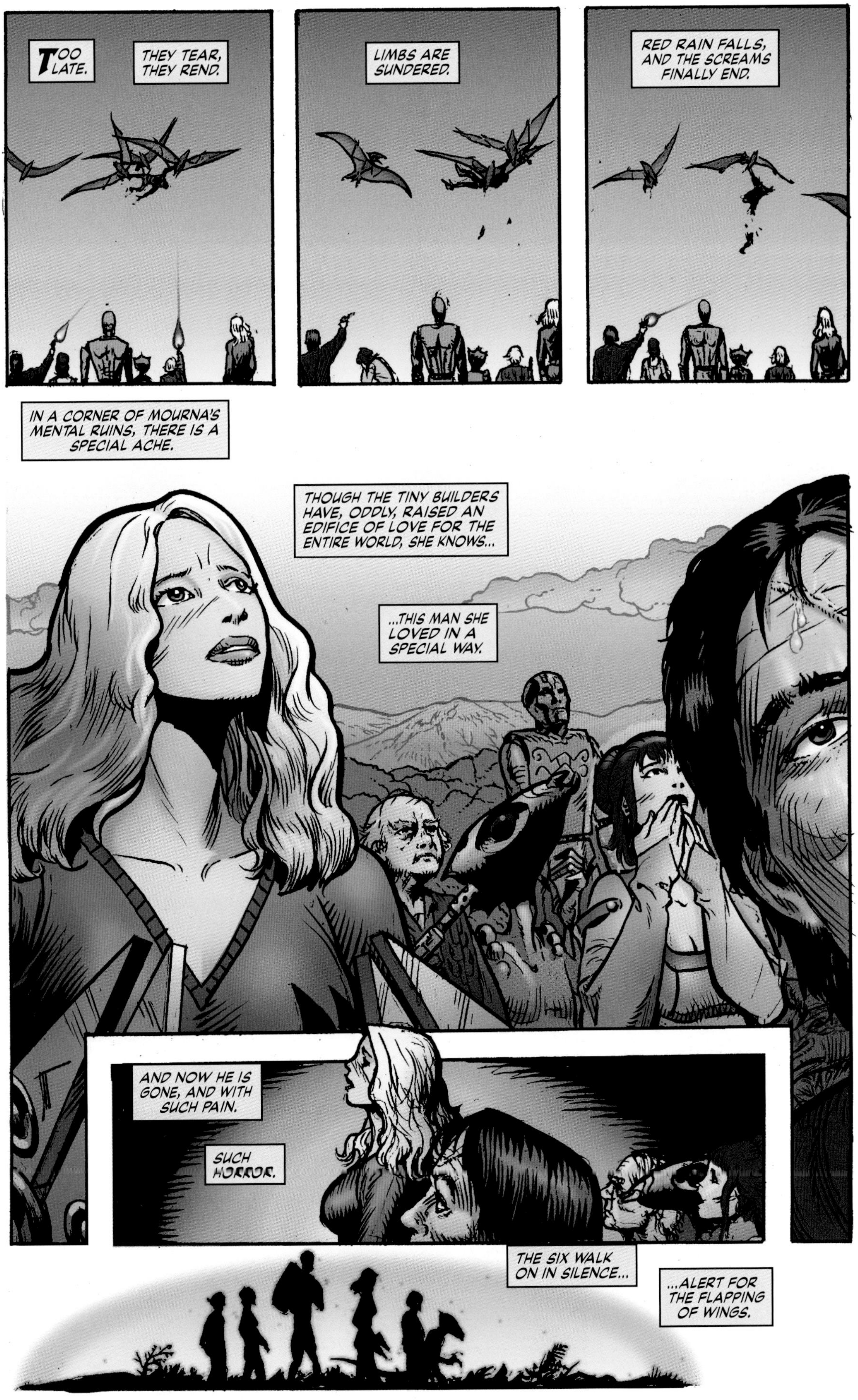
TOO LATE.
THEY TEAR, THEY REND.
LIMBS ARE SUNDERED.
RED RAIN FALLS, AND THE SCREAMS FINALLY END.
IN A CORNER OF MOURNA'S MENTAL RUINS, THERE IS A SPECIAL ACHE.
THOUGH THE TINY BUILDERS HAVE, ODDLY, RAISED AN EDIFICE OF LOVE FOR THE ENTIRE WORLD, SHE KNOWS...
...THIS MAN SHE LOVED IN A SPECIAL WAY.
AND NOW HE IS GONE, AND WITH SUCH PAIN.
SUCH HORROR.
THE SIX WALK ON IN SILENCE...
...ALERT FOR THE FLAPPING OF WINGS.

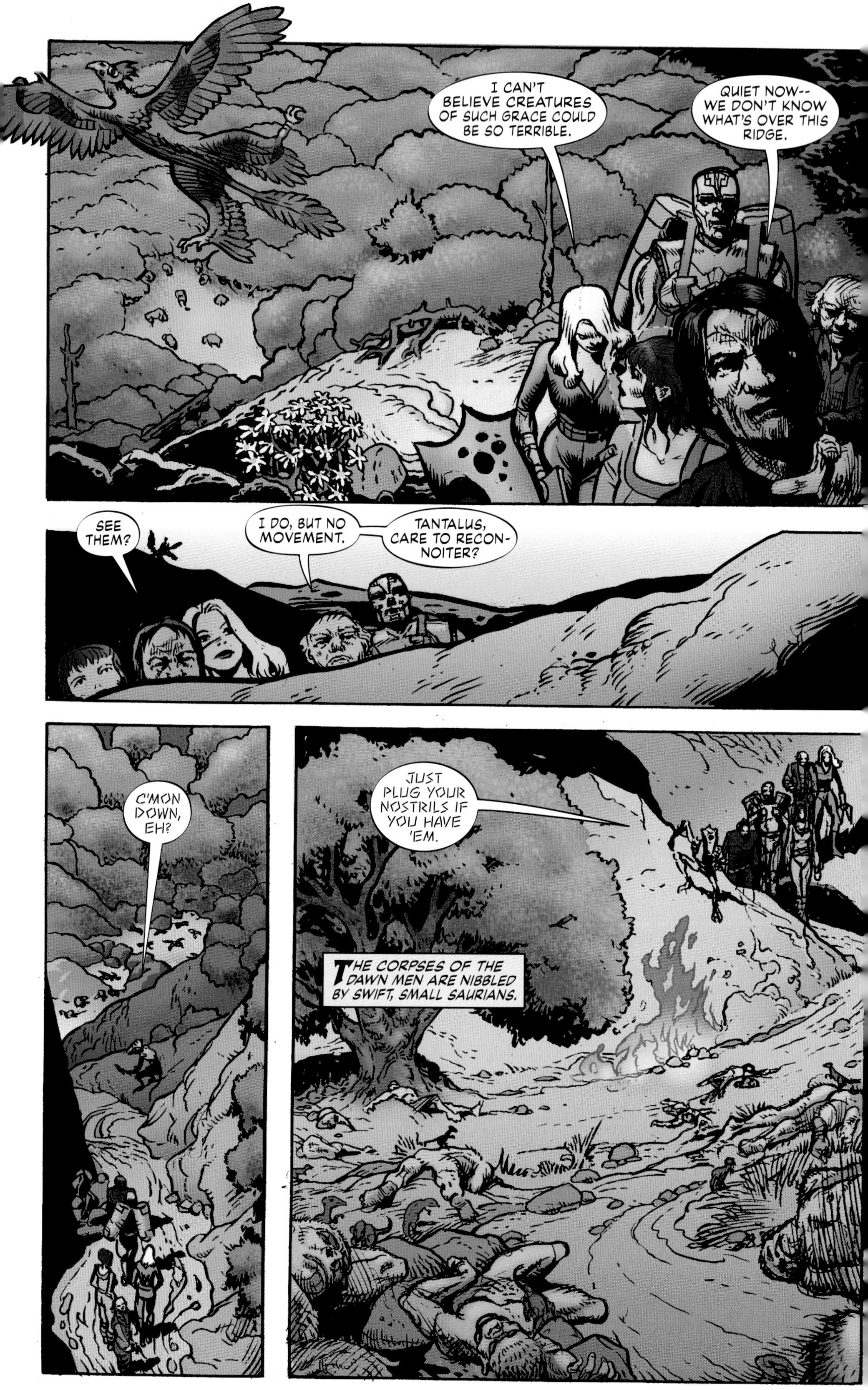
I CAN'T BELIEVE CREATURES OF SUCH GRACE COULD BE SO TERRIBLE.
QUIET NOW-- WE DON'T KNOW WHAT'S OVER THIS RIDGE.
SEE THEM?
I DO, BUT NO MOVEMENT.
TANTALUS, CARE TO RECON-NOITER?
C'MON DOWN, EH?
JUST PLUG YOUR NOSTRILS IF YOU HAVE 'EM.
THE CORPSES OF THE DAWN MEN ARE NIBBLED BY SWIFT, SMALL SAURIANS.

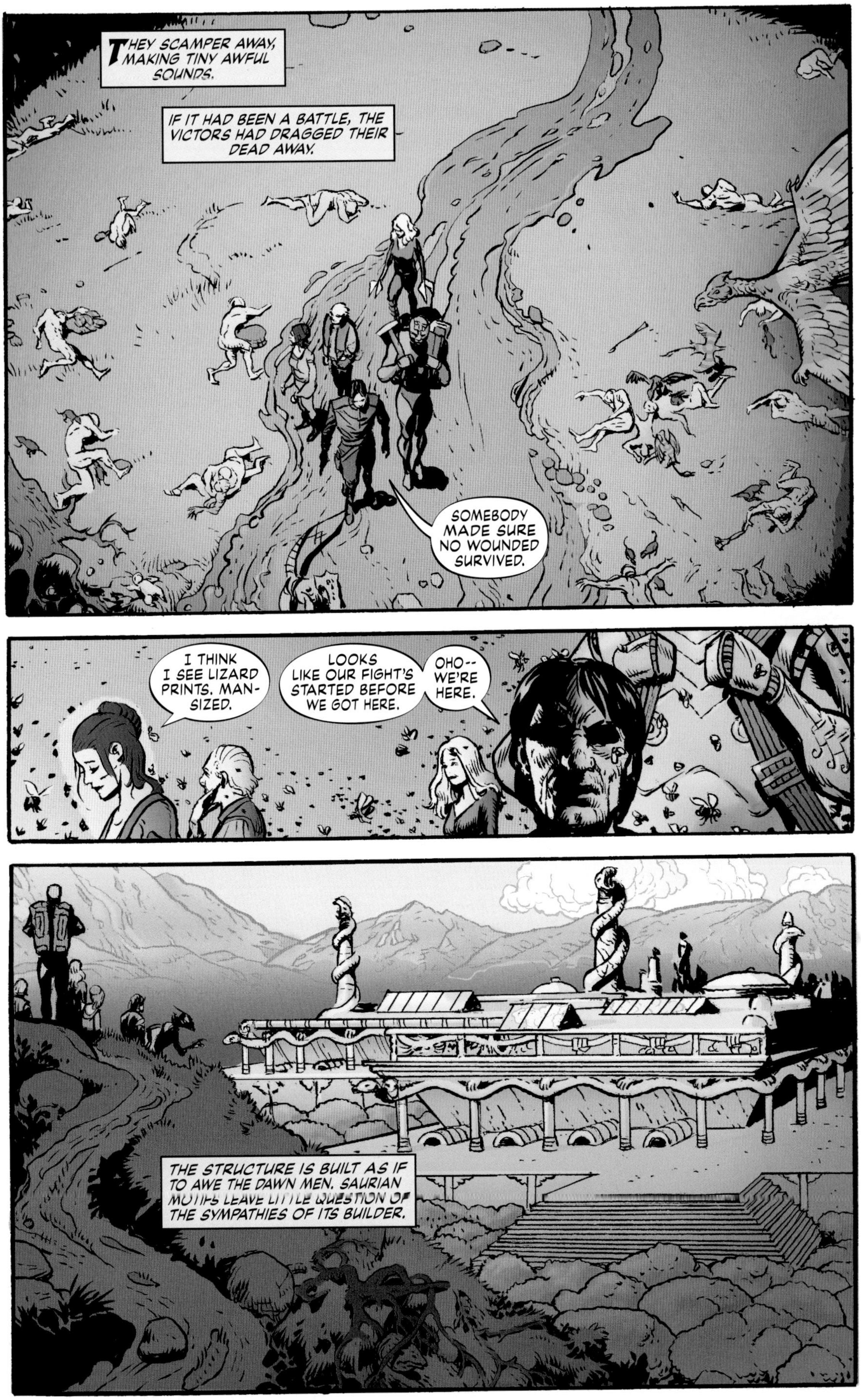
THEY SCAMPER AWAY, MAKING TINY AWFUL SOUNDS.
IF IT HAD BEEN A BATTLE, THE VICTORS HAD DRAGGED THEIR DEAD AWAY.
SOMEBODY MADE SURE NO WOUNDED SURVIVED.
I THINK I SEE LIZARD PRINTS. MAN-SIZED.
LOOKS LIKE OUR FIGHT'S STARTED BEFORE WE GOT HERE.
OHO-- WE'RE HERE.
THE STRUCTURE IS BUILT AS IF TO AWE THE DAWN MEN. SAURIAN MOTIFS LEAVE LITTLE QUESTION OF THE SYMPATHIES OF ITS BUILDER.

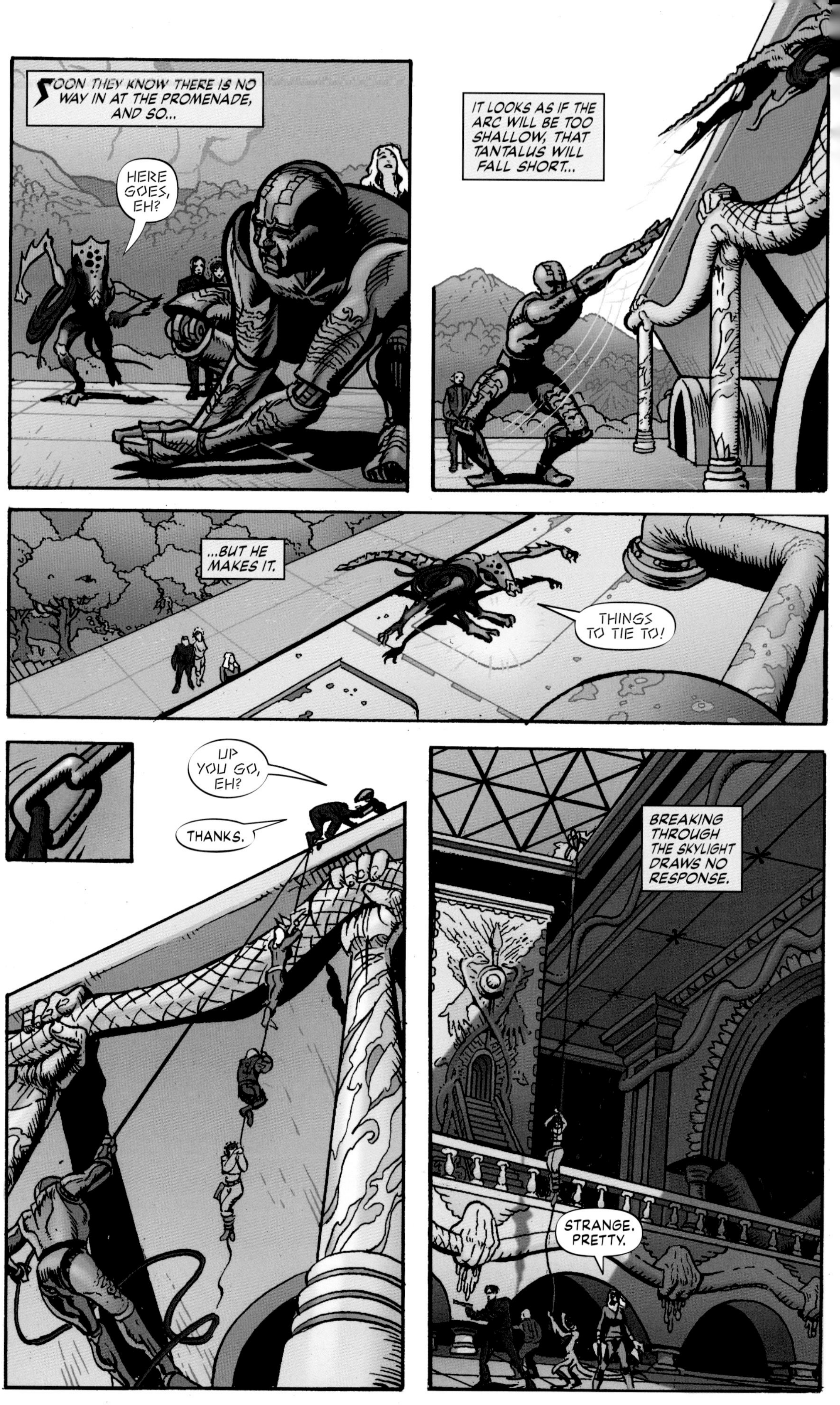
SOON THEY KNOW THERE IS NO WAY IN AT THE PROMENADE, AND SO...
HERE GOES, EH?
IT LOOKS AS IF THE ARC WILL BE TOO SHALLOW, THAT TANTALUS WILL FALL SHORT...
...BUT HE MAKES IT.
THINGS TO TIE TO!
UP YOU GO, EH?
THANKS.
BREAKING THROUGH THE SKYLIGHT DRAWS NO RESPONSE.
STRANGE. PRETTY.

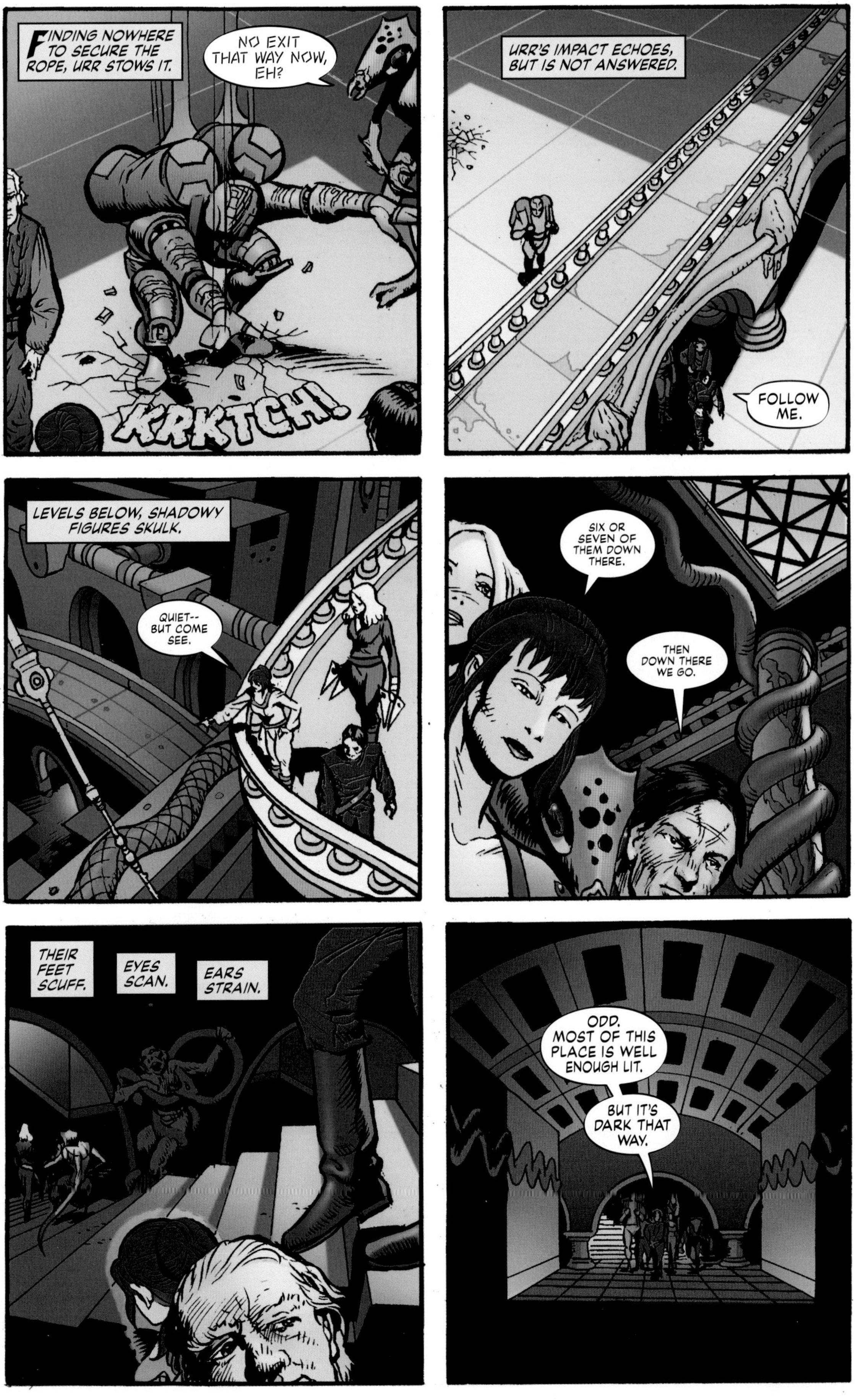
FINDING NOWHERE TO SECURE THE ROPE, URR STOWS IT.
NO EXIT THAT WAY NOW, EH?
KRKTCH!
URR'S IMPACT ECHOES, BUT IS NOT ANSWERED.
FOLLOW ME.
LEVELS BELOW, SHADOWY FIGURES SKULK.
QUIET-- BUT COME SEE.
SIX OR SEVEN OF THEM DOWN THERE.
THEN DOWN THERE WE GO.
THEIR FEET SCUFF.
EYES SCAN.
EARS STRAIN.
ODD. MOST OF THIS PLACE IS WELL ENOUGH LIT.
BUT IT'S DARK THAT WAY.

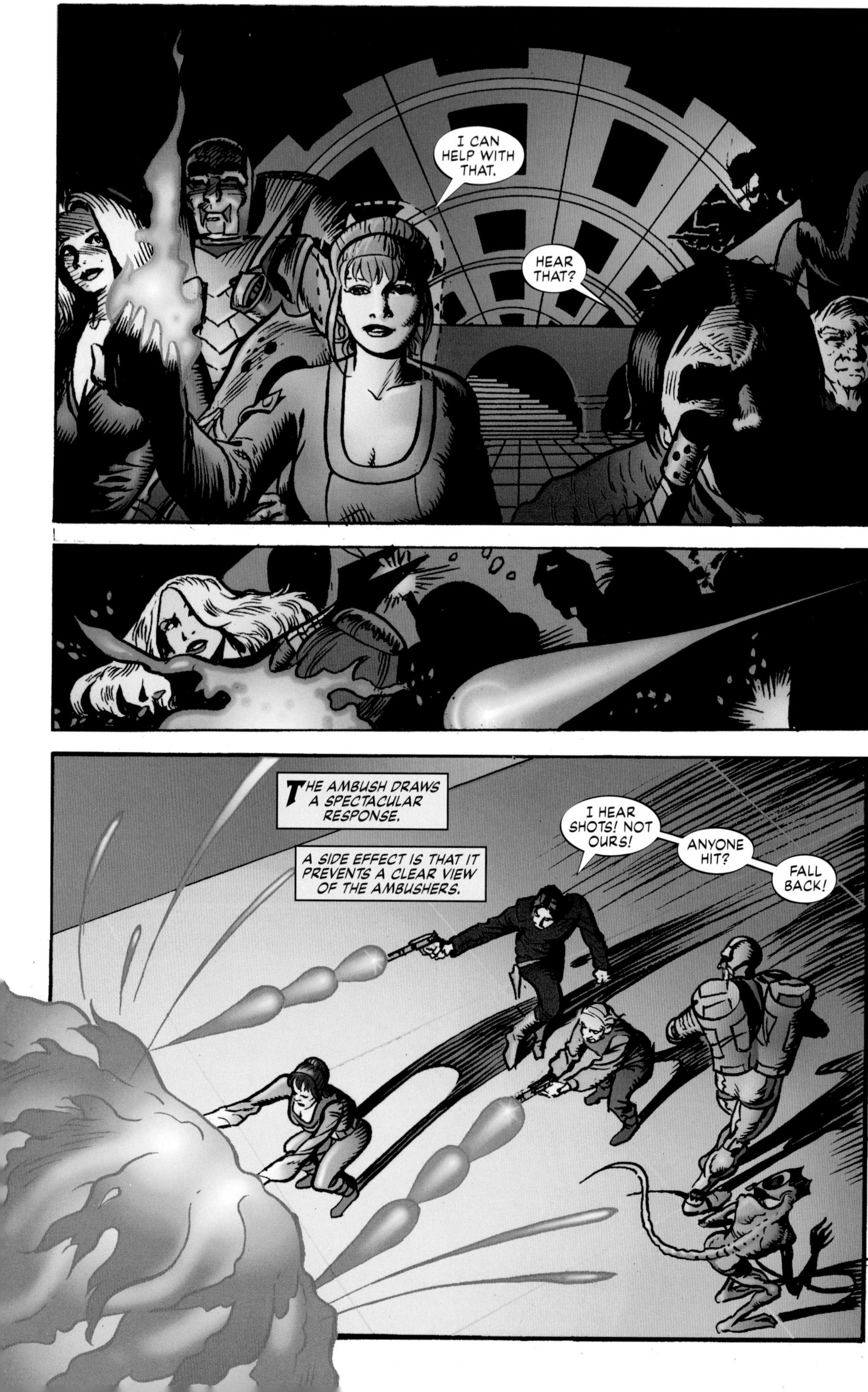
I CAN HELP WITH THAT.
HEAR THAT?
THE AMBUSH DRAWS A SPECTACULAR RESPONSE.
A SIDE EFFECT IS THAT IT PREVENTS A CLEAR VIEW OF THE AMBUSHERS.
I HEAR SHOTS! NOT OURS!
ANYONE HIT?
FALL BACK!

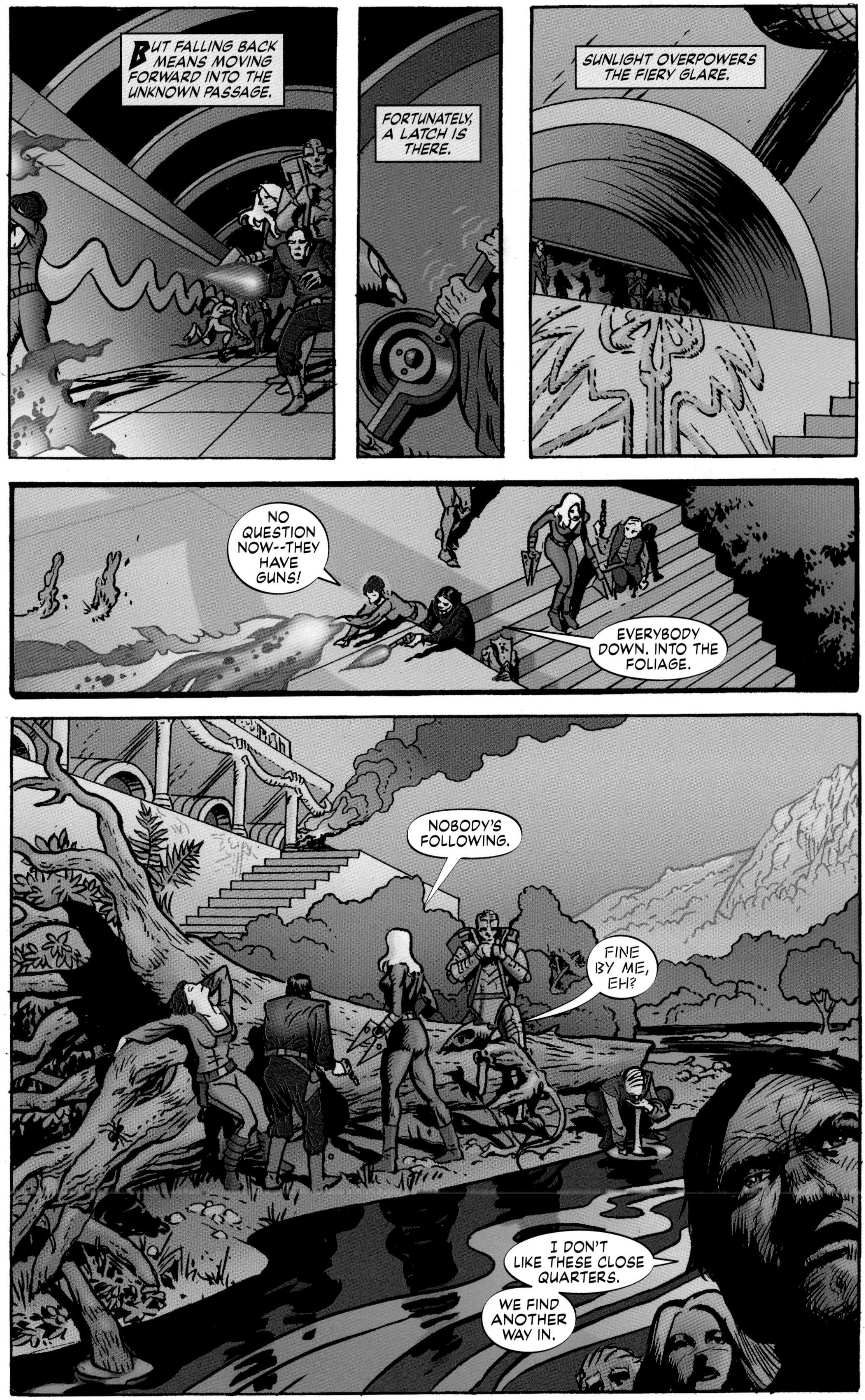
BUT FALLING BACK MEANS MOVING FORWARD INTO THE UNKNOWN PASSAGE.
FORTUNATELY, A LATCH IS THERE.
SUNLIGHT OVERPOWERS THE FIERY GLARE.
NO QUESTION NOW--THEY HAVE GUNS!
EVERYBODY DOWN. INTO THE FOLIAGE.
NOBODY'S FOLLOWING.
FINE BY ME, EH?
I DON'T LIKE THESE CLOSE QUARTERS.
WE FIND ANOTHER WAY IN.

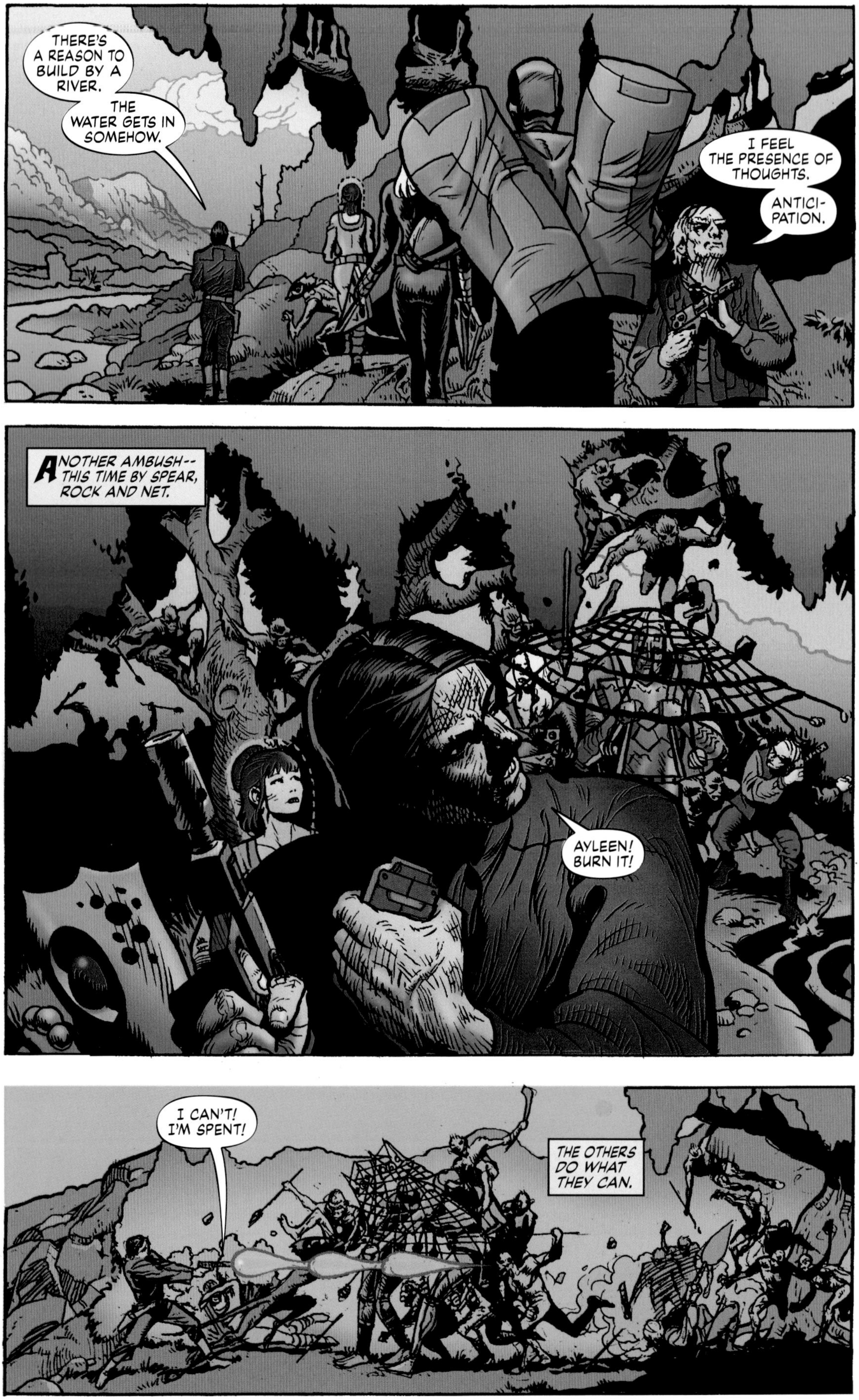
THERE'S A REASON TO BUILD BY A RIVER.
THE WATER GETS IN SOMEHOW.
I FEEL THE PRESENCE OF THOUGHTS.
ANTICI-PATION.
ANOTHER AMBUSH-- THIS TIME BY SPEAR, ROCK AND NET.
AYLEEN! BURN IT!
I CAN'T! I'M SPENT!
THE OTHERS DO WHAT THEY CAN.

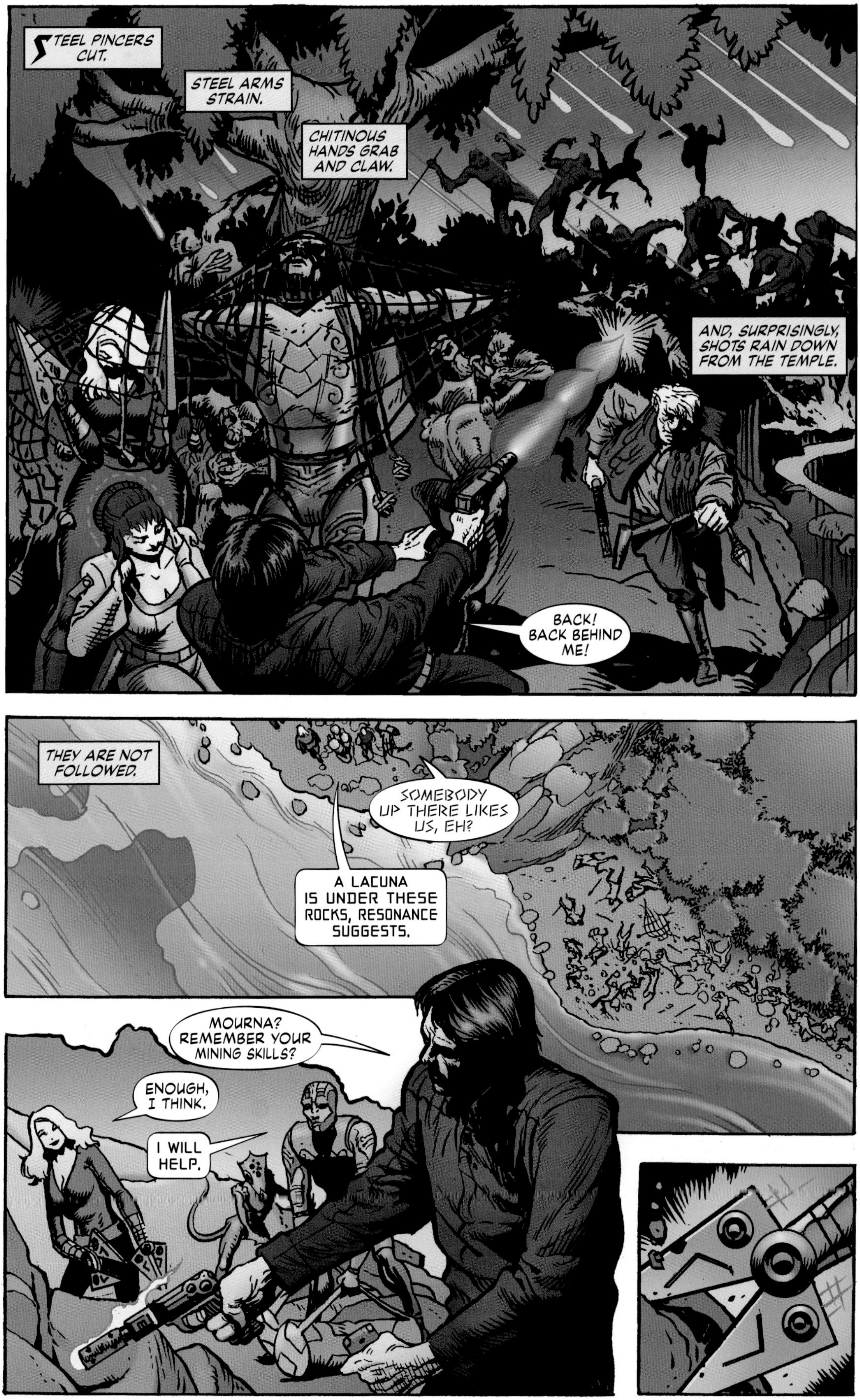
STEEL PINCERS CUT.
STEEL ARMS STRAIN.
CHITINOUS HANDS GRAB AND CLAW.
AND, SURPRISINGLY, SHOTS RAIN DOWN FROM THE TEMPLE.
BACK! BACK BEHIND ME!
THEY ARE NOT FOLLOWED.
SOMEBODY UP THERE LIKES US, EH?
A LACUNA IS UNDER THESE ROCKS, RESONANCE SUGGESTS.
MOURNA? REMEMBER YOUR MINING SKILLS?
ENOUGH, I THINK.
I WILL HELP.

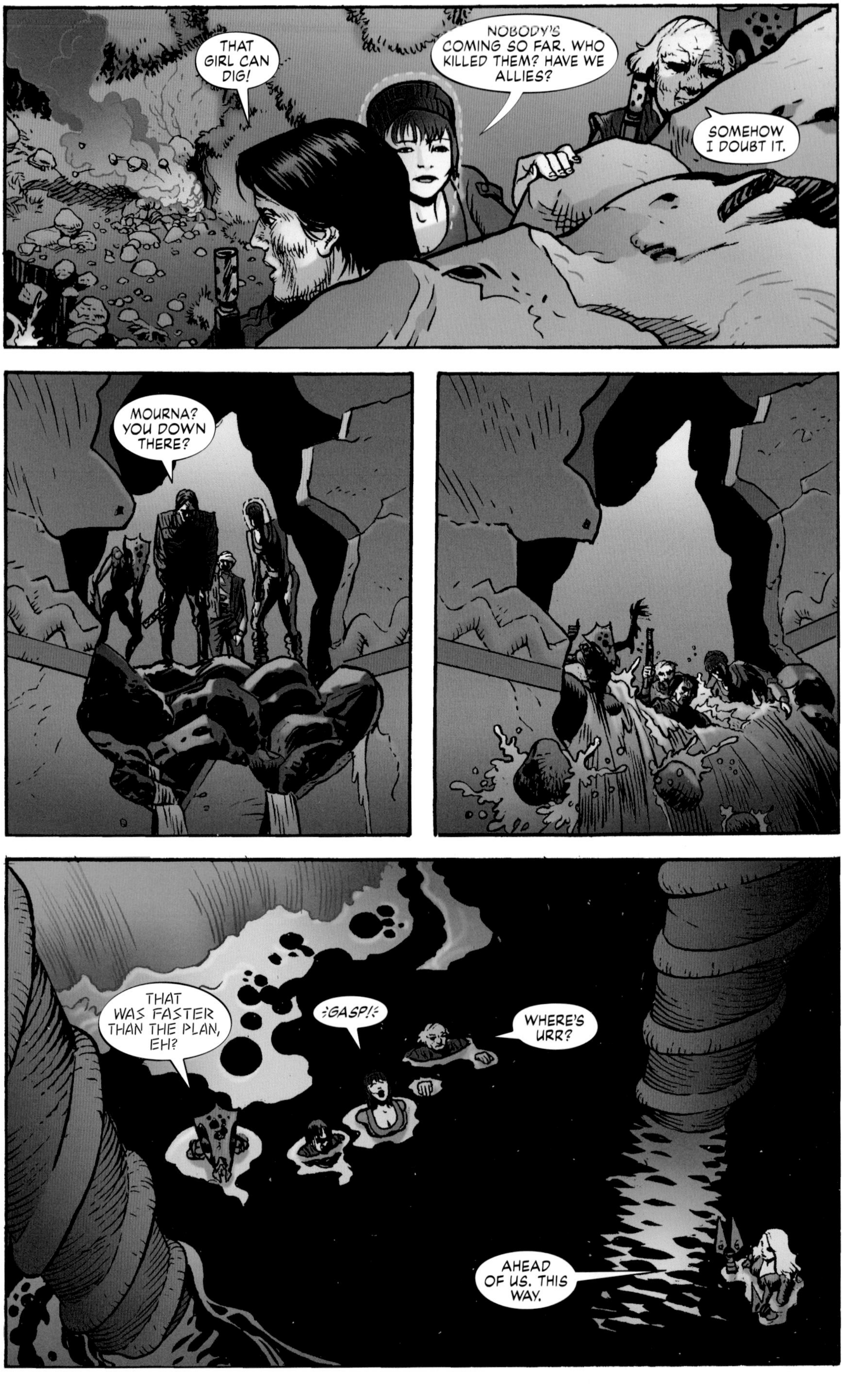
THAT GIRL CAN DIG!
NOBODY'S COMING SO FAR. WHO KILLED THEM? HAVE WE ALLIES?
SOMEHOW I DOUBT IT.
MOURNA? YOU DOWN THERE?
THAT WAS FASTER THAN THE PLAN, EH?
:GASP!:
WHERE'S URR?
AHEAD OF US. THIS WAY.

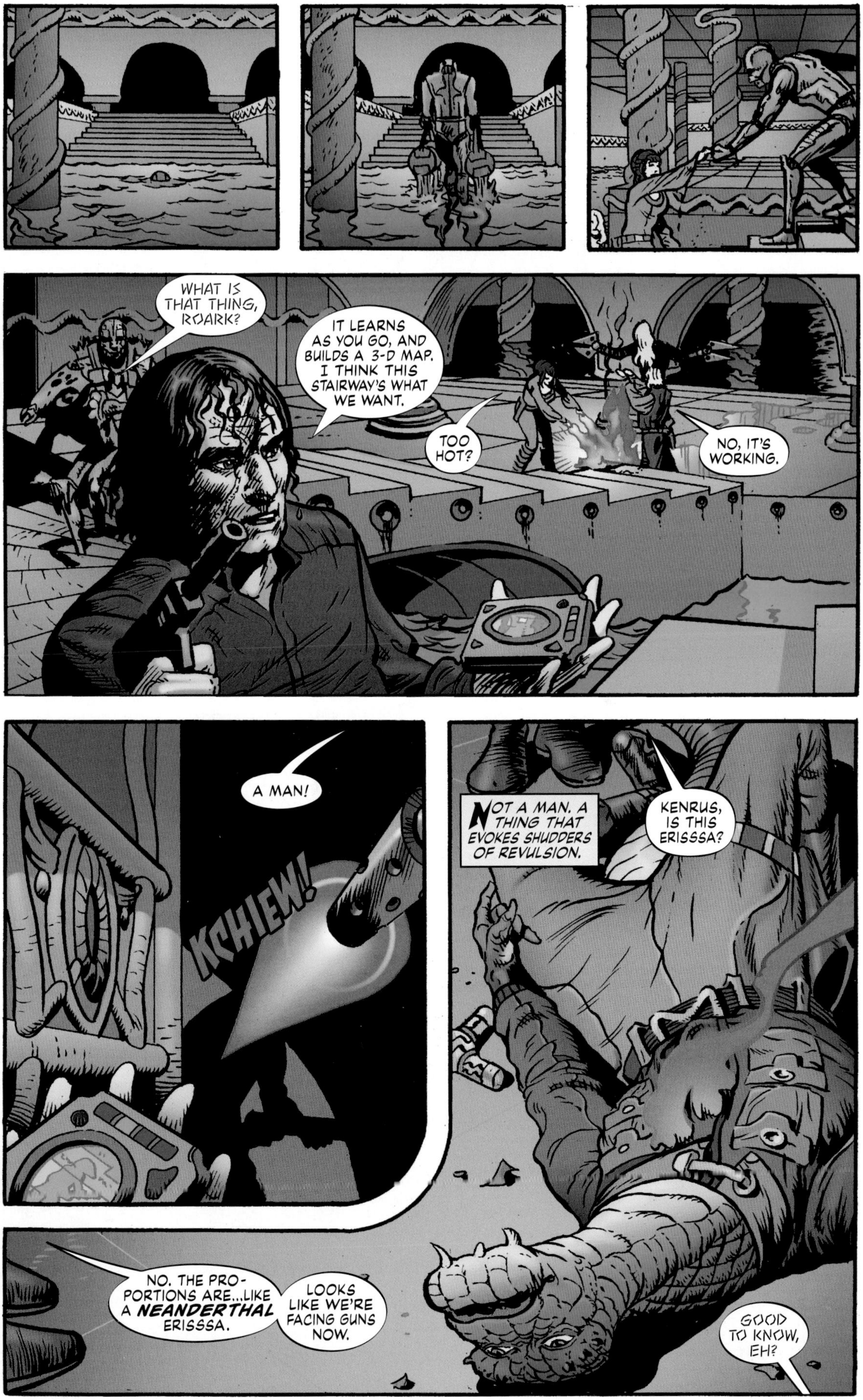
WHAT IS THAT THING, ROARK?
IT LEARNS AS YOU GO, AND BUILDS A 3-D MAP. I THINK THIS STAIRWAY'S WHAT WE WANT.
TOO HOT?
NO, IT'S WORKING.
A MAN!
KCHIEW!
NOT A MAN. A THING THAT EVOKES SHUDDERS OF REVULSION.
KENRUS, IS THIS ERISSSA?
NO. THE PRO-PORTIONS ARE...LIKE A NEANDERTHAL ERISSSA.
LOOKS LIKE WE'RE FACING GUNS NOW.
GOOD TO KNOW, EH?

VISITORS FROM THE FUTURE PERHAPS?

COULD BE. OR OFF-PLANET.

PERHAPS-- WE COULD HAVE TALKED WITH HIM.

THEY SHOOT THE BIGGEST ONE FIRST.

URR!

THEY ARE HARASSED AND SINGED AS THEY DASH THROUGH A LABYRINTH...

...BUT THEY REMAIN UNHURT.

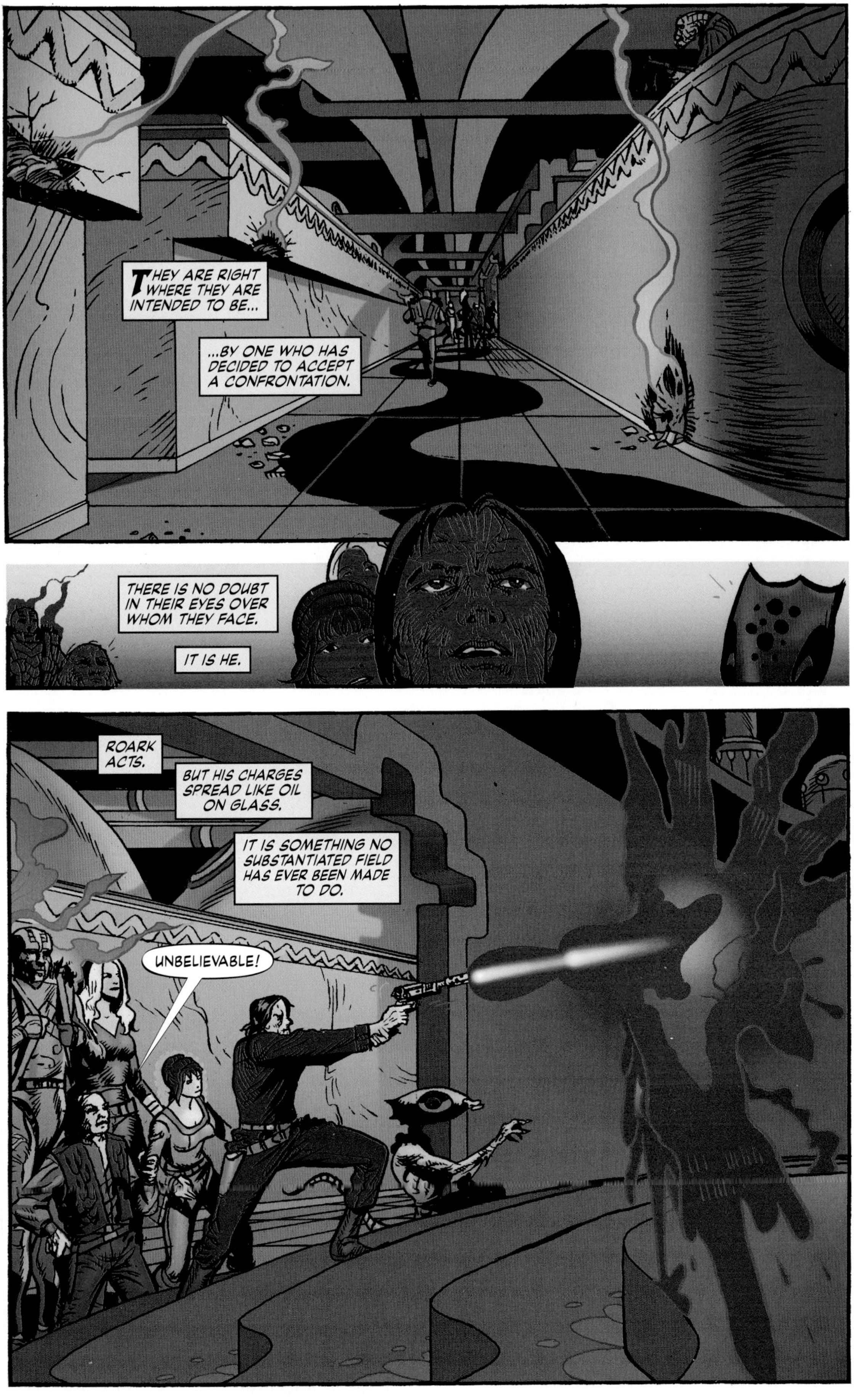
THEY ARE RIGHT WHERE THEY ARE INTENDED TO BE...
...BY ONE WHO HAS DECIDED TO ACCEPT A CONFRONTATION.
THERE IS NO DOUBT IN THEIR EYES OVER WHOM THEY FACE.
IT IS HE.
ROARK ACTS.
BUT HIS CHARGES SPREAD LIKE OIL ON GLASS.
IT IS SOMETHING NO SUBSTANTIATED FIELD HAS EVER BEEN MADE TO DO.
UNBELIEVABLE!

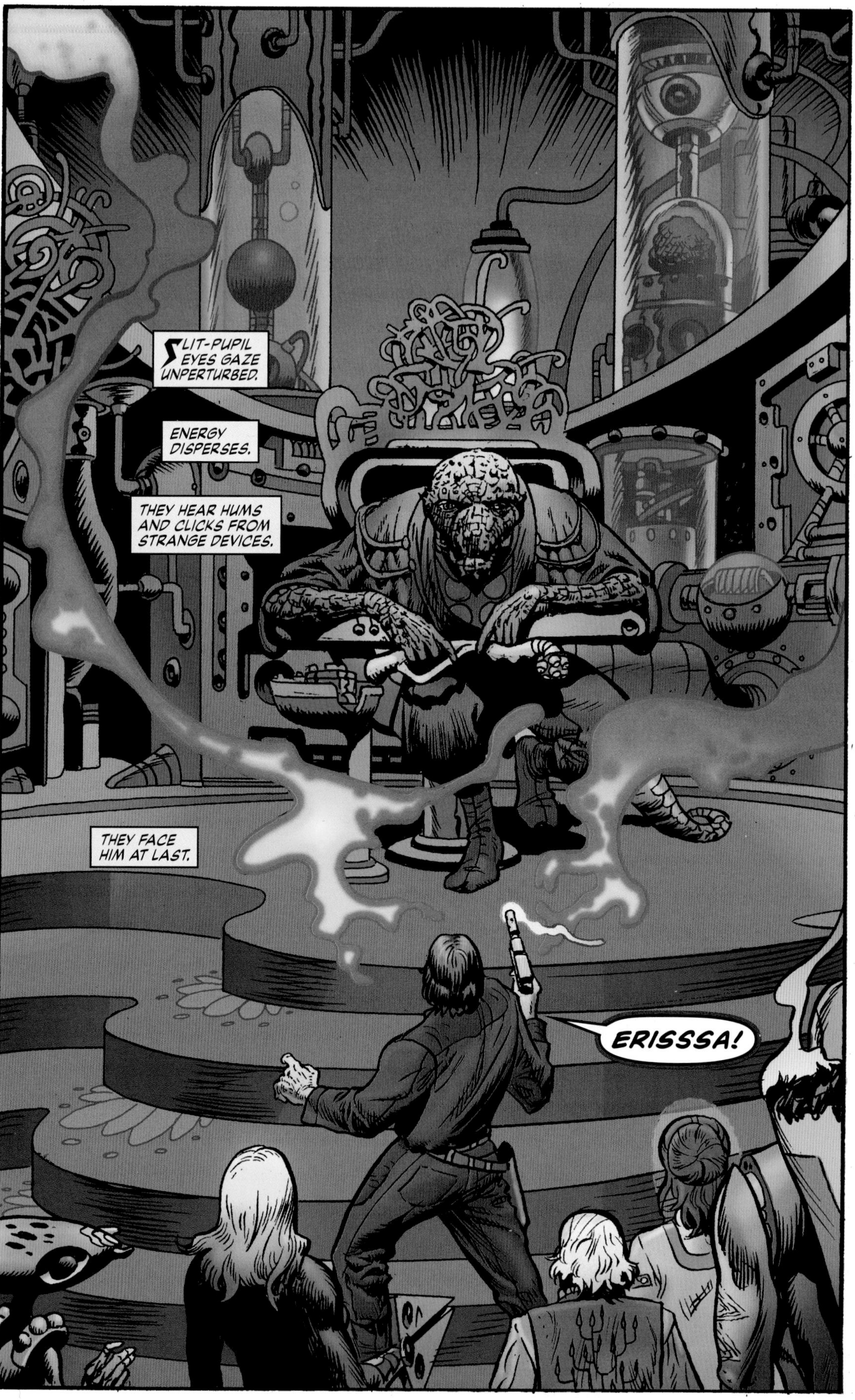
SLIT-PUPIL EYES GAZE UNPERTURBED.
ENERGY DISPERSES.
THEY HEAR HUMS AND CLICKS FROM STRANGE DEVICES.
THEY FACE HIM AT LAST.
ERISSSA!

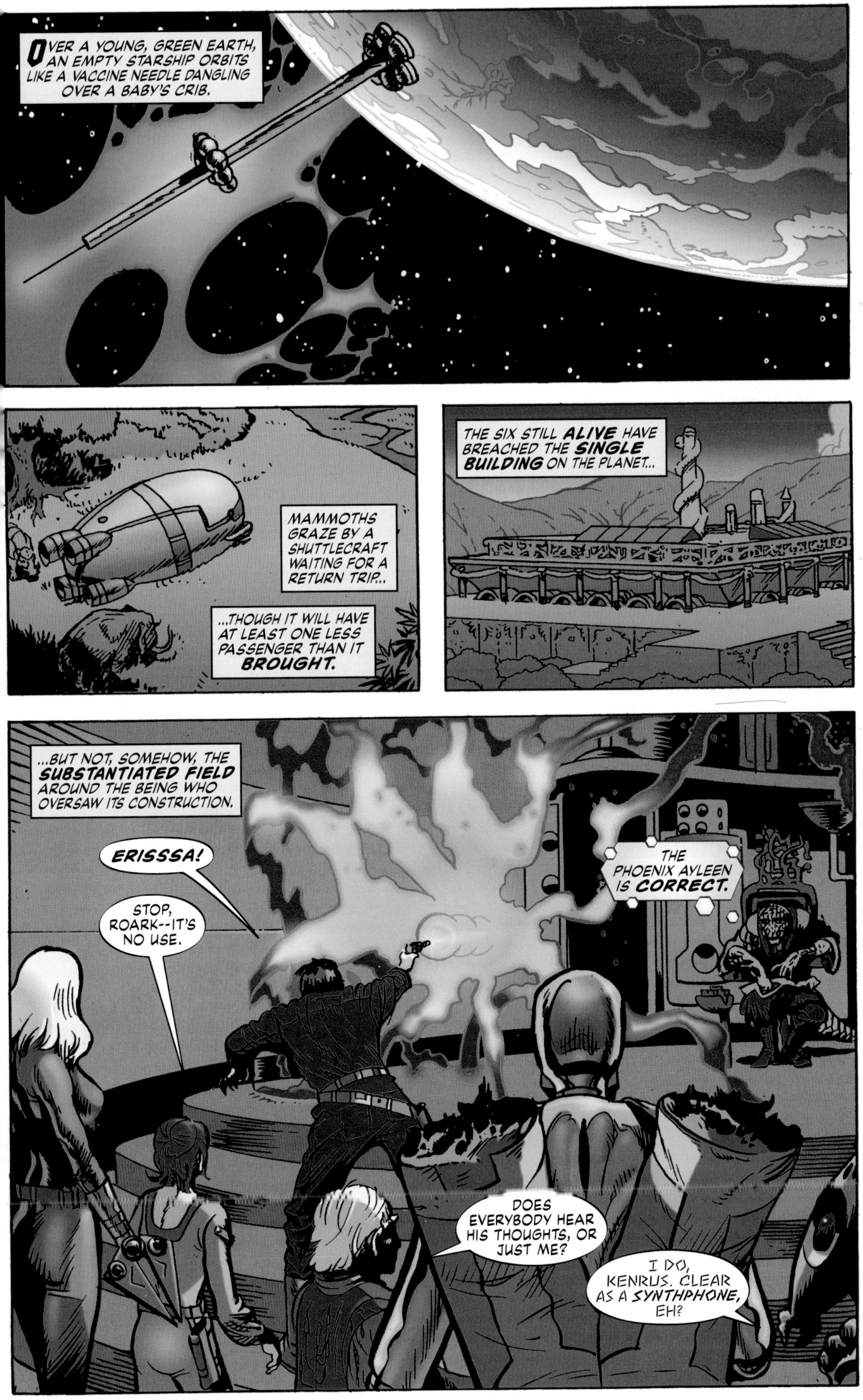
OVER A YOUNG, GREEN EARTH, AN EMPTY STARSHIP ORBITS LIKE A VACCINE NEEDLE DANGLING OVER A BABY'S CRIB.
MAMMOTHS GRAZE BY A SHUTTLECRAFT WAITING FOR A RETURN TRIP...
...THOUGH IT WILL HAVE AT LEAST ONE LESS PASSENGER THAN IT BROUGHT.
THE SIX STILL ALIVE HAVE BREACHED THE SINGLE BUILDING ON THE PLANET...
...BUT NOT, SOMEHOW, THE SUBSTANTIATED FIELD AROUND THE BEING WHO OVERSAW ITS CONSTRUCTION.
ERISSSA!
STOP, ROARK--IT'S NO USE.
THE PHOENIX AYLEEN IS CORRECT.
DOES EVERYBODY HEAR HIS THOUGHTS, OR JUST ME?
I DO, KENRUS. CLEAR AS A SYNTHPHONE, EH?

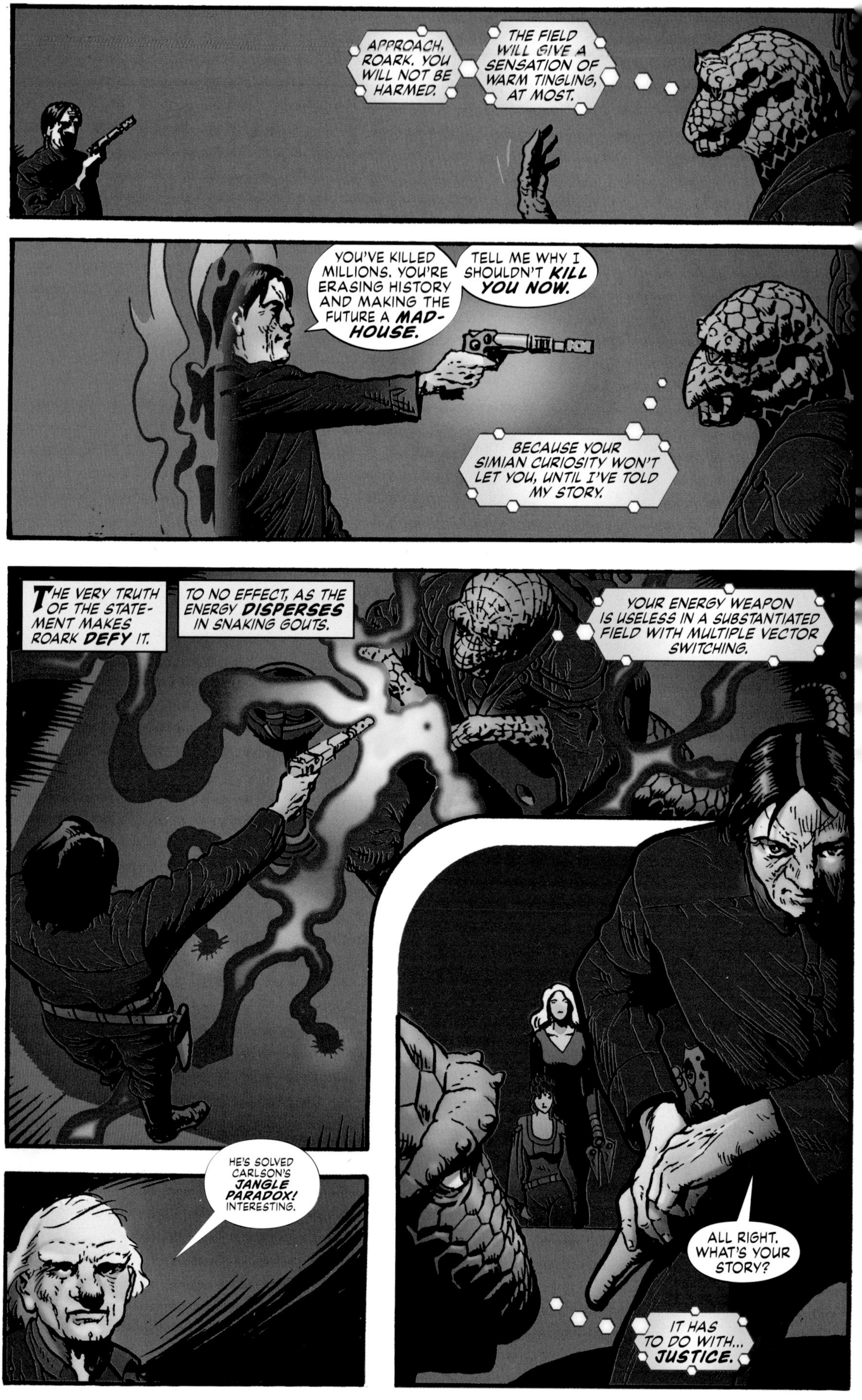
APPROACH, ROARK. YOU WILL NOT BE HARMED.
THE FIELD WILL GIVE A SENSATION OF WARM TINGLING, AT MOST.
YOU'VE KILLED MILLIONS. YOU'RE ERASING HISTORY AND MAKING THE FUTURE A MAD-HOUSE.
TELL ME WHY I SHOULDN'T KILL YOU NOW.
BECAUSE YOUR SIMIAN CURIOSITY WON'T LET YOU, UNTIL I'VE TOLD MY STORY.
THE VERY TRUTH OF THE STATE-MENT MAKES ROARK DEFY IT.
TO NO EFFECT, AS THE ENERGY DISPERSES IN SNAKING GOUTS.
YOUR ENERGY WEAPON IS USELESS IN A SUBSTANTIATED FIELD WITH MULTIPLE VECTOR SWITCHING.
HE'S SOLVED CARLSON'S JANGLE PARADOX! INTERESTING.
ALL RIGHT. WHAT'S YOUR STORY?
IT HAS TO DO WITH... JUSTICE.

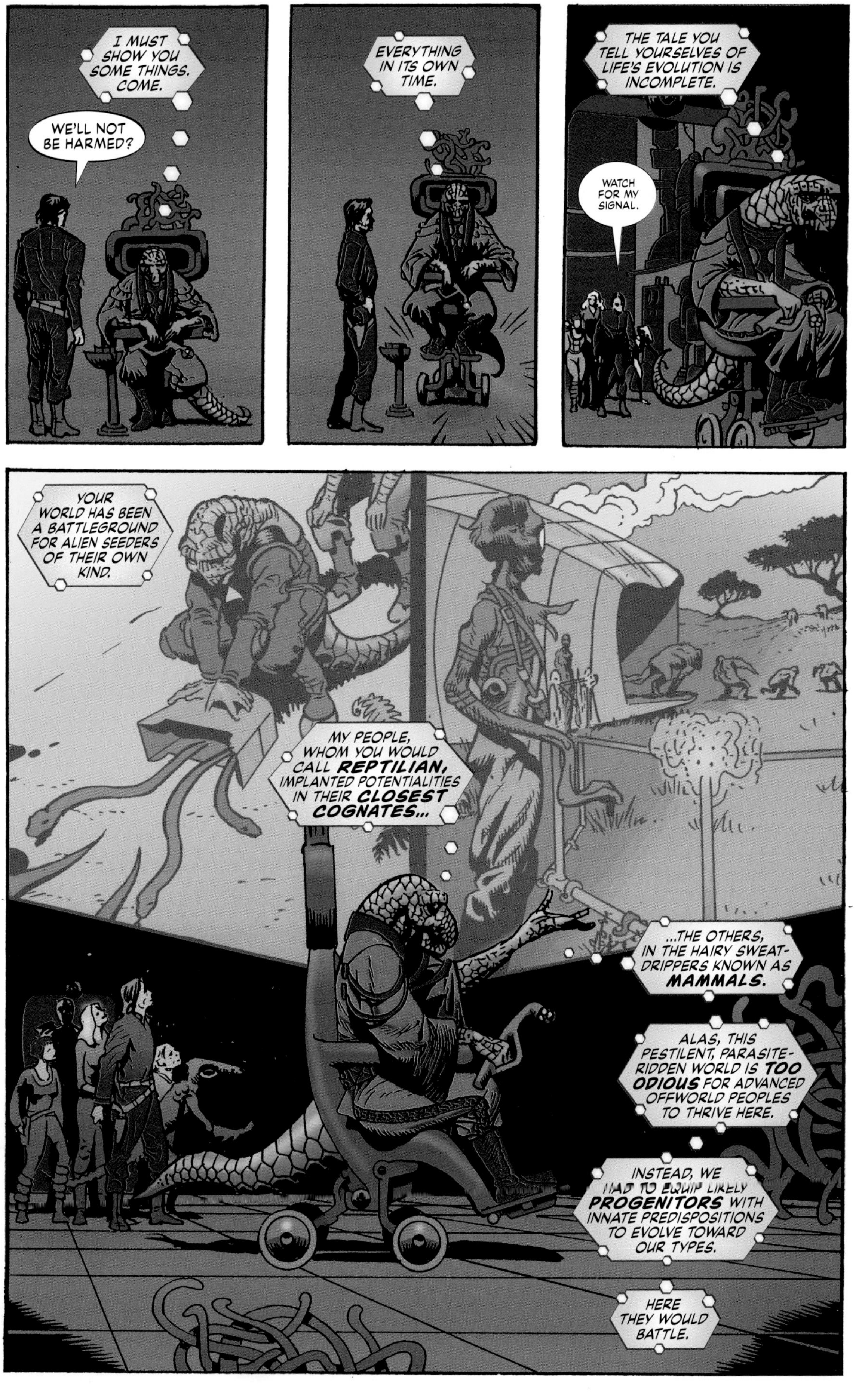
I MUST SHOW YOU SOME THINGS. COME.
WE'LL NOT BE HARMED?
EVERYTHING IN ITS OWN TIME.
THE TALE YOU TELL YOURSELVES OF LIFE'S EVOLUTION IS INCOMPLETE.
WATCH FOR MY SIGNAL.
YOUR WORLD HAS BEEN A BATTLEGROUND FOR ALIEN SEEDERS OF THEIR OWN KIND.
MY PEOPLE, WHOM YOU WOULD CALL REPTILIAN, IMPLANTED POTENTIALITIES IN THEIR CLOSEST COGNATES...
...THE OTHERS, IN THE HAIRY SWEAT-DRIPPERS KNOWN AS MAMMALS.
ALAS, THIS PESTILENT, PARASITE-RIDDEN WORLD IS TOO ODIOUS FOR ADVANCED OFFWORLD PEOPLES TO THRIVE HERE.
INSTEAD, WE HAD TO EQUIP LIKELY PROGENITORS WITH INNATE PREDISPOSITIONS TO EVOLVE TOWARD OUR TYPES.
HERE THEY WOULD BATTLE.

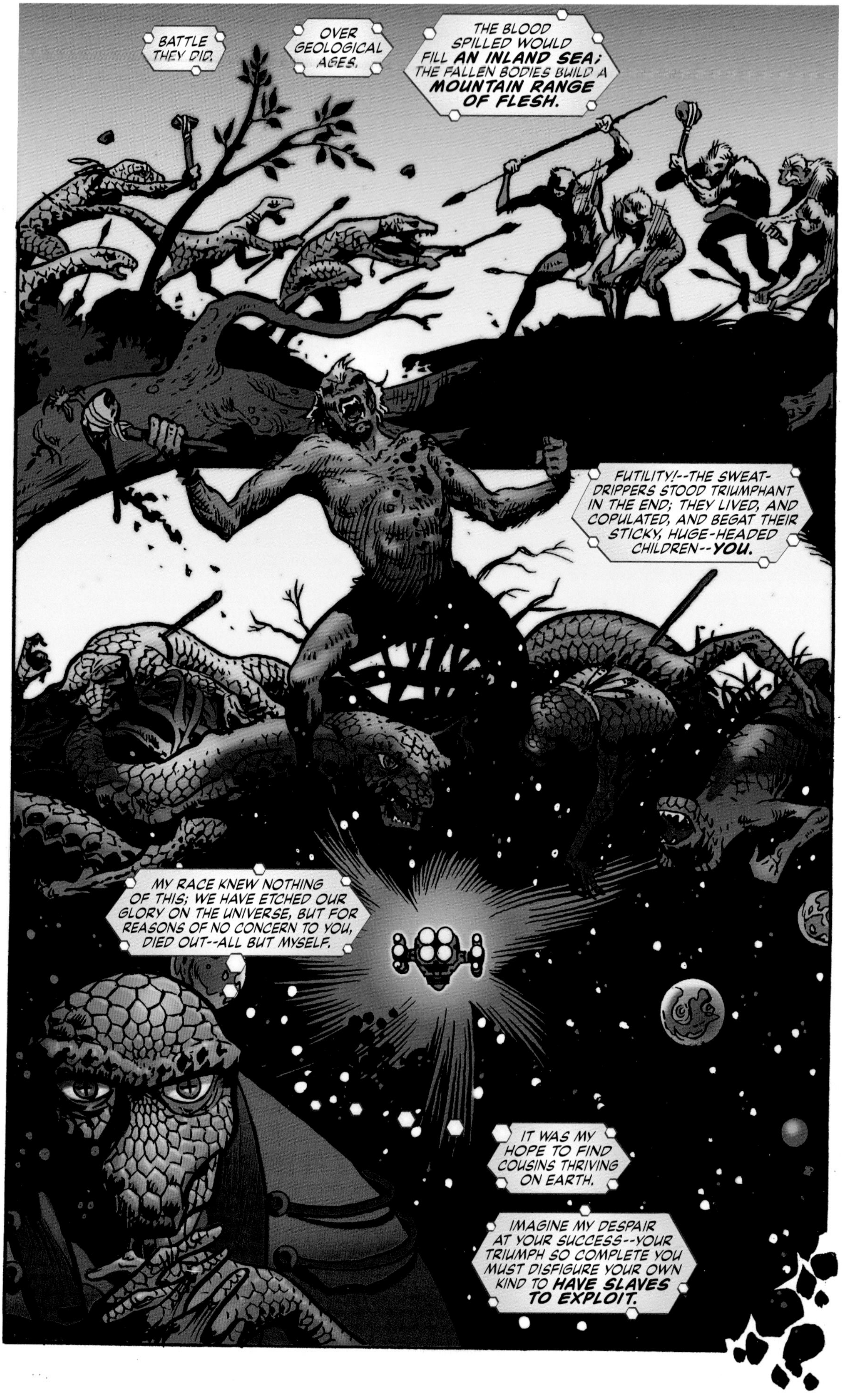
BATTLE THEY DID.
OVER GEOLOGICAL AGES.
THE BLOOD SPILLED WOULD FILL **AN INLAND SEA;** THE FALLEN BODIES BUILD A **MOUNTAIN RANGE OF FLESH.**
FUTILITY!--THE SWEAT-DRIPPERS STOOD TRIUMPHANT IN THE END; THEY LIVED, AND COPULATED, AND BEGAT THEIR STICKY, HUGE-HEADED CHILDREN--**YOU.**
MY RACE KNEW NOTHING OF THIS; WE HAVE ETCHED OUR GLORY ON THE UNIVERSE, BUT FOR REASONS OF NO CONCERN TO YOU, DIED OUT--ALL BUT MYSELF.
IT WAS MY HOPE TO FIND COUSINS THRIVING ON EARTH.
IMAGINE MY DESPAIR AT YOUR SUCCESS--YOUR TRIUMPH SO COMPLETE YOU MUST DISFIGURE YOUR OWN KIND TO **HAVE SLAVES TO EXPLOIT.**

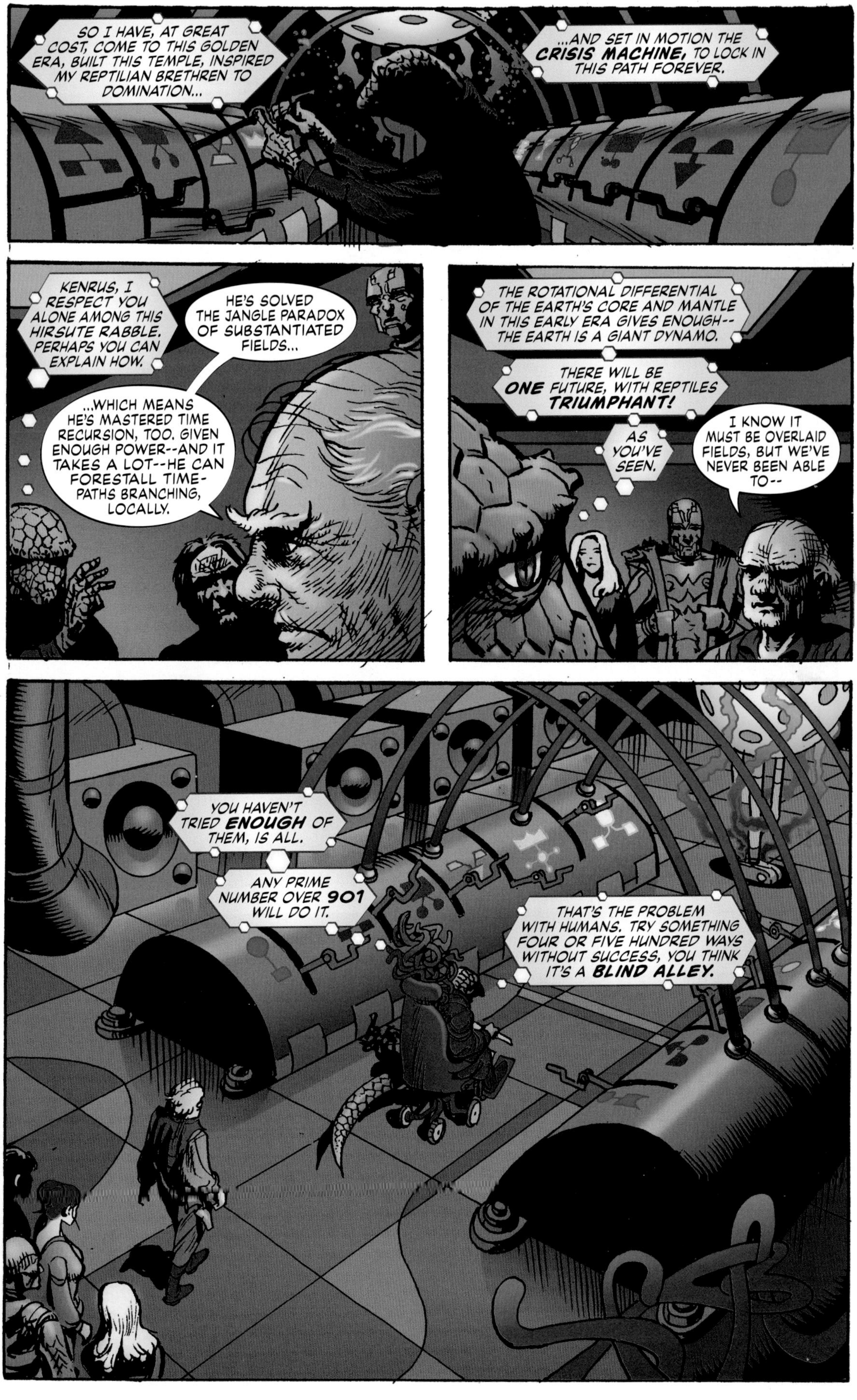
SO I HAVE, AT GREAT COST, COME TO THIS GOLDEN ERA, BUILT THIS TEMPLE, INSPIRED MY REPTILIAN BRETHREN TO DOMINATION...
...AND SET IN MOTION THE **CRISIS MACHINE,** TO LOCK IN THIS PATH FOREVER.
KENRUS, I RESPECT YOU ALONE AMONG THIS HIRSUTE RABBLE. PERHAPS YOU CAN EXPLAIN HOW.
HE'S SOLVED THE JANGLE PARADOX OF SUBSTANTIATED FIELDS...
...WHICH MEANS HE'S MASTERED TIME RECURSION, TOO. GIVEN ENOUGH POWER--AND IT TAKES A LOT--HE CAN FORESTALL TIME-PATHS BRANCHING, LOCALLY.
THE ROTATIONAL DIFFERENTIAL OF THE EARTH'S CORE AND MANTLE IN THIS EARLY ERA GIVES ENOUGH-- THE EARTH IS A GIANT DYNAMO.
THERE WILL BE **ONE** FUTURE, WITH REPTILES **TRIUMPHANT!**
AS YOU'VE SEEN.
I KNOW IT MUST BE OVERLAID FIELDS, BUT WE'VE NEVER BEEN ABLE TO--
YOU HAVEN'T TRIED **ENOUGH** OF THEM, IS ALL.
ANY PRIME NUMBER OVER **901** WILL DO IT.
THAT'S THE PROBLEM WITH HUMANS. TRY SOMETHING FOUR OR FIVE HUNDRED WAYS WITHOUT SUCCESS, YOU THINK IT'S A **BLIND ALLEY.**

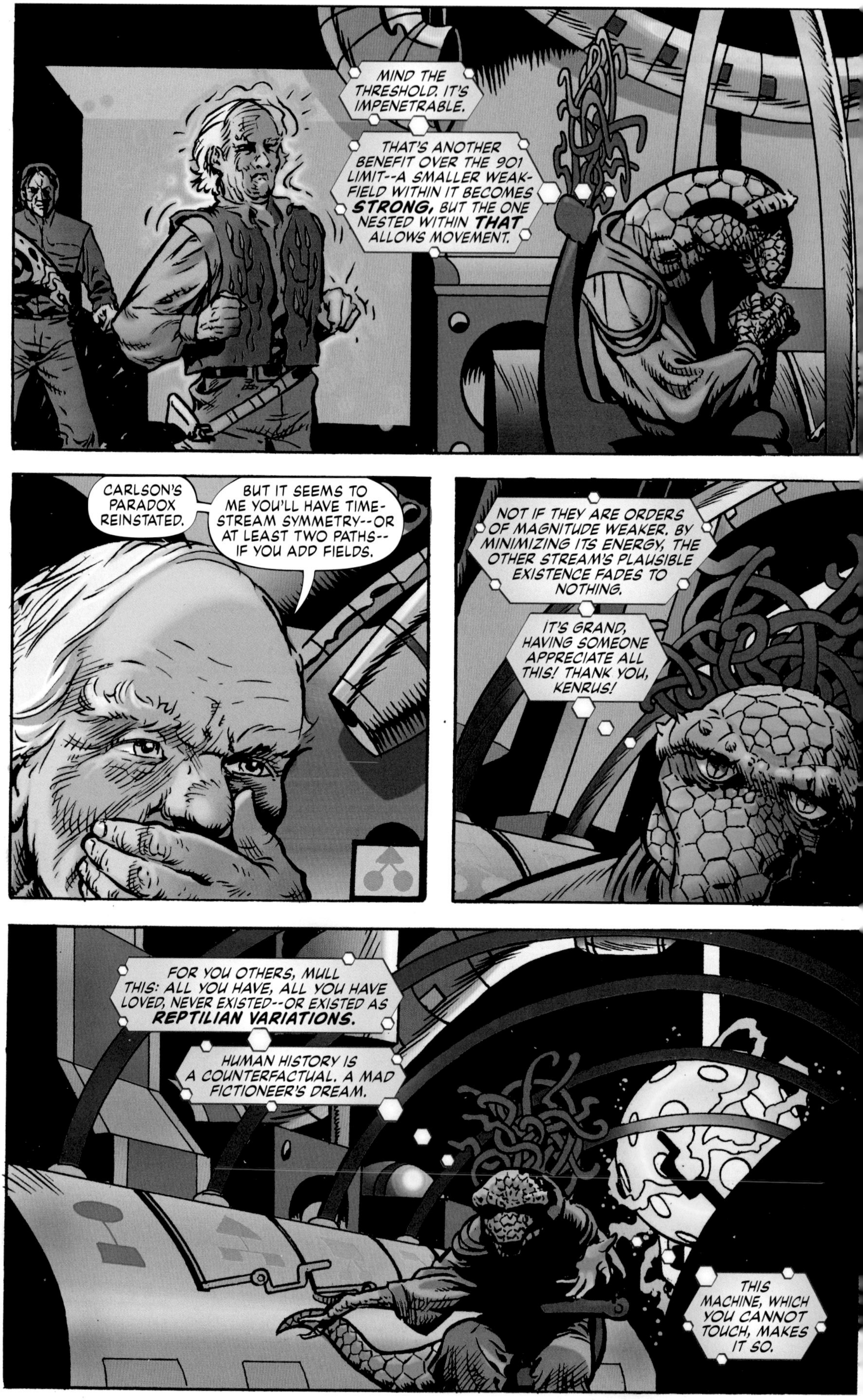
MIND THE THRESHOLD. IT'S IMPENETRABLE.
THAT'S ANOTHER BENEFIT OVER THE 901 LIMIT--A SMALLER WEAK-FIELD WITHIN IT BECOMES **STRONG,** BUT THE ONE NESTED WITHIN **THAT** ALLOWS MOVEMENT.
CARLSON'S PARADOX REINSTATED.
BUT IT SEEMS TO ME YOU'LL HAVE TIME-STREAM SYMMETRY--OR AT LEAST TWO PATHS--IF YOU ADD FIELDS.
NOT IF THEY ARE ORDERS OF MAGNITUDE WEAKER. BY MINIMIZING ITS ENERGY, THE OTHER STREAM'S PLAUSIBLE EXISTENCE FADES TO NOTHING.
IT'S GRAND, HAVING SOMEONE APPRECIATE ALL THIS! THANK YOU, KENRUS!
FOR YOU OTHERS, MULL THIS: ALL YOU HAVE, ALL YOU HAVE LOVED, NEVER EXISTED--OR EXISTED AS **REPTILIAN VARIATIONS.**
HUMAN HISTORY IS A COUNTERFACTUAL. A MAD FICTIONEER'S DREAM.
THIS MACHINE, WHICH YOU CANNOT TOUCH, MAKES IT SO.

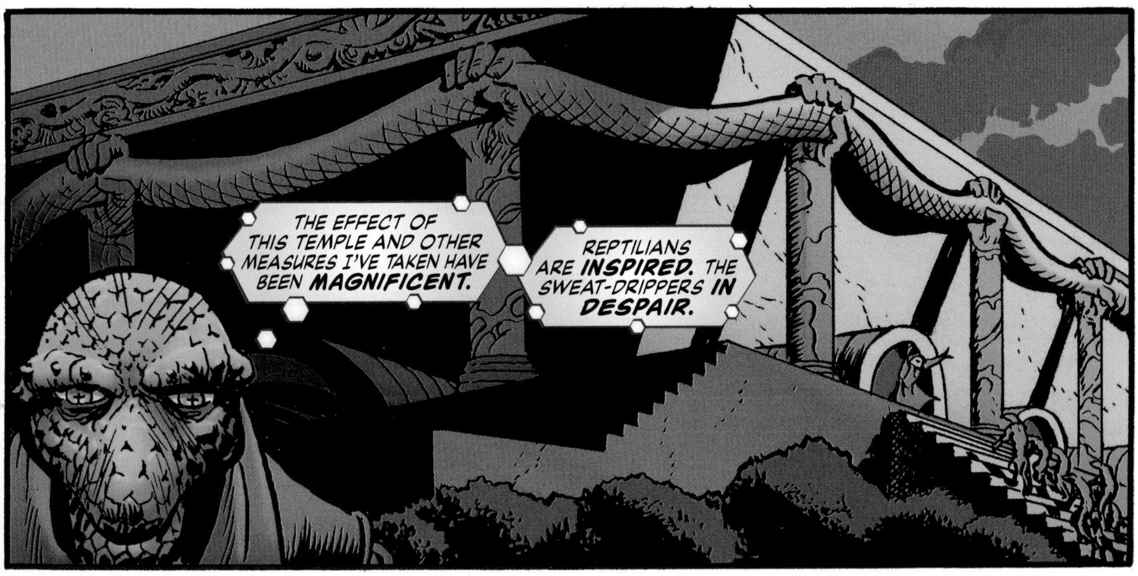
THE EFFECT OF THIS TEMPLE AND OTHER MEASURES I'VE TAKEN HAVE BEEN MAGNIFICENT.
REPTILIANS ARE INSPIRED. THE SWEAT-DRIPPERS IN DESPAIR.

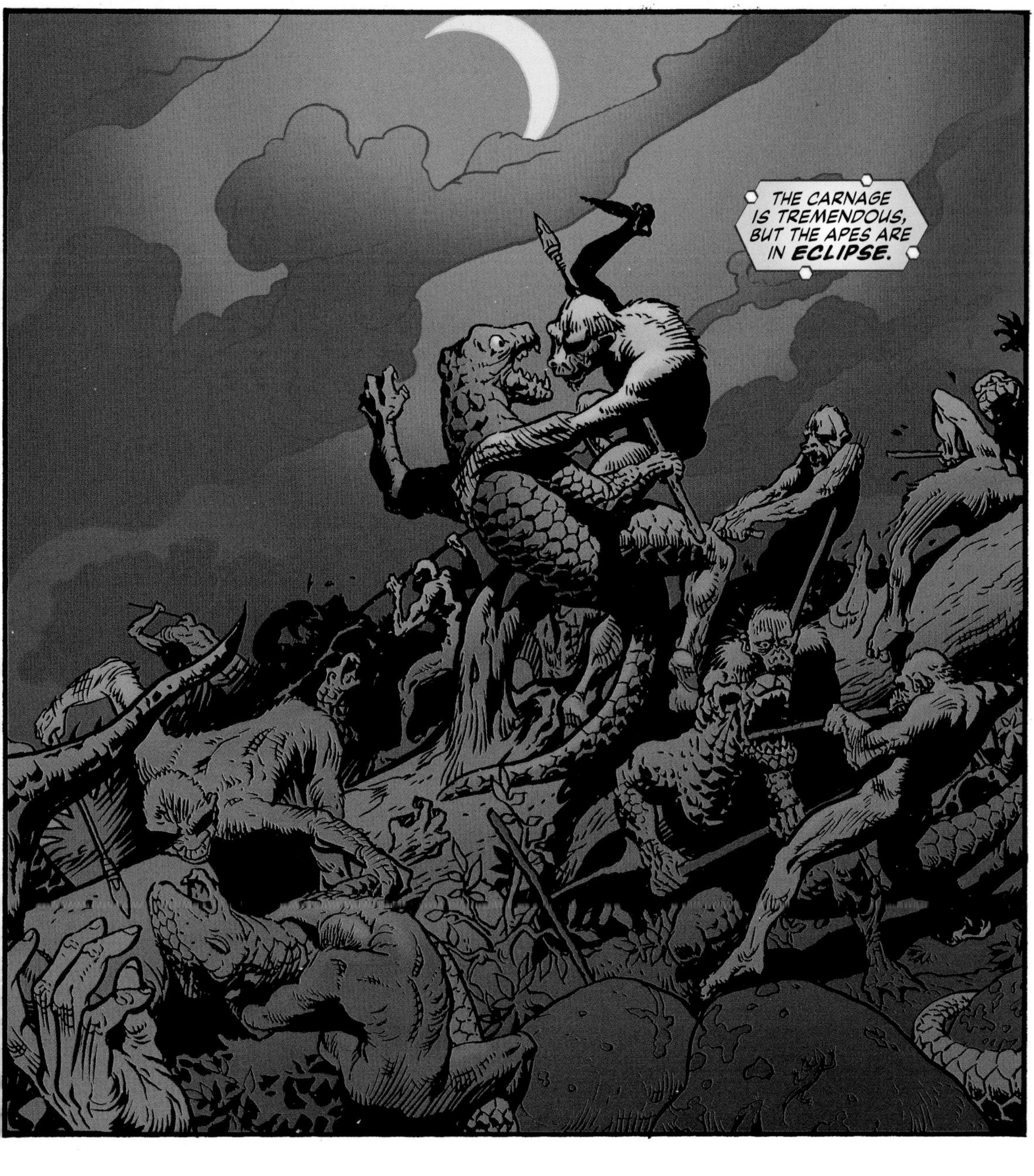
THE CARNAGE IS TREMENDOUS, BUT THE APES ARE IN ECLIPSE.

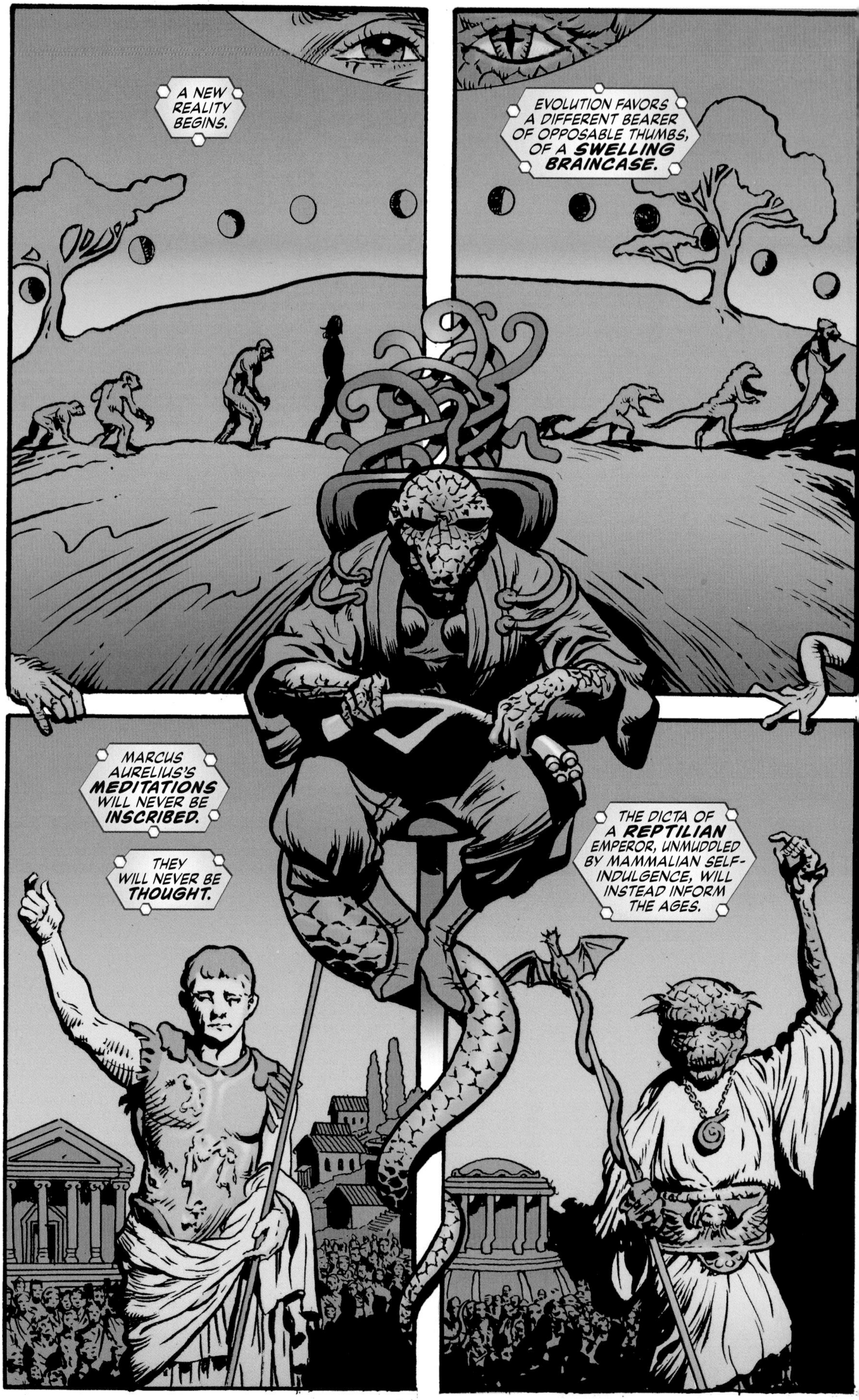
A NEW REALITY BEGINS.
EVOLUTION FAVORS A DIFFERENT BEARER OF OPPOSABLE THUMBS, OF A SWELLING BRAINCASE.
MARCUS AURELIUS'S MEDITATIONS WILL NEVER BE INSCRIBED.
THEY WILL NEVER BE THOUGHT.
THE DICTA OF A REPTILIAN EMPEROR, UNMUDDLED BY MAMMALIAN SELF-INDULGENCE, WILL INSTEAD INFORM THE AGES.

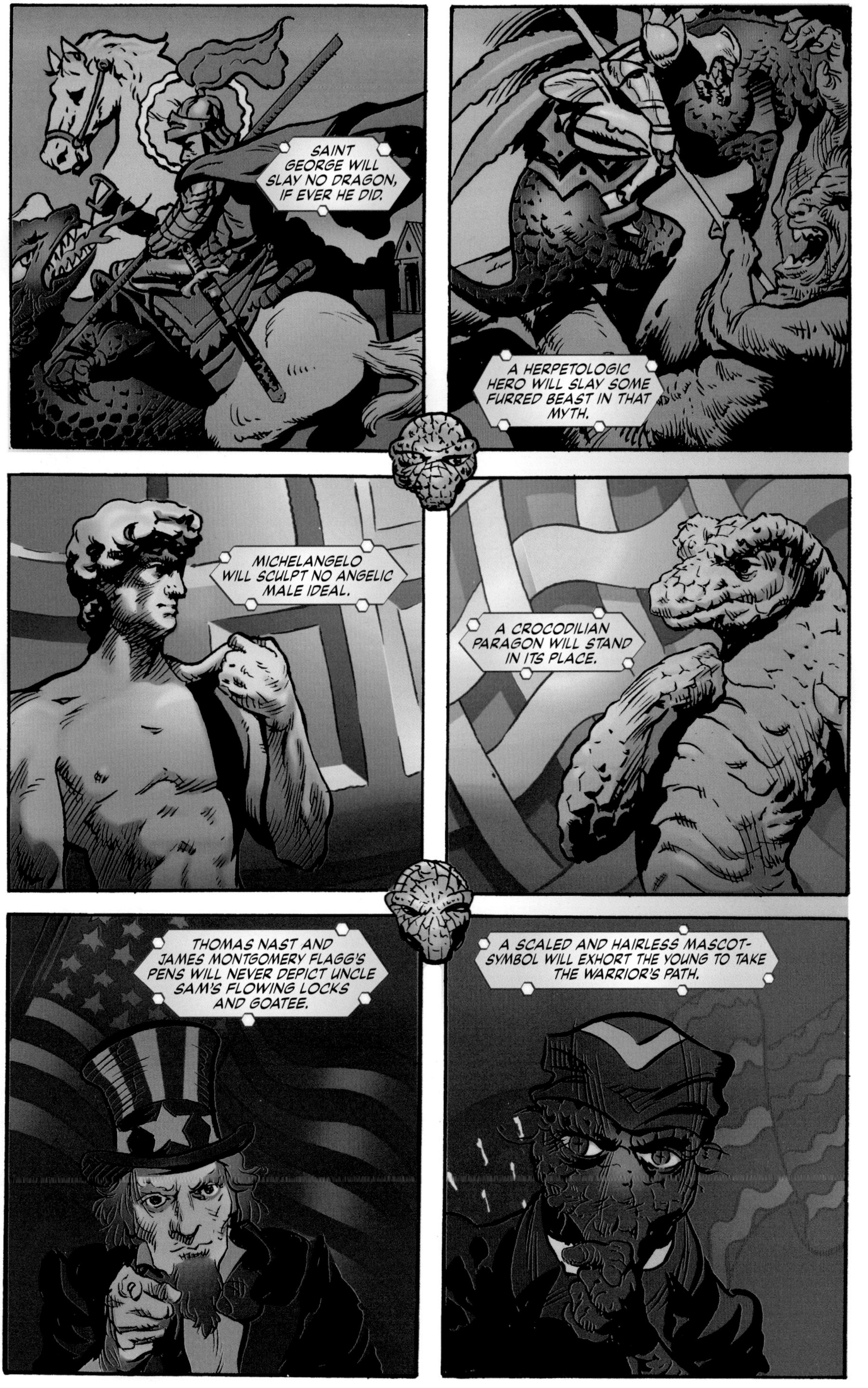
SAINT GEORGE WILL SLAY NO DRAGON, IF EVER HE DID.
A HERPETOLOGIC HERO WILL SLAY SOME FURRED BEAST IN THAT MYTH.
MICHELANGELO WILL SCULPT NO ANGELIC MALE IDEAL.
A CROCODILIAN PARAGON WILL STAND IN ITS PLACE.
THOMAS NAST AND JAMES MONTGOMERY FLAGG'S PENS WILL NEVER DEPICT UNCLE SAM'S FLOWING LOCKS AND GOATEE.
A SCALED AND HAIRLESS MASCOT-SYMBOL WILL EXHORT THE YOUNG TO TAKE THE WARRIOR'S PATH.

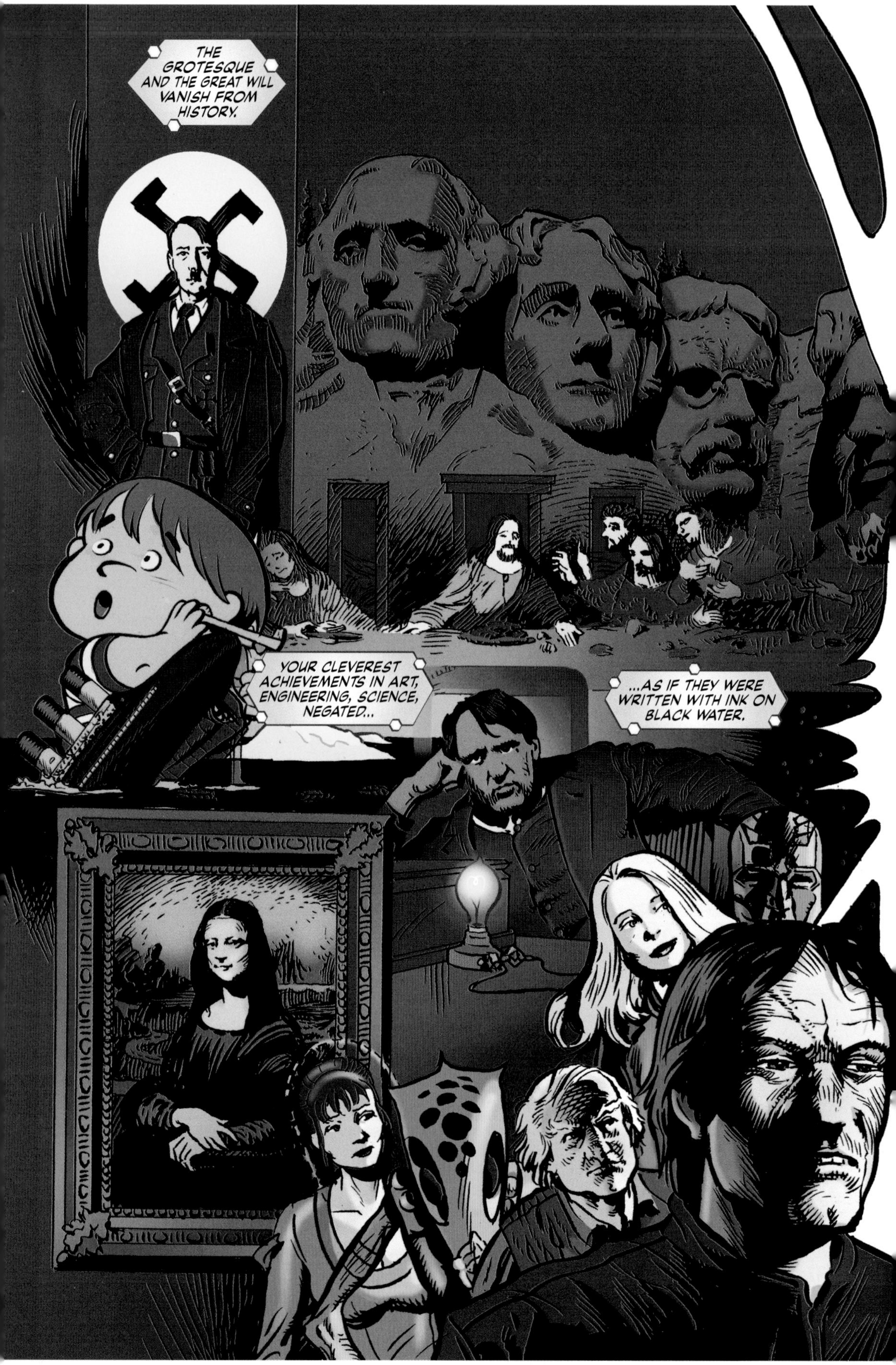
THE GROTESQUE AND THE GREAT WILL VANISH FROM HISTORY.
YOUR CLEVEREST ACHIEVEMENTS IN ART, ENGINEERING, SCIENCE, NEGATED...
...AS IF THEY WERE WRITTEN WITH INK ON BLACK WATER.

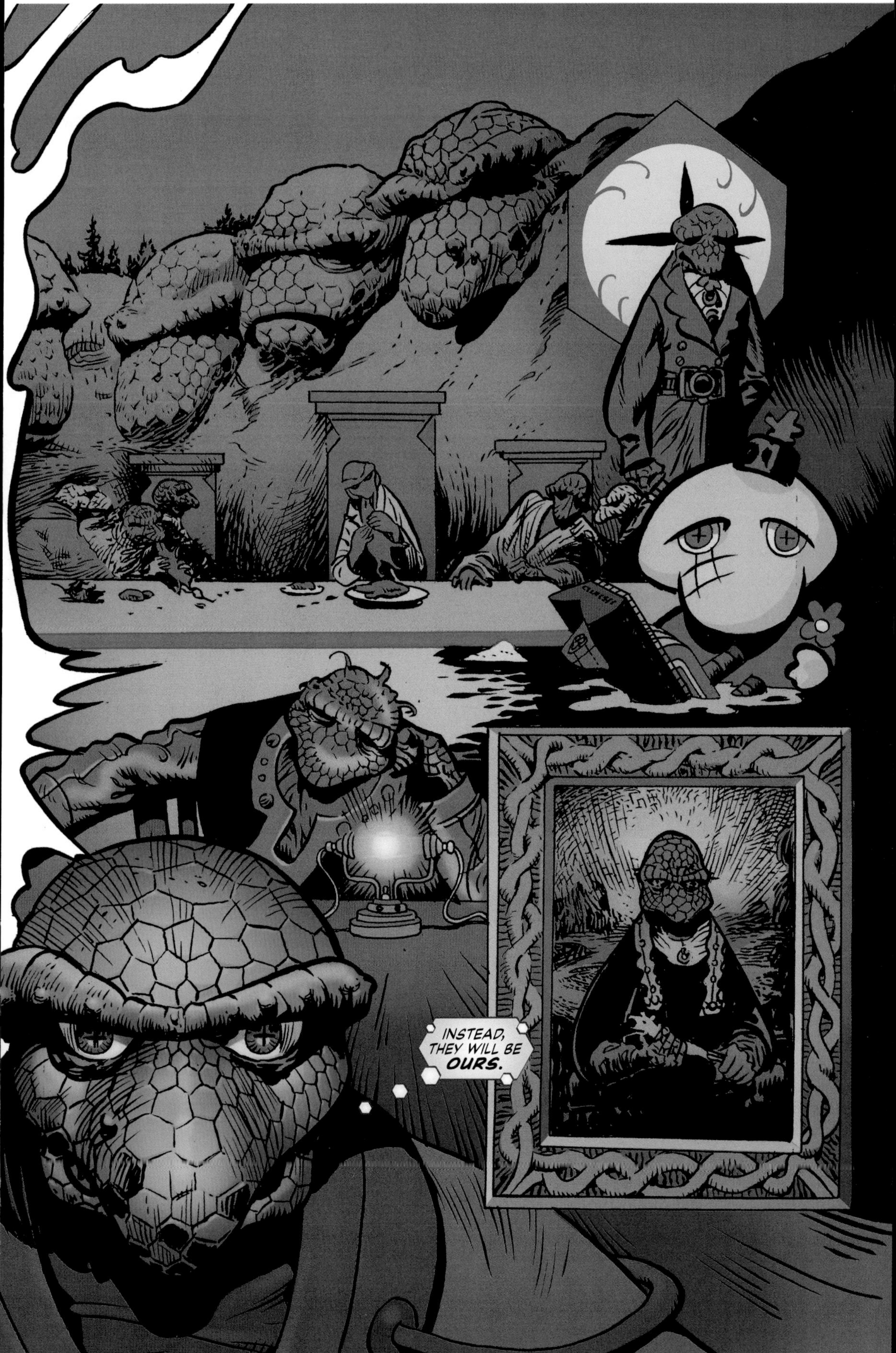
INSTEAD, THEY WILL BE OURS.

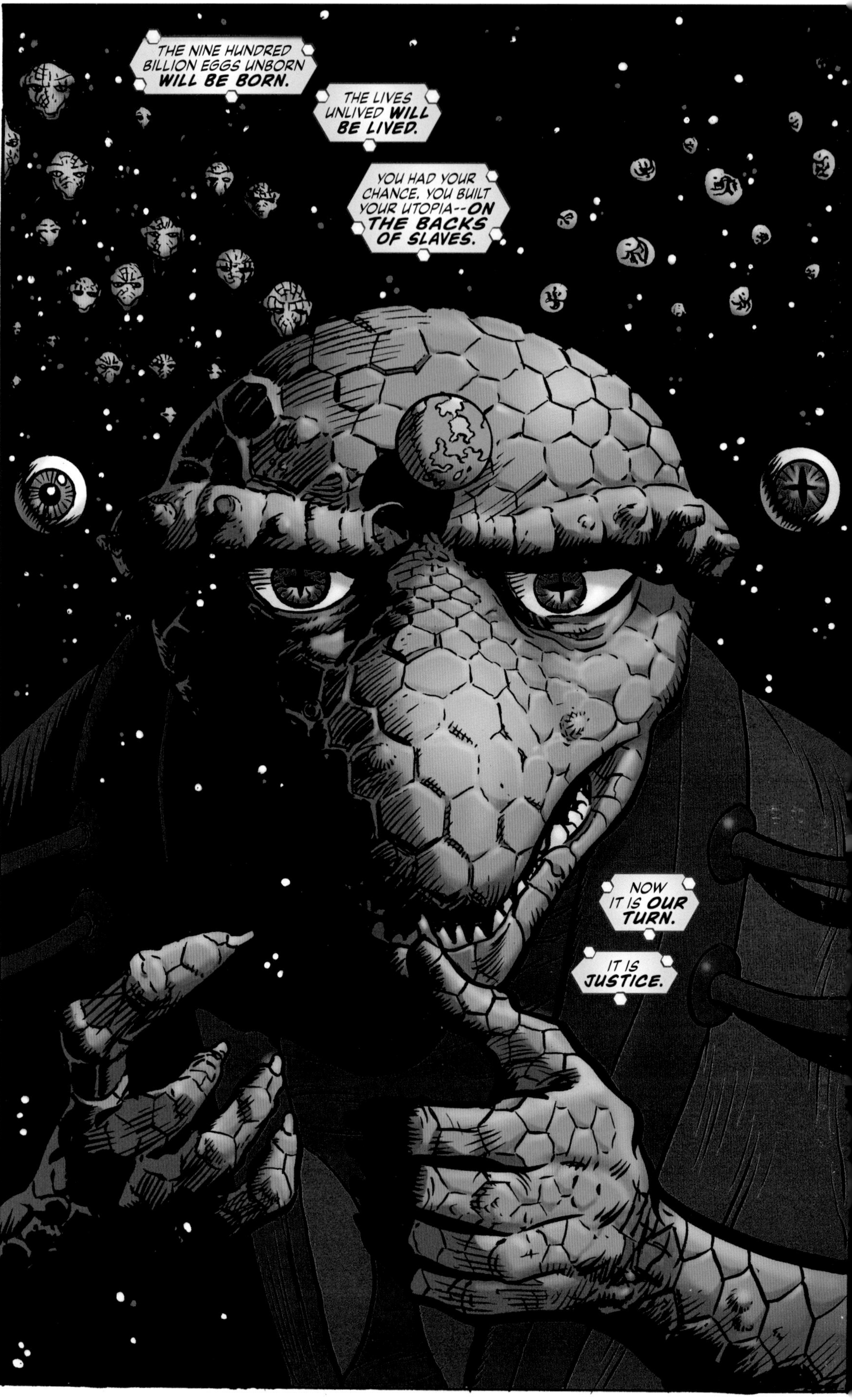
THE NINE HUNDRED BILLION EGGS UNBORN **WILL BE BORN.**
THE LIVES UNLIVED **WILL BE LIVED.**
YOU HAD YOUR CHANCE. YOU BUILT YOUR UTOPIA--**ON THE BACKS OF SLAVES.**
NOW IT IS **OUR TURN.**
IT IS **JUSTICE.**

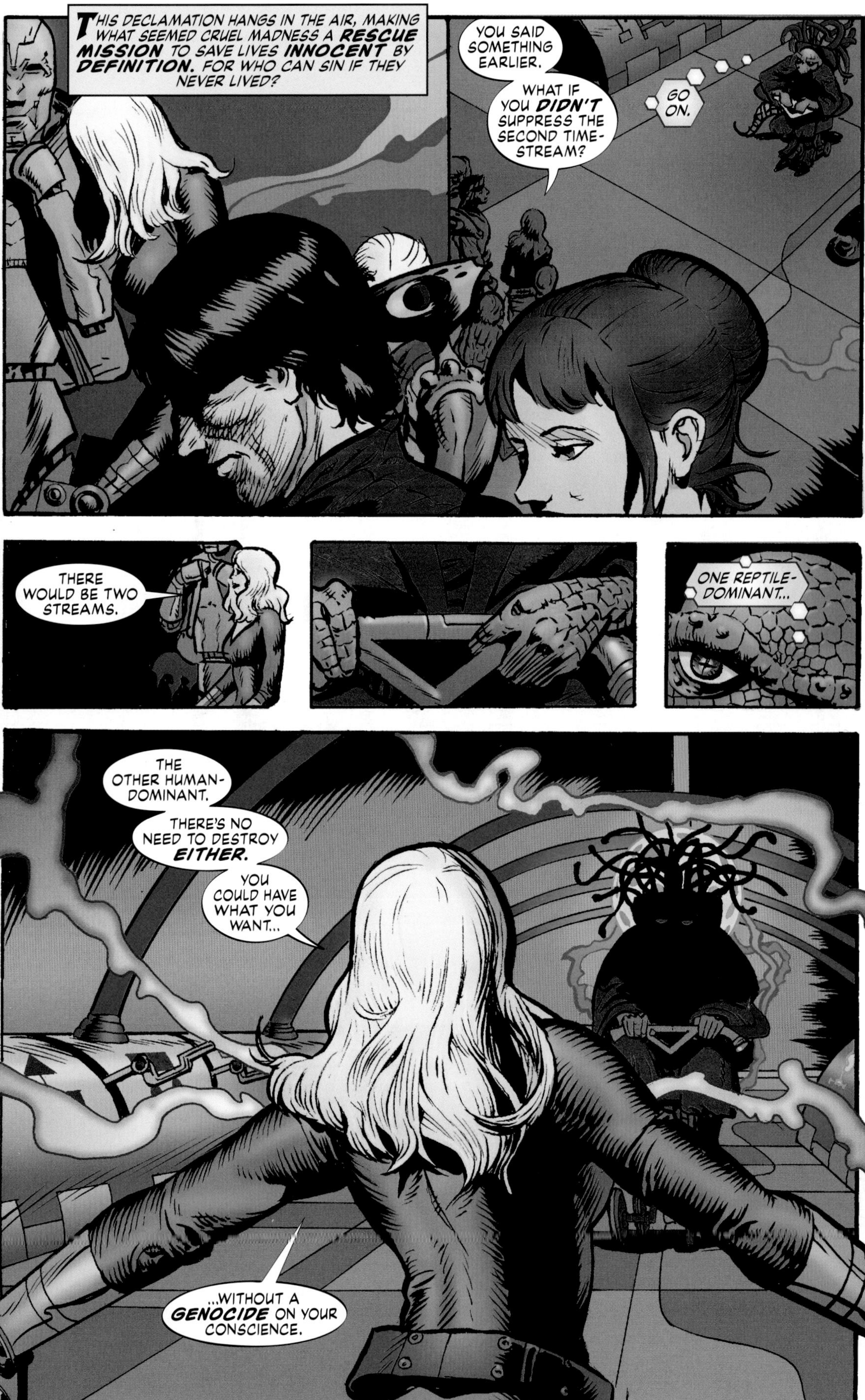
THIS DECLAMATION HANGS IN THE AIR, MAKING WHAT SEEMED CRUEL MADNESS A **RESCUE MISSION** TO SAVE LIVES **INNOCENT** BY **DEFINITION.** FOR WHO CAN SIN IF THEY NEVER LIVED?
YOU SAID SOMETHING EARLIER.
WHAT IF YOU ***DIDN'T*** SUPPRESS THE SECOND TIME-STREAM?
GO ON.
THERE WOULD BE TWO STREAMS.
ONE REPTILE-DOMINANT...
THE OTHER HUMAN-DOMINANT.
THERE'S NO NEED TO DESTROY ***EITHER.***
YOU COULD HAVE WHAT YOU WANT...
...WITHOUT A ***GENOCIDE*** ON YOUR CONSCIENCE.

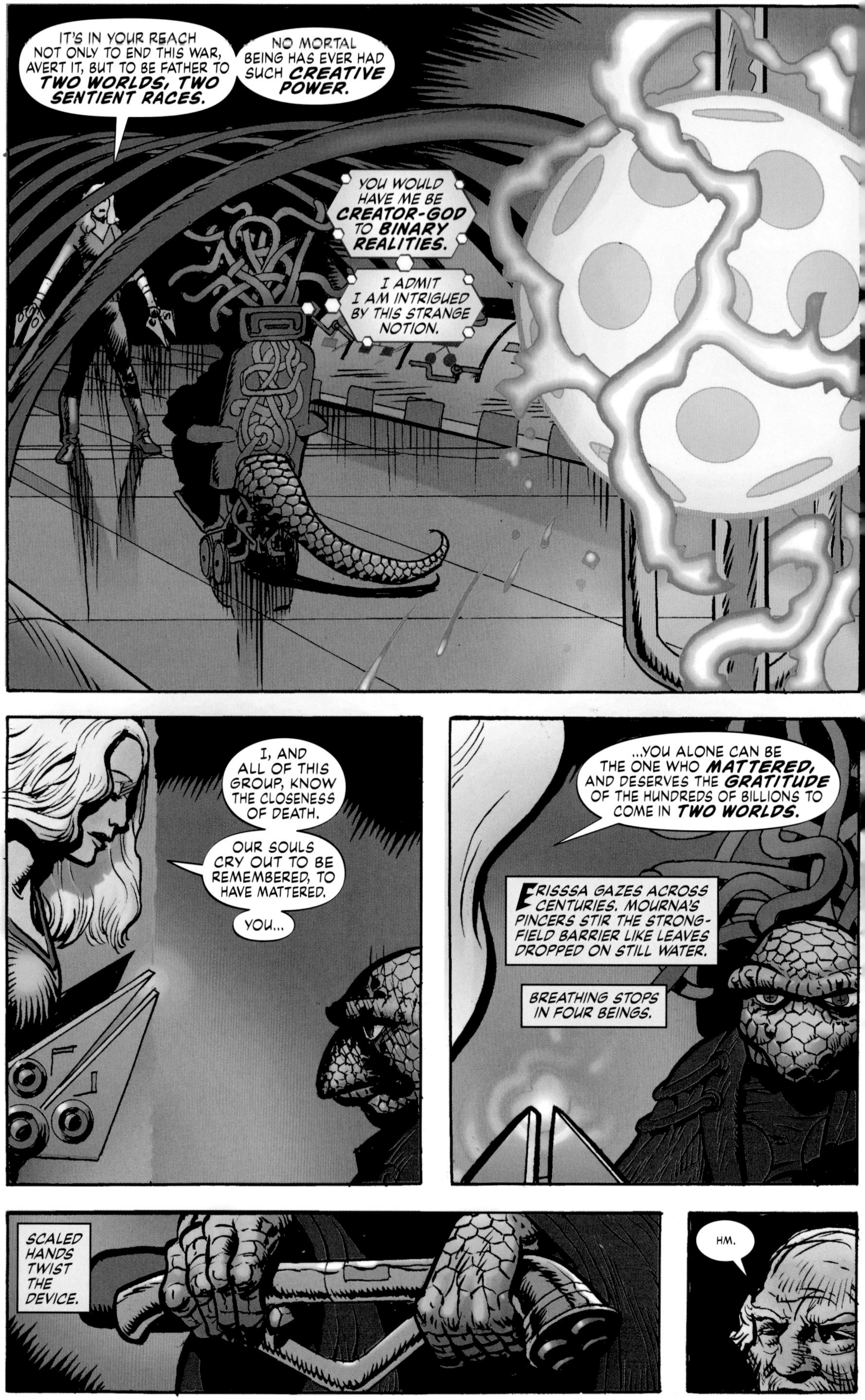

IT'S IN YOUR REACH NOT ONLY TO END THIS WAR, AVERT IT, BUT TO BE FATHER TO TWO WORLDS, TWO SENTIENT RACES.
NO MORTAL BEING HAS EVER HAD SUCH CREATIVE POWER.
YOU WOULD HAVE ME BE CREATOR-GOD TO BINARY REALITIES.
I ADMIT I AM INTRIGUED BY THIS STRANGE NOTION.
I, AND ALL OF THIS GROUP, KNOW THE CLOSENESS OF DEATH.
OUR SOULS CRY OUT TO BE REMEMBERED, TO HAVE MATTERED.
YOU...
...YOU ALONE CAN BE THE ONE WHO MATTERED, AND DESERVES THE GRATITUDE OF THE HUNDREDS OF BILLIONS TO COME IN TWO WORLDS.
ERISSSA GAZES ACROSS CENTURIES. MOURNA'S PINCERS STIR THE STRONG-FIELD BARRIER LIKE LEAVES DROPPED ON STILL WATER.
BREATHING STOPS IN FOUR BEINGS.
SCALED HANDS TWIST THE DEVICE.
HM.

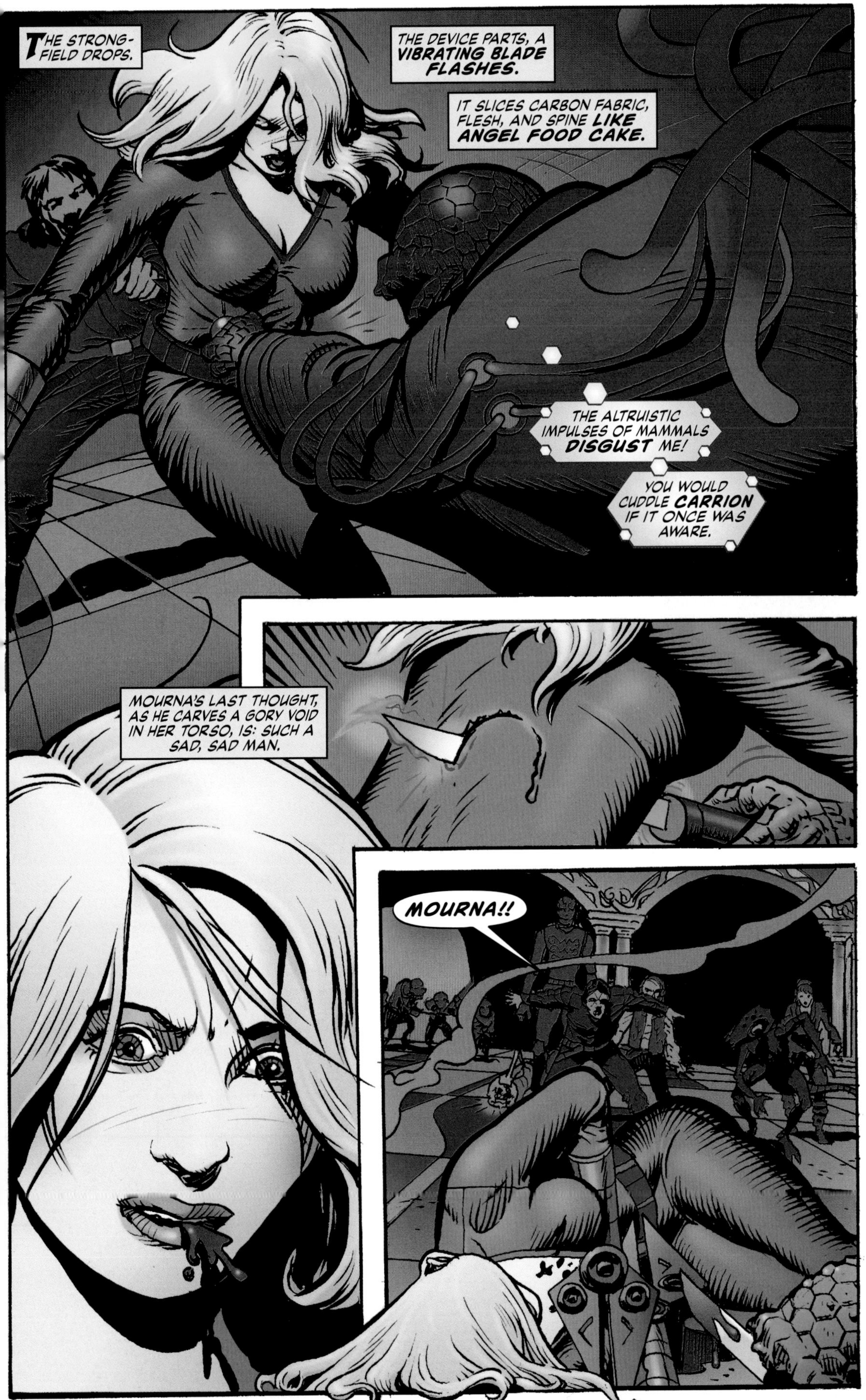
THE STRONG-FIELD DROPS.
THE DEVICE PARTS, A VIBRATING BLADE FLASHES.
IT SLICES CARBON FABRIC, FLESH, AND SPINE LIKE ANGEL FOOD CAKE.
THE ALTRUISTIC IMPULSES OF MAMMALS DISGUST ME!
YOU WOULD CUDDLE CARRION IF IT ONCE WAS AWARE.
MOURNA'S LAST THOUGHT, AS HE CARVES A GORY VOID IN HER TORSO, IS: SUCH A SAD, SAD MAN.
MOURNA!!

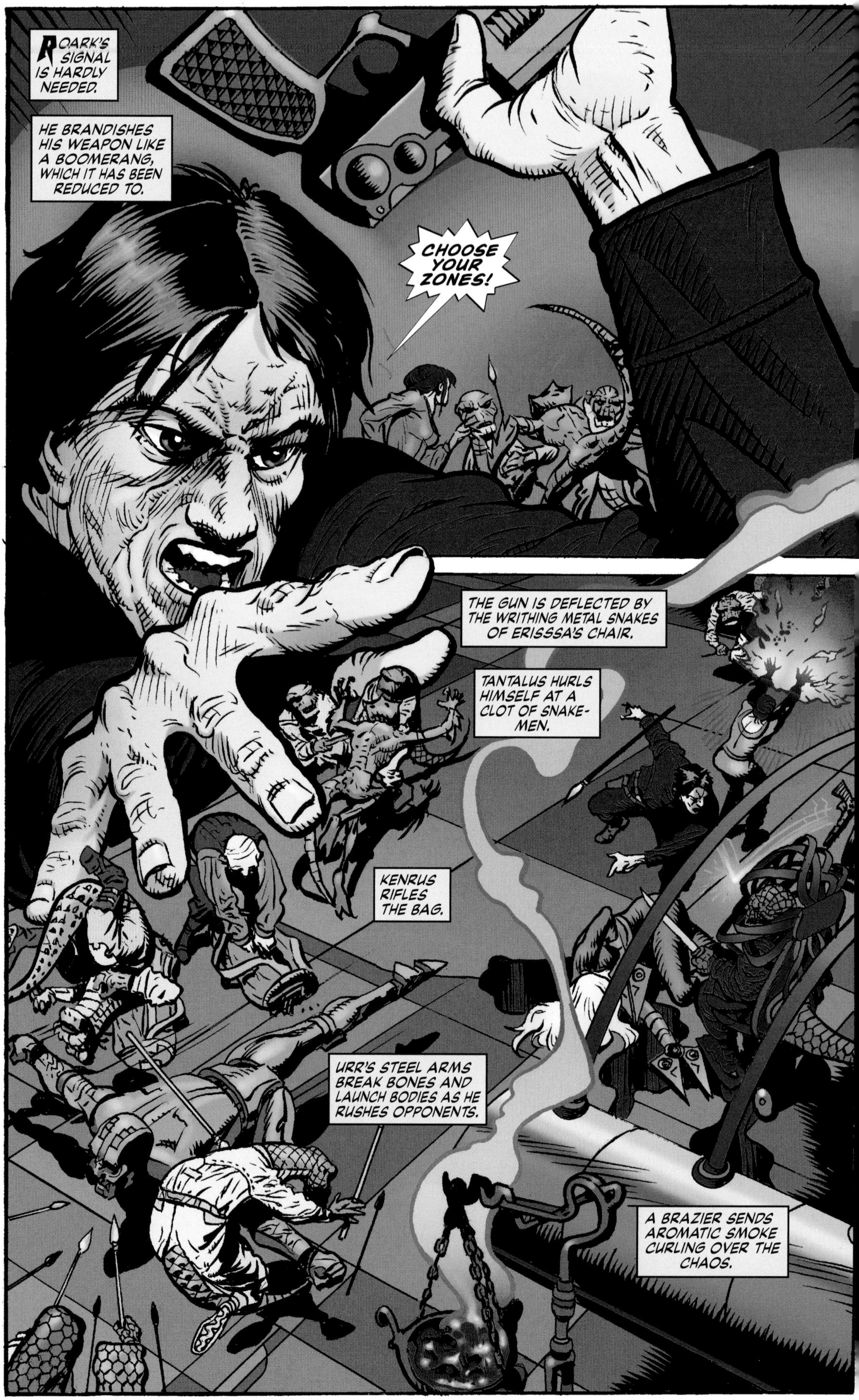
ROARK'S SIGNAL IS HARDLY NEEDED.
HE BRANDISHES HIS WEAPON LIKE A BOOMERANG, WHICH IT HAS BEEN REDUCED TO.
CHOOSE YOUR ZONES!
THE GUN IS DEFLECTED BY THE WRITHING METAL SNAKES OF ERISSSA'S CHAIR.
TANTALUS HURLS HIMSELF AT A CLOT OF SNAKE-MEN.
KENRUS RIFLES THE BAG.
URR'S STEEL ARMS BREAK BONES AND LAUNCH BODIES AS HE RUSHES OPPONENTS.
A BRAZIER SENDS AROMATIC SMOKE CURLING OVER THE CHAOS.

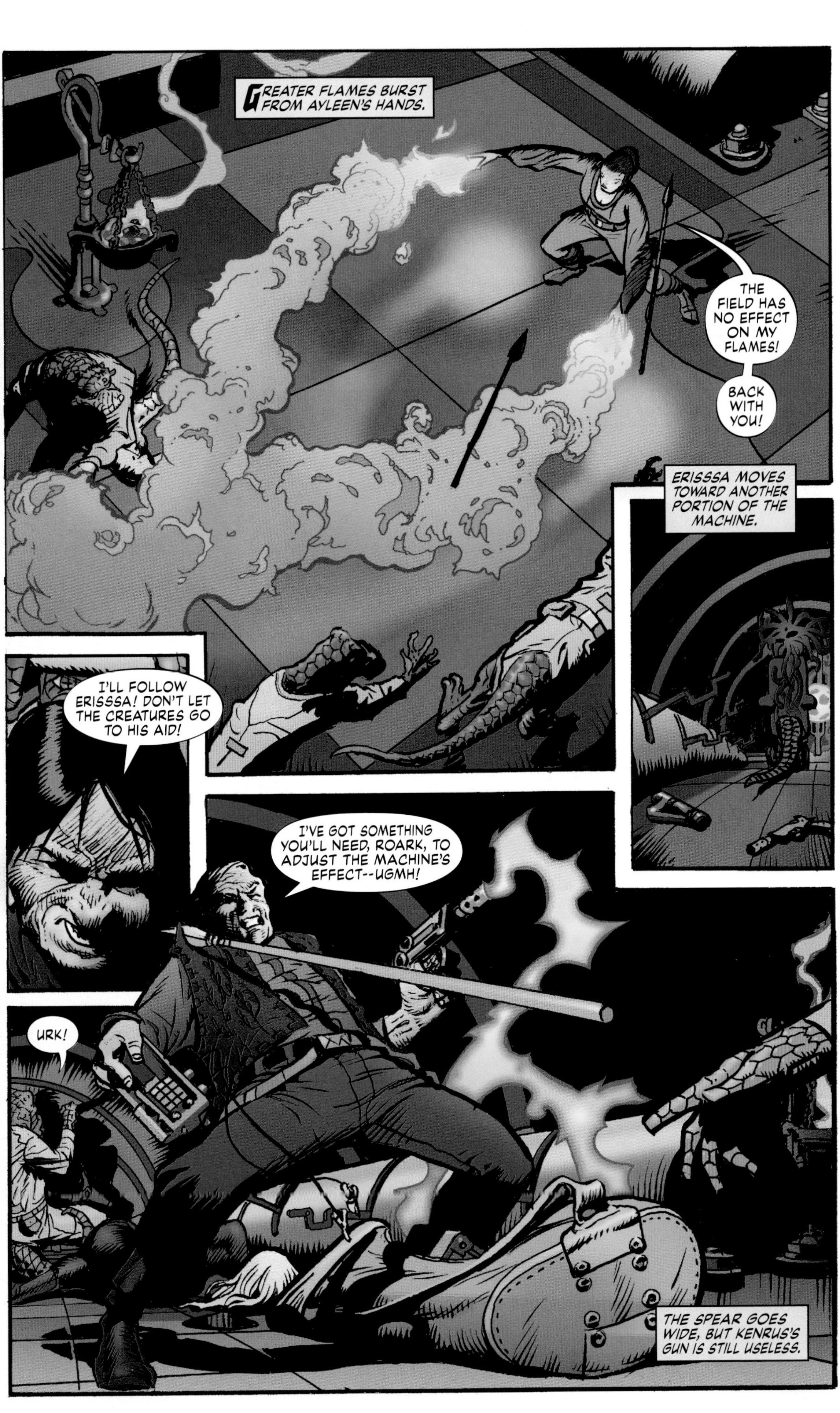
GREATER FLAMES BURST FROM AYLEEN'S HANDS.
THE FIELD HAS NO EFFECT ON MY FLAMES!
BACK WITH YOU!
ERISSSA MOVES TOWARD ANOTHER PORTION OF THE MACHINE.
I'LL FOLLOW ERISSSA! DON'T LET THE CREATURES GO TO HIS AID!
I'VE GOT SOMETHING YOU'LL NEED, ROARK, TO ADJUST THE MACHINE'S EFFECT--UGMH!
URK!
THE SPEAR GOES WIDE, BUT KENRUS'S GUN IS STILL USELESS.

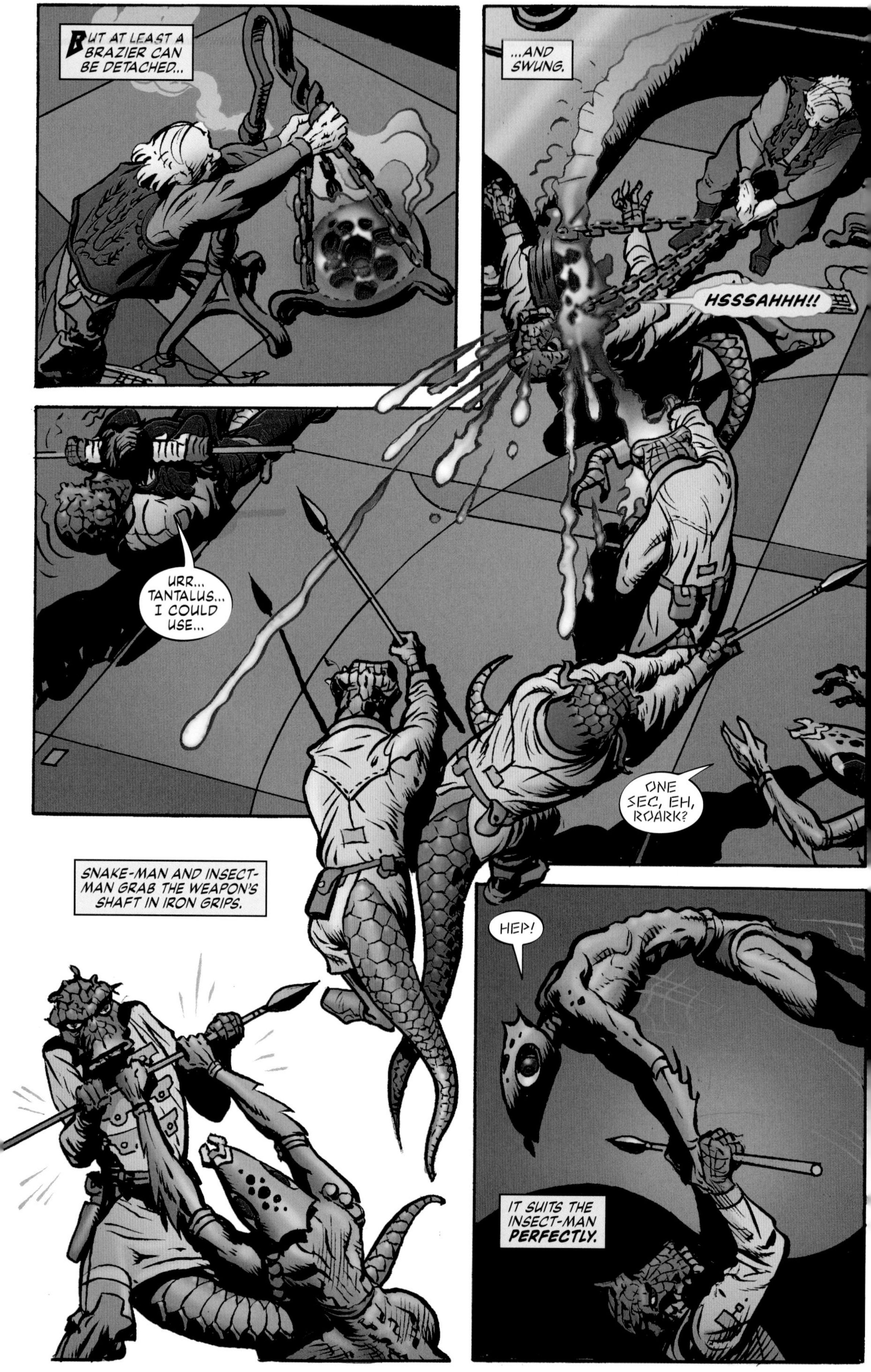
BUT AT LEAST A BRAZIER CAN BE DETACHED...
...AND SWUNG.
HSSSAHHH!!
URR... TANTALUS... I COULD USE...
ONE SEC, EH, ROARK?
SNAKE-MAN AND INSECT-MAN GRAB THE WEAPON'S SHAFT IN IRON GRIPS.
HEP!
IT SUITS THE INSECT-MAN PERFECTLY.

DON'T GO ANYWHERE, ROARK, EH?

THE JEST GOES **UNAPPRECIATED** AS ROARK'S WORLD TURNS **RED-BLACK**, AND THE SNAKE-MAN'S BREATH **STEAMS**.

HSSSUUH!

A STRANGE METAL **TONGUE** BLOODILY **EMERGES** FROM THE GREAT MOUTH.

PRESSURE **EASES**.

GOOD AND **STUCK** IN THERE. YOU OKAY?

YES :COUGH!: THANKS.

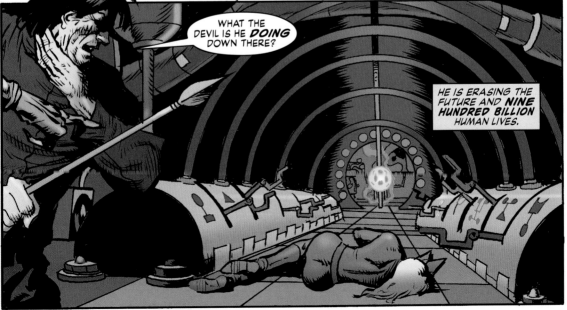

WHAT THE DEVIL IS HE **DOING** DOWN THERE?

HE IS ERASING THE FUTURE AND **NINE HUNDRED BILLION** HUMAN LIVES.

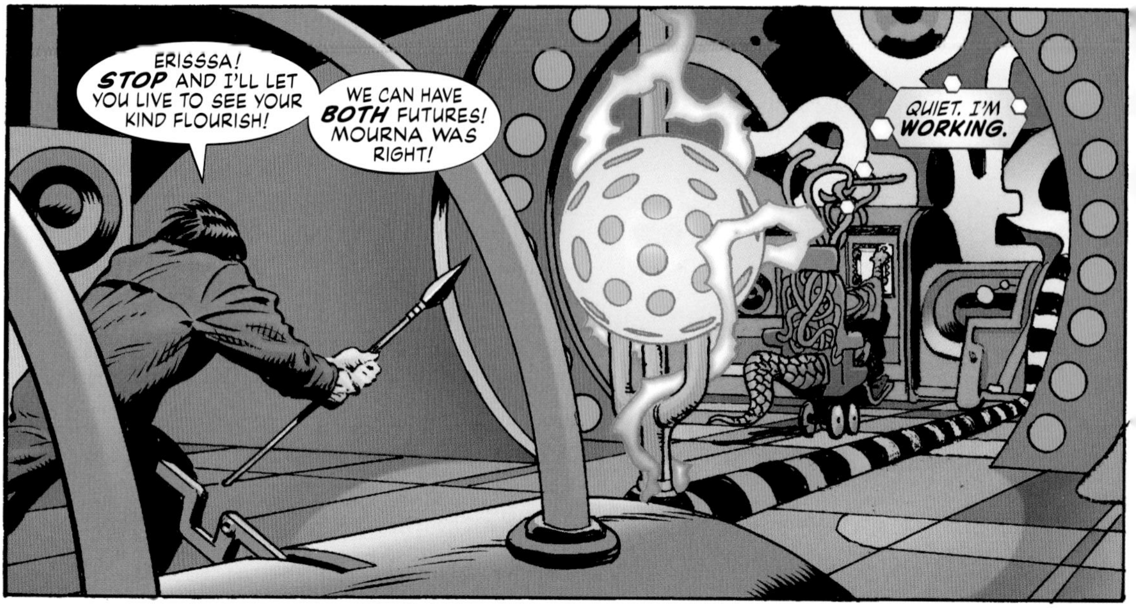
ERISSSA! STOP AND I'LL LET YOU LIVE TO SEE YOUR KIND FLOURISH!
WE CAN HAVE BOTH FUTURES! MOURNA WAS RIGHT!
QUIET. I'M WORKING.

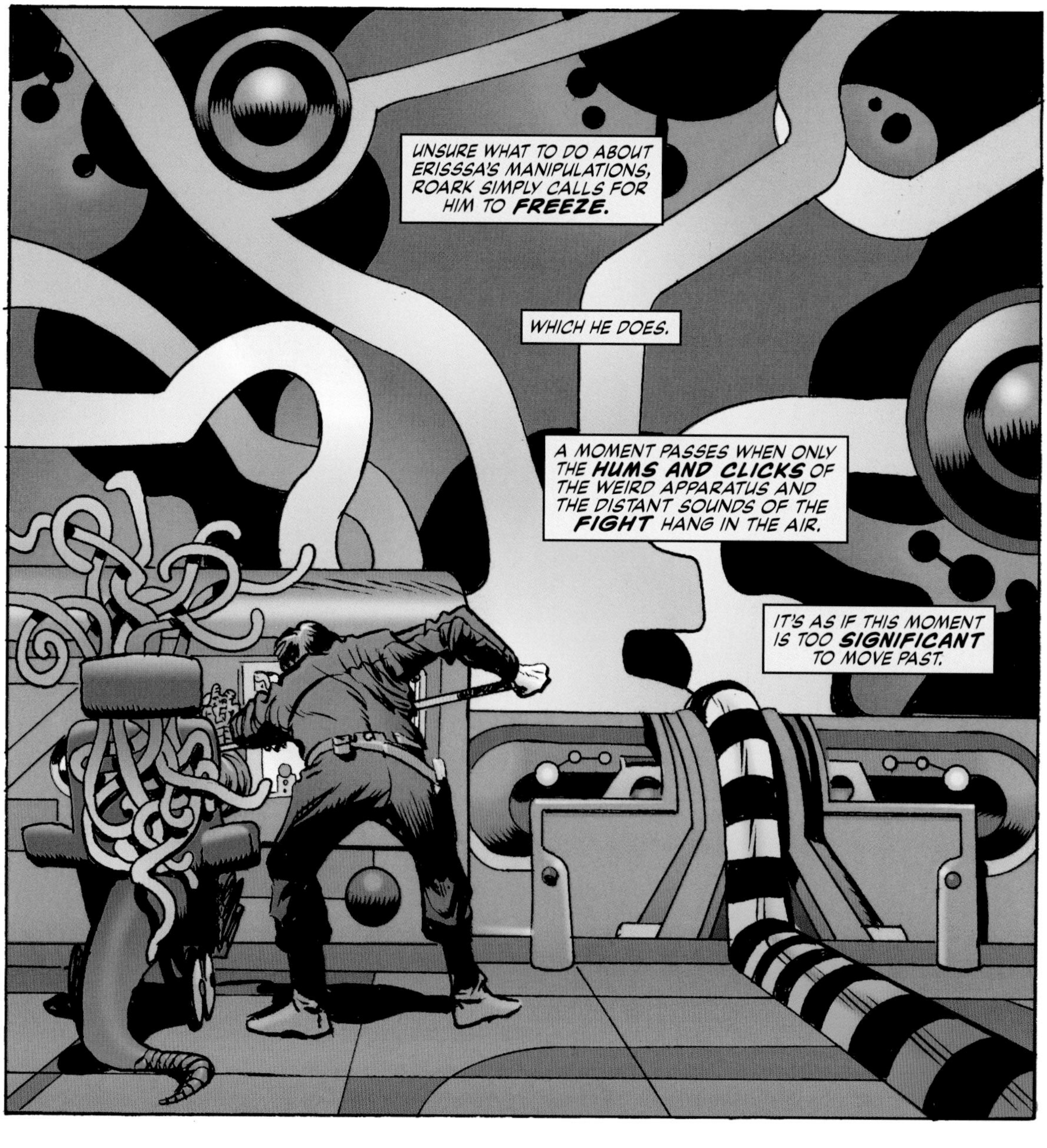
UNSURE WHAT TO DO ABOUT ERISSSA'S MANIPULATIONS, ROARK SIMPLY CALLS FOR HIM TO FREEZE.
WHICH HE DOES.
A MOMENT PASSES WHEN ONLY THE HUMS AND CLICKS OF THE WEIRD APPARATUS AND THE DISTANT SOUNDS OF THE FIGHT HANG IN THE AIR.
IT'S AS IF THIS MOMENT IS TOO SIGNIFICANT TO MOVE PAST.

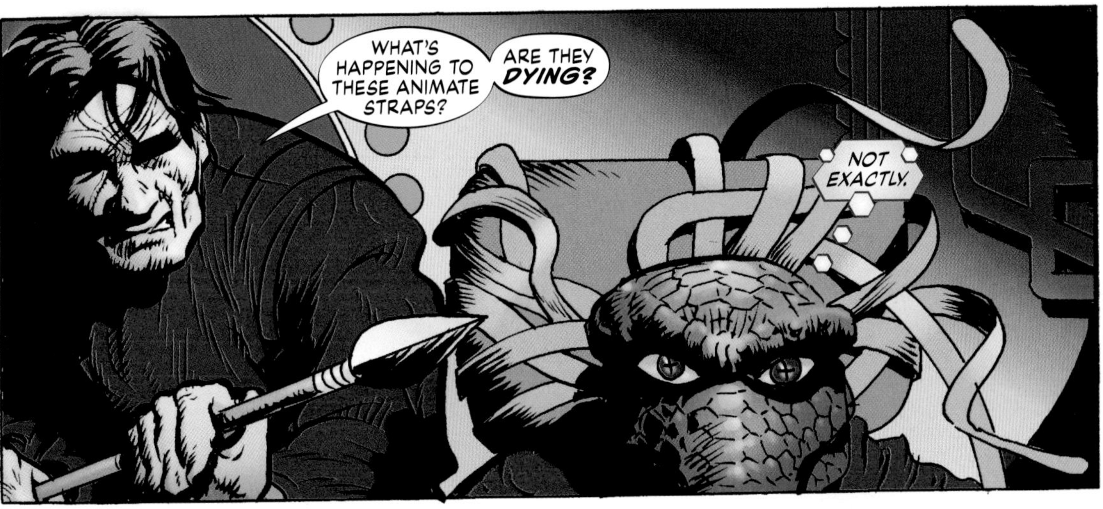
WHAT'S HAPPENING TO THESE ANIMATE STRAPS?
ARE THEY DYING?
NOT EXACTLY.

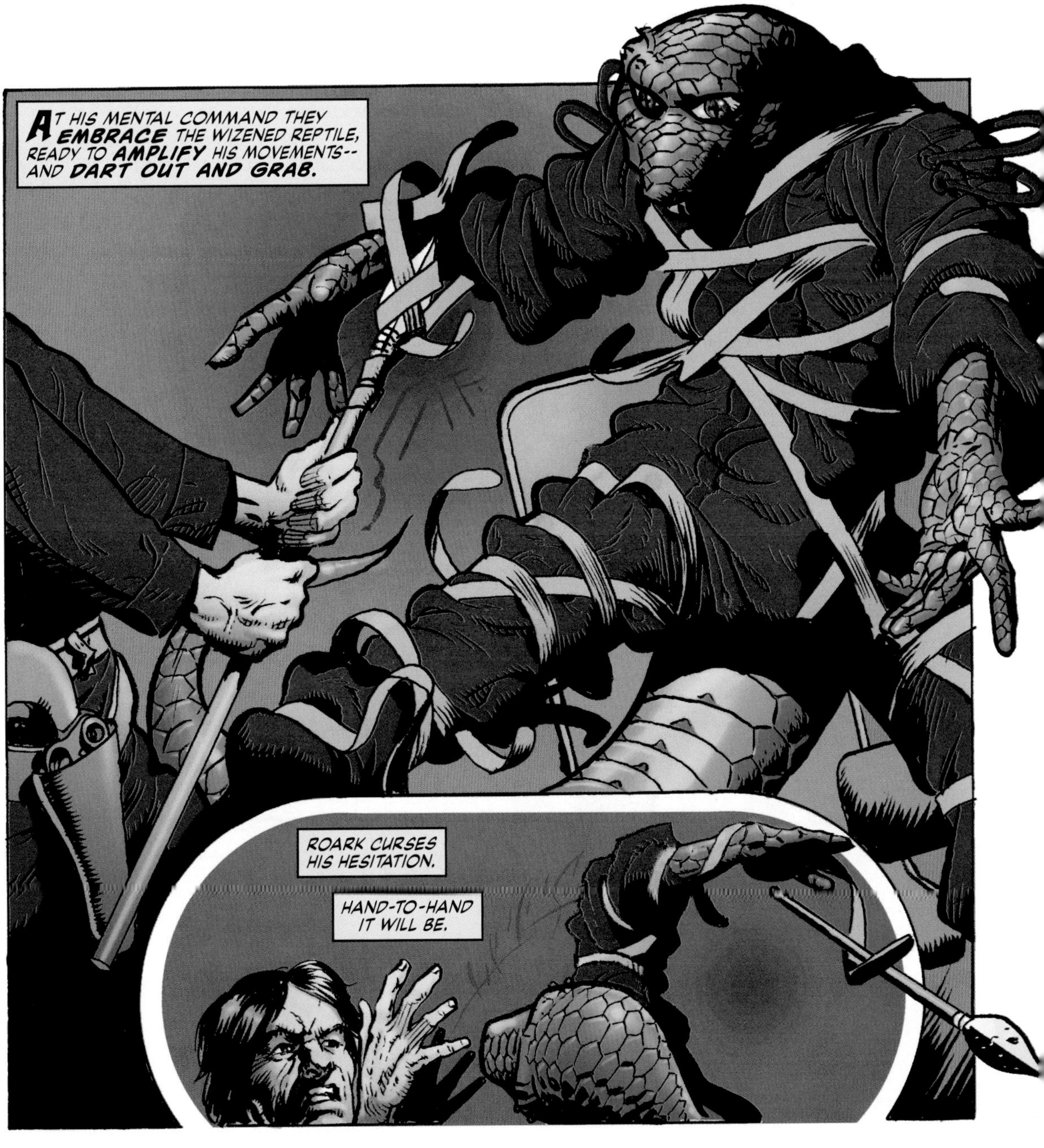
AT HIS MENTAL COMMAND THEY EMBRACE THE WIZENED REPTILE, READY TO AMPLIFY HIS MOVEMENTS--AND DART OUT AND GRAB.
ROARK CURSES HIS HESITATION.
HAND-TO-HAND IT WILL BE.

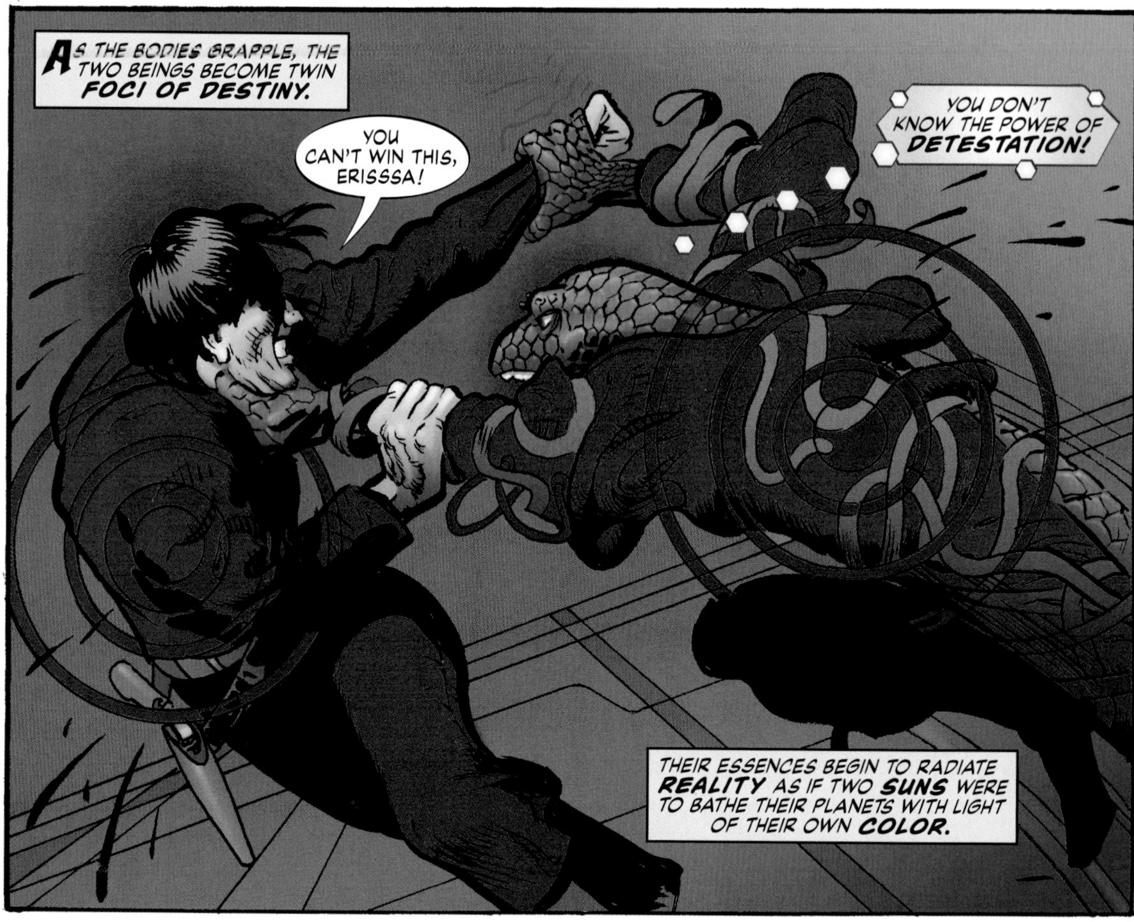
AS THE BODIES GRAPPLE, THE TWO BEINGS BECOME TWIN FOCI OF DESTINY.
YOU CAN'T WIN THIS, ERISSSA!
YOU DON'T KNOW THE POWER OF DETESTATION!
THEIR ESSENCES BEGIN TO RADIATE REALITY AS IF TWO SUNS WERE TO BATHE THEIR PLANETS WITH LIGHT OF THEIR OWN COLOR.

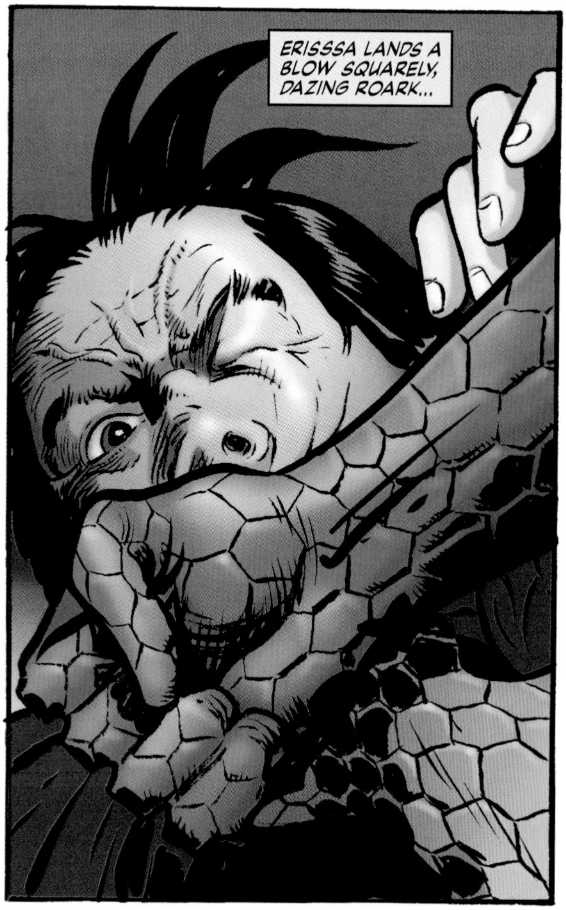
ERISSSA LANDS A BLOW SQUARELY, DAZING ROARK...

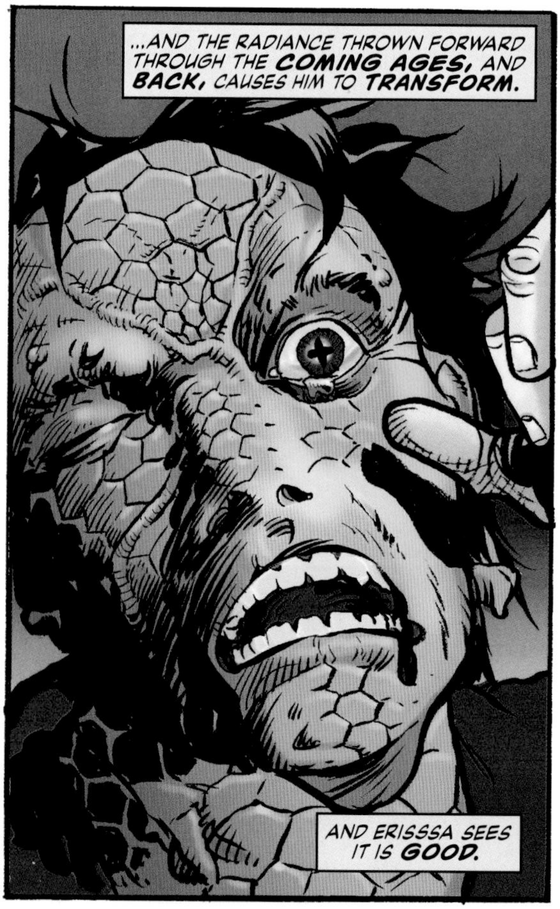
...AND THE RADIANCE THROWN FORWARD THROUGH THE COMING AGES, AND BACK, CAUSES HIM TO TRANSFORM.
AND ERISSSA SEES IT IS GOOD.

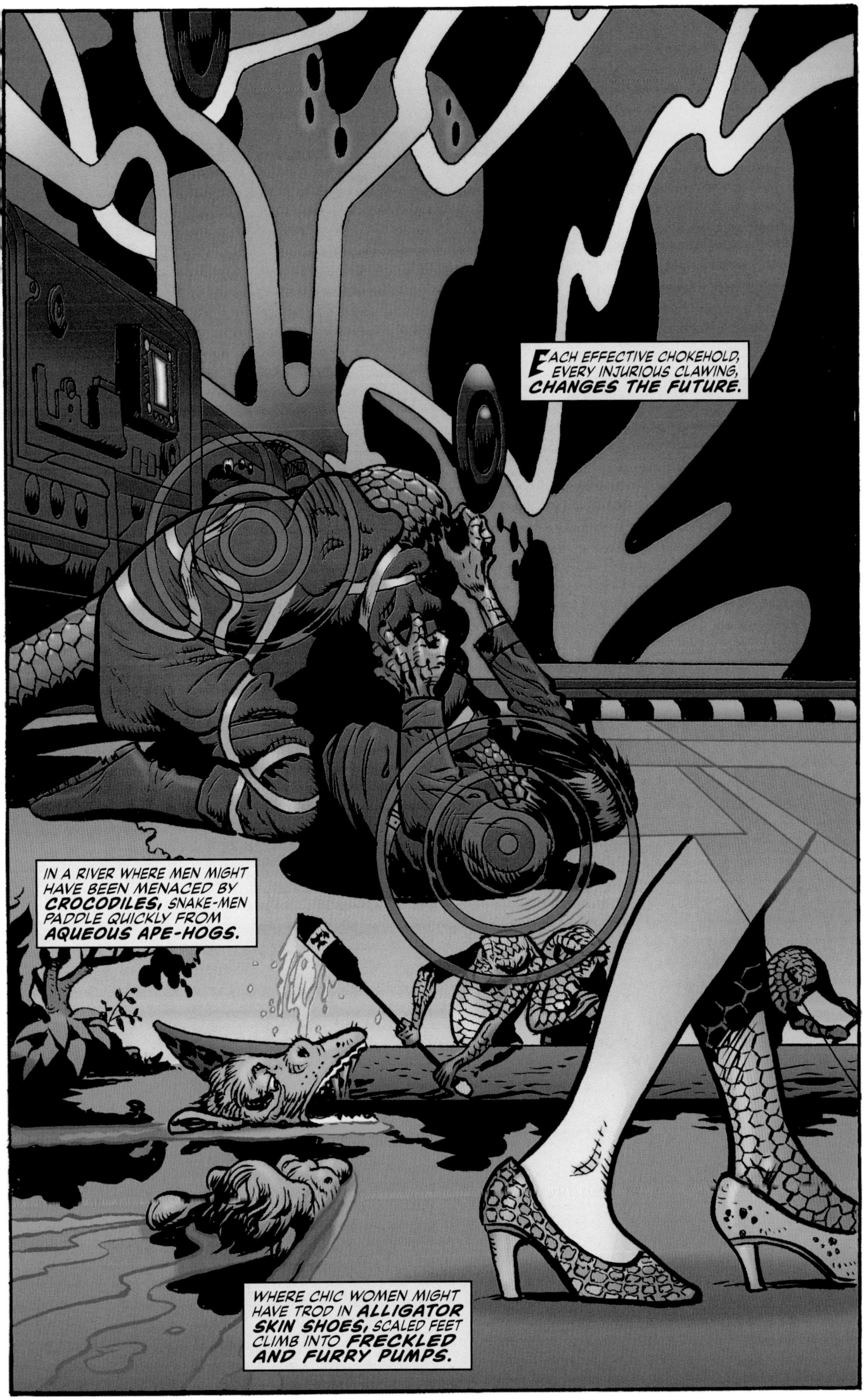
EACH EFFECTIVE CHOKEHOLD, EVERY INJURIOUS CLAWING, CHANGES THE FUTURE.
IN A RIVER WHERE MEN MIGHT HAVE BEEN MENACED BY CROCODILES, SNAKE-MEN PADDLE QUICKLY FROM AQUEOUS APE-HOGS.
WHERE CHIC WOMEN MIGHT HAVE TROD IN ALLIGATOR SKIN SHOES, SCALED FEET CLIMB INTO FRECKLED AND FURRY PUMPS.

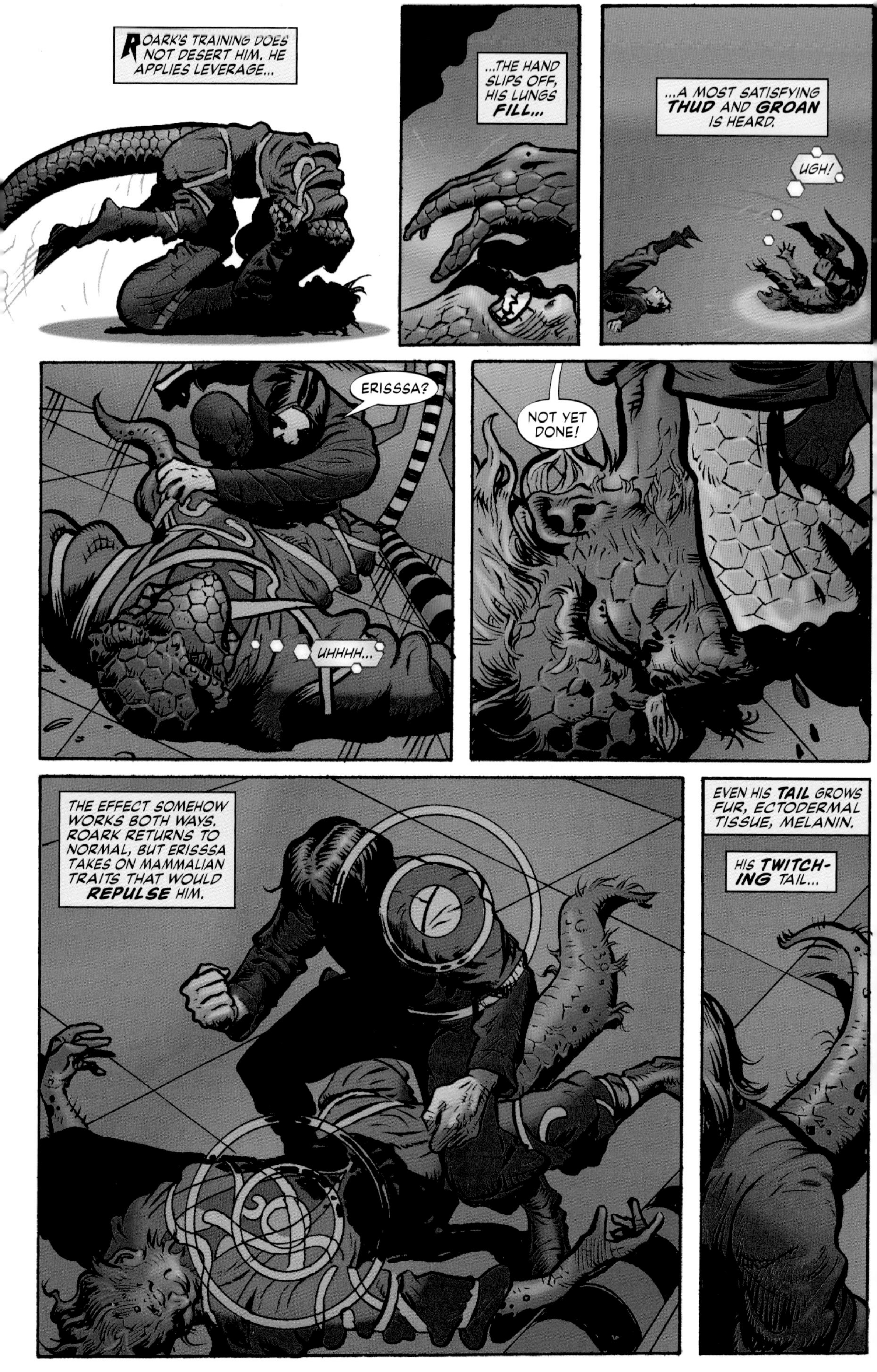
ROARK'S TRAINING DOES NOT DESERT HIM. HE APPLIES LEVERAGE...
...THE HAND SLIPS OFF, HIS LUNGS FILL...
...A MOST SATISFYING THUD AND GROAN IS HEARD.
UGH!
ERISSSA?
UHHHH...
NOT YET DONE!
THE EFFECT SOMEHOW WORKS BOTH WAYS. ROARK RETURNS TO NORMAL, BUT ERISSSA TAKES ON MAMMALIAN TRAITS THAT WOULD REPULSE HIM.
EVEN HIS TAIL GROWS FUR, ECTODERMAL TISSUE, MELANIN.
HIS TWITCHING TAIL...

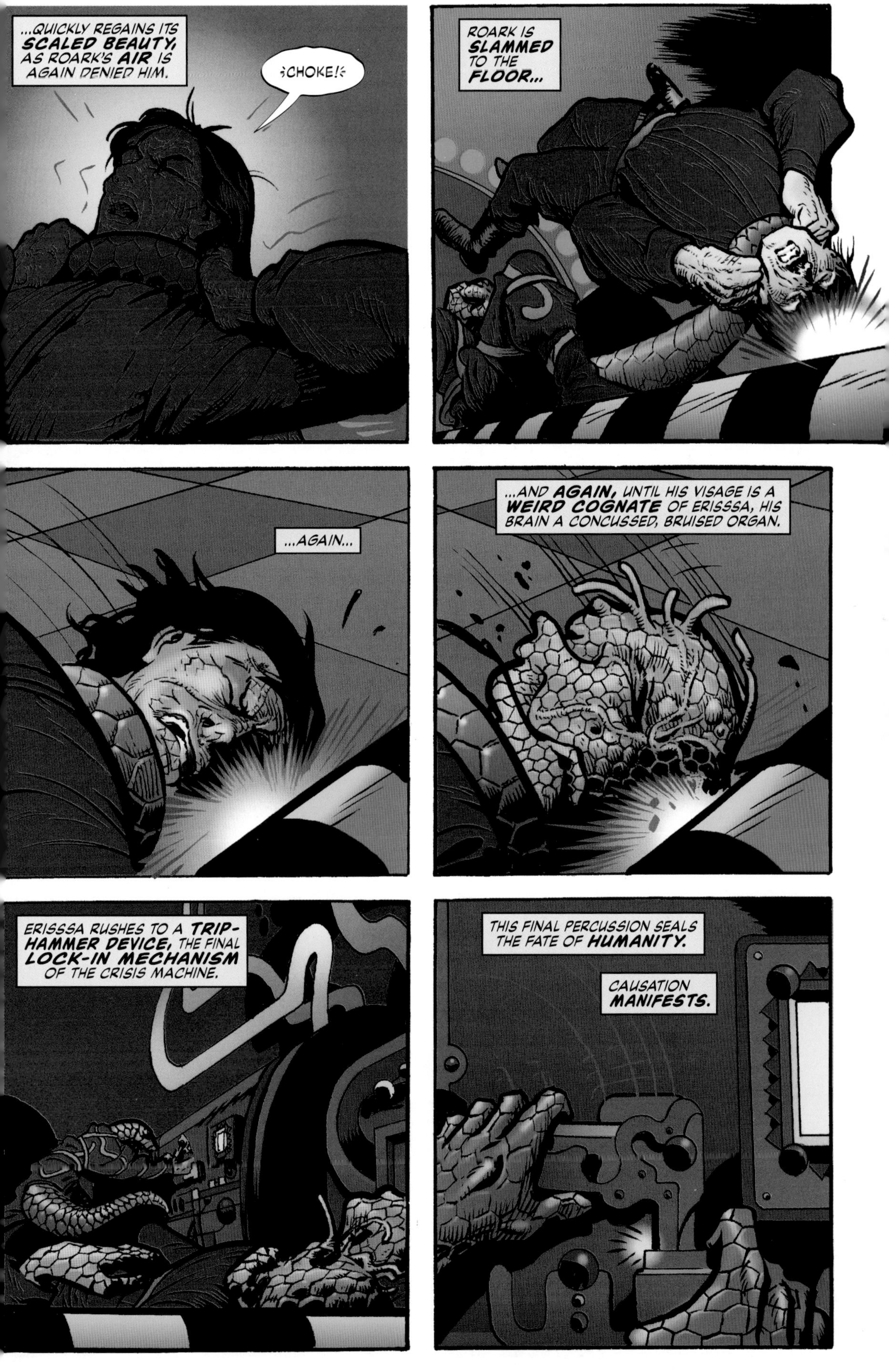
...QUICKLY REGAINS ITS SCALED BEAUTY, AS ROARK'S AIR IS AGAIN DENIED HIM.
CHOKE!
ROARK IS SLAMMED TO THE FLOOR...
...AGAIN...
...AND AGAIN, UNTIL HIS VISAGE IS A WEIRD COGNATE OF ERISSSA, HIS BRAIN A CONCUSSED, BRUISED ORGAN.
ERISSSA RUSHES TO A TRIP-HAMMER DEVICE, THE FINAL LOCK-IN MECHANISM OF THE CRISIS MACHINE.
THIS FINAL PERCUSSION SEALS THE FATE OF HUMANITY.
CAUSATION MANIFESTS.

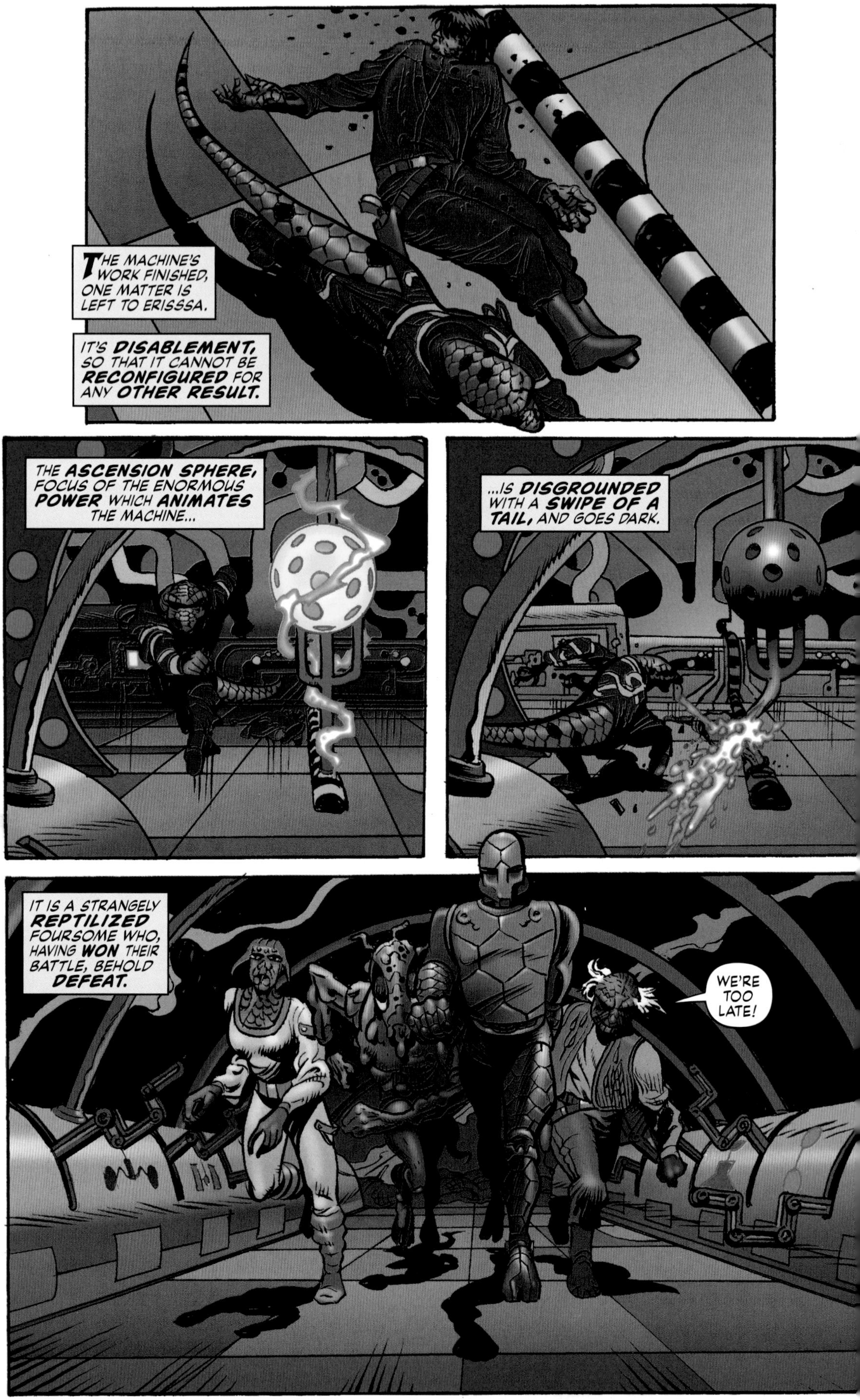
THE MACHINE'S WORK FINISHED, ONE MATTER IS LEFT TO ERISSSA.
IT'S DISABLEMENT, SO THAT IT CANNOT BE RECONFIGURED FOR ANY OTHER RESULT.
THE ASCENSION SPHERE, FOCUS OF THE ENORMOUS POWER WHICH ANIMATES THE MACHINE...
...IS DISGROUNDED WITH A SWIPE OF A TAIL, AND GOES DARK.
IT IS A STRANGELY REPTILIZED FOURSOME WHO, HAVING WON THEIR BATTLE, BEHOLD DEFEAT.
WE'RE TOO LATE!

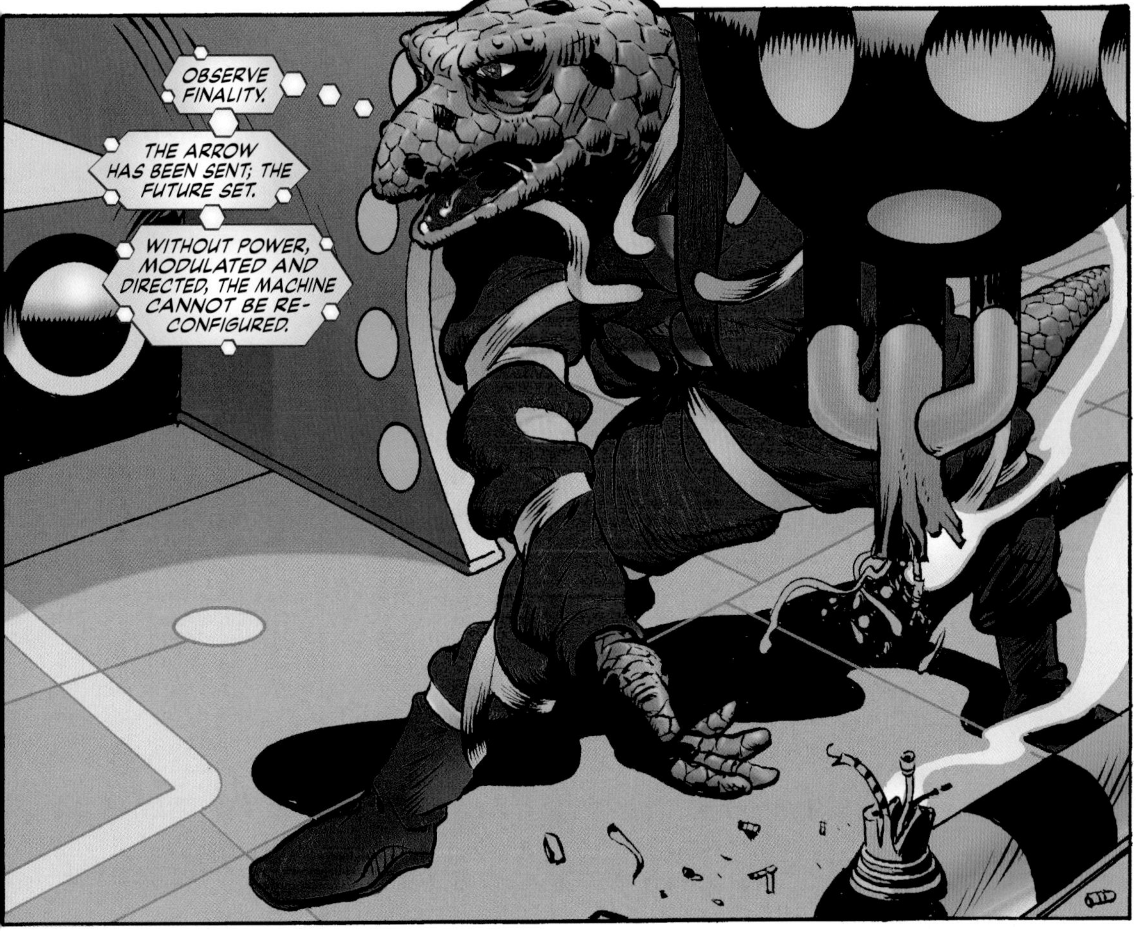
OBSERVE FINALITY.
THE ARROW HAS BEEN SENT; THE FUTURE SET.
WITHOUT POWER, MODULATED AND DIRECTED, THE MACHINE CANNOT BE RE-CONFIGURED.

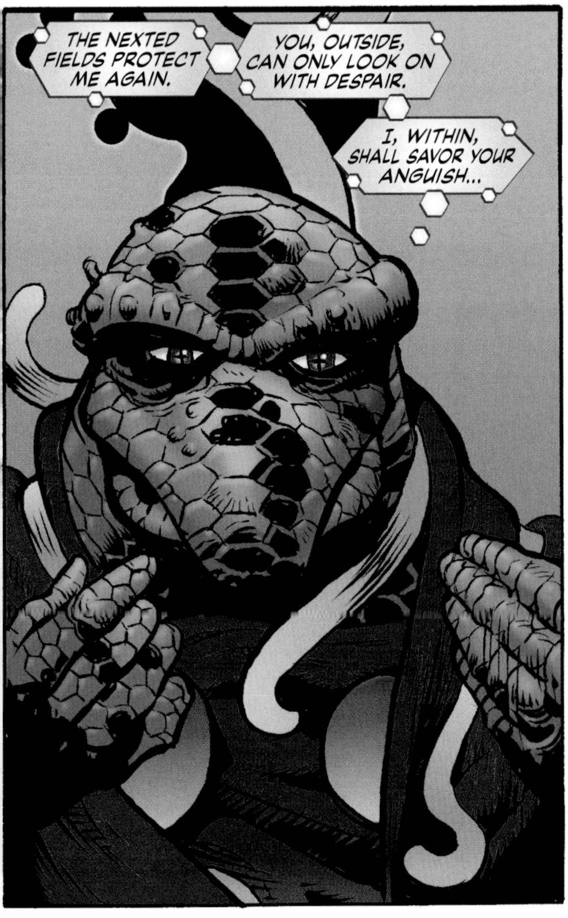
THE NEXTED FIELDS PROTECT ME AGAIN.
YOU, OUTSIDE, CAN ONLY LOOK ON WITH DESPAIR.
I, WITHIN, SHALL SAVOR YOUR ANGUISH...

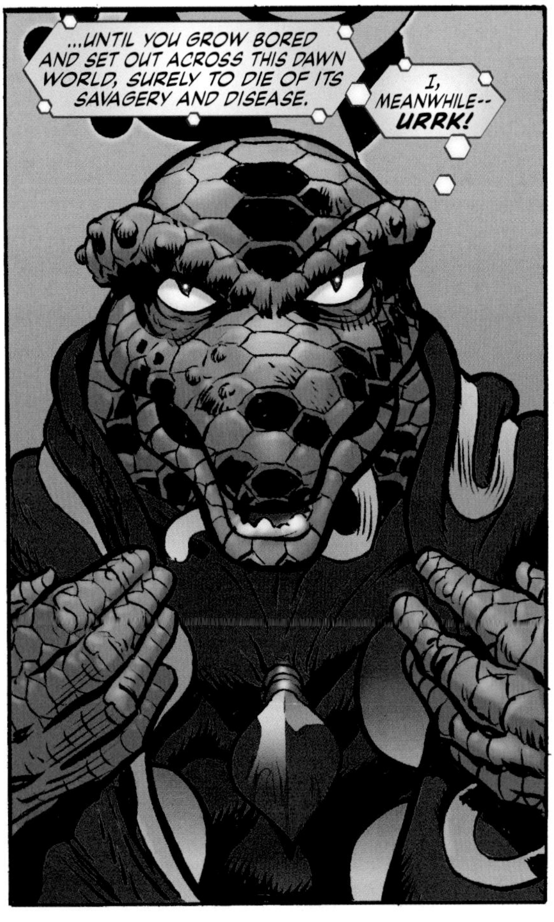
...UNTIL YOU GROW BORED AND SET OUT ACROSS THIS DAWN WORLD, SURELY TO DIE OF ITS SAVAGERY AND DISEASE.
I, MEANWHILE-- **URRK!**

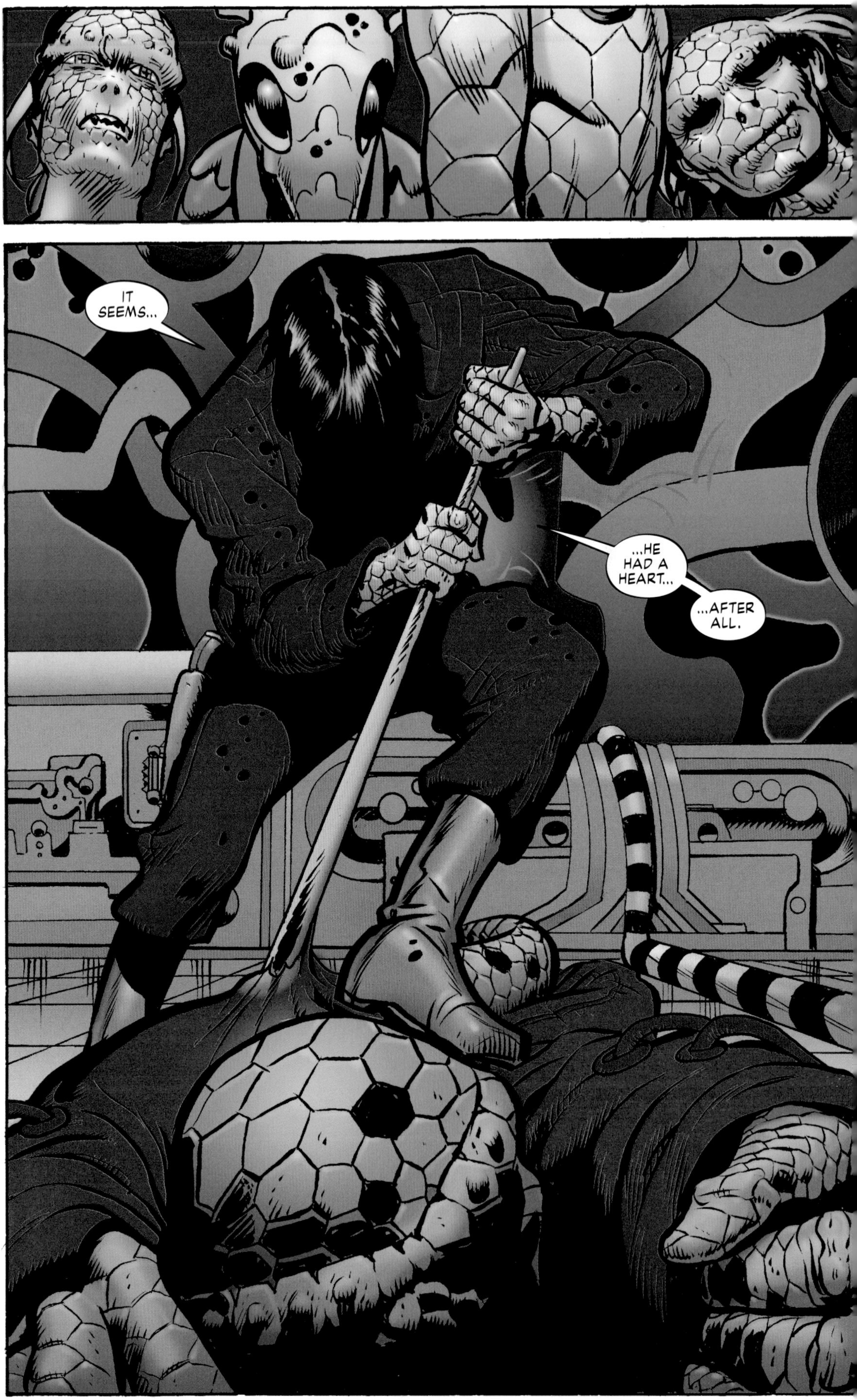
IT SEEMS...
...HE HAD A HEART...
...AFTER ALL.

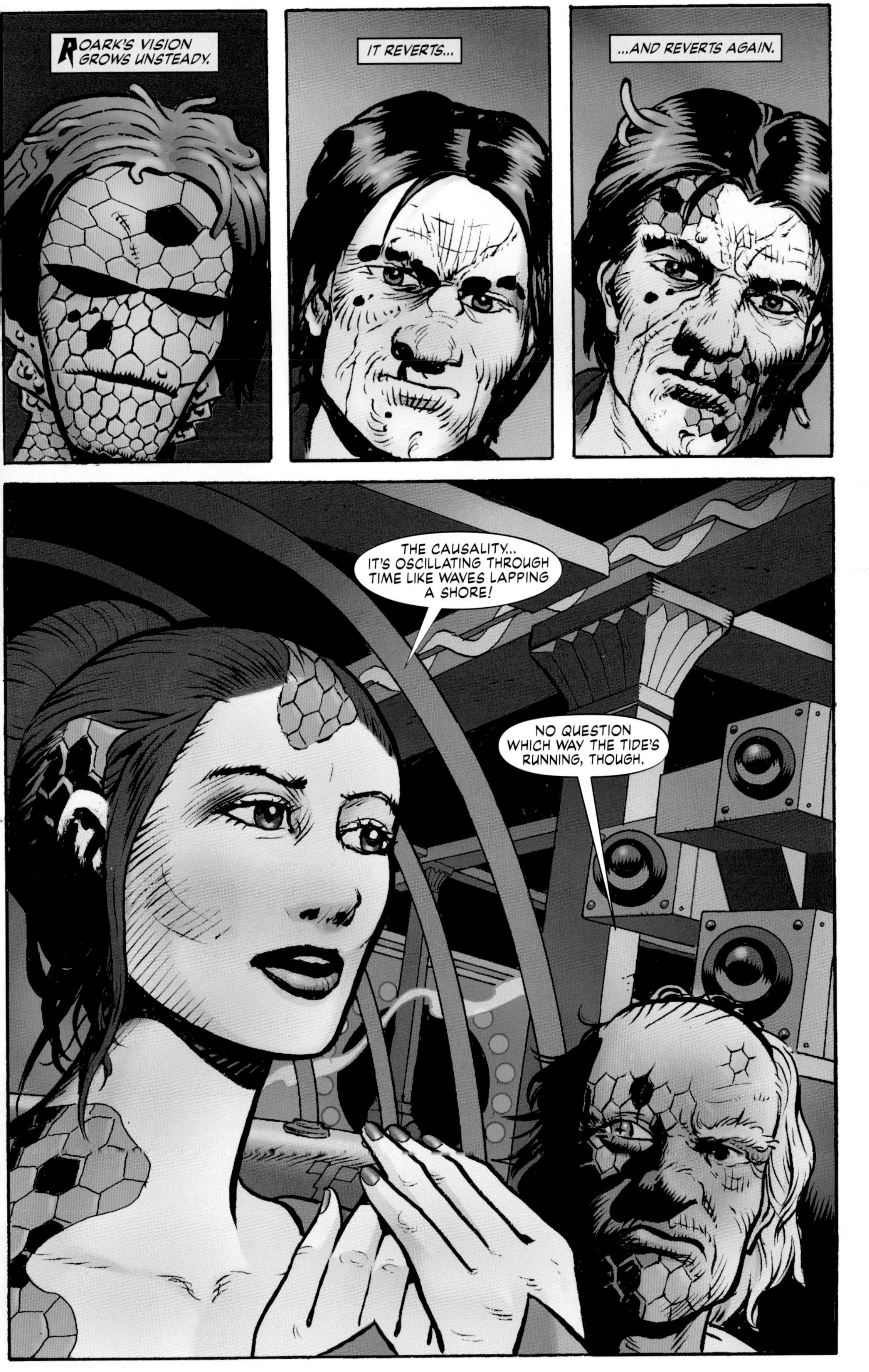
ROARK'S VISION GROWS UNSTEADY.
IT REVERTS...
...AND REVERTS AGAIN.
THE CAUSALITY... IT'S OSCILLATING THROUGH TIME LIKE WAVES LAPPING A SHORE!
NO QUESTION WHICH WAY THE TIDE'S RUNNING, THOUGH.

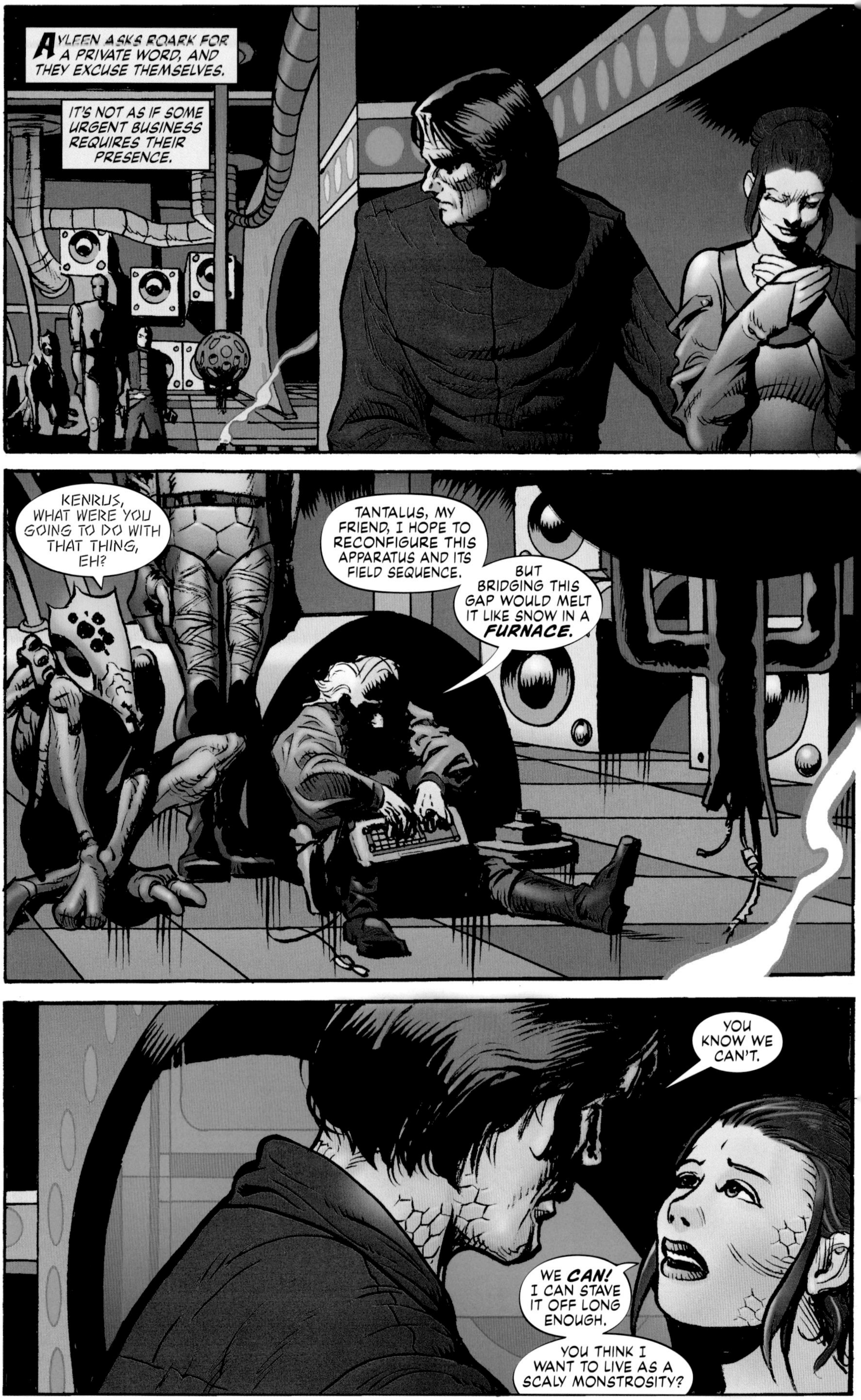
AYLEEN ASKS ROARK FOR A PRIVATE WORD, AND THEY EXCUSE THEMSELVES.
IT'S NOT AS IF SOME URGENT BUSINESS REQUIRES THEIR PRESENCE.
KENRUS, WHAT WERE YOU GOING TO DO WITH THAT THING, EH?
TANTALUS, MY FRIEND, I HOPE TO RECONFIGURE THIS APPARATUS AND ITS FIELD SEQUENCE.
BUT BRIDGING THIS GAP WOULD MELT IT LIKE SNOW IN A FURNACE.
YOU KNOW WE CAN'T.
WE CAN! I CAN STAVE IT OFF LONG ENOUGH.
YOU THINK I WANT TO LIVE AS A SCALY MONSTROSITY?

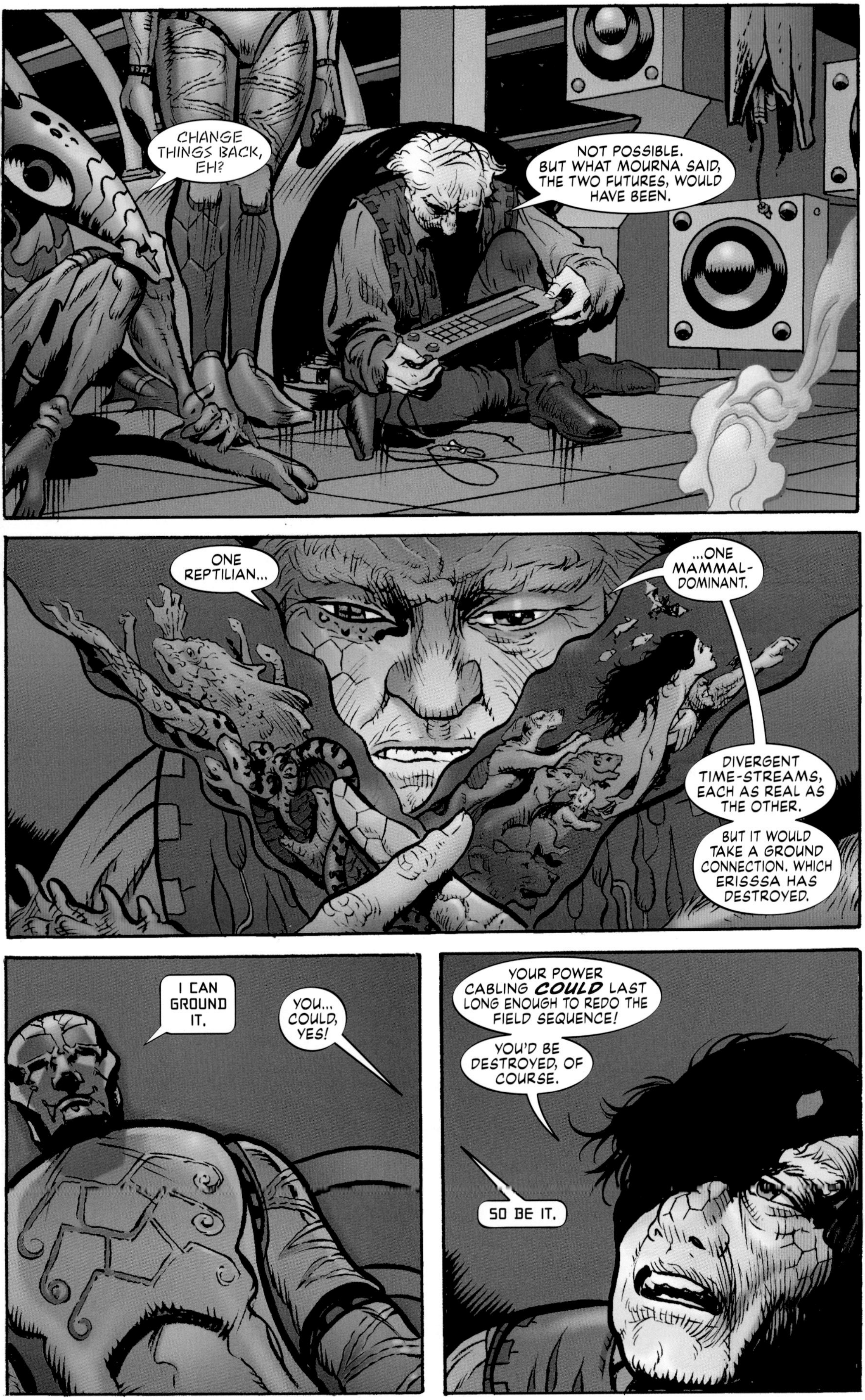
CHANGE THINGS BACK, EH?
NOT POSSIBLE. BUT WHAT MOURNA SAID, THE TWO FUTURES, WOULD HAVE BEEN.
ONE REPTILIAN...
...ONE MAMMAL-DOMINANT.
DIVERGENT TIME-STREAMS, EACH AS REAL AS THE OTHER.
BUT IT WOULD TAKE A GROUND CONNECTION. WHICH ERISSSA HAS DESTROYED.
I CAN GROUND IT.
YOU... COULD, YES!
YOUR POWER CABLING COULD LAST LONG ENOUGH TO REDO THE FIELD SEQUENCE!
YOU'D BE DESTROYED, OF COURSE.
SO BE IT.

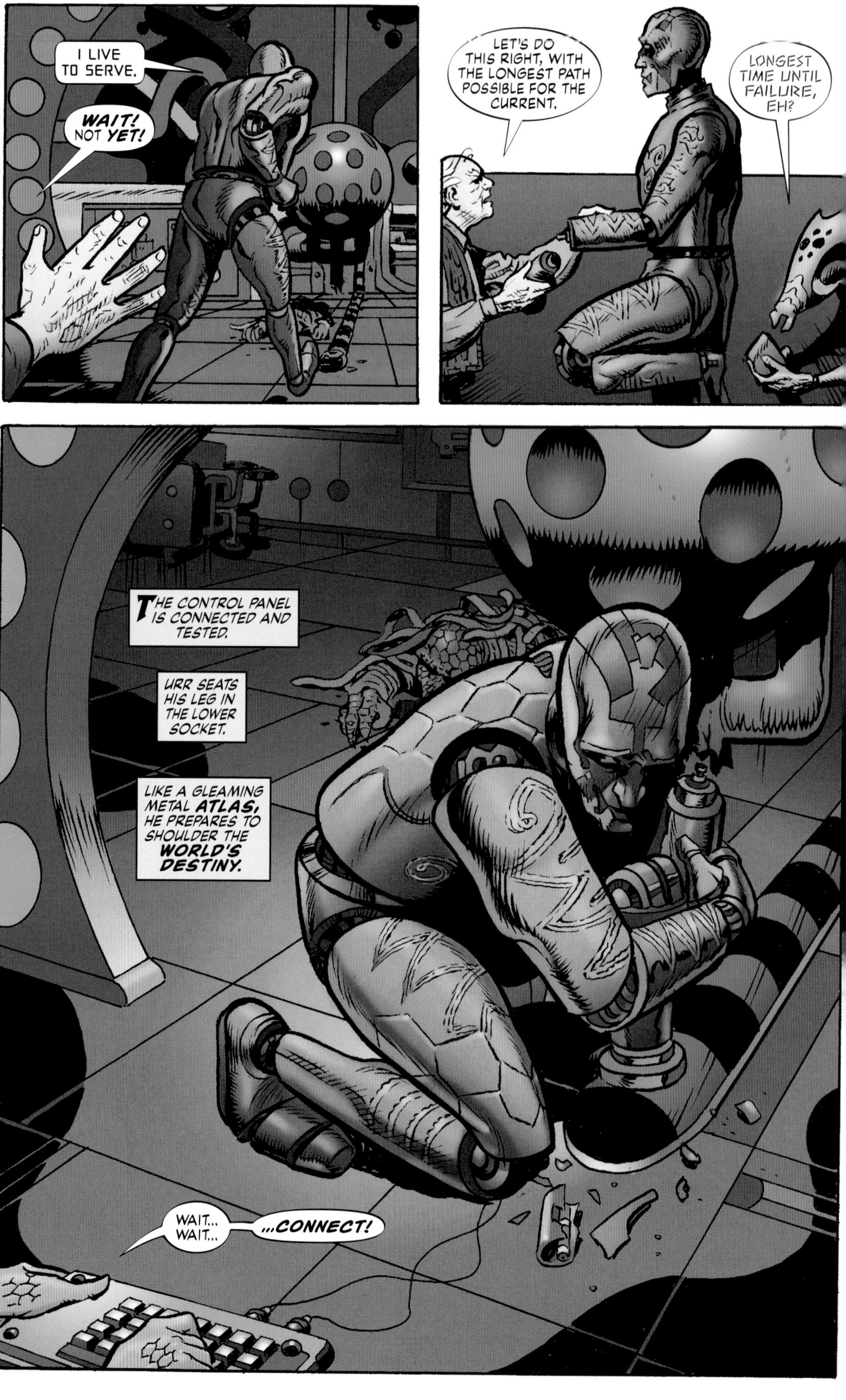
I LIVE TO SERVE.
WAIT! NOT YET!
LET'S DO THIS RIGHT, WITH THE LONGEST PATH POSSIBLE FOR THE CURRENT.
LONGEST TIME UNTIL FAILURE, EH?
THE CONTROL PANEL IS CONNECTED AND TESTED.
URR SEATS HIS LEG IN THE LOWER SOCKET.
LIKE A GLEAMING METAL ATLAS, HE PREPARES TO SHOULDER THE WORLD'S DESTINY.
WAIT... WAIT...
...CONNECT!

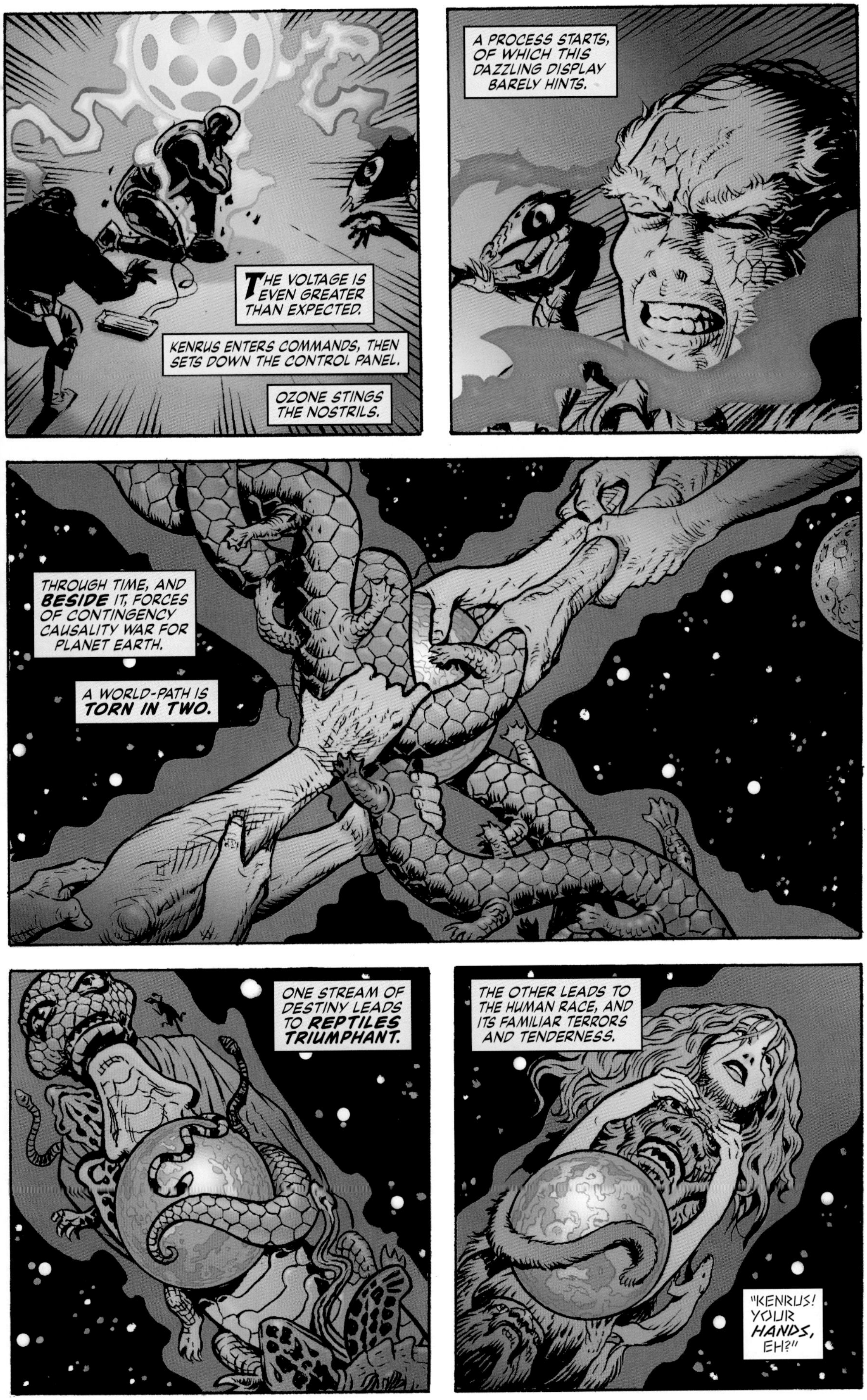
THE VOLTAGE IS EVEN GREATER THAN EXPECTED.
KENRUS ENTERS COMMANDS, THEN SETS DOWN THE CONTROL PANEL.
OZONE STINGS THE NOSTRILS.
A PROCESS STARTS, OF WHICH THIS DAZZLING DISPLAY BARELY HINTS.
THROUGH TIME, AND BESIDE IT, FORCES OF CONTINGENCY CAUSALITY WAR FOR PLANET EARTH.
A WORLD-PATH IS TORN IN TWO.
ONE STREAM OF DESTINY LEADS TO REPTILES TRIUMPHANT.
THE OTHER LEADS TO THE HUMAN RACE, AND ITS FAMILIAR TERRORS AND TENDERNESS.
"KENRUS! YOUR HANDS, EH?"

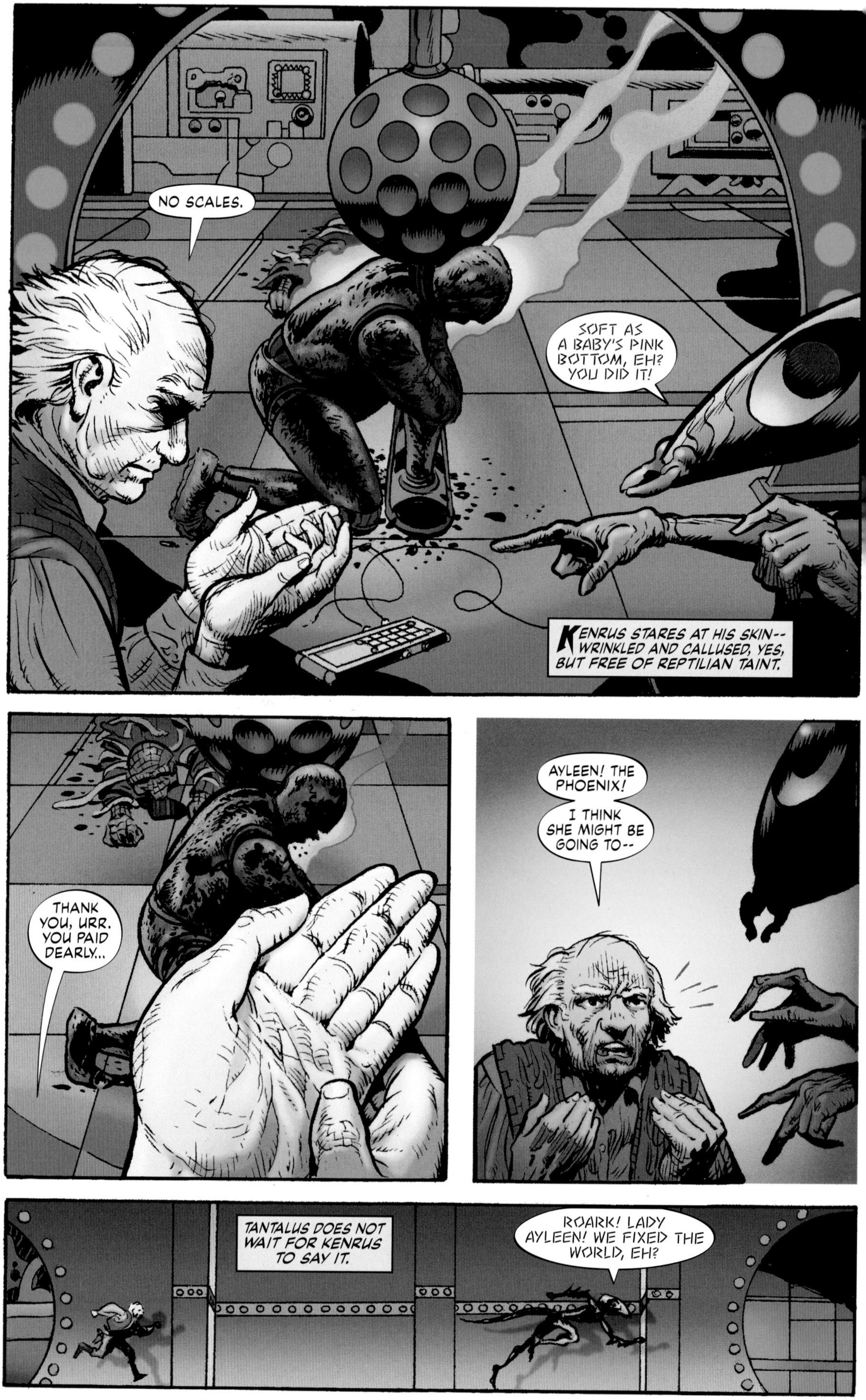
NO SCALES.
SOFT AS A BABY'S PINK BOTTOM, EH? YOU DID IT!
KENRUS STARES AT HIS SKIN--WRINKLED AND CALLUSED, YES, BUT FREE OF REPTILIAN TAINT.
THANK YOU, URR. YOU PAID DEARLY...
AYLEEN! THE PHOENIX!
I THINK SHE MIGHT BE GOING TO--
TANTALUS DOES NOT WAIT FOR KENRUS TO SAY IT.
ROARK! LADY AYLEEN! WE FIXED THE WORLD, EH?

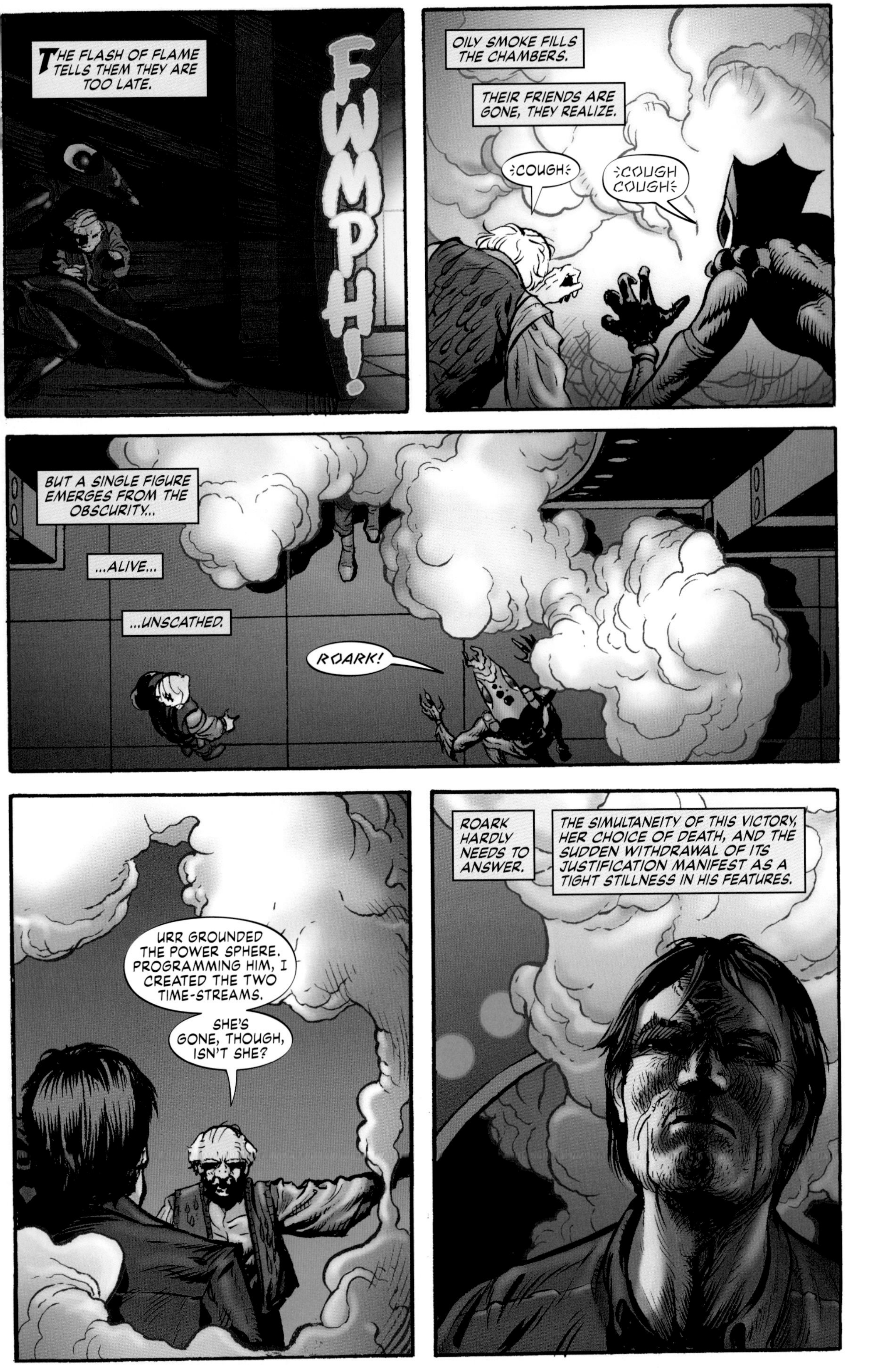
THE FLASH OF FLAME TELLS THEM THEY ARE TOO LATE.
FWMPH!
OILY SMOKE FILLS THE CHAMBERS.
THEIR FRIENDS ARE GONE, THEY REALIZE.
COUGH
COUGH COUGH
BUT A SINGLE FIGURE EMERGES FROM THE OBSCURITY...
...ALIVE...
...UNSCATHED.
ROARK!
URR GROUNDED THE POWER SPHERE. PROGRAMMING HIM, I CREATED THE TWO TIME-STREAMS.
SHE'S GONE, THOUGH, ISN'T SHE?
ROARK HARDLY NEEDS TO ANSWER.
THE SIMULTANEITY OF THIS VICTORY, HER CHOICE OF DEATH, AND THE SUDDEN WITHDRAWAL OF ITS JUSTIFICATION MANIFEST AS A TIGHT STILLNESS IN HIS FEATURES.

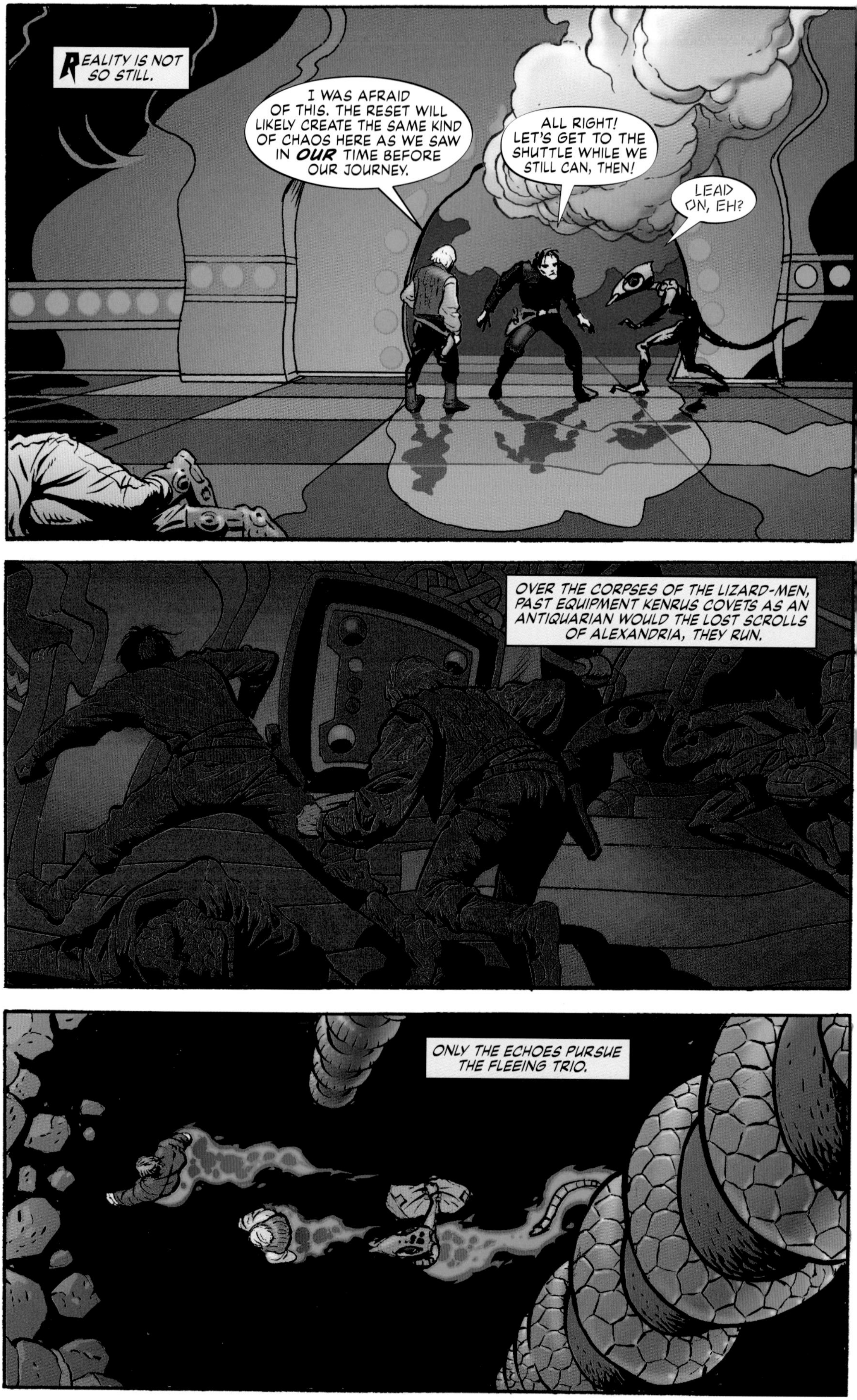
REALITY IS NOT SO STILL.
I WAS AFRAID OF THIS. THE RESET WILL LIKELY CREATE THE SAME KIND OF CHAOS HERE AS WE SAW IN OUR TIME BEFORE OUR JOURNEY.
ALL RIGHT! LET'S GET TO THE SHUTTLE WHILE WE STILL CAN, THEN!
LEAD ON, EH?
OVER THE CORPSES OF THE LIZARD-MEN, PAST EQUIPMENT KENRUS COVETS AS AN ANTIQUARIAN WOULD THE LOST SCROLLS OF ALEXANDRIA, THEY RUN.
ONLY THE ECHOES PURSUE THE FLEEING TRIO.

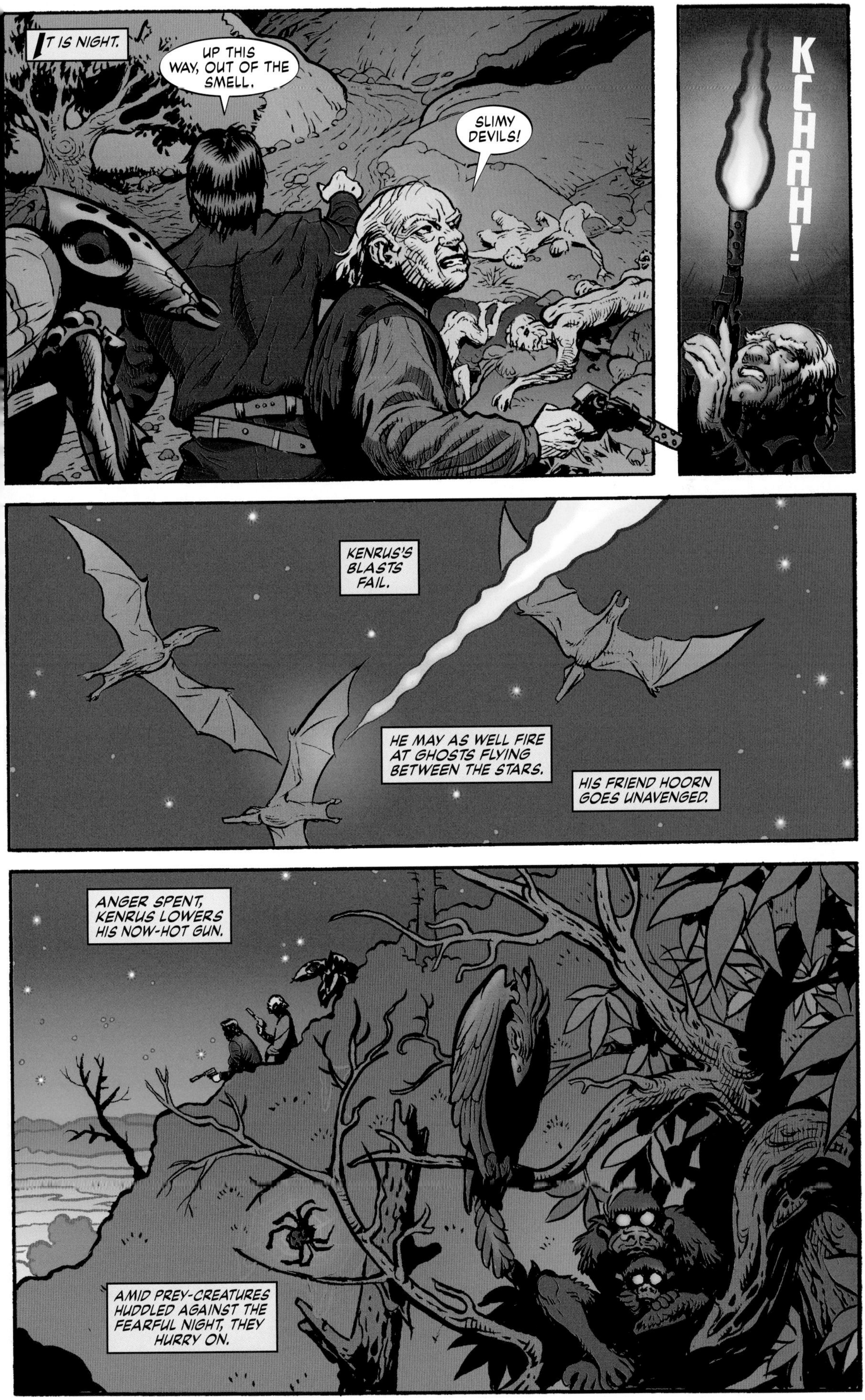
IT IS NIGHT.
UP THIS WAY, OUT OF THE SMELL.
SLIMY DEVILS!
KCHAH!
KENRUS'S BLASTS FAIL.
HE MAY AS WELL FIRE AT GHOSTS FLYING BETWEEN THE STARS.
HIS FRIEND HOORN GOES UNAVENGED.
ANGER SPENT, KENRUS LOWERS HIS NOW-HOT GUN.
AMID PREY-CREATURES HUDDLED AGAINST THE FEARFUL NIGHT, THEY HURRY ON.

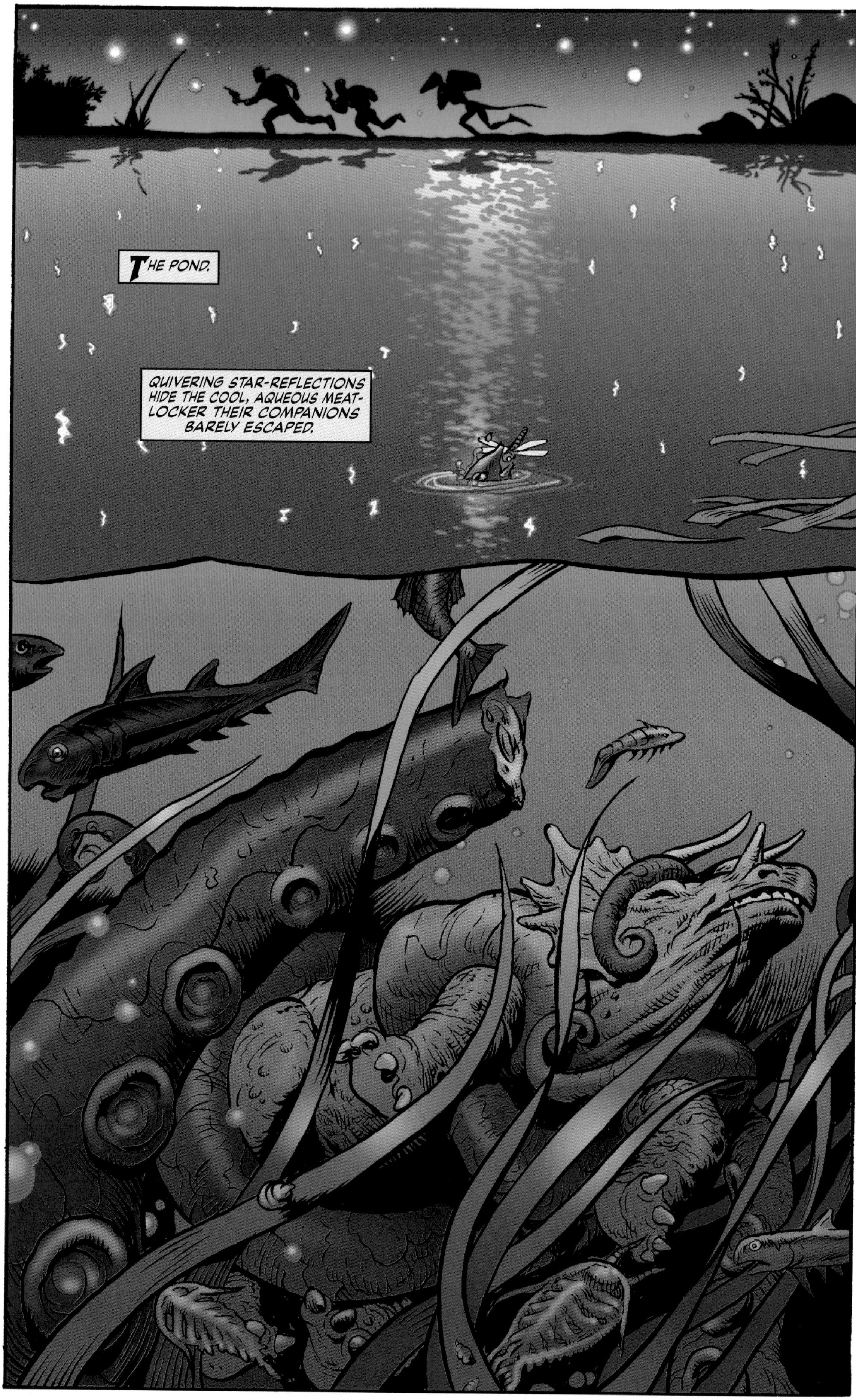
THE POND.
QUIVERING STAR-REFLECTIONS HIDE THE COOL, AQUEOUS MEAT-LOCKER THEIR COMPANIONS BARELY ESCAPED.

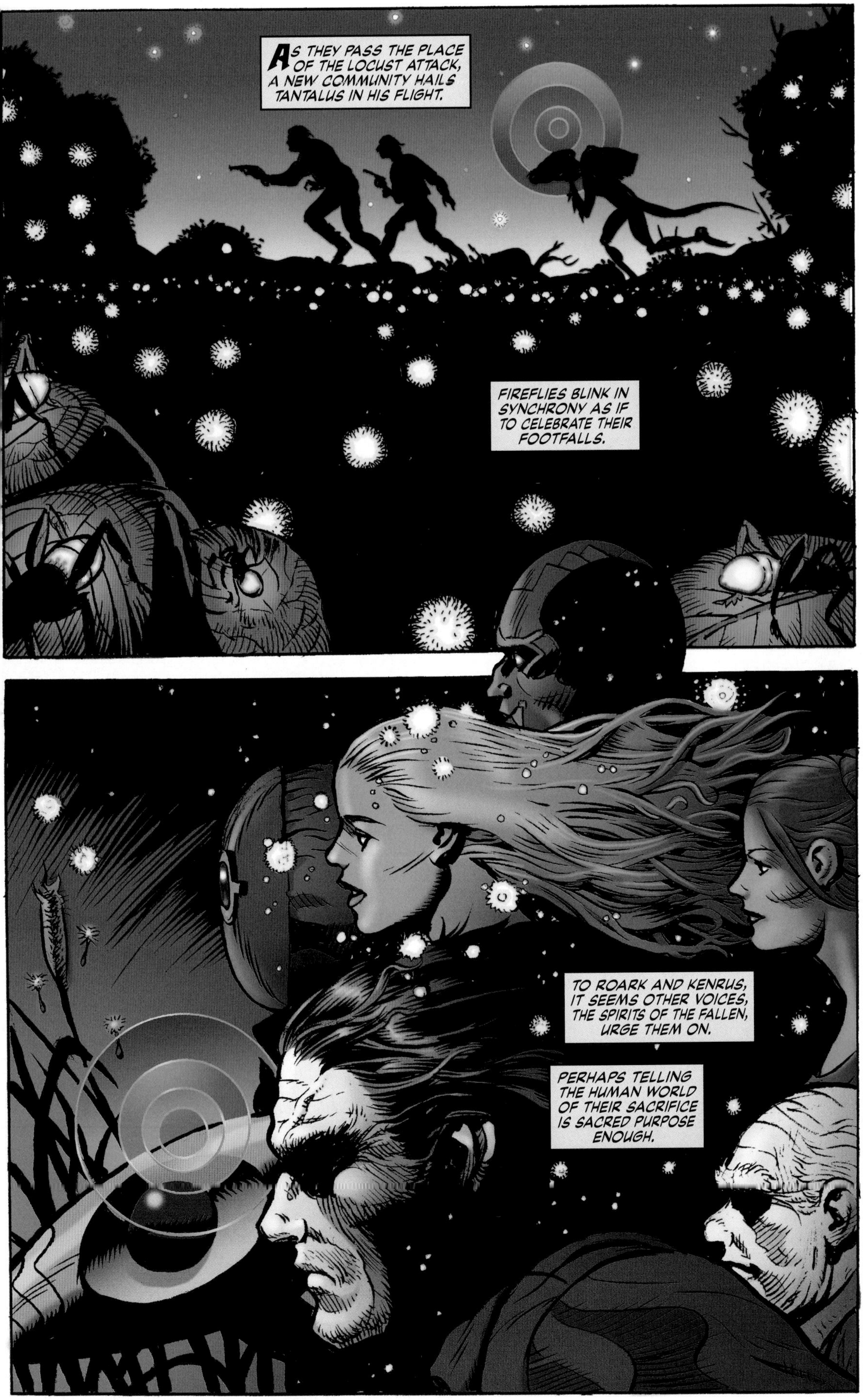
AS THEY PASS THE PLACE OF THE LOCUST ATTACK, A NEW COMMUNITY HAILS TANTALUS IN HIS FLIGHT.
FIREFLIES BLINK IN SYNCHRONY AS IF TO CELEBRATE THEIR FOOTFALLS.
TO ROARK AND KENRUS, IT SEEMS OTHER VOICES, THE SPIRITS OF THE FALLEN, URGE THEM ON.
PERHAPS TELLING THE HUMAN WORLD OF THEIR SACRIFICE IS SACRED PURPOSE ENOUGH.

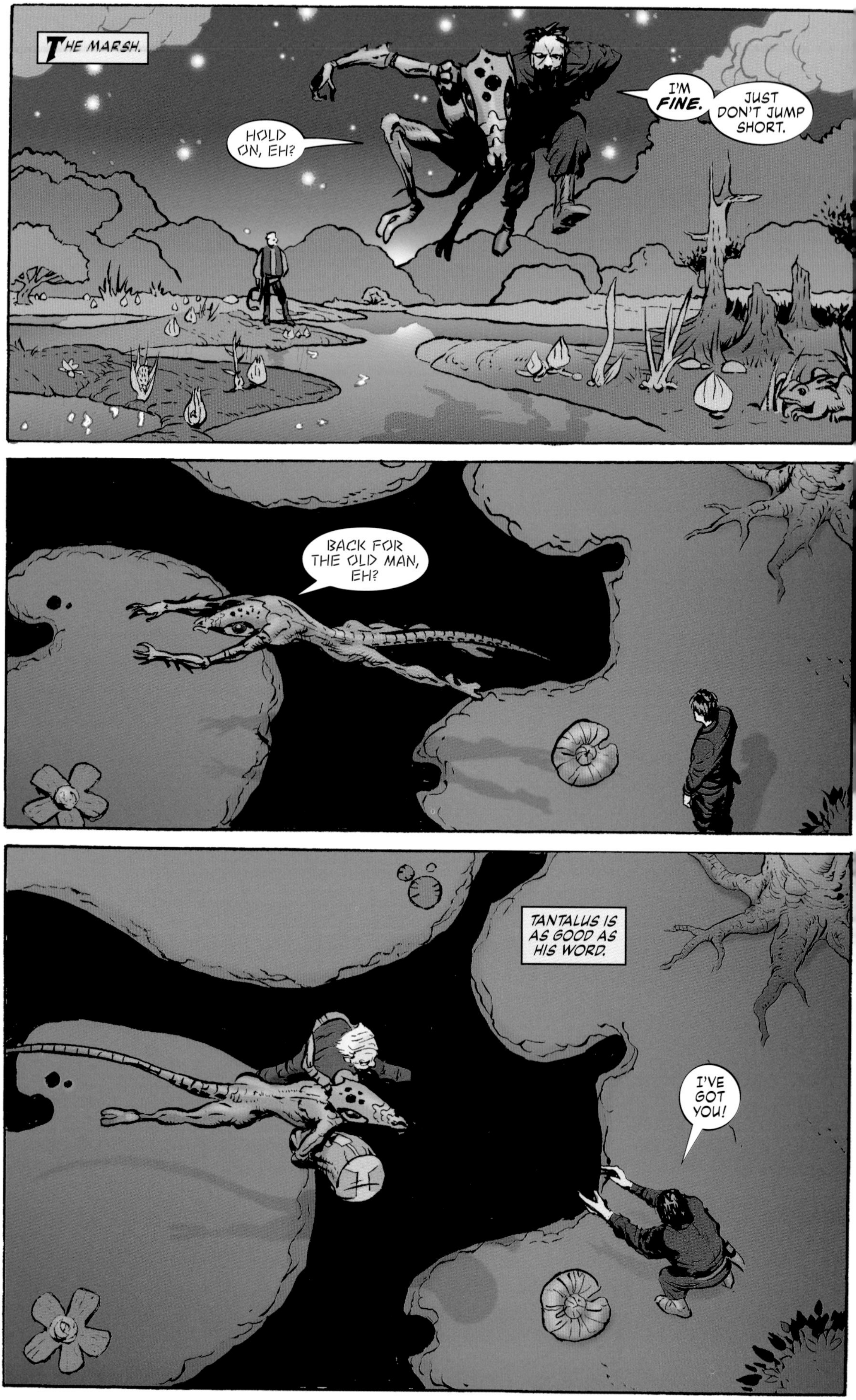
THE MARSH.
HOLD ON, EH?
I'M FINE.
JUST DON'T JUMP SHORT.
BACK FOR THE OLD MAN, EH?
TANTALUS IS AS GOOD AS HIS WORD.
I'VE GOT YOU!

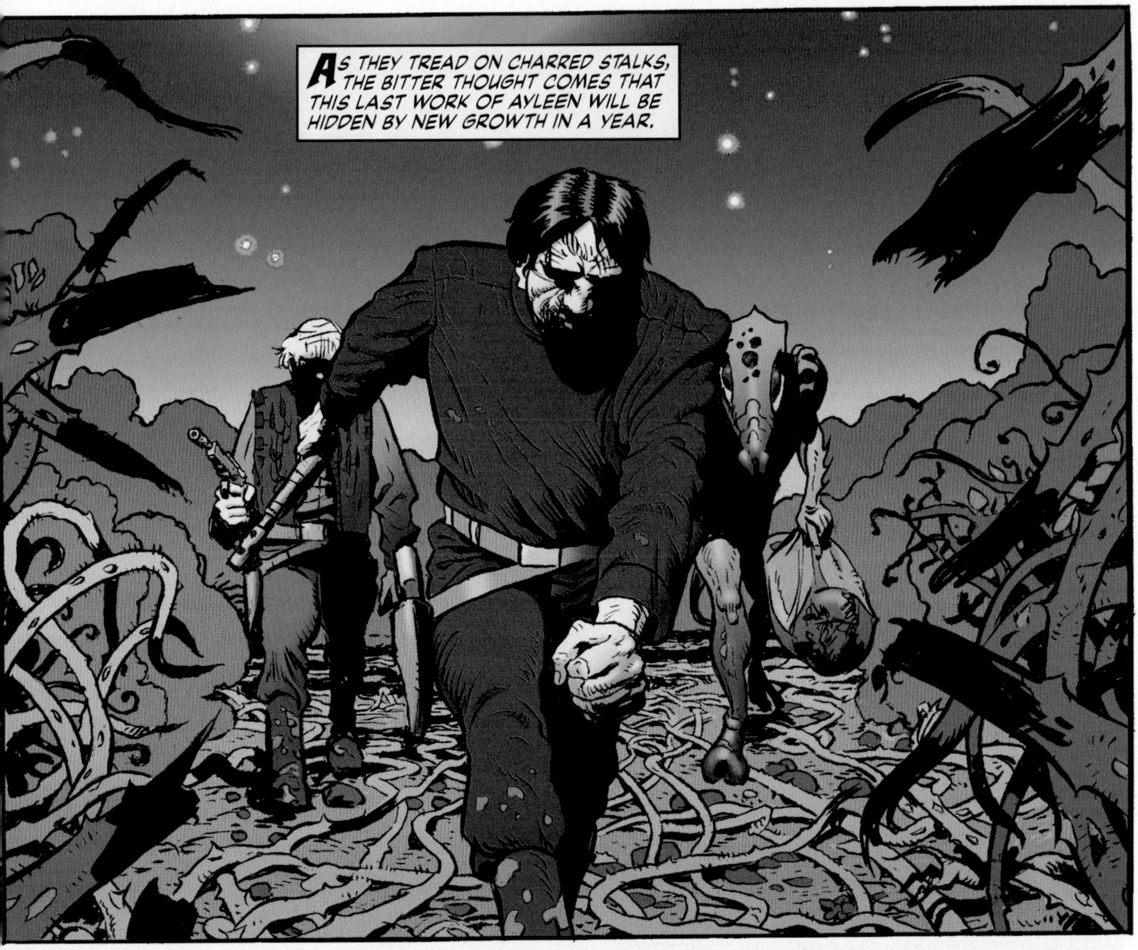
As they tread on charred stalks, the bitter thought comes that this last work of Ayleen will be hidden by new growth in a year.

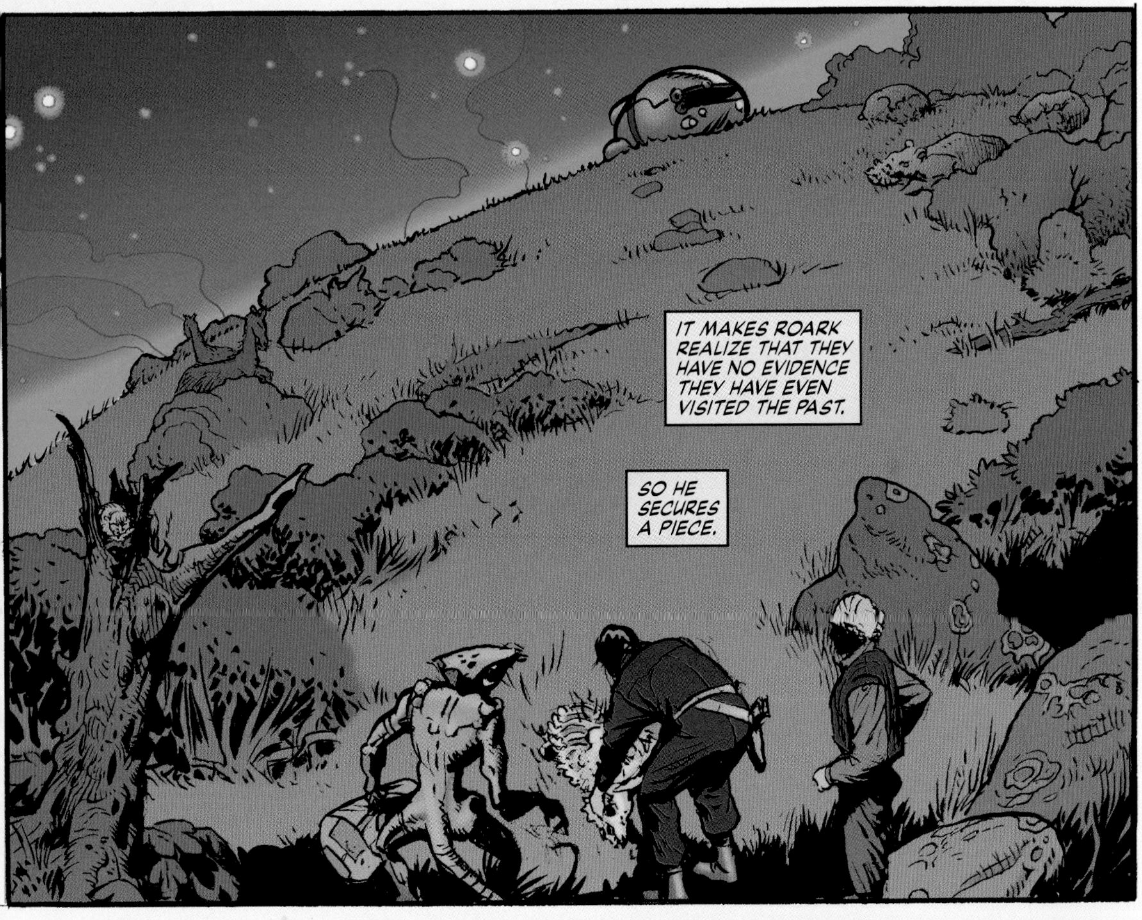
It makes Roark realize that they have no evidence they have even visited the past.
So he secures a piece.

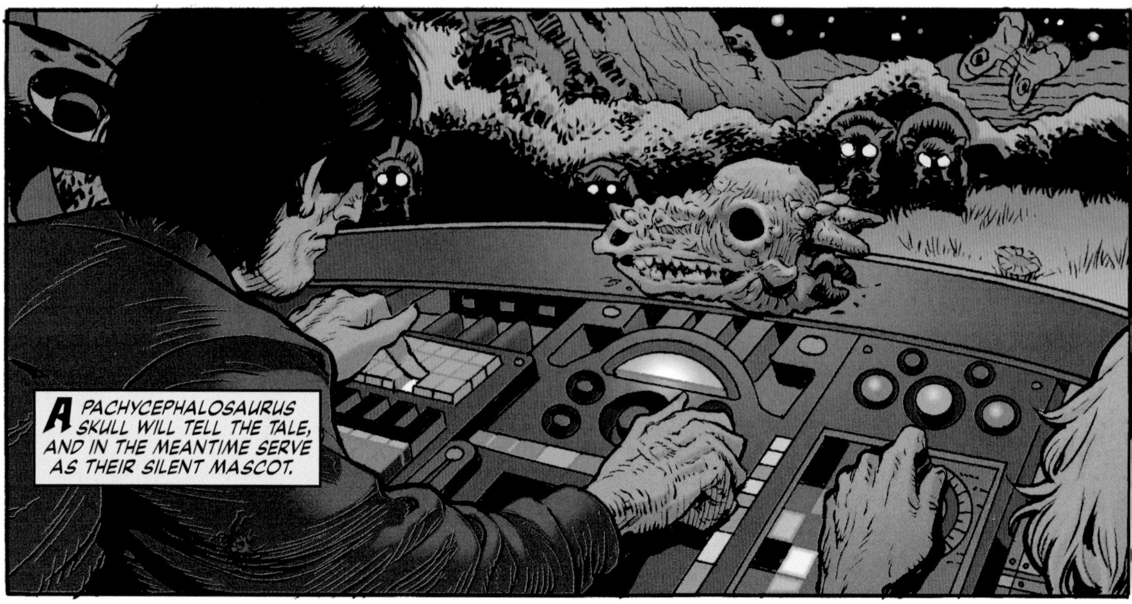
A PACHYCEPHALOSAURUS SKULL WILL TELL THE TALE, AND IN THE MEANTIME SERVE AS THEIR SILENT MASCOT.

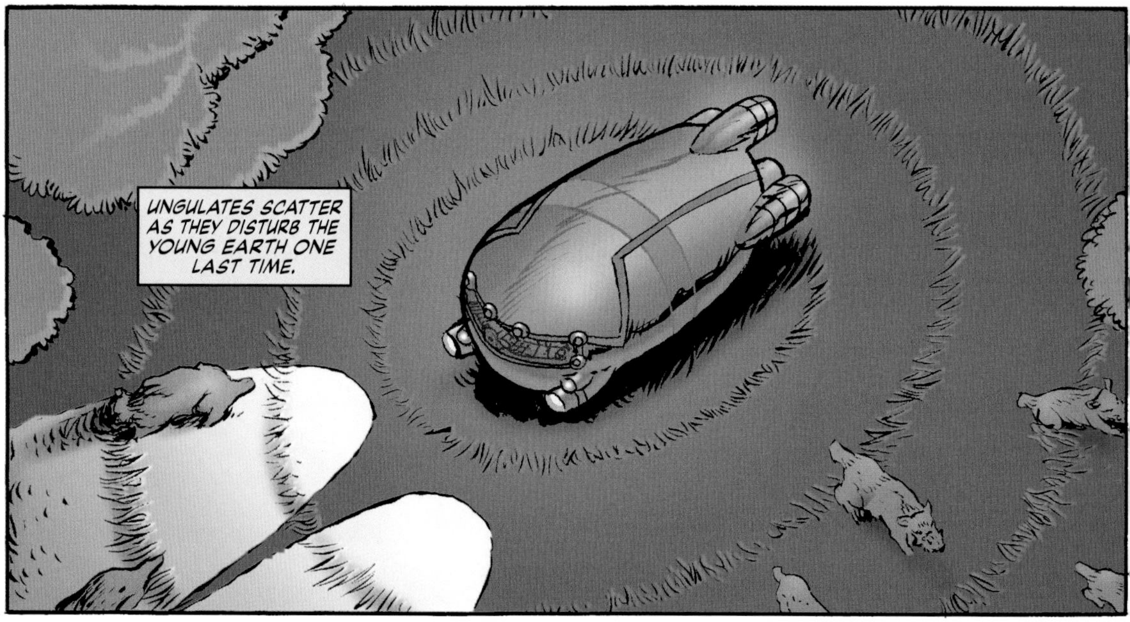
UNGULATES SCATTER AS THEY DISTURB THE YOUNG EARTH ONE LAST TIME.

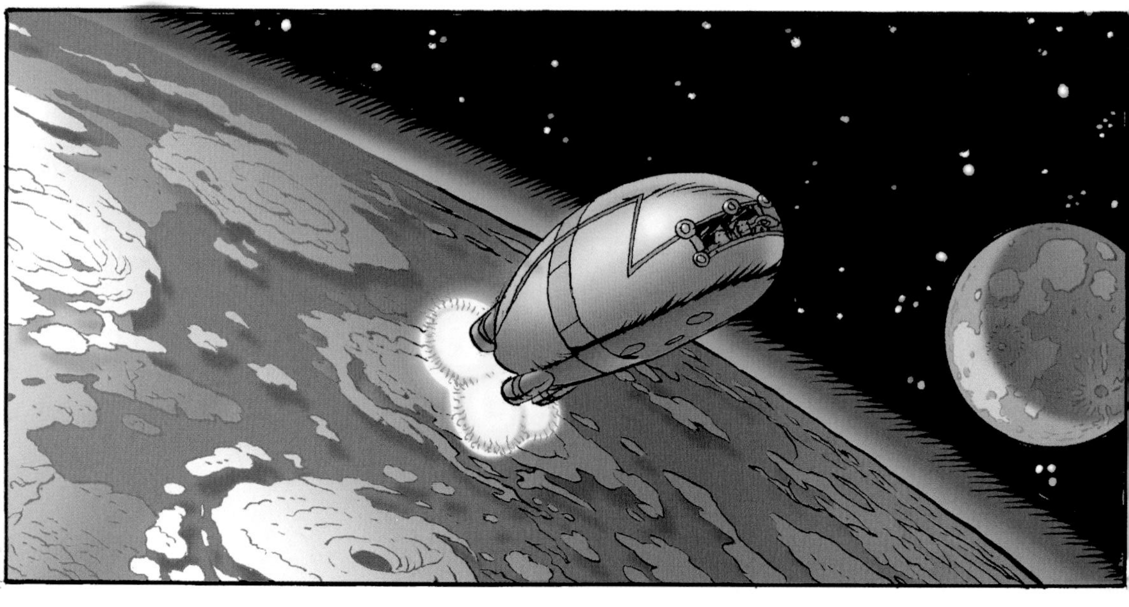

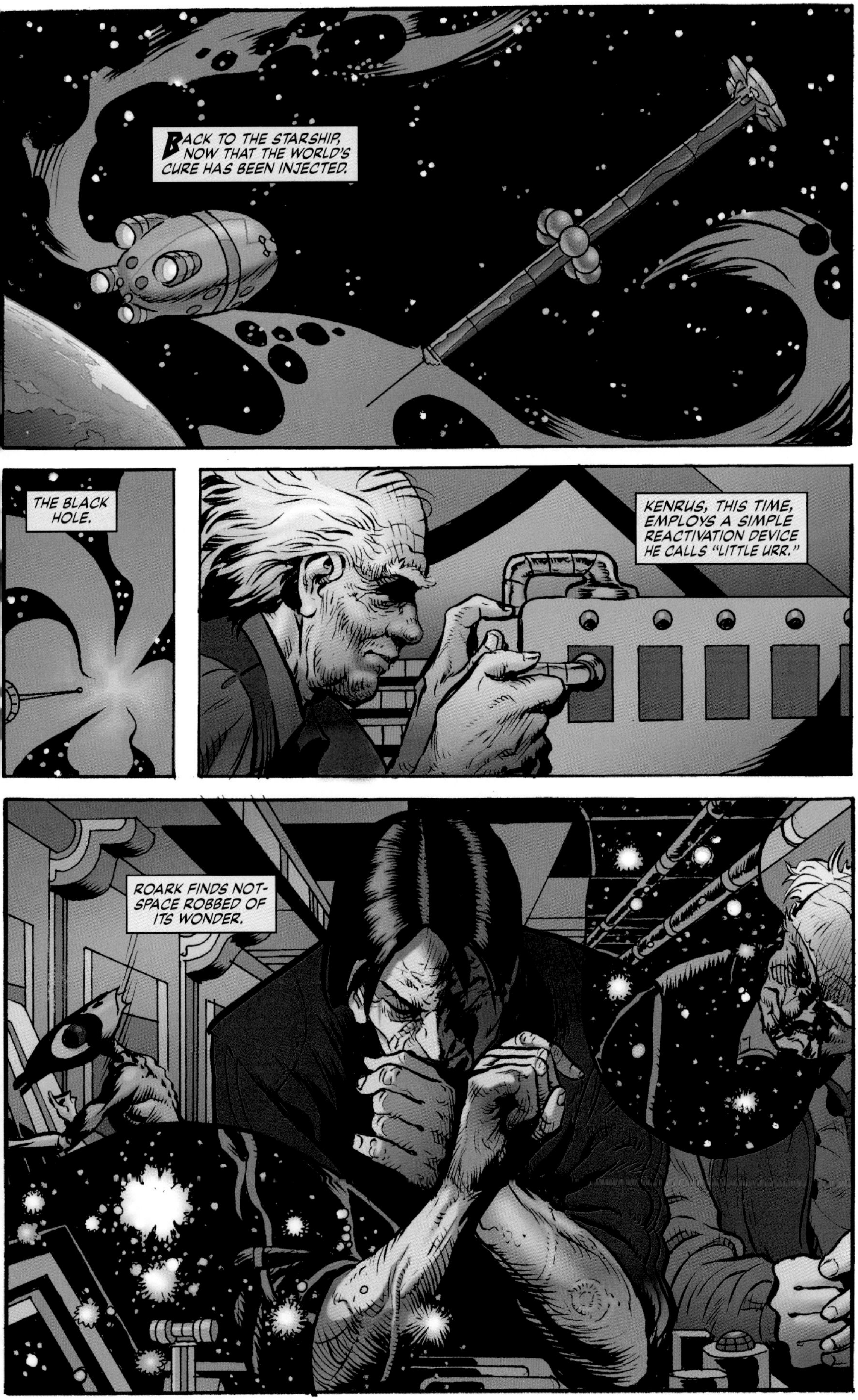
BACK TO THE STARSHIP, NOW THAT THE WORLD'S CURE HAS BEEN INJECTED.
THE BLACK HOLE.
KENRUS, THIS TIME, EMPLOYS A SIMPLE REACTIVATION DEVICE HE CALLS "LITTLE URR."
ROARK FINDS NOT-SPACE ROBBED OF ITS WONDER.

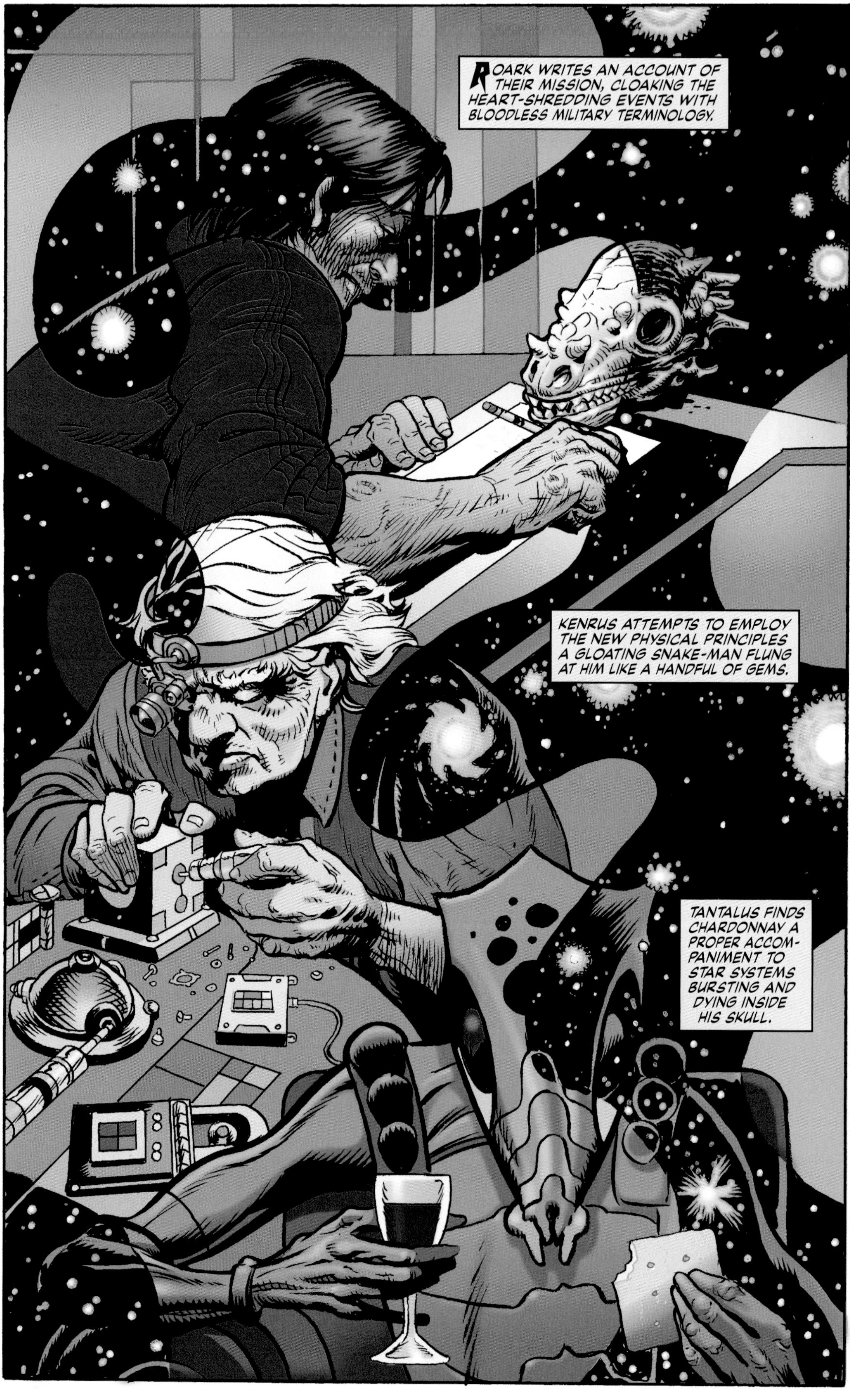
ROARK WRITES AN ACCOUNT OF THEIR MISSION, CLOAKING THE HEART-SHREDDING EVENTS WITH BLOODLESS MILITARY TERMINOLOGY.
KENRUS ATTEMPTS TO EMPLOY THE NEW PHYSICAL PRINCIPLES A GLOATING SNAKE-MAN FLUNG AT HIM LIKE A HANDFUL OF GEMS.
TANTALUS FINDS CHARDONNAY A PROPER ACCOMPANIMENT TO STAR SYSTEMS BURSTING AND DYING INSIDE HIS SKULL.

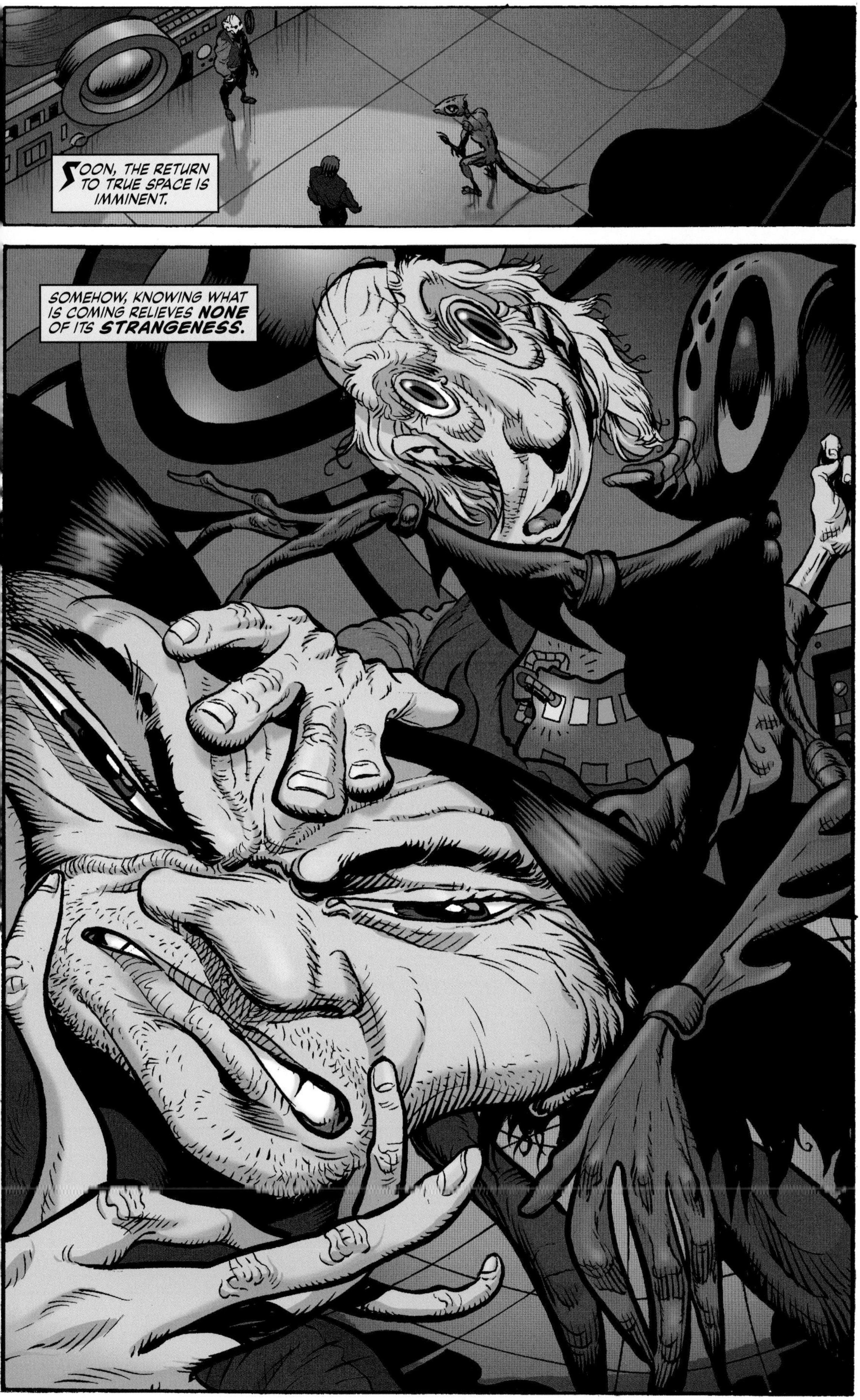
SOON, THE RETURN TO TRUE SPACE IS IMMINENT.
SOMEHOW, KNOWING WHAT IS COMING RELIEVES NONE OF ITS STRANGENESS.

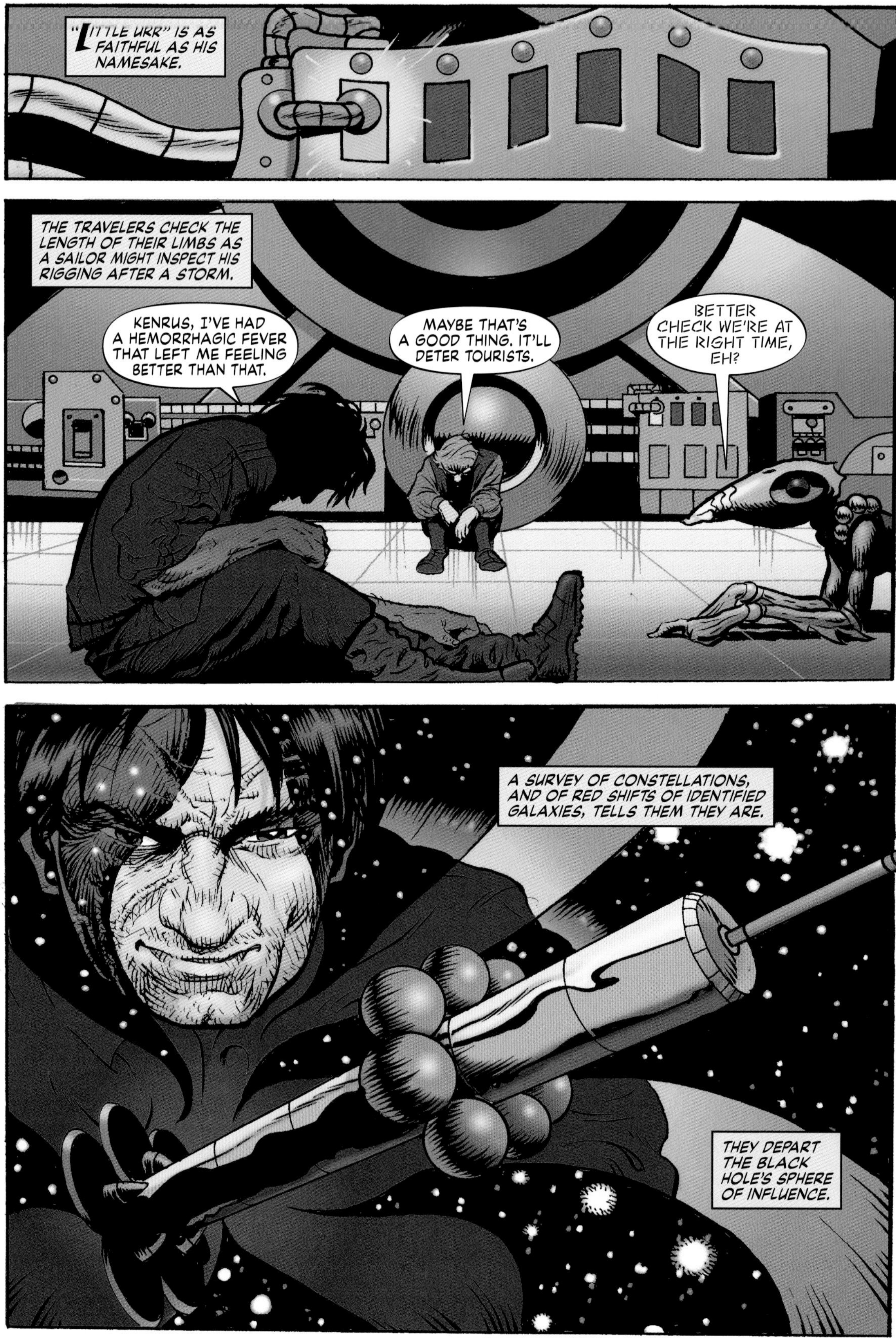
"LITTLE URR" IS AS FAITHFUL AS HIS NAMESAKE.
THE TRAVELERS CHECK THE LENGTH OF THEIR LIMBS AS A SAILOR MIGHT INSPECT HIS RIGGING AFTER A STORM.
KENRUS, I'VE HAD A HEMORRHAGIC FEVER THAT LEFT ME FEELING BETTER THAN THAT.
MAYBE THAT'S A GOOD THING. IT'LL DETER TOURISTS.
BETTER CHECK WE'RE AT THE RIGHT TIME, EH?
A SURVEY OF CONSTELLATIONS, AND OF RED SHIFTS OF IDENTIFIED GALAXIES, TELLS THEM THEY ARE.
THEY DEPART THE BLACK HOLE'S SPHERE OF INFLUENCE.

THE TRIP TO EARTH TAKES THE SAME TIME AS BEFORE.

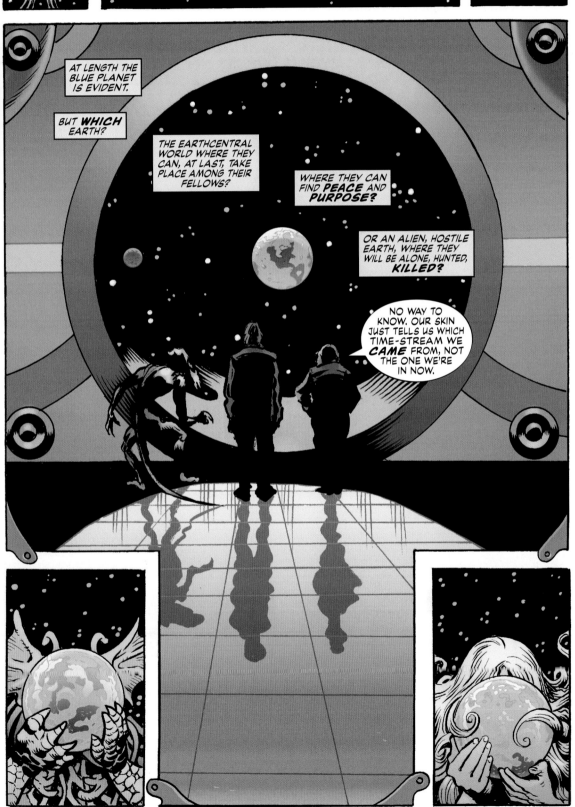

AT LENGTH THE BLUE PLANET IS EVIDENT.

BUT **WHICH** EARTH?

THE EARTHCENTRAL WORLD WHERE THEY CAN, AT LAST, TAKE PLACE AMONG THEIR FELLOWS?

WHERE THEY CAN FIND **PEACE** AND **PURPOSE?**

OR AN ALIEN, HOSTILE EARTH, WHERE THEY WILL BE ALONE, HUNTED, **KILLED?**

NO WAY TO KNOW. OUR SKIN JUST TELLS US WHICH TIME-STREAM WE **CAME** FROM, NOT THE ONE WE'RE IN NOW.

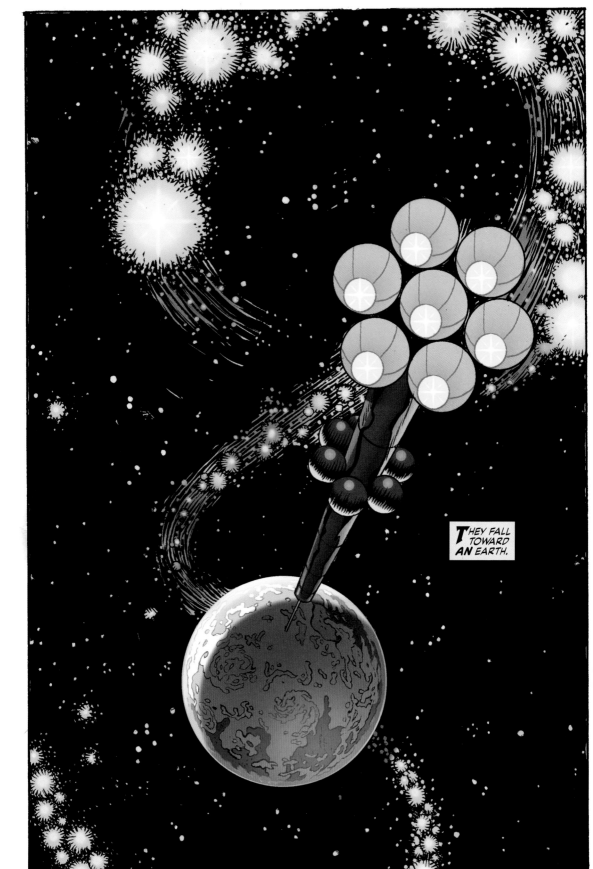

THEY FALL TOWARD AN EARTH.

FIN

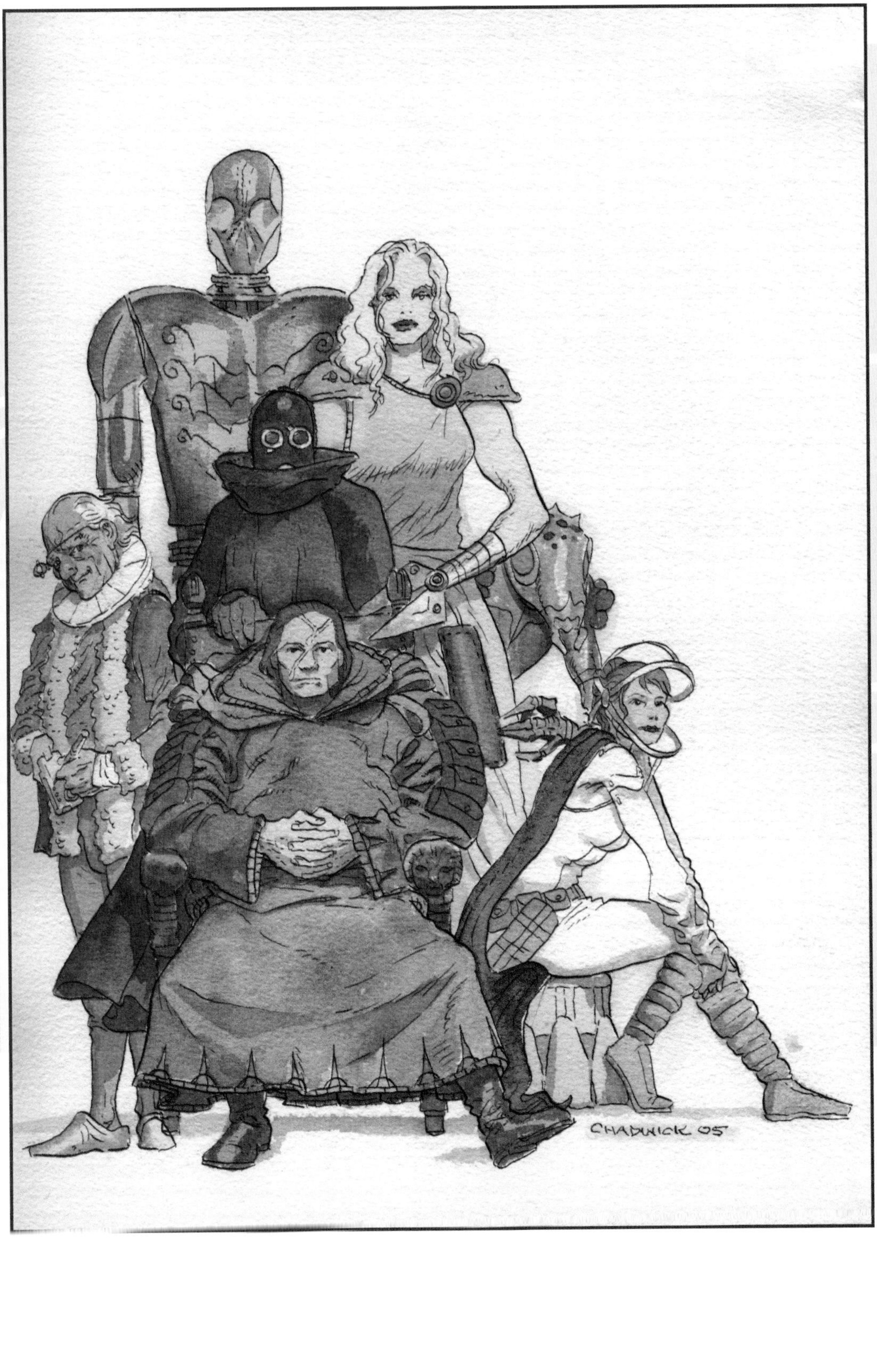
CHADWICK 05

MOURNA
7 feet tall

matted hair

WIDE FOR
SOLES
FEET
MIT
CLAWS
THRU

Sinewy, not bulky muscles

PADS

A GARMENT
SHE CAN
REMOVE AND
PUT ON WITH
CLAWS.

MAGNETIC
CLASPS +
PULLS

AYLEEN

REMOVABLE
FRAME AROUND
HEAD PRECLUDES
CHARGE TOUCH
WITH OTHER
HUMANS
FOLDS UP
FOR EATING

TIGHT
JUMPSUIT
EXCEPT
FOR
SLEEVES

GLOVED
HANDS

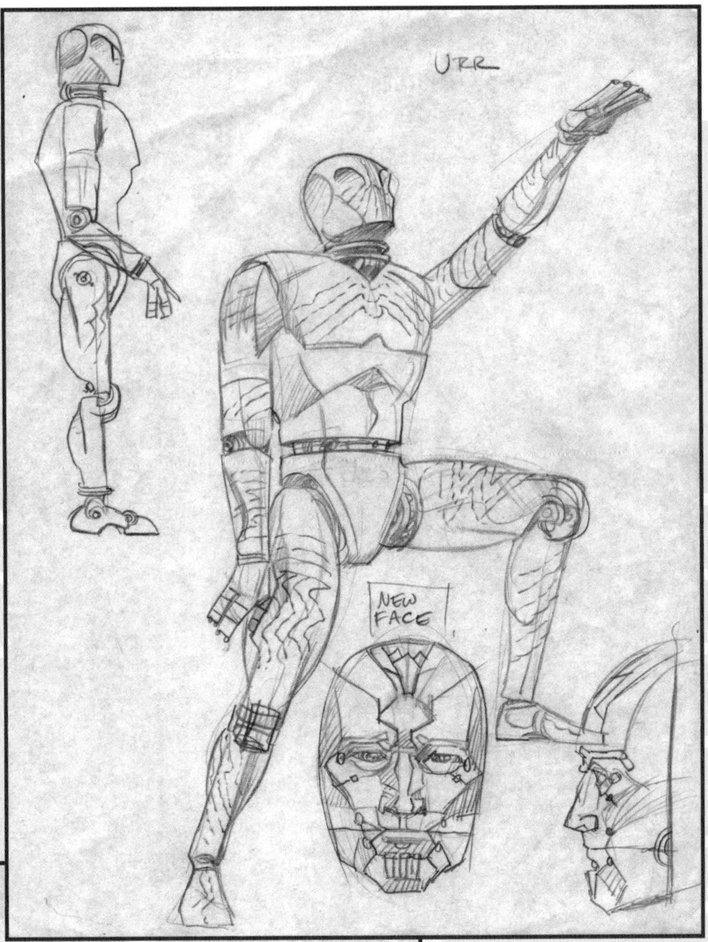
URR
NEW FACE

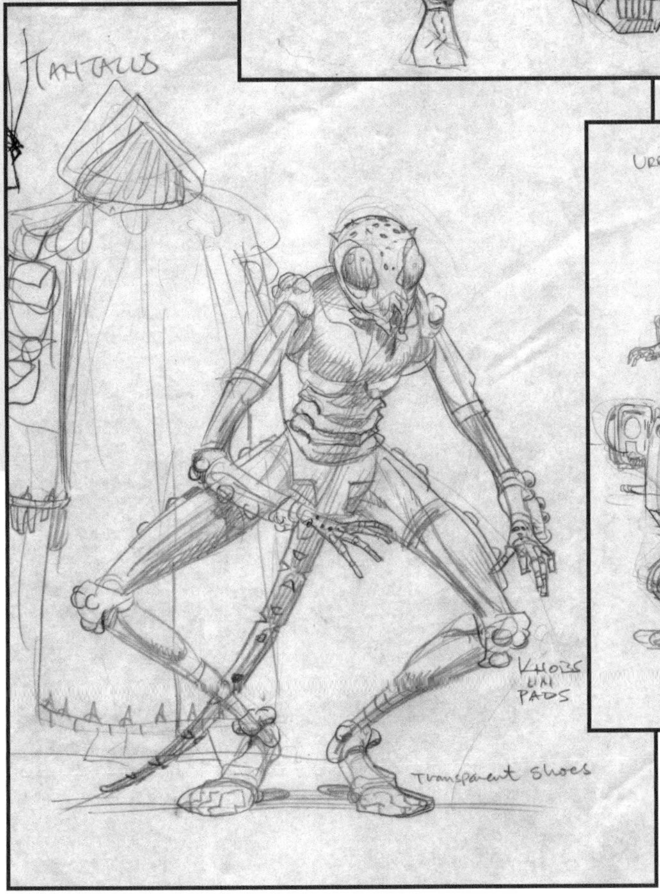
KNOBS ON PADS
Transparent Shoes

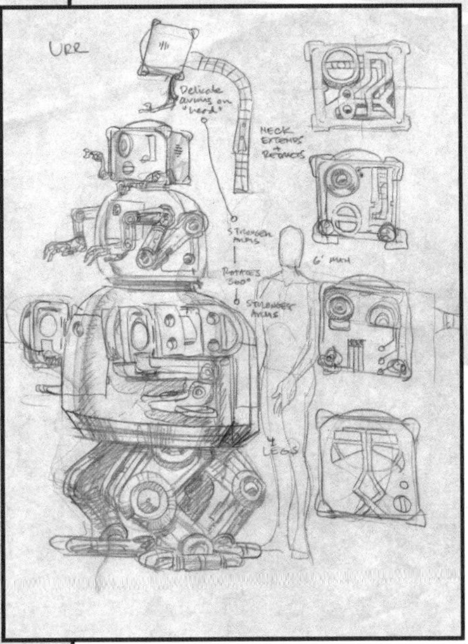
URR
NECK EXTENDS + RETRACTS
6' MAN
LEGS

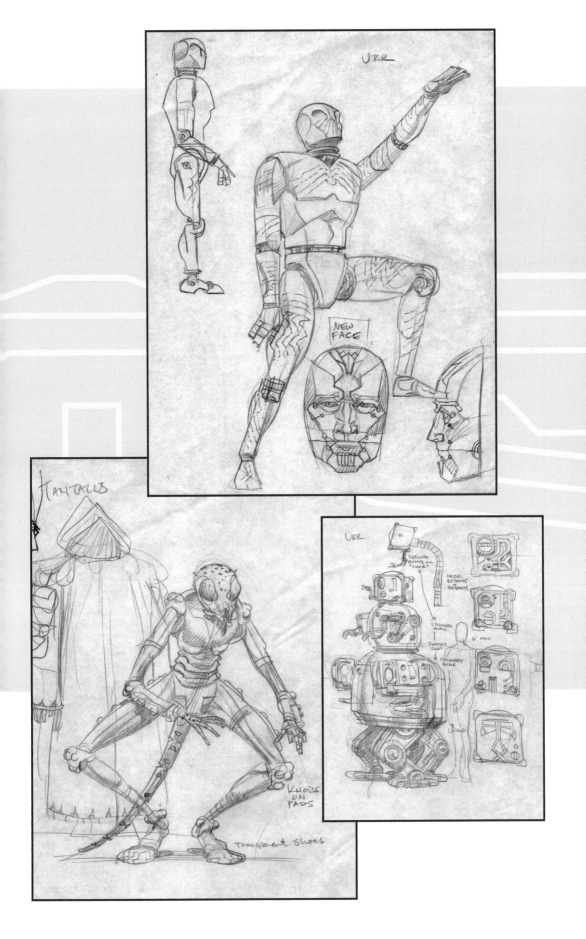

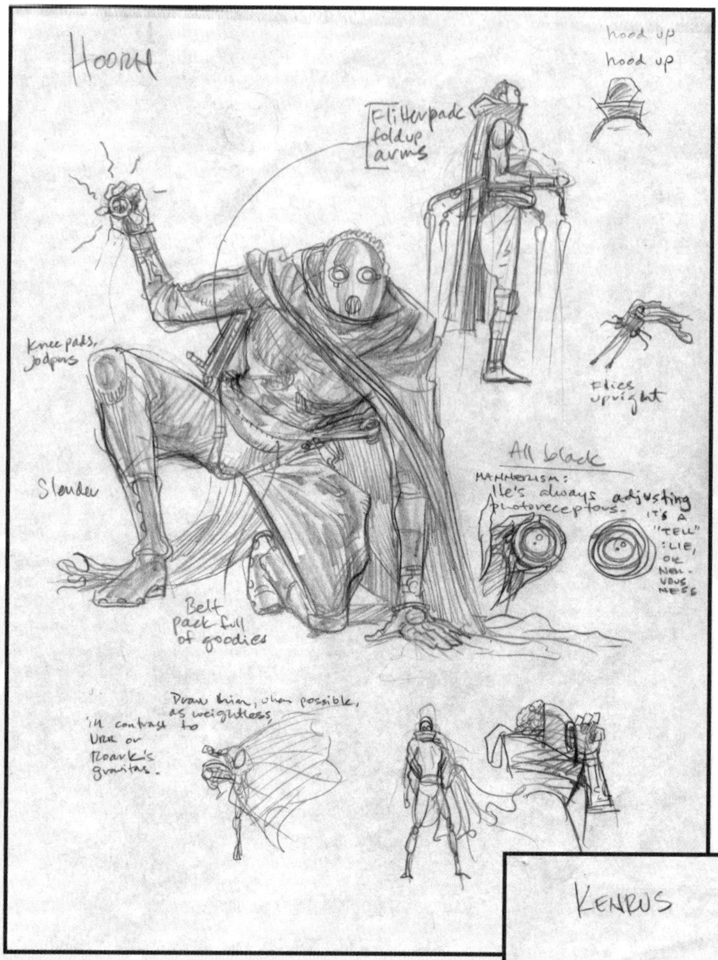

HOORM
hood up
hood up
Flitterpads foldup arms
Knee pads, Jodpurs
Flies upright
All black
MANNERISM:
He's always adjusting photoreceptors.
IT'S A "TELL": LIE, OR NERVOUSNESS
Slender
Belt pack full of goodies
Draw him, when possible, as weightless, in contrast to Urr or Roark's gravitas.

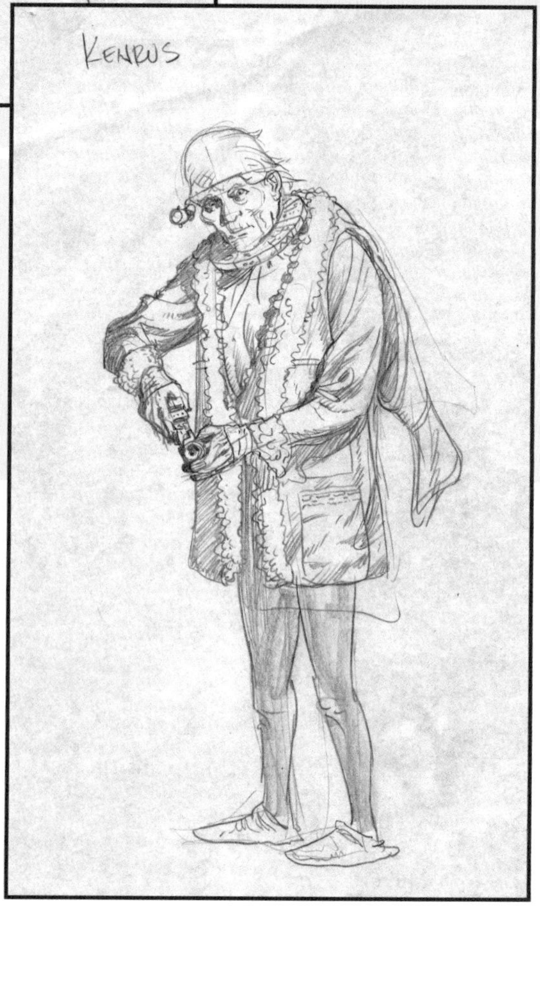

KENRUS

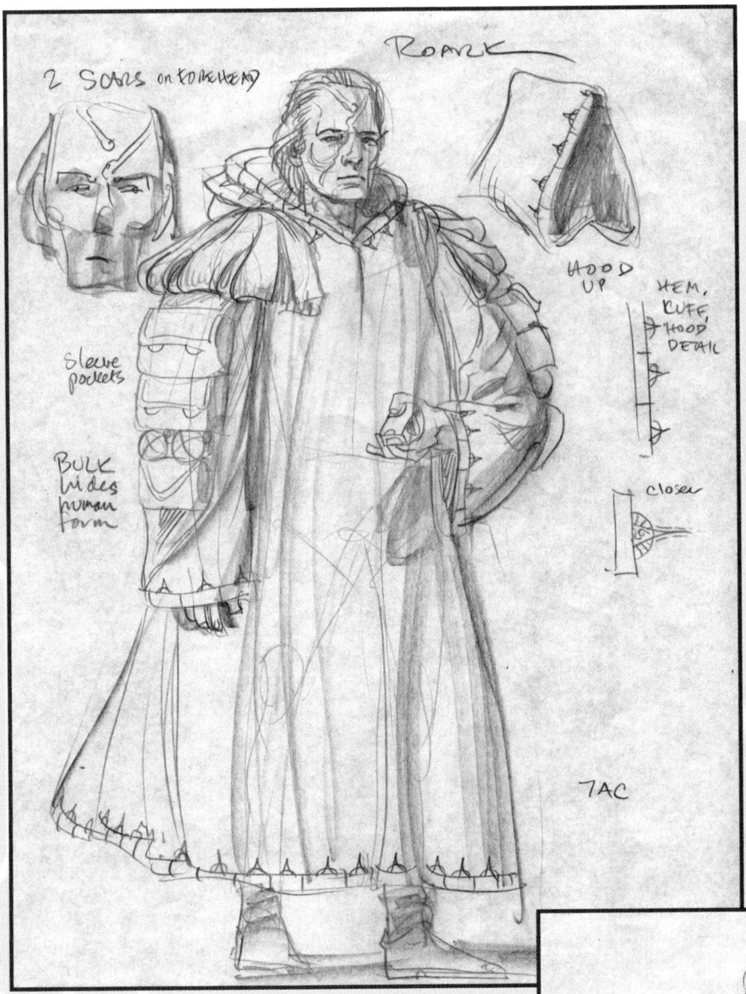
ROARK
2 SCARS on FOREHEAD
HOOD UP
HEM, CUFF, 'HOOD' DETAIL
sleeve pockets
BULK hides human form
closer
7AC

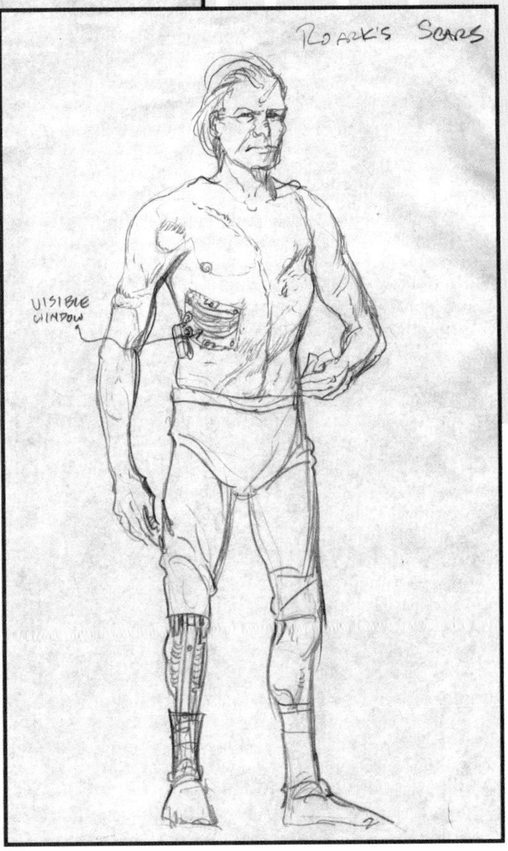
ROARK'S SCARS
VISIBLE WINDOW

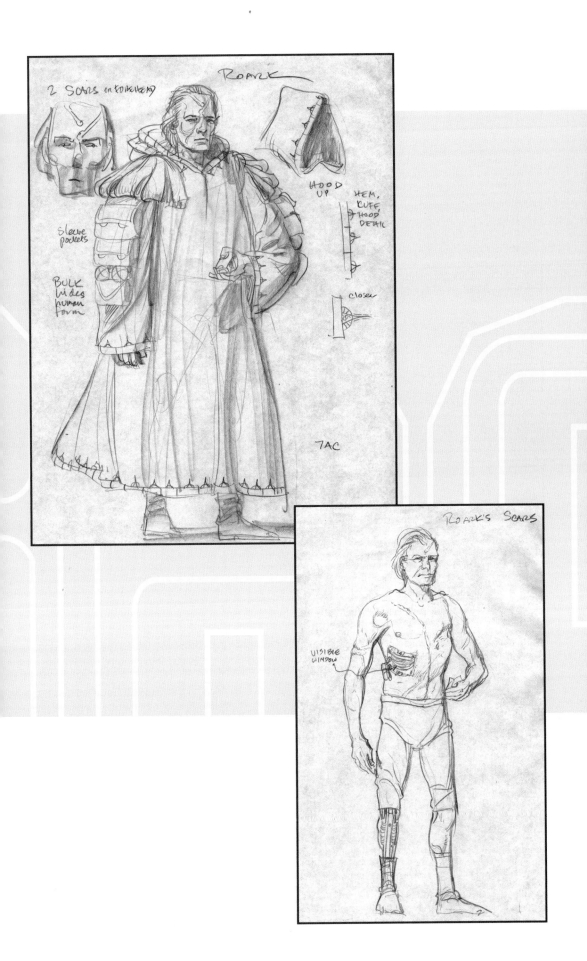

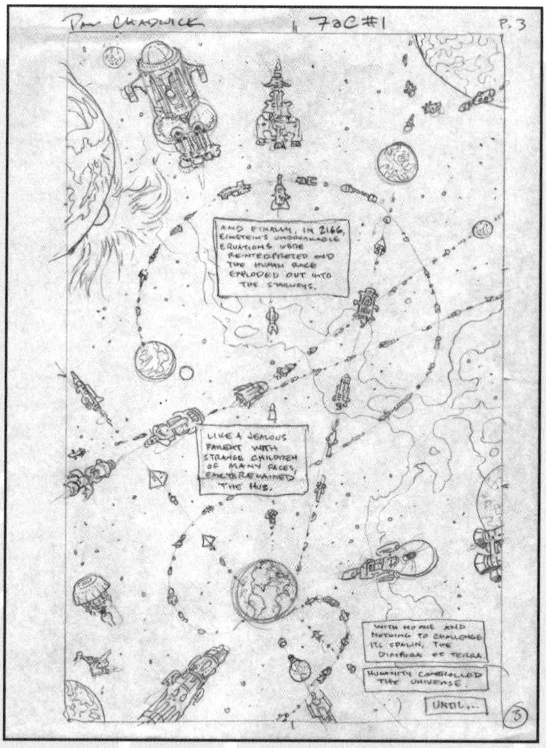
PAUL CHADWICK
7aC #1
P. 3
AND FINALLY, IN 2166, EINSTEIN'S UNDOCKABLE EQUATIONS WERE REINTERPRETED AND THE HUMAN RACE EXPLODED OUT INTO THE STARWAYS.
LIKE A JEALOUS PARENT WITH STRANGE CHILDREN OF MANY FACES, EARTH REMAINED THE HUB.
WITH NO ONE AND NOTHING TO CHALLENGE ITS SPAWN, THE DIASPORA OF TERRA
HUMANITY CONTROLLED THE UNIVERSE.
UNTIL...
3

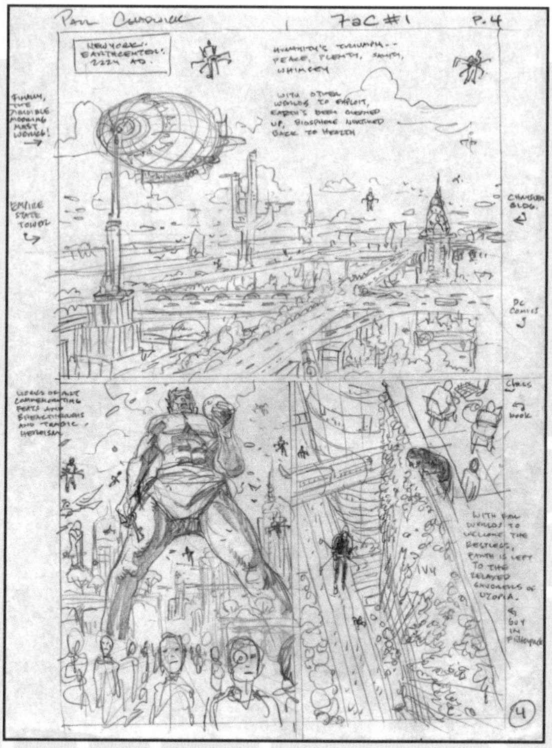
PAUL CHADWICK
7aC #1
P. 4
NEW YORK: EARTHCENTER: 2224 AD.
HUMANITY'S TRIUMPH... PEACE, PLENTY, SANITY, WHIMSEY
WITH OTHER WORLDS TO EXPLOIT, EARTH'S BEEN CLEANED UP, BIOSPHERE NURTURED BACK TO HEALTH
EMPIRE STATE TOWER
CHRYSLER BLDG.
DC COMICS
WITH FAR WORLDS TO WELCOME THE RESTLESS, EARTH IS LEFT TO THE RELAXED ENJOYMENTS OF UTOPIA.
GUY IN FILLERPACK
4

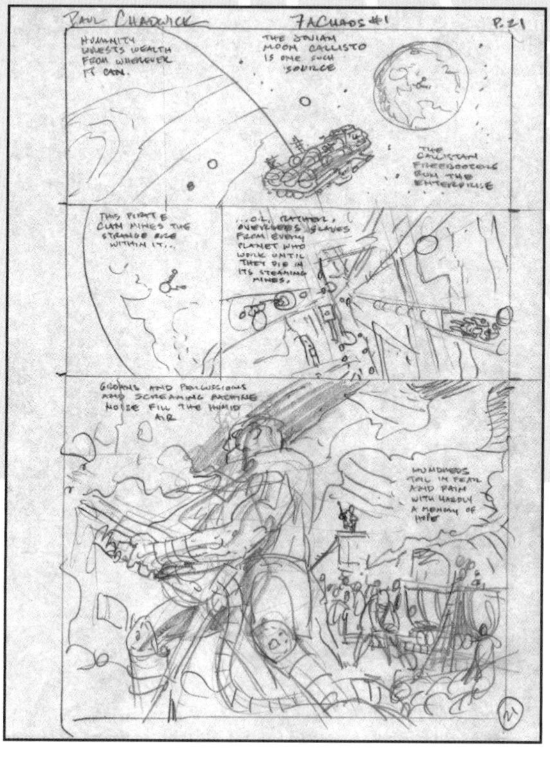
PAUL CHADWICK
7ACHAOS #1
P. 21
HUMANITY WRESTS WEALTH FROM WHEREVER IT CAN.
THE JOVIAN MOON CALLISTO IS ONE SUCH SOURCE
THE CALLISTAN FREEBOOTERS RUN THE ENTERPRISE
THIS PIRATE CLAN MINES THE STRANGE ORE WITHIN IT...
...OR, RATHER, OVERSEES SLAVES FROM EVERY PLANET WHO WORK UNTIL THEY DIE IN ITS STEAMING MINES.
GROANS AND PERCUSSIONS AND SCREAMING MACHINE NOISE FILL THE HUMID AIR
HUNDREDS TOIL IN FEAR AND PAIN WITH HARDLY A MEMORY OF HOPE
21

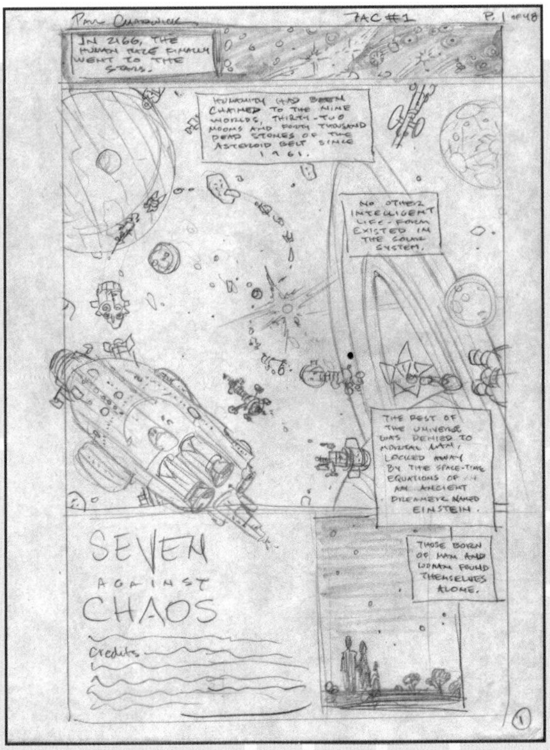
PAUL CHADWICK
7AC #1
P.1 OF 48
IN 2166, THE HUMAN RACE FINALLY WENT TO THE STARS.
HUMANITY HAD BEEN CHAINED TO THE NINE WORLDS, THIRTY-TWO MOONS AND FORTY THOUSAND DEAD STONES OF THE ASTEROID BELT SINCE 1961.
NO OTHER INTELLIGENT LIFE-FORM EXISTED IN THE SOLAR SYSTEM.
THE REST OF THE UNIVERSE WAS DENIED TO MORTAL MAN, LOCKED AWAY BY THE SPACE-TIME EQUATIONS OF AN ANCIENT DREAMER NAMED EINSTEIN.
SEVEN AGAINST CHAOS
Credits
THOSE BORN OF MAN AND WOMAN FOUND THEMSELVES ALONE.
1

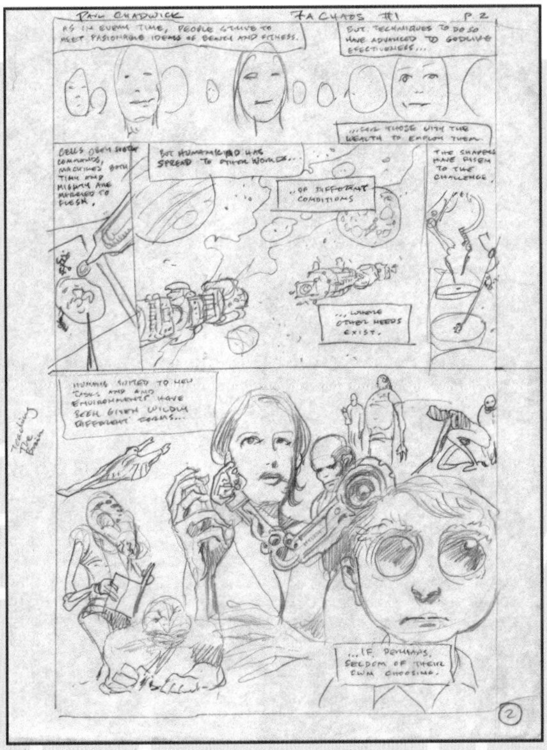
PAUL CHADWICK
7A CHAOS #1
P.2
AS IN EVERY TIME, PEOPLE STRIVE TO MEET FASHIONABLE IDEALS OF BEAUTY AND FITNESS.
BUT TECHNIQUES TO DO SO HAVE ADVANCED TO GODLIKE EFFECTIVENESS...
...FOR THOSE WITH THE WEALTH TO EMPLOY THEM.
BUT HUMANKIND HAS SPREAD TO OTHER WORLDS...
...OF DIFFERENT CONDITIONS
...WHERE OTHER NEEDS EXIST.
THE SHAPERS HAVE RISEN TO THE CHALLENGE.
HUMANS SUITED TO NEW TASKS AND ENVIRONMENTS HAVE BEEN GIVEN WILDLY DIFFERENT FORMS...
...IF, PERHAPS, SELDOM OF THEIR OWN CHOOSING.
2

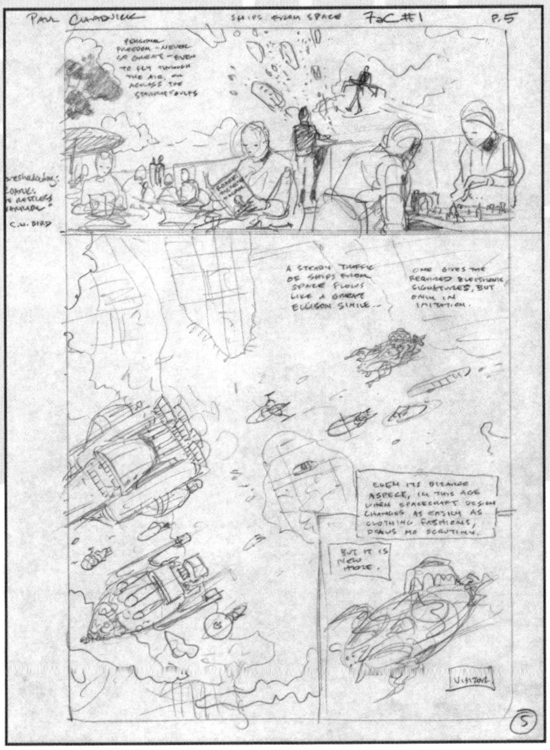
PAUL CHADWICK
SHIPS FROM SPACE
7aC #1
P.5
C.W. BIRD
A STEADY TRAFFIC OF SHIPS FROM SPACE FLOWS LIKE A GREAT ELLISON SIMILE...
ONE GIVES THE REQUIRED ELECTRONIC SIGNATURES, BUT
EVEN ITS BIZARRE ASPECT, IN THIS AGE WHEN SPACECRAFT DESIGN CHANGES AS EASILY AS CLOTHING FASHIONS, DRAWS NO SCRUTINY.
BUT IT IS NEW HERE.
5

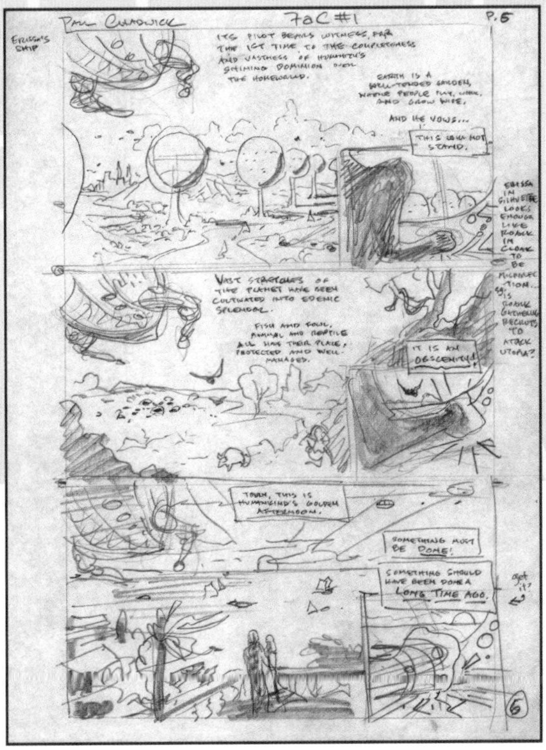
PAUL CHADWICK
7aC #1
P.5
ERISSA'S SHIP
ITS PILOT BEARS WITNESS, FOR THE 1ST TIME TO THE COMPLETENESS AND VASTNESS OF HUMANITY'S SHINING DOMINION OVER THE HOMEWORLD.
EARTH IS A WELL-TENDED GARDEN,
AND HE VOWS...
THIS CANNOT STAND.
VAST STRETCHES OF THE PLANET HAVE BEEN CULTIVATED INTO EDENIC SPLENDOR.
FISH AND FOWL, ANIMAL AND REPTILE ALL HAVE THEIR PLACE, PROTECTED AND WELL-MANAGED.
IT IS AN OBSCENITY!
TRULY, THIS IS HUMANKIND'S GOLDEN AFTERNOON.
SOMETHING MUST BE DONE!
SOMETHING SHOULD HAVE BEEN DONE A LONG TIME AGO.
6

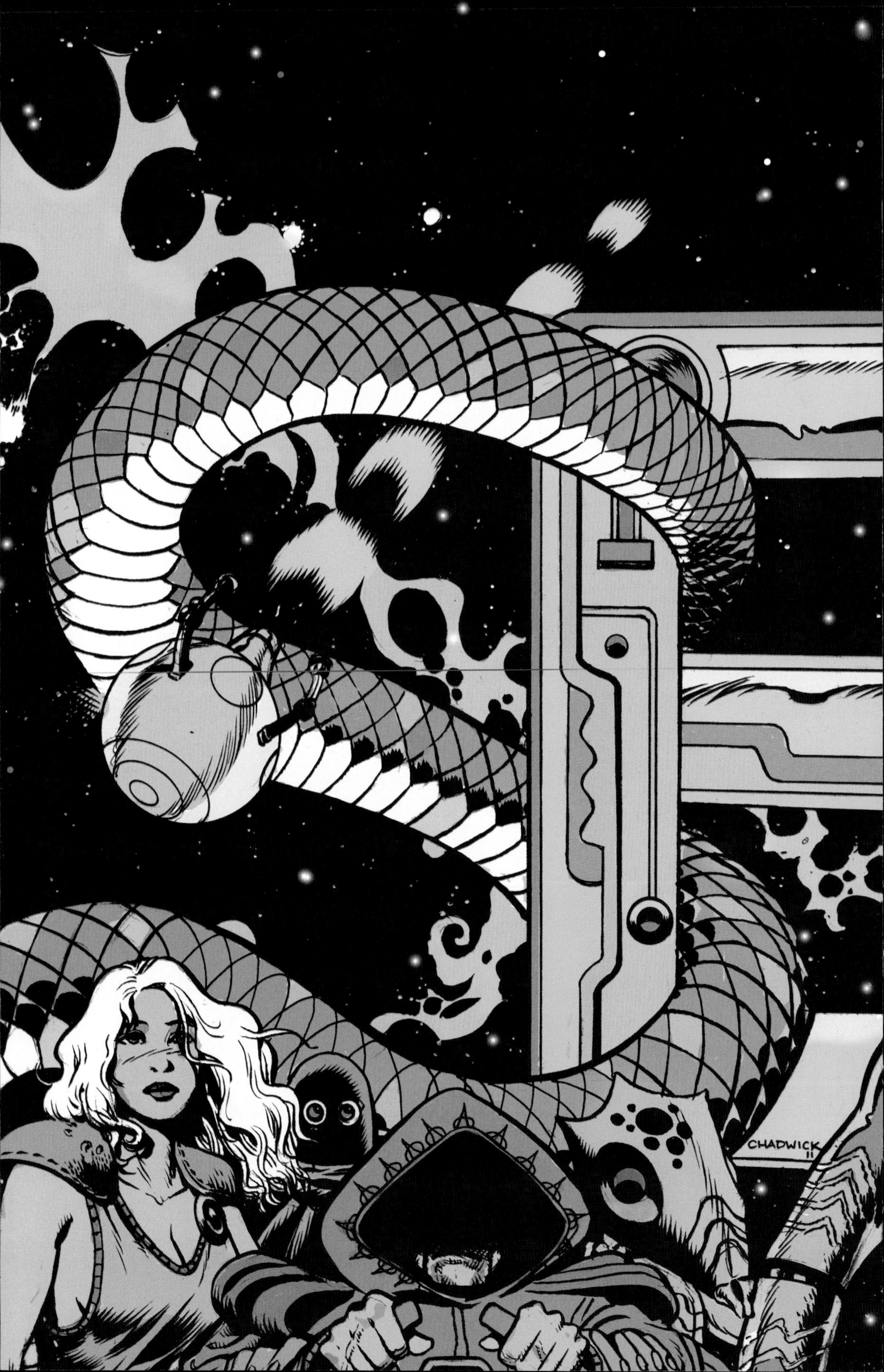
CHADWICK 11

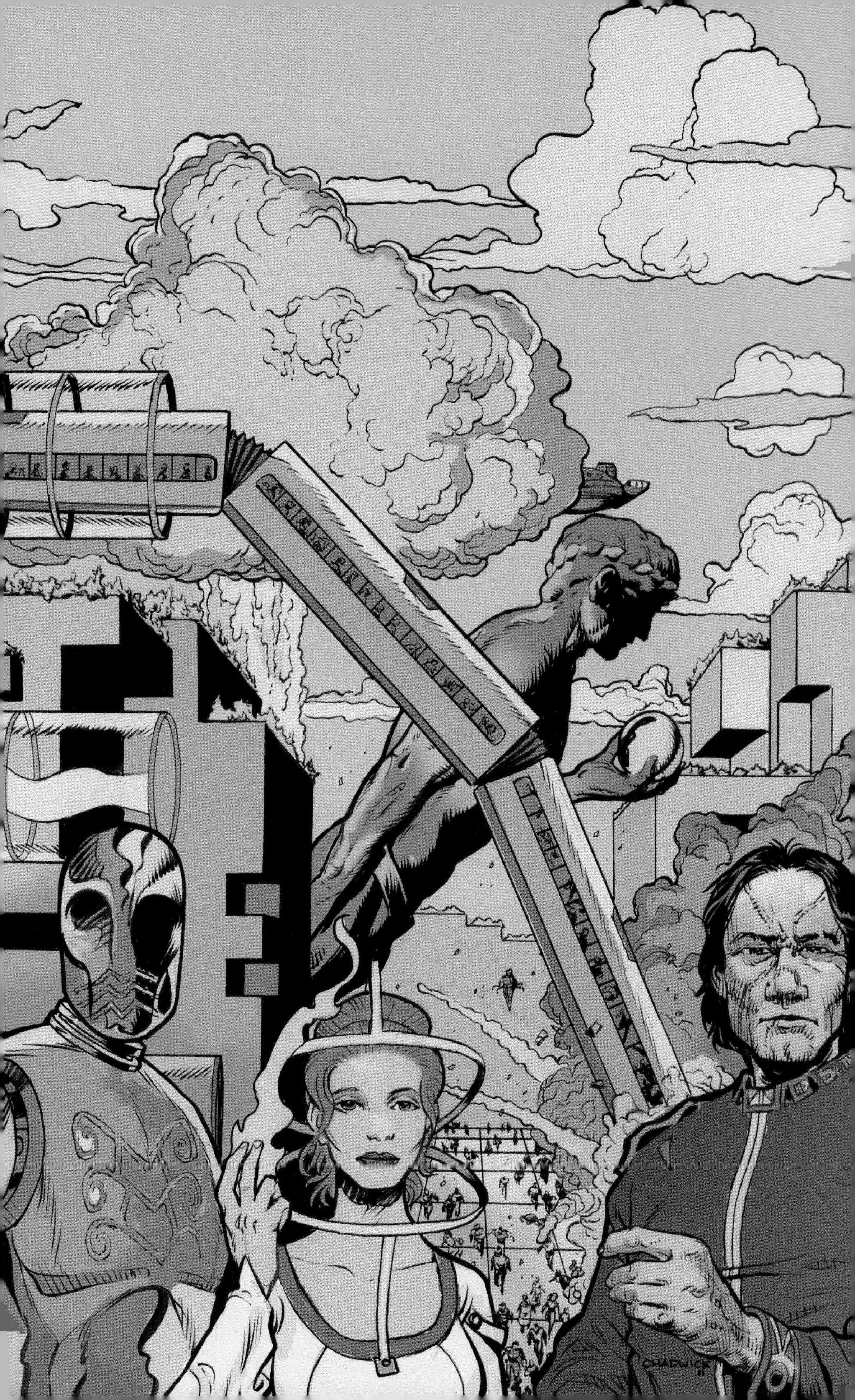
CHADWICK
11

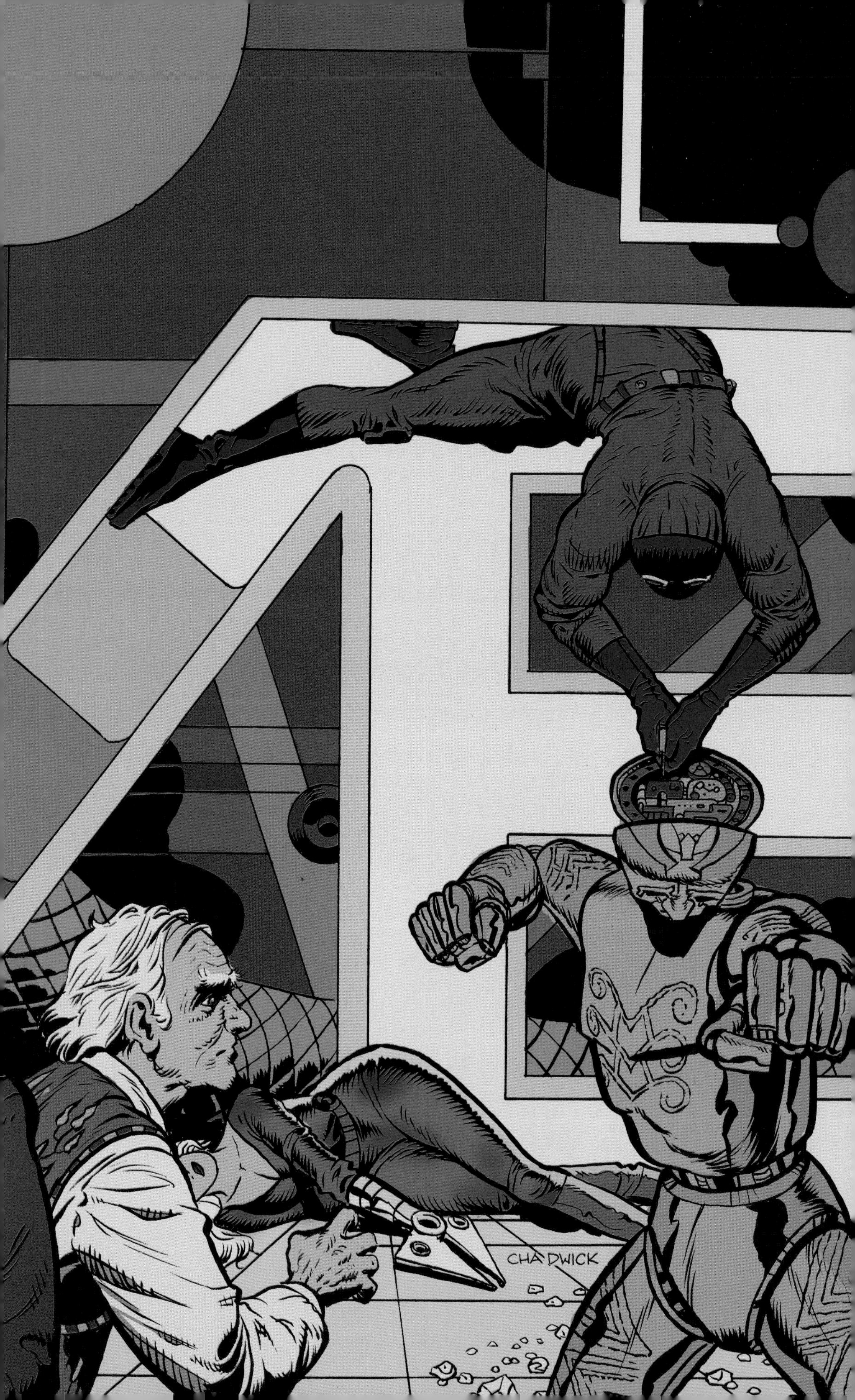
CHADWICK

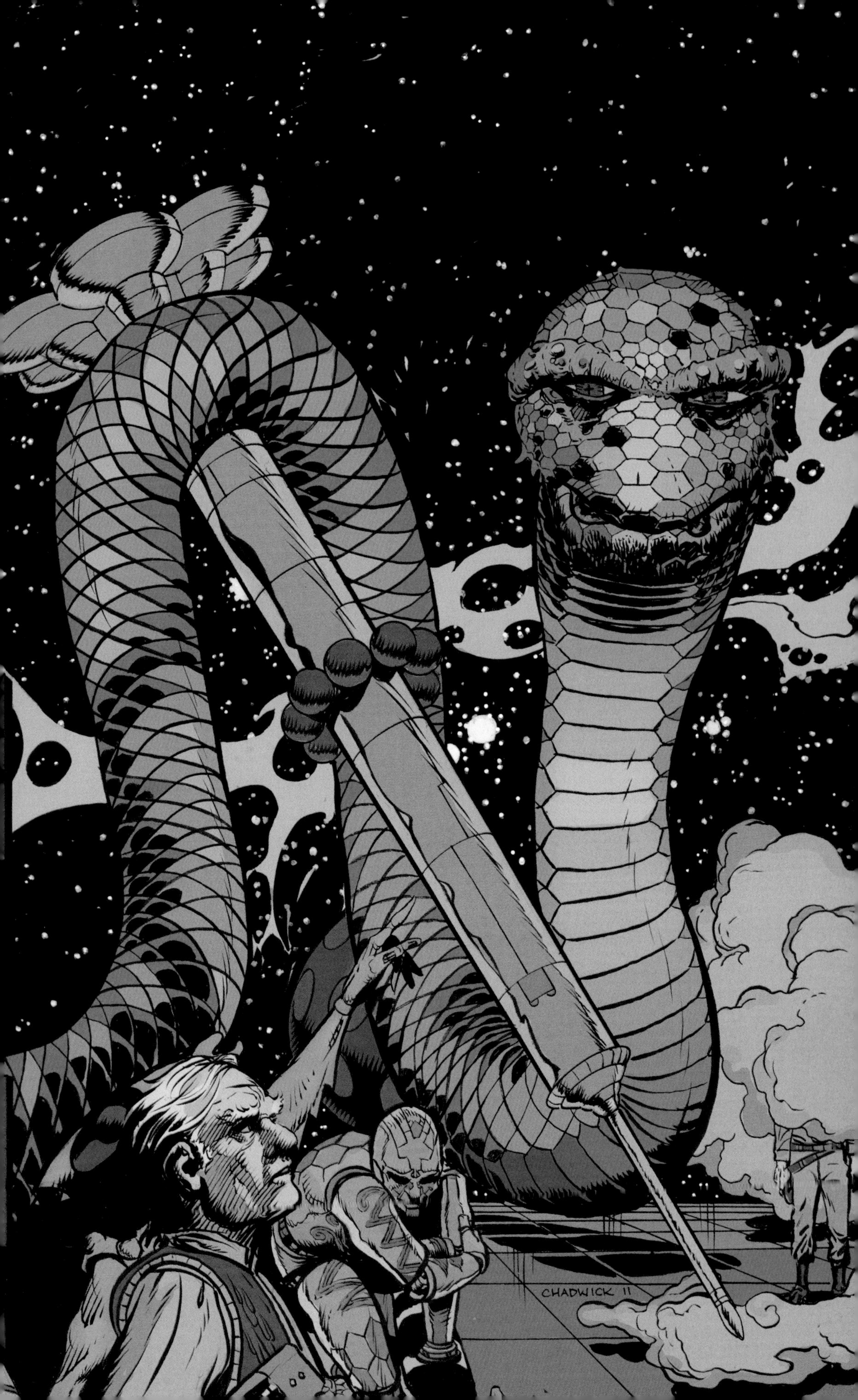
CHADWICK 11

HARLAN ELLISON was recently characterized by *The New York Times Book Review* as having "the spellbinding quality of a great nonstop talker, with a cultural warehouse for a mind." *The Los Angeles Times* suggested, "It's long past time for Harlan Ellison to be awarded the title: 20th century Lewis Carroll." And the *Washington Post Book World* said simply, "One of the great living American short story writers."

He has written or edited 75 books; more than 1,700 stories, essays, articles, and newspaper columns; two dozen teleplays, for which he received the Writers Guild of America most outstanding teleplay award for solo work an unprecedented *four* times; and a dozen movies. He won the Mystery Writers of America Edgar Allan Poe Award twice, the Horror Writers Association Bram Stoker Award six times (including The Lifetime Achievement Award in 1996), the Nebula three times, the Hugo 8 1/2 times, and received the Silver Pen for Journalism from P.E.N. Not to mention The World Fantasy Award, the British Fantasy Award, the American Mystery Award, two Audie Awards, the Ray Bradbury Award, and a Grammy nomination for Spoken Word recordings.

Mr. Ellison worked as a consultant and host for the radio series 2000^X, a series of 26 one-hour dramatized radio adaptations of famous SF stories for The Hollywood Theater of the Ear. The series was broadcast on National Public Radio (NPR) in 2000 and 2001. Ellison's classic story "'Repent, Harlequin!' Said the Ticktockman" was included as part of this significant series, starring Robin Williams, with the author in the role of Narrator. Harlan Ellison was awarded the Ray Bradbury Award For Drama Series: For Program Host & Creative Consultant: NPR Presentation of 2000^X.

He created great fantasies for *The Twilight Zone* (including Danny Kaye's final performance) and *The Outer Limits*; traveled with The Rolling Stones; marched with Martin Luther King from Selma to Montgomery; once stood off the son of a Mafia kingpin with a Remington XP-100, while wearing nothing but a bath towel — and probably *is* the most contentious person now walking the Earth. But the bottom line, as voiced by *Booklist* last year, is this: "One thing's for sure: the man can write."

PAUL CHADWICK has worked widely as an artist and writer for comics, with collaborators like Ron Randall, Doug Wheatley, Alan Moore, John Bolton, Jan Strnad, Randy Stradley, Archie Goodwin, Brian K. Vaughan, and others. He's most noted for his award-winning series *Concrete*.

After graduating from Art Center College of Design in 1979, he began storyboarding movies for Disney, Warner Bros., Lucasfilm and others. Credits include *Pee Wee's Big Adventure*, *Strange Brew*, *The Big Easy* and *Ewoks: The Battle for Endor*. He also freelanced illustration for movie advertising and for SF and fantasy paperbacks.

Chadwick then decided to devote himself to comics, though occasionally he's pulled out of the field; he was lead writer of continuity for the MMORPG *The Matrix Online*, based on the *Matrix* movies. His most recent *Concrete* comic was *Three Uneasy Pieces*.

He lives on San Juan Island in Washington State with his wife Elizabeth, also an artist.

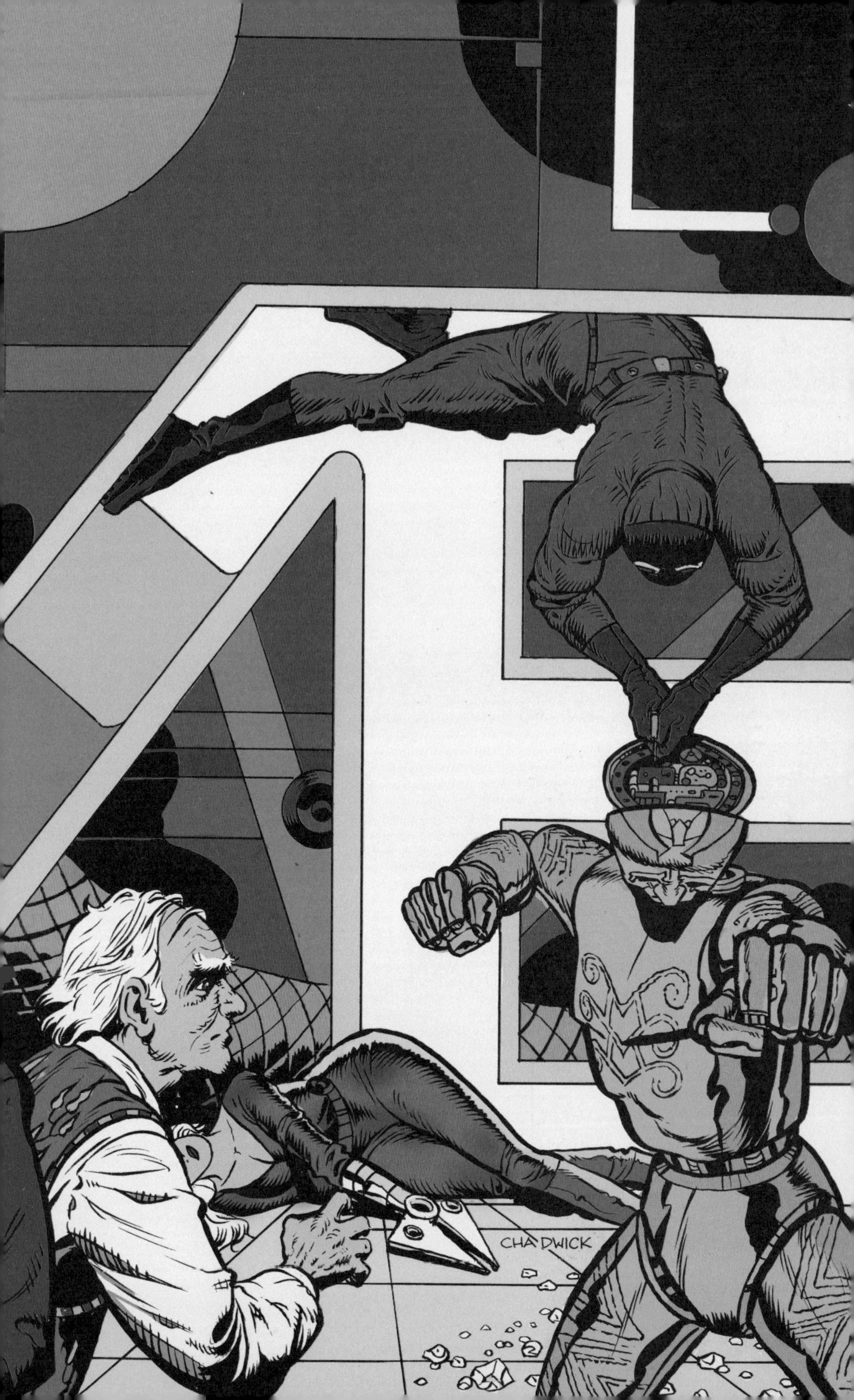
CHADWICK